D0435093

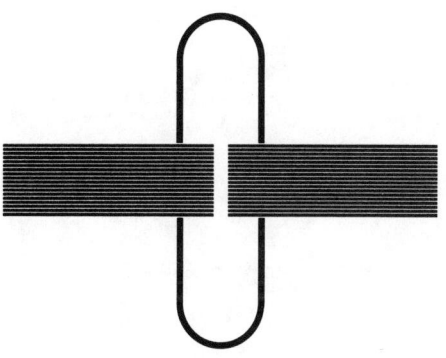

A COMPANION TO YOUR STUDY OF THE BOOK OF MORMON

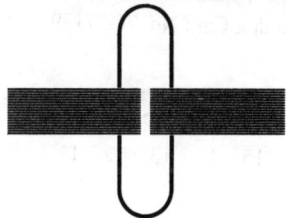

Daniel H. Ludlow

Deseret Book Company
Salt Lake City, Utah

Library of Congress Catalog Card No. 76-27139

ISBN 0-87747-610-1

Printed in the United States of America   18961

20   19   18   17   16   15   14   13   12   11

CONTENTS

Preface

Part I Introduction to the Book of Mormon

1   The Story of the Coming Forth of the Book of Mormon

44   Major Purposes of the Book of Mormon

56   The Major Sets of Plates

60   Historical Background Leading to the Period of the Book of Mormon

65   A Secular History of the Book of Mormon Peoples

Part II A Companion to Your Study of the Book of Mormon

88   First Nephi

124   Second Nephi

154   Jacob

162   Enos

165   Jarom

166   Omni

169   The Words of Mormon

171   Mosiah

192   Alma

237   Helaman

250   Third Nephi

293   Fourth Nephi

296   Mormon

306   Ether

328   Moroni

Appendixes

342   A. The Book of Mormon as a Part of God's System of Witnesses

349   B. Background Information Related to the Book of Mormon

352   C. The Book of Mormon as a Power of Conversion

361   D. The Lamanite and the Gospel, by President Spencer W. Kimball

371   E. A Pure Heart and Clean Hands, by President Marion G. Romney

Charts and Maps

381   Compilation of the Book of Mormon

382   Analytical Chart of the Book of Mormon

383   Possible Book of Mormon Sites

384   Some Significant Journeys in the Book of Mormon

385   Major Leaders During the Last 500 Years
of Nephite History - 91 B.C. to 421 A.D.

386   Index

PREFACE

A Companion to Your Study of the Book of Mormon is exactly what the name indicates: It is designed to assist the reader as he studies the Book of Mormon.

The Book of Mormon has been presented to the world with special credentials. The Three Witnesses testified that the Book of Mormon was "translated by the gift and power of God" and that "the work is true." (See "The Testimony of Three Witnesses," in the introductory pages of the Book of Mormon.) The Prophet Joseph Smith stated that the Book of Mormon was "the most correct of any book on earth, and the keystone of our religion, and a man would get nearer to God by abiding by its precepts than by any other book." (*History of the Church,* 4:461.) The Book of Mormon itself claims to contain the precious truths of the gospel of Jesus Christ, written in plainness and simplicity. Thus, the Book of Mormon is probably one of the easiest scriptures to read and understand.

The Book of Mormon was written originally by persons far removed from us today not only by time, but also by language and culture. Thus, some of their expressions, idioms, manners, and customs might be difficult for the person of the twentieth century to understand. Many of these difficult passages, however, have been explained by modern prophets. Other possible confusing sections have been illuminated through research and study of Latter-day Saint scholars. Still other obscure passages have been clarified by perceptive and discerning teachers. The major portion of the *Companion* is a compilation of explanations concerning the more challenging and difficult verses.

The *Companion* is much more than this, however. The first two chapters (pages 1-55) provides background information on the Prophet Joseph Smith and on the events associated with the coming forth of the Book of Mormon. The materials in this section are largely arranged chronologically.

The next chapter (pages 56-59) discusses the major sets of plates associated with the Book of Mormon and describes their relationship to each other and to the present printed scripture.

Another chapter (pages 60-64) provides historical background to the biblical world where the Book of Mormon first began, and still another (pages 65-85) gives a brief review of the secular history of the peoples of the Book of Mormon.

The longest and perhaps the most helpful section, however, is the one which provides additional information on selected verses and topics (pages 88-339). This material is arranged consecutively according to the books, chapters, and verses in the Book of Mormon. A year's course of study in the Book of Mormon is required of all freshmen and other new students at colleges and universities sponsored by the Church. Thus, tens of thousands of students have taken courses in the Book of Mormon at Brigham Young University, and their questions have been compiled over the years by some of the BYU faculty. Such questions were anticipated in the preparation of this *Companion,* and possible answers and explanations are included. Thus, after a reader has read a chapter in the Book of Mormon, he might want to refer to the *Companion* to see if any helps are included for any of the material in that chapter.

Still another section includes a series of appendixes that provide additional information related to the purposes and the messages of the Book of Mormon (pages 340-78).

The *Companion* concludes with some charts, maps, and diagrams that help to provide overview information on such diverse topics as the possible movements and locations of these people, the various sets of plates, and a chronological listing of Book of Mormon prophets and major political leaders.

The *Companion* is designed to be used *only* with the Book of Mormon, and its greatest value will be when it is used as a companion to the study of this sacred record. If the goals and purposes of the compiler and the publisher are achieved, then this volume will truly be a companion to your study of the Book of Mormon.

PART I

INTRODUCTION
TO THE
BOOK OF MORMON

THE STORY OF THE COMING FORTH OF THE BOOK OF MORMON

The story of how the Book of Mormon came to be, as we have it today, is most fascinating and challenging. Following are some brief statements concerning the coming forth of the Book of Mormon as told by the Prophet Joseph Smith himself and by those who knew him and his story.

Family background of Joseph Smith

It is difficult to understand fully the drama of the coming forth, translation, and publication of our present Book of Mormon without knowing something about Joseph Smith and his family. The story begins with his ancestors. An early Church historian, B. H. Roberts, lists one reason why it is important to become acquainted with the family background of Joseph Smith:

The study of his ancestry becomes important, since no pains are spared in making systematic pathological studies of that ancestry in the hope of finding some abnormalities that would justify the theory that the Prophet's revelations were but hallucinations, the product of a mind diseased. It may be well, therefore, to state what is known of the line of men from whom the Prophet descended, as also to inquire concerning his maternal ancestors. (*A Comprehensive History of the Church,* 1:1.)

The following statements have been selected to introduce the immediate ancestors of the Prophet and to indicate the type of people they were. Concerning his ancestors on his father's side of the family, Carter E. Grant has written:

The early coming of Joseph Smith's ancestors and associates to a new land of freedom planted indelibly within their hearts an unbounded determination to overthrow every tyrannical force that had dominated them in the Old World—coercions that were already beginning to chafe them in the New World.

The descent of the Smiths in America began with Robert, who in 1638, as a boy of fifteen, sailed into Boston Harbor. He later married Mary French and had ten children. Their son Samuel,

2 Sen., born January 26, 1666, married Rebecca Curtis and became the father of nine children. Samuel, Jun., known sometimes as "Captain Samuel Smith," born January 26, 1714, married Priscilla Gould and had five children. After Samuel's first wife's death, he married her cousin by the same name.

During the decisive years of the Revolutionary conflict, Samuel Smith joined the colonial forces and became an ardent champion of freedom. Chief among the many offices that he held was chairman of the Committee of Safety, with headquarters at Concord, Massachusetts. He also had the honor of signing the orders that released to his countrymen the first muskets and ammunition used in the opening battles of the Revolution, April 19, 1775, at Lexington and Concord. Captain Smith fought under the command of General George Washington, and later became prominent in the affairs of his community.

Asael Smith, Samuel's son, who was the Prophet's grandfather, was a man of liberal views, far in advance of his time. He was born March 7, 1744 at Topsfield, Massachusetts; and at the age of thirty-two he joined his father's regiment. Together they struggled valiantly to obtain political and religious freedom in America.

Joseph Smith, Sen., son of Asael, was born at Topsfield, July 12, 1771. He was five years old when his father and grandfather marched off to war—a testing, seven-year conflict. . . .

Several of the major objectives obtained by the colonies during their decisive struggle for freedom are referred to in terms of gratitude in a letter January 14, 1796, written by Asael Smith to Mr. Jacob Town. "He (God) has conducted us through a glorious revolution and has brought us into the Promised Land of Peace and Liberty; and I believe he is about to bring all the world into the same beatitude in His own time and way." To his family, a year later, he wrote: "Bless God that you live in a land of Liberty, and bear yourselves dutifully . . . toward the authority under which you live. See God's providence in the appointment of the Federal Constitution, and hold union and order precious jewels. . . . As to your marriages, I do not think it worth while to say much about them, for I believe God hath created the persons for each other and that nature will find its own."

Upon another occasion the spirit of prophecy rested upon Joseph's grandfather, causing him to predict: "It has been borne in upon my soul that one of my descendants will promulgate a work to revolutionize the world of religious faith."

In Asael's old age he was converted to the restored gospel by his son Joseph Smith, Sen., and the Prophet's brother Don Carlos. These elders baptized the Prophet's grandmother but did not baptize the grandfather because of his age and ill health. (*The Kingdom of God Restored* [Deseret Book Co., 1965], pp. 12-13.)   3

The maiden name of the Prophet's mother was Lucy Mack. The following has been written concerning her father, Solomon, and other members on her side of the family:

Solomon, son of Ebenezer Mack, was born in Lyme, Conn., Sept. 26, 1735. At the age of twenty-one years he enlisted in the services of his country under the command of Captain Henry, and the regiment of Col. Whiting. He was engaged in the king's service with two teams carrying supplies to Fort Edwards. In 1748 he enlisted under Major Spenser and was engaged in several bloody engagements in which his life was spared miraculously. He served until the spring of 1759, when he received his honorable discharge at Crown Point. That same year he met a young schoolteacher, Lydia Gates, daughter of Nathan Gates, a wealthy citizen of East Haddam, Connecticut. The friendship of these young people ripened and they were married after a short acquaintance. In 1761 Solomon and his young wife moved to Marlow where they took up their residence in a wilderness. Only four other families resided within forty miles of them. It was while here he learned to fully appreciate the excellent virtues of his wife, "For," he writes, "as our children were deprived of schools she assumed charge of their education, and performed the duties of instructress as none, save a mother, is capable of. Precepts, accompanied with examples such as theirs, were calculated to make impressions on the minds of the young, never to be forgotten. She, besides instructing them in the various branches of an ordinary education, was in the habit of calling them together both morning and evening, and teaching them to pray, meanwhile urging upon them the necessity of love towards each other as well as devotional feelings towards Him who made them."

In this manner their children became confirmed in the virtues and were established in faith in their Redeemer.

In 1776, Solomon Mack enlisted in the American army. For some time he served in the land forces and later was transferred to the navy. With his two sons, Jason and Stephen, he was engaged in a privateering expedition commanded by Captain Havens. In this service they passed through some thrilling experiences, but escaped without great harm. His service in the war covered a period of about four years. After his discharge he went to Gilsum, New Hampshire, to make his home. Owing to the rigorous campaigns through two wars, he became broken in health and suffered considerably in his declining years. His son Stephen moved to Vermont and later to Detroit, where he engaged in mercantile pursuits and was one of the founders of Detroit. During the war of 1812

4   Stephen again entered the service of his country. He held the commission of a captain at the time of the siege of Detroit and was ordered by his superior officer to surrender, which he boldly refused to do. Breaking his sword across his knee he threw the parts into the lake and said he would not submit to such a disgraceful compromise while the blood of an American ran in his veins.

Such is the character of the forebears of Joseph Smith. (Joseph Fielding Smith, *Essentials in Church History* [Deseret Book Co., 1950], pp. 26-27.)

The boyhood of Joseph Smith

The Prophet's account of his own birth and boyhood is brief but important. He writes:

I was born in the year of our Lord one thousand eight hundred and five, on the twenty-third day of December, in the town of Sharon, Windsor county, State of Vermont. . . My father, Joseph Smith, Sen., left the State of Vermont, and moved to Palmyra, Ontario (now Wayne) county, in the State of New York, when I was in my tenth year, or thereabouts. In about four years after my father's arrival in Palmyra, he moved with his family into Manchester in the same county of Ontario—

His family consisting of eleven souls, namely, my father, Joseph Smith; my mother, Lucy Smith (whose name, previous to her marriage, was Mack, daughter of Solomon Mack); my brothers, Alvin (who died November 19th, 1824, in the 27th year of his age), Hyrum, myself, Samuel Harrison, William, Don Carlos; and my sisters, Sophronia, Catherine, and Lucy. (Pearl of Great Price, Joseph Smith 2:3-4.)

In connection with the family of Joseph Smith, Sr., B. H. Roberts has written the following:

During Joseph Smith's early childhood there were removals of the family from Sharon to Tunbridge, and thence to Royalton; but nevertheless these were years of prosperity. In 1811 the family settled in Lebanon, Grafton county, New Hampshire, just over the Vermont line, in the beautiful valley of the Connecticut river. Here the parents hoped for even larger prosperity than had come from their labors in the past. "Here we settled our selves down," says Lucy Smith, "and began to contemplate with joy and satisfaction the prosperity which had attended our recent exertions; and we doubled our diligence, in order to obtain more of this world's goods, with a view of assisting our children when they should need it; and, as is quite natural, we looked forward to the decline of life and were providing for its wants as well as striving to procure those things which contribute much to the comfort of old age."

Hyrum Smith, the second son, was sent to an academy in 5
Hanover, a few miles north from Lebanon; and the other children
of sufficient age, to the near common school in Lebanon. The
affairs of the family were in this happy condition when an epidemic
of typhus fever passed over the neighborhood. The Smiths were
sorely afflicted by the fever. Hyrum was stricken while in school·in
Hanover, and brought home; and all the children one after the
other fell victims to the scourge. Sophronia, a daughter, narrowly
escaped dying; the mother attributes her recovery to the blessing of
God obtained through prayer. Joseph recovered from the fever, but
some two weeks after his recovery was suddenly seized with a
severe pain in his shoulder. A wrong diagnosis by the physician attributed the trouble to a sprain, when in reality there had been
none; but after two weeks of suffering there developed between the
breast and shoulder a fever sore which, on being lanced, discharged
large quantities of pus. The pain then shifted into the leg, causing
great suffering; and so continued from bad to worse despite the
efforts of physicians, until finally amputation was decided upon by
the surgeons, and was only avoided by the protests and determination of the lad himself and the mother. An operation was
performed, however, by a large piece of one of the bones between
the knee and ankle being removed. Of course the operation was
performed with the crude instruments of the times, without the use
of anesthetics; and as the boy refused to take stimulants or to be
tied down to the bed, the manner in which he passed through the
trying ordeal was a rare exhibition of pluck and power of endur-
ance. After the operation the lad quickly recovered, and was sent to
Salem, Massachusetts, to the home of his uncle, Jesse Smith, in the
hope that the sea air would help in his restoration to perfect health,
a hope that was not disappointed. (*A Comprehensive History of the
Church,* 1:29-30.)

Under the influence of the Lord, the Smith family
moved from Vermont to the western part of New York state,
where they located at Palmyra. Concerning these movements
of the Smith family, B. H. Roberts has written:

Something like a year of sickness played havoc with the
fortunes of the family of Joseph Smith, Sen., and they removed to
Norwich in the state of Vermont—just over the state line, and some
ten or twelve miles distant from Lebanon. Here three successive
crop failures still further reduced the fortunes of the family. Meantime, Joseph Smith, Sen., having heard of the richer lands and
milder climate of western New York, determined upon removing to
that state. . . . After a painful separation from her mother at
Royalton . . . Lucy Smith and her family made their way to

6

Palmyra, New York, where they were welcomed by the father, and all rejoiced in the reunion of the family.

It was a serious condition that confronted this family on its arrival in Palmyra. More than a year of sickness, followed by three successive crop failures—not because of idleness or lack of skill in husbandry, but through drought or frosts, causes beyond their control—together with the necessary expense of removing from New Hampshire to Palmyra, a distance of some three hundred miles, had exhausted all their resources, and they were penniless. It need create no special wonderment that the elder Smith at this period is described as being "of gaunt and haggard visage," and wearing "rusty clothes." A family consultation resulted in the determination to unite their efforts in purchasing a tract of one hundred acres of land some two miles south of Palmyra, on the north border of Manchester township, belonging to minor heirs of the Everson estate, whose agent resided at Canandaigua, Ontario county. "In a year," says Lucy Smith, "we made nearly all of the first payment, erected a log house, and commenced clearing. I believe something like thirty acres of land were made ready for cultivation the first year." Meanwhile, to meet the immediate necessities of the family, the male members engaged in occasional day's work among the neighboring farmers or in the town; while the mother, skilled in hand-painting oil-cloth covers for tables and stands, etc., met a large part of the family expenses.

Finally the family moved from the town of Palmyra, to the new log house on the farm, in Manchester township. . . .

The amount of cleared land gradually increased from thirty to sixty acres, and there were from twelve to fifteen hundred sugar trees on the place from which sap was gathered in the spring and converted into molasses and sugar. The farm thus redeemed from a wilderness and a commodious house built upon it, attracted the attention of the covetous. . . . (*A Comprehensive History of the Church,* 1:30-34.)

After describing in considerable detail the usual conditions in many of these early settlements, Francis Kirkham adds these words, which pertain specifically to Joseph Smith and his family:

Such was the early life and environment of the youth chosen by our Heavenly Father to initiate His great latter-day work. The time had now come when "His Spirit was to be poured out upon all flesh." Joseph Smith grew to manhood among God's noblemen, men of faith, self reliance, initiative and determination. They worked twelve hours a day with hand tools to build their homes and supply food and clothing for their families. Travel for pleasure was unknown. The first railroad had not yet competed with the horse-drawn vehicle. Roads were poor and usually maintained by a tax or a toll. A journey of one hundred miles was an unusual event. Wheat that sold at seventy-five cents a bushel in Western New York, sold for two dollars and fifty cents a bushel at Albany on the Hudson River, because of the cost of transportation on the Erie Canal. Books were few. In addition to the Bible, one might find in the home the almanac, and a few books of travel. Children went to school for about three months a year, until they could "read, write and cipher."

Modern science was unknown. Persons suffering with fever were denied water, and people were bled when blood infusion would have saved their lives. Children died from communicable diseases, now prevented by inoculation.

People lived near to nature and believed in the love and mercies of God. They were kind, helpful and considerate to all. To them, Jesus was the Christ, and the Bible was the word of God to all men. It contained His commandments. These they accepted and sought to obey. (Francis W. Kirkham, *A New Witness for Christ in America* [Independence, Mo.: Zion's Printing and Publishing Co., 1942], 1:36-37.)

The mother of the Prophet wrote these brief words concerning the boyhood and family environment of her son:

. . . I shall say nothing respecting him until he arrived at the age of fourteen. However, in this I am aware that some of my readers will be disappointed, for I suppose, from questions which are frequently asked me, that it is thought by some that I shall be likely to tell many very remarkable incidents which attended his childhood; but, as nothing occurred during his early life, except those trivial circumstances which are common to that state of human existence, I pass them in silence. (Ibid., 1:62.)

The First Vision

Although the Prophet's early boyhood may not have contained "many very remarkable incidents," certainly the story of his life from the spring of 1820 to his death in 1844 at Carthage was "remarkable." Concerning his life during 1820 he wrote:

Some time in the second year after our removal to Manchester, there was in the place where we lived an unusual excitement on the subject of religion. It commenced with the Methodists, but soon became general among all the sects in that region of country. Indeed, the whole district of country seemed affected by it, and great multitudes united themselves to the different religious parties, which

8   created no small stir and division amongst the people, some crying, "Lo, here!" and others, "Lo, there!" Some were contending for the Methodist faith, some for the Presbyterian, and some for the Baptist.

For, notwithstanding the great love which the converts to these different faiths expressed at the time of their conversion, and the great zeal manifested by the respective clergy, who were active in getting up and promoting this extraordinary scene of religious feeling, in order to have everybody converted, as they were pleased to call it, let them join what sect they pleased; yet when the converts began to file off, some to one party and some to another, it was seen that the seemingly good feelings of both the priests and the converts were more pretended than real; for a scene of great confusion and bad feeling ensued—priest contending against priest, and convert against convert; so that all their good feelings one for another, if they ever had any, were entirely lost in a strife of words and a contest about opinions.

I was at this time in my fifteenth year. My father's family was proselyted to the Presbyterian faith, and four of them joined that church, namely, my mother, Lucy; my brothers Hyrum and Samuel Harrison; and my sister Sophronia.

During this time of great excitement my mind was called up to serious reflection and great uneasiness; but though my feelings were deep and often poignant, still I kept myself aloof from all these parties, though I attended their several meetings as often as occasion would permit. In process of time my mind became somewhat partial to the Methodist sect, and I felt some desire to be united with them; but so great were the confusion and strife among the different denominations, that it was impossible for a person young as I was, and so unacquainted with men and things, to come to any certain conclusion who was right and who was wrong.

My mind at times was greatly excited, the cry and tumult were so great and incessant. The Presbyterians were most decided against the Baptists and Methodists, and used all the powers of both reason and sophistry to prove their errors, or, at least, to make the people think they were in error. On the other hand, the Baptists and Methodists in their turn were equally zealous in endeavoring to establish their own tenets and disprove all others.

In the midst of this war of words and tumult of opinions, I often said to myself: What is to be done? Who of all these parties are right; or, are they all wrong together? If any one of them be right, which is it, and how shall I know it?

While I was laboring under the extreme difficulties caused by the contests of these parties of religionists, I was one day reading the Epistle of James, first chapter and fifth verse, which reads: *If*

any of you lack wisdom, let him ask of God, that giveth to all men 9
*liberally, and upbraideth not; and it shall be given him.**

Never did any passage of scripture come with more power to the heart of man than this did at this time to mine. It seemed to enter with great force into every feeling of my heart. I reflected on it again and again, knowing that if any person needed wisdom from God, I did; for how to act I did not know, and unless I could get more wisdom than I then had, I would never know; for the teachers of religion of the different sects understood the same passages of scripture so differently as to destroy all confidence in settling the question by an appeal to the Bible.

At length I came to the conclusion that I must either remain in darkness and confusion, or else I must do as James directs, that is, ask of God. I at length came to the determination to "ask of God," concluding that if he gave wisdom to them that lacked wisdom, and would give liberally, and not upbraid, I might venture.

So, in accordance with this, my determination to ask of God, I retired to the woods to make the attempt. It was on the morning of a beautiful, clear day, early in the spring of eighteen hundred and twenty. It was the first time in my life that I had made such an attempt, for amidst all my anxieties I had never as yet made the attempt to pray vocally.

After I had retired to the place where I had previously designed to go, having looked around me, and finding myself alone, I kneeled down and began to offer up the desire of my heart to God. I had scarcely done so, when immediately I was seized upon by some power which entirely overcame me, and had such an astonishing influence over me as to bind my tongue so that I could not speak. Thick darkness gathered around me, and it seemed to me for a time as if I were doomed to sudden destruction.

But, exerting all my powers to call upon God to deliver me out of the power of this enemy which had seized upon me, and at the very moment when I was ready to sink into despair and abandon

---

*When the Prophet's brother William was later asked "What caused Joseph to ask for guidance as to what church he ought to join," he replied as follows:

"Why, there was a joint revival . . . in the neighborhood between the Baptists, Methodists, and Presbyterians, and they had succeeded in stirring up quite a feeling and after the meeting the question arose which church should have the converts. Rev. Stockton was the president of the meeting and suggested that it was their meeting and under their care, and they had a church there and they ought to join the Presbyterians, but as father did not like Rev. Stockton very well, our folks hesitated and the next evening a Rev. Mr. Lane of the Methodists preached a sermon on 'what church shall I join,' and the burden of his discourses was to ask God, using as a text, 'If any man lack wisdom let him ask of God, who giveth to all men liberally.' And of course when Joseph went home and was looking over the text, he was impressed to do just what the preacher had said. . . ." (Kirkham, *A New Witness for Christ in America,* 1:44.)

10   myself to destruction—not to an imaginary ruin, but to the power of some actual being from the unseen world, who had such marvelous power as I had never before felt in any being—just at this moment of great alarm, I saw a pillar of light exactly over my head, above the brightness of the sun, which descended gradually until it fell upon me.

It no sooner appeared than I found myself delivered from the enemy which held me bound. When the light rested upon me I saw two Personages, whose brightness and glory defy all description, standing above me in the air. One of them spake unto me, calling me by name and said, pointing to the other—*This is My Beloved Son. Hear Him!*

My object in going to inquire of the Lord was to know which of all the sects was right, that I might know which to join. No sooner, therefore, did I get possession of myself, so as to be able to speak, than I asked the Personages who stood above me in the light, which of all the sects was right—and which I should join.

I was answered that I must join none of them, for they were all wrong; and the Personage who addressed me said that all their creeds were an abomination in his sight; that those professors were all corrupt; that: "they draw near to me with their lips, but their hearts are far from me, they teach for doctrines the commandments of men, having a form of godliness, but they deny the power thereof."

He again forbade me to join with any of them; and many other things did he say unto me, which I cannot write at this time. When I came to myself again, I found myself lying on my back, looking up into heaven. When the light had departed, I had no strength; but soon recovering in some degree, I went home. And as I leaned up to the fireplace, mother inquired what the matter was. I replied, "Never mind, all is well—I am well enough off." I then said to my mother, "I have learned for myself that Presbyterianism is not true." It seems as though the adversary was aware, at a very early period of my life, that I was destined to prove a disturber and an annoyer of his kingdom; else why should the powers of darkness combine against me? Why the opposition and persecution that arose against me, almost in my infancy?

Some few days after I had this vision, I happened to be in company with one of the Methodist preachers, who was very active in the before mentioned religious excitement; and, conversing with him on the subject of religion, I took occasion to give him an account of the vision which I had had. I was greatly surprised at his behavior; he treated my communication not only lightly, but with great contempt, saying it was all of the devil, that there were no such things as visions or revelations in these days; that all such things had ceased with the apostles, and that there would never be any more of them.   11

I soon found, however, that my telling the story had excited a great deal of prejudice against me among professors of religion, and was the cause of great persecution, which continued to increase; and though I was an obscure boy, only between fourteen and fifteen years of age, and my circumstances in life such as to make a boy of no consequence in the world, yet men of high standing would take notice sufficient to excite the public mind against me, and create a bitter persecution; and this was common among all the sects—all united to persecute me.

It caused me serious reflection then, and often has since, how very strange it was that an obscure boy, of a little over fourteen years of age, and one, too, who was doomed to the necessity of obtaining a scanty maintenance by his daily labor, should be thought a character of sufficient importance to attract the attention of the great ones of the most popular sects of the day, and in a manner to create in them a spirit of the most bitter persecution and reviling. But strange or not, so it was, and it was often the cause of great sorrow to myself.

However, it was nevertheless a fact that I had beheld a vision. I have thought since, that I felt much like Paul, when he made his defense before King Agrippa, and related the account of the vision he had when he saw a light, and heard a voice; but still there were but few who believed him; some said he was dishonest, others said he was mad; and he was ridiculed and reviled. But all this did not destroy the reality of his vision. He had seen a vision, he knew he had, and all the persecution under heaven could not make it otherwise; and though they should persecute him unto death, yet he knew, and would know to his latest breath, that he had both seen a light and heard a voice speaking unto him, and all the world could not make him think or believe otherwise.

So it was with me. I had actually seen a light, and in the midst of that light I saw two Personages, and they did in reality speak to me; and though I was hated and persecuted for saying that I had seen a vision, yet it was true; and while they were persecuting me, reviling me, and speaking all manner of evil against me falsely for so saying, I was led to say in my heart: Why persecute me for telling the truth? I have actually seen a vision; and who am I that I can withstand God, or why does the world think to make me deny what I have actually seen? For I had seen a vision; I knew it, and I knew that God knew it, and I could not deny it, neither dared I do it; at least I knew that by so doing I would offend God, and come under condemnation.

I had now got my mind satisfied so far as the sectarian world was concerned—that it was not my duty to join with any of them, but to continue as I was until further directed. I had found the testimony of James to be true—that a man who lacked wisdom might ask of God, and obtain, and not be upbraided. (Pearl of Great Price, Joseph Smith 2:5-26.)

The Prophet bore testimony many times of the sacred experience he had when he talked with the Father and the Son. Edward Stevenson recorded the following vivid description of his experience when he heard the Prophet bear his testimony of this incident:

The Prophet Joseph Smith (was) a plain but noble looking man of large frame and about six feet high. With him were his father, Joseph Smith, his brother, Hyrum, Oliver Cowdery, David Whitmer, and Martin Harris whose sister, Sophia Kellogg lived in our settlement. A great stir was made in this settlement at so distinguished visitors. The meetings held were crowded to see and hear the testimonies given, which were very powerful. I will here relate my own experience on the occasion of a meeting in our old log schoolhouse. The Prophet stood at a table, for the pulpit, where he began relating his vision, and before he got through, he was in the midst of the congregation with uplifted hand. I do believe that there was not one person present who was not (convinced) of the truth of his vision of an angel (coming) to him. His countenance seemed to me to assume a heavenly whiteness and his voice was so piercing and forcible—for my part, it so impressed me as to become indelible imprinted on my mind.

. . . Here are some of the Prophet's words, as uttered in the schoolhouse. With uplifted hand he said, "I am a witness that there is a God, for I saw Him in open day, while praying in a silent grove, in the spring of 1820." He further testified that God, the Eternal Father, pointing to a separate personage, in the likeness of Himself, said, "This is my Beloved Son; hear ye Him." O how these words thrilled my entire system, and filled me with joy unspeakable—to behold one who, like Paul the apostle of olden time, could with boldness testify that he had been in the presence of Jesus Christ! (Joseph Grant Stevenson, *Stevenson Family History* [Provo: Joseph Grant Stevenson, 1955], 1:19-21.)

On another occasion, Edward Stevenson made the following statement concerning the testimony offered by the Prophet:

I first saw him in 1834 at Pontiac (Michigan). . . .

In that same year, 1834, in the midst of many large congregations, the Prophet testified with great power concerning the visit of the Father and the Son, and the conversation he had with them.

Never before did I feel such power as was manifested on these oc-   13
casions, and, although only a small percentage of those who saw
and heard him accepted the restored gospel, there was not one who
dared to refute it. (William E. Berrett and Alma H. Burton, *Readings in L.D.S. Church History* [Deseret Book Co., 1953], 1:17.)

In his letter of March 1, 1842, to John Wentworth, the
editor of the Chicago *Democrat,* the Prophet wrote of his first
vision as follows:

"They (the two Heavenly Personages,) told me that all religious
denominations were believing in incorrect doctrines, and that none
of them was acknowledged of God as His church and kingdom.
And I was expressly commanded to 'go not after them' at the same
time receiving a promise that the fulness of the gospel should at
some future time be made known unto me." (Kirkham, *A New Witness for Christ in America,* 1:52.)

Appearance of the angel Moroni

The vision of the Father and the Son eventually proved
to be only the first of a series of heavenly manifestations that
the Prophet received, but he did not receive his next instructions from a heavenly messenger for over three years. He
records this dramatic event as follows:

I continued to pursue my common vocations in life until the
twenty-first of September, one thousand eight hundred and twenty-
three, all the time suffering severe persecution at the hands of all
classes of men, both religious and irreligious, because I continued
to affirm that I had seen a vision.

During the space of time which intervened between the time I
had the vision and the year eighteen hundred and twenty-three—
having been forbidden to join any of the religious sects of the day,
and being of very tender years, and persecuted by those who ought
to have been my friends and to have treated me kindly, and if they
suppose me to be deluded to have endeavored in a proper and
affectionate manner to have reclaimed me—I was left to all kinds
of temptations; and, mingling with all kinds of society, I frequently
fell into many foolish errors, and displayed the weakness of youth,
and the foibles of human nature; which, I am sorry to say, led me
into divers temptations, offensive in the sight of God. In making
this confession, no one need suppose me guilty of any great or ma-
lignant sins. A disposition to commit such was never in my nature.
But I was guilty of levity, and sometimes associated with jovial
company, etc., not consistent with that character which ought to be
maintained by one who was called of God as I had been. But this
will not seem very strange to any one who recollects my youth, and

is acquainted with my native cheery temperament.

In consequence of these things, I often felt condemned for my weakness and imperfections; when, on the evening of the above-mentioned twenty-first of September, after I had retired to my bed for the night, I betook myself to prayer and supplication to Almighty God for forgiveness of all my sins and follies, and also for a manifestation to me, that I might know of my state and standing before him; for I had full confidence in obtaining a divine manifestation, as I previously had one.

While I was thus in the act of calling upon God, I discovered a light appearing in my room, which continued to increase until the room was lighter than at noonday, when immediately a personage appeared at my bedside, standing in the air, for his feet did not touch the floor.

He had on a loose robe of most exquisite whiteness. It was a whiteness beyond anything earthly I had ever seen; nor do I believe that any earthly thing could be made to appear so exceedingly white and brilliant. His hands were naked, and his arms also, a little above the wrist; so, also, were his feet naked, as were his legs, a little above the ankles. His head and neck were also bare. I could discover that he had no other clothing on but this robe, as it was open, so that I could see into his bosom.

Not only was his robe exceedingly white, but his whole person was glorious beyond description, and his countenance truly like lightning. The room was exceedingly light, but not so very bright as immediately around his person. When I first looked upon him, I was afraid; but the fear soon left me.

He called me by name, and said unto me that he was a messenger sent from the presence of God to me, and that his name was Moroni; that God had a work for me to do; and that my name should be had for good and evil among all nations, kindreds, and tongues, or that it should be both good and evil spoken of among all people.

He said there was a book deposited, written upon gold plates, giving an account of the former inhabitants of this continent, and the source from whence they sprang. He also said that the fulness of the everlasting Gospel was contained in it, as delivered by the Savior to the ancient inhabitants;

Also, that there were two stones in silver bows—and these stones, fastened to a breastplate, constituted what is called the Urim and Thummim—deposited with the plates; and the possession and use of these stones were what constituted "seers" in ancient or former times; and that God had prepared them for the purpose of translating the book.

After telling me these things, he commenced quoting the

prophecies of the Old Testament. He first quoted part of the third 15
chapter of Malachi; and he quoted also the fourth or last chapter of
the same prophecy, though with a little variation from the way it
reads in our Bibles. Instead of quoting the first verse as it reads in
our books, he quoted it thus:

*For behold, the day cometh that shall burn as an oven, and all the
proud, yea, and all that do wickedly shall burn as stubble; for they
that come shall burn them, saith the Lord of Hosts, that it shall leave
them neither root nor branch.*

And again, he quoted the fifth verse thus: *Behold, I will reveal
unto you the Priesthood, by the hand of Elijah the prophet, before the
coming of the great and dreadful day of the Lord.*

He also quoted the next verse differently: *And he shall plant in
the hearts of the children the promises made to the fathers, and the
hearts of the children shall turn to their fathers. If it were not so, the
whole earth would be utterly wasted at his coming.*

In addition to these, he quoted the eleventh chapter of Isaiah,
saying that it was about to be fulfilled. He quoted also the third
chapter of Acts, twenty-second and twenty-third verses, precisely as
they stand in our New Testament. He said that that prophet was
Christ; but the day had not yet come when "they who would not
hear his voice should be cut off from among the people," but soon
would come.

He also quoted the second chapter of Joel, from the twenty-
eighth verse to the last. He also said that this was not yet fulfilled,
but was soon to be. And he further stated that the fulness of the
Gentiles was soon to come in. He quoted many other passages of
scripture, and offered many explanations which cannot be mentioned here.

Again, he told me, that when I got those plates of which he had
spoken—for the time that they should be obtained was not yet
fulfilled—I should not show them to any person; neither the breast-
plate with the Urim and Thummim; only to those to whom I
should be commanded to show them; if I did I should be destroyed.
While he was conversing with me about the plates, the vision was
opened to my mind that I could see the place where the plates were
deposited, and that so clearly and distinctly that I knew the place
again when I visited it.

After this communication, I saw the light in the room begin to
gather immediately around the person of him who had been speaking to me, and it continued to do so until the room was again left
dark, except just around him; when, instantly I saw, as it were, a
conduit open right up into heaven, and he ascended till he entirely
disappeared, and the room was left as it had been before this
heavenly light had made its appearance.

16   I lay musing on the singularity of the scene, and marveling greatly at what had been told to me by this extraordinary messenger; when, in the midst of my meditation, I suddenly discovered that my room was again beginning to get lighted, and in an instant, as it were, the same heavenly messenger was again by my bedside.

He commenced, and again related the very same things which he had done at his first visit, without the least variation; which having done, he informed me of great judgments which were coming upon the earth, with great desolations by famine, sword, and pestilence; and that these grievous judgments would come on the earth in this generation. Having related these things, he again ascended as he had done before.

By this time, so deep were the impressions made on my mind, that sleep had fled from my eyes, and I lay overwhelmed in astonishment at what I had both seen and heard. But what was my surprise when again I beheld the same messenger at my bedside, and heard him rehearse or repeat over again to me the same things as before; and added a caution to me, telling me that Satan would try to tempt me (in consequence of the indigent circumstances of my father's family), to get the plates for the purpose of getting rich. This he forbade me, saying that I must have no other object in view in getting the plates but to glorify God, and must not be influenced by any other motive than that of building his kingdom; otherwise I could not get them.

After this third visit, he again ascended into heaven as before, and I was again left to ponder on the strangeness of what I had just experienced; when almost immediately after the heavenly messenger had ascended from me for the third time, the cock crowed, and I found that day was approaching, so that our interviews must have occupied the whole of that night.

I shortly after arose from my bed, and, as usual, went to the necessary labors of the day; but, in attempting to work as at other times, I found my strength so exhausted as to render me entirely unable. My father, who was laboring along with me, discovered something to be wrong with me, and told me to go home. I started with the intention of going to the house; but, in attempting to cross the fence out of the field where we were, my strength entirely failed me, and I fell helpless on the ground, and for a time was quite unconscious of anything.

The first thing that I can recollect was a voice speaking unto me, calling me by name. I looked up, and beheld the same messenger standing over my head, surrounded by light as before. He then again related unto me all that he had related to me the previous night, and commanded me to go to my father and tell him of the vision and commandments which I had received.   17

I obeyed; I returned to my father in the field, and rehearsed the whole matter to him. He replied to me that it was of God, and told me to go and do as commanded by the messenger. I left the field, and went to the place where the messenger had told me the plates were deposited; and owing to the distinctness of the vision which I had had concerning it, I knew the place the instant that I arrived there. (Joseph Smith 2:27-50.)*

Joseph acquires the plates

Convenient to the village of Manchester, Ontario county, New York, stands a hill of considerable size, and the most elevated of any in the neighborhood. On the west side of this hill, not far from the top, under a stone of considerable size, lay the plates, deposited in a stone box. This stone was thick and rounding in the middle of the upper side, and thinner towards the edges, so that the middle part of it was visible above the ground, but the edge all around was covered with earth.

Having removed the earth, I obtained a lever, which I got fixed under the edge of the stone, and with a little exertion raised it up. I looked in, and there indeed did I behold the plates, the Urim and Thummim, and the breastplate, as stated by the messenger. The box in which they lay was formed by laying stones together in some kind of cement. In the bottom of the box were laid two stones crossways of the box, and on these stones lay the plates and the other things with them.

I made an attempt to take them out, but was forbidden by the messenger, and was again informed that the time for bringing them forth had not yet arrived, neither would it, until four years from

---

*In addition to the Prophet's account of the momentous event of the appearance of the angel Moroni, Oliver Cowdery has recorded the following concerning Joseph's description of the angel:

. . . on a sudden a light like that of day, only of a purer and far more glorious appearance and brightness burst into the room. Indeed, to use his own description, the first sight was as though the house was filled with consuming and unquenchable fire. This sudden appearance of a light so bright, as must naturally be expected, occasioned a shock or sensation, visible to the extremities of the body. It was, however, followed with a calmness and serenity of mind, and an overwhelming rapture of joy that surpassed understanding, and in a moment a personage stood before him.

Notwithstanding the room was previously filled with light above the brightness of the sun, as I have before described, yet there seemed to be an additional glory surrounding or accompanying this personage, which shone with an increased degree of brilliancy, of which he was in the midst; and though his countenance was as lightning, yet it was of a pleasing, innocent and glorious appearance, so much so, that every fear was banished from the heart, and nothing but calmness pervaded the soul.

It is no easy task to describe the appearance of a messenger from the skies—indeed, I doubt there being an individual clothed with perishable clay, who is capable to do this work. . . . (Berrett and Burton, *Readings in L.D.S. Church History,* 1:24.)

18   that time; but he told me that I should come to that place precisely
in one year from that time, and that he would there meet with me,
and that I should continue to do so until the time should come for
obtaining the plates.

Accordingly, as I had been commanded, I went at the end of
each year, and at each time I found the same messenger there, and
received instruction and intelligence from him at each of our interviews, respecting what the Lord was going to do, and how and in
what manner his kingdom was to be conducted in the last days.

As my father's worldly circumstances were very limited, we
were under the necessity of laboring with our hands, hiring out by
day's work and otherwise, as we could get opportunity. Sometimes
we were at home, and sometimes abroad, and by continuous labor
were enabled to get a comfortable maintenance.

At length the time arrived for obtaining the plates, the Urim
and Thummim, and the breastplate. On the twenty-second day of
September, one thousand eight hundred and twenty-seven, having
gone as usual at the end of another year to the place where they
were deposited, the same heavenly messenger delivered them up to
me with this charge: that I should be responsible for them; that if I
should let them go carelessly, or through any neglect of mine, I
should be cut off; but that if I would use all my endeavors to
preserve them, until he, the messenger, should call for them, they
should be protected.

I soon found out the reason why I had received such strict
charges to keep them safe, and why it was that the messenger had
said that when I had done what was required at my hand, he would
call for them. For no sooner was it known that I had them, than the
most strenuous exertions were used to get them from me. Every
stratagem that could be invented was resorted to for that purpose.
The persecution became more bitter and severe than before, and
multitudes were on the alert continually to get them from me if
possible. But by the wisdom of God, they remained safe in my
hands, until I had accomplished by them what was required at my
hand. When, according to arrangements, the messenger called for
them, I delivered them up to him; and he has them in his charge
until this day, being the second day of May, one thousand eight
hundred and thirty-eight. (Joseph Smith 2:51-55, 59-60.)

Concerning the important events of this period, the
Prophet's mother adds the following incidents and descriptions to the record:

The plates were secreted about three miles from home, in the
following manner: Finding an old birch log much decayed, except-
ing the bark, which was in a measure sound, he took his pocket

knife and cut the bark with some care, then turned it back, and   19
made a hole of sufficient size to receive the plates, and, laying them
in the cavity thus formed, he replaced the bark; after which he laid
across the log, in several places, some old stuff that happened to lay
near, in order to conceal, as much as possible, the place in which
they were deposited.

Joseph, on coming to them, took them from their secret place,
and, wrapping them in his linen frock, placed them under his arm
and started for home.

After proceeding a short distance, he thought it would be more
safe to leave the road and go through the woods. Traveling some
distance after he left the road, he came to a large windfall, and as
he was jumping over a log, a man sprang up from behind it and
gave him a heavy blow with a gun. Joseph turned around and
knocked him down, then ran at the top of his speed. About half a
mile further he was attacked again in the same manner as before;
he knocked this man down in like manner as the former, and ran
on again; and before he reached home he was assaulted the third
time. In striking the last one, he dislocated his thumb, which,
however, he did not notice until he came within sight of the house,
when he threw himself down in the corner of the fence in order to
recover his breath. As soon as he was able, he arose and came to
the house. He was still altogether speechless from fright and the
fatigue of running.

After resting a few moments, he desired me to send Carlos for
my husband [Joseph Smith, Sen.], Mr. Knight, and his friend Stoal,
and have them go immediately and see if they could find the men
who had been pursuing him. And after Carlos had done this, he
wished to have him sent to Hyrum's, to tell him to bring the chest.

I did as I was requested, and when Carlos arrived at Hyrum's,
he found him at tea, with two of his wife's sisters. Just as Hyrum
was raising a cup to his mouth, Carlos touched his shoulder. Without waiting to hear one word from the child, he dropped the cup,
sprang from the table, caught the chest, turned it upside down, and
emptying its contents on the floor, left the house instantly with the
chest on his shoulder.

The young ladies were greatly astonished at his singular behavior, and declared to his wife—who was then confined to her
bed, her eldest daughter, Lovina, being but four days old—that he
was certainly crazy.

His wife laughed heartily, and replied, "Oh, not in the least; he
has just thought of something which he has neglected; and it is just
like him to fly off in a tangent when he thinks of anything in that
way."

When the chest came, Joseph locked up the Record, then threw himself upon the bed, and after resting a little, so that he could converse freely, he arose and went into the kitchen, where he related his recent adventure to his father, Mr. Knight, and Mr. Stoal, besides many others, who had by this time collected, with the view of hearing something in regard to the strange circumstance which had taken place. . . .

After bringing home the plates, Joseph commenced working with his father and brothers on the farm, in order to be as near as possible to the treasure which was confided to his care.

Soon after this, he came in from work, one afternoon, and after remaining a short time, he put on his great coat, and left the house. I was engaged at the time, in an upper room, in preparing some oil-cloths for painting. When he returned, he requested me to come down stairs. I told him that I could not leave my work just then, yet, upon his urgent request, I finally concluded to go down and see what he wanted, upon which he handed me the breast-plate spoken of in his history.

It was wrapped in a thin muslin handkerchief, so thin that I could feel its proportions without any difficulty.

It was concave on one side, and convex on the other, and extended from the neck downwards, as far as the center of the stomach of a man of extraordinary size. It had four straps of the same material, for the purpose of fastening it to the breast, two of which ran back to go over the shoulders, and the other two were designed to fasten to the hips. They were just the width of two of my fingers, (for I measured them) and they had holes in the end of them, to be convenient in fastening. After I had examined it, Joseph placed it in the chest with the Urim and Thummim.

Shortly after this circumstance, Joseph came to the house in great haste, and inquired, if there had been a company of men about. I told him, not a single individual had come to the house since he left. He then said, that a mob would be there that night, if they did not come before that time, to search for the Record, and that it must be removed immediately. . . .

In view of this, it was determined that a portion of the hearth should be taken up, and that the Record and breast-plate should be buried under the same, and then the hearth be relaid, to prevent suspicion.

This was done as speedily as possible, but the hearth was scarcely relaid when a large company of men well armed came rushing up to the house. Joseph threw open the doors, and taking a hint from the stratagem of his grandfather Mack, halloed as if he had a legion at hand, in the meanwhile, giving the word of command with great emphasis; while all the male portion of the family, from the father down to little Carlos, ran out of the house with such fury upon the mob, that it struck them with terror and dismay, and they fled before the little Spartan band into the woods, where they dispersed themselves to their several homes.

In a short time Joseph received another intimation of the approach of a mob, also of the necessity of removing the Record and breast-plate from the place wherein they were secreted, consequently he took them out of the box in which they were placed, and wrapping them in clothes, carried them across the road to a cooper's shop, and laid them in a quantity of flax which was stowed in the shop loft. After which he nailed up the box again, then tore up the floor of the shop, and put it under the same.

As soon as night came, the mob came also, and commenced ransacking the place. They rummaged round the house, and all over the premises, but did not come into the house. After making satisfactory search, they went away. (*History of Joseph Smith by His Mother, Lucy Mack Smith* [Bookcraft, 1958 ed.], pp. 107-9, 111-13.)*

Joseph begins translating

As soon as Joseph acquired the plates he desired to begin translating, but because of the severe persecution he was forced to leave New York. His brief account of this trying period follows:

---

*In connection with the foregoing accounts, Brigham Young records:

There were a great many treasures hid up by the Nephites. . . . I lived right in the country where the plates were found from which the Book of Mormon was translated, and I know a great many things pertaining to that country. I believe I will take the liberty to tell you of another circumstance that will be as marvelous as anything can be. This is an incident in the life of Oliver Cowdery, but he did not take the liberty of telling such things in meeting as I take. I tell these things to you, and I have a motive for doing so. I want to carry them to the ears of my brethren and sisters, and the children also, that they may grow to an understanding of some things that seem to be entirely hidden from the human family, Oliver Cowdery went with the Prophet Joseph when he deposited these plates. Joseph did not translate all of the plates; there was a portion of these sealed which you can learn from the Doctrine and Covenants. When Joseph got the plates, the angel instructed him to carry them back to the Hill Cumorah, which he did. Oliver says that when Joseph and Oliver went there, the hill opened, and they walked into a cave, in which there was a large and spacious room. . . . They laid the plates on the table; it was a large table that stood in the room. Under this table there was a pile of plates as much as two feet high, and there were altogether in this room more plates than probably many wagon loads; they were piled up in the corners and along the walls. . . .

Also the following entry by Edward Stevenson:

It was stated to me by David Whitmer in the year 1877 that Oliver Cowdery told him that the Prophet Joseph and himself had seen this room and that it was filled with treasure, and on a table therein were the breast plate and the sword of Laban, as well as the portion of the gold plates not yet translated, and that these plates were bound by three small gold rings. . . . (Berrett and Burton, *Readings in L.D.S. Church History,* 1:36-37.)

22   The excitement, however, still continued, and rumor with her thousand tongues was all the time employed in circulating falsehoods about my father's family, and about myself. If I were to relate a thousandth part of them, it would fill up volumes. The persecution, however, became so intolerable that I was under the necessity of leaving Manchester, and going with my wife to Susquehanna county, in the State of Pennsylvania. While preparing to start—being very poor, and the persecution so heavy upon us that there was no probability that we would ever be otherwise—in the midst of our afflictions we found a friend in a gentleman by the name of Martin Harris, who came to us and gave me fifty dollars to assist us on our journey. Mr. Harris was a resident of Palmyra township, Wayne county, in the State of New York, and a farmer of respectability.

By this timely aid was I enabled to reach the place of my destination in Pennsylvania; and immediately after my arrival there I commenced copying the characters off the plates. I copied a considerable number of them, and by means of the Urim and Thummim I translated some of them, which I did between the time I arrived at the house of my wife's father, in the month of December, and the February following. (Joseph Smith 2:61-62.)

Martin Harris visits Professor Anthon

The word that Joseph had started translating the record was evidently conveyed back to the Smith family at Palmyra. At any rate, Martin Harris heard of the Prophet's work and soon followed the Prophet to Harmony, Pennsylvania.

Sometime in this month of February, the aforementioned Mr. Martin Harris came to our place, got the characters which I had drawn off the plates, and started with them to the city of New York. For what took place relative to him and the characters, I refer to his own account of the circumstances, as he related them to me after his return, which was as follows:

"I went to the city of New York, and presented the characters which had been translated, with the translation thereof, to Professor Charles Anthon, a gentleman celebrated for his literary attainments. Professor Anthon stated that the translation was correct, more so than any he had before seen translated from the Egyptian. I then showed him those which were not yet translated, and he said that they were Egyptian, Chaldaic, Assyriac, and Arabic; and he said they were true characters. He gave me a certificate, certifying to the people of Palmyra that they were true characters, and that the translation of such of them as had been translated was also correct. I took the certificate and put it into my pocket, and was just leaving the house, when Mr. Anthon called me

back, and asked me how the young man found out that there were   23
gold plates in the place where he found them. I answered that an
angel of God had revealed it unto him.

"He then said to me, 'Let me see that certificate.' I accordingly
took it out of my pocket and gave it to him, when he took it and
tore it to pieces, saying that there was no such thing now as ministering of angels, and that if I would bring the plates to him he
would translate them. I informed him that part of the plates were
sealed, and that I was forbidden to bring them. He replied, 'I cannot read a sealed book.' I left him and went to Dr. Mitchell, who
sanctioned what Professor Anthon had said respecting both the
characters and the translation." (Joseph Smith 2:63-65.)

Loss of 116 pages of manuscript

Following his visit to the East, Martin Harris seemed to
be satisfied with the Prophet's story of the gold plates. Thus,
he became the first scribe for the Prophet Joseph in the
translation of the Book of Mormon. This service was short
lived, however, because of the following event.

The impression made on the mind of Martin Harris by this in-
terview, resulted in his removal to Harmony to give further aid to
Joseph Smith. He arrived about the 12th of April, 1828, and immediately commenced to write as the Prophet dictated his translation of the record. Martin continued in this work until the 14th of
June, at which time one hundred and sixteen pages of manuscript
on foolscap paper had been prepared. Some time after Martin
Harris commenced to write he importuned the Prophet for the
privilege of taking the manuscript home and showing it to some
skeptical friends, who had sorely criticized him for the part he was
taking in the work. He was desirous of convincing them; and they
had, without doubt, pleaded with him to do this thing. Especially
had his wife implored him for a look at the manuscript.

The Prophet inquired by Urim and Thummim, and the request
of Martin was denied. However, he was not satisfied and importuned and pleaded with Joseph again to inquire of the Lord.
This he did, but the answer was the same as before. Still Martin implored, and so insistent and prolonged were his pleadings that Joseph Smith again, the third time, inquired of the Lord. This time
the answer was favorable. The request was granted on certain positive conditions. Martin was to show the manuscript to his brother,
Preserved Harris, his wife, his father and mother and his wife's
sister, Mrs. Cobb. No other person was to see the writings. In a
most solemn covenant Martin bound himself to this agreement.
When he arrived home, and pressure was brought to bear upon
him, he forgot his solemn oath and permitted others to view the

24 manuscript, with the result that by stratagem it passed out of his hands.

The Lord was displeased with Joseph Smith for his constant importuning, and took from him the Urim and Thummim after the departure of Martin Harris with the partial translation from the plates. When the fact was known that Martin had lost the manuscript, the Prophet suffered the torments of the damned. He found no rest; there was no peace of conscience. In the bitterness of his soul he feared to approach the Lord. This condition continued for some time until one day the angel appeared to him, and returned the Urim and Thummim, that he might through them receive a revelation from the Lord. (Doc and Cov. Sec. 3.) In this revelation it was made known that the purposes of the Lord were not frustrated, but the designs of men. Joseph was soundly rebuked and warned against yielding to temptation. Nevertheless the mercy of the Lord was extended to him because of his severe punishment and sore repentance. After the revelation was received, both the Urim and Thummim and the plates were taken from him, but in a few days were restored again. This was the most bitter lesson Joseph Smith ever received. It seemed necessary to prepare him for the great responsibilities yet before him.

In May of 1829 Joseph received another revelation (Doc. and Cov. Sec. 10) in which he was forbidden again to translate the portion of the record which had been lost. Satan had put it into the hearts of wicked men, the revelation declared, to alter the writings of the manuscript and then, if Joseph Smith should translate again, they would say that he could not do it twice alike, and thus they would catch him in his words which he had pretended to translate.

The lost manuscript contained the abridgment made by Mormon of the record of [Lehi], from the time Lehi left Jerusalem down to the reign of King Benjamin, or to the words of Mormon, in the Book of Mormon. When Mormon made his abridgment of the records of the Nephites, the Lord directed him to attach also the small plates of Nephi, which contained the record of the people covering the same period of time as the abridgment down to the reign of King Benjamin. In this manner there were two accounts of that history, the abridgment and the original. Now the translation of the abridgment was lost; but the better account could still be translated, and the designs of Satan be defeated. Thus the "wise purpose" of the Lord, in directing Mormon to include Nephi's plates, was made known to Joseph Smith. (Joseph Fielding Smith, *Essentials in Church History,* pp. 55-56.)

Joseph resumes translating with Emma Smith as scribe

The Prophet was now without the services of Martin

Harris. He resumed translating the record at this time with 25
his wife Emma acting as scribe until the Lord provided
another full-time scribe. Emma later told her son of her
experience as a scribe:

My belief is that the Book of Mormon is of divine
authenticity—I have not the slightest doubt of it. I am satisfied that
no man could have dictated the writing of the manuscript unless he
was inspired: for, when [I was acting] as his scribe, your father
would dictate to me hour after hour; and when returning after
meals, or after interruptions, he would at once begin where he had
left off, without either seeing the manuscript or having any portion
of it read to him. It would have been improbable that a learned
man could do this; and, for one so . . . unlearned as he was, it was
simply impossible. (Kirkham, *A New Witness for Christ in America*,
1:195-96.)

However, the wife of the Prophet was so involved in her
housework that she was not able to spend much time assisting her husband in writing as he continued the translation.
The Prophet's mother makes the following comment concerning this period:

Joseph had been so hurried with his secular affairs, that he
could not proceed with his spiritual concerns so fast as was
necessary for the speedy completion of the work; there was also
another disadvantage under which he labored; his wife had so
much of her time taken up with the care of her house, that she
could write for him but a small portion of the time. On account of
these embarrassments, Joseph called upon the Lord, three days
before the arrival of Samuel and Oliver, to send him a scribe.
(Ibid., p. 212.)

Oliver Cowdery meets Joseph Smith and becomes his scribe

The Prophet evidently felt the work of translation must
go more rapidly than it was going with his wife acting as
scribe. Therefore, he asked the Lord to send someone to
assist him, as is noted in this quotation:

For a time the Prophet was without assistance. For several months
he was under the necessity of "laboring with his hands" on his
small farm in Harmony and otherwise seeking employment. The
work of the Lord was lagging. He must be about his mission. He
prayed to the Lord for help. On the 5th of April, 1829, a young
school teacher, Oliver Cowdery, came to Harmony to inquire of Joseph Smith regarding his work. Oliver Cowdery had been teaching

26   school near the home of the Smiths in Manchester, and part of the time boarded with that family. From them he learned of the Prophet's vision, the coming of Moroni, and of the plates. He had a feeling that these stories were true and desired to investigate at close quarters. He was convinced of the truth of Joseph's story, and two days after his arrival in Harmony, commenced to write as the Prophet translated from the record. Later in the month of April the Lord gave to Oliver a revelation through Joseph Smith in which he was called to the work. In that revelation things were revealed that only Oliver Cowdery knew. From that time forth he continued to act as the amanuensis for Joseph Smith, until the Book of Mormon was finished. (Joseph Fielding Smith, *Essentials in Church History,* pp. 56-57.)

Oliver Cowdery himself has left the following record of his first meeting the Prophet and starting to act as his scribe.

Near the time of the setting of the sun, Sabbath evening, April 5th, 1829, my natural eyes for the first time beheld this brother. He then resided in Harmony, Susquehanna County, Pennsylvania. On Monday, the 6th, I assisted him in arranging some business of a temporal nature and on Tuesday, the 7th, commenced to write the Book of Mormon. These days were never to be forgotten—to sit under the sound of a voice dictated by the inspiration of heaven, awakened the utmost gratitude of this bosom. Day after day I continued, uninterrupted, to write from his mouth, as he translated with the Urim and Thummim, or, as the Nephites would have said, "Interpreters," the history or record called the "Book of Mormon." (Kirkham, *A New Witness for Christ in America,* 1:81.)

Although Oliver Cowdery left the Church for a few years, he came back into full membership before his death. On the occasion of his reentering the Church, he addressed about two thousand Latter-day Saints at Council Bluffs, Iowa; he then recalled his early work as a scribe to the Prophet:

My name is Cowdery, Oliver Cowdery. In the early history of this Church I stood identified with her, and one in her councils. True it is that the gifts and callings of God are without repentance; not because I was better than the rest of mankind was I called; but, to fulfill the purposes of God, he called me to a high and holy calling.

I wrote, with my own pen, the entire Book of Mormon (save a few pages) as it fell from the lips of the Prophet Joseph Smith, as he translated it by the gift and power of God, by the means of the Urim and Thummim, or, as it is called by that book "Holy Interpreters." I beheld with my eyes, and handled with my hands, the gold plates from which it was transcribed. I also saw with my eyes and handled with my hands the "Holy Interpreters." That book is true. Sidney Rigdon did not write it; Mr. Spaulding did not write it. I wrote it myself as it fell from the lips of the Prophet. It contains the everlasting gospel, and came forth to the children of men in fulfillment of the revelations of John, where he says he saw an angel come, with the everlasting gospel to preach to every nation, kindred, tongue, and people. It contains principles of salvation; and if you, my hearers, will walk by its light and obey its precepts, you will be saved with an everlasting salvation in the Kingdom of God on high. . . . (Kirkham, *A New Witness for Christ in America,* 1:71.)

The Prophet continues the translation

Joseph Smith did not provide the world with very much information concerning the actual process of translating the plates. In fact, he specifically said it was not expedient for him to relate such things, as is indicated in Francis Kirkham's commentary and Joseph Smith's answer to the following questions:

"How and where did you obtain the Book of Mormon?" . . . "I am answering these questions," wrote the Prophet, "by publication for the reason they are asked me thousands of times.

"Moroni, the person who deposited the plates from whence the Book of Mormon was translated, in a hill in Manchester, Ontario County, New York, being dead, and raised again therefrom, appeared unto me, and told me where they were; and gave me directions how to obtain them. *I obtained them and the Urim and Thummim with them, by the means of which I translated the plates and thus came the Book of Mormon.*"

In recording the first visit of Moroni, the immortal messenger, to him, the Prophet writes, *"That God had prepared them [the Urim and Thummim] for the purpose of translating the book."*

Another short statement by the Prophet of the origin and translation of the Book of Mormon is a letter dated Nauvoo, Illinois, March 1, 1842, addressed to John Wentworth, editor and proprietor of the Chicago *Democrat.* This letter was published at Nauvoo, May 1, 1842. Speaking of the visit to him of Moroni, the immortal messenger, on September 21, 1823, the Prophet writes:

"I was also told where there were deposited some plates, on which was engraved an abridgment of the records of the ancient peoples that had existed on this continent. The angel appeared to me three times the same night and unfolded the same things. After having received many visits from the angel of God, unfolding the

28 majesty and glory of the events that should transpire in the last days, on the morning of the 22nd of September, A.D. 1827, the angel of the Lord delivered the records into my hands.

"These records were engraven on plates which had the appearance of gold: each plate was six inches wide and eight inches long, and not quite so thick as common tin. They were filled with engravings in Egyptian characters and bound together in a volume as the leaves of a book, with three rings running through the whole. The volume was something over six inches in thickness, part of which was sealed. The characters on the unsealed part were small and beautifully engraved. The whole book exhibited many marks of antiquity in its construction, and much skill in the art of engraving. With the records was found a curious instrument which the ancients called 'Urim and Thummim,' which consisted of two transparent stones set in the rim of a bow fastened to a breastplate. *Through the medium of the Urim and Thummim I translated the record, by the gift and power of God.*"...

About a year and a half after the publication of the Book of Mormon, forty-four elders, ten priests and ten teachers were in conference at the home of Brother Sirenes Burnett, at Orange, Cuyahoga County, Ohio, (Oct. 25, 1831). In the minutes of this conference the following appears:

"Brother Hyrum Smith said, 'That he thought best that the information of the coming forth of the Book of Mormon be related by Joseph himself, to the elders present, that all might know for themselves.'

"Brother Joseph Smith, Jr., said, 'That it was not intended to tell the world all the particulars of the coming forth of the Book of Mormon,' and also said, 'that it was not expedient for him to relate these things, etc.' "...

A careful reading of the writings of the Prophet and Oliver Cowdery, his scribe, reveals no information regarding the manner of translating the Book of Mormon, except that "It was translated by the gift and power of God by the aid of the Urim and Thummim." This is also the conclusion of Brigham H. Roberts.

After a lapse of forty years of time, both David Whitmer and Martin Harris attempted to give the method of the translation. Evidently the Prophet did not tell them the method, for he states positively it was not expedient "for him to relate these things."

The conclusion is that no one knows the procedure or exact method of the translation. All that is known is contained in these words, "It was translated by the gift and power of God, with the aid of the Urim and Thummim." Beyond this statement, it is only conjecture. The dictation was continuous without correction. It was not human. It was divine. (Kirkham, *A New Witness for Christ in America*, 1:190-91, 194, 196.)

Restoration of the priesthood

While the Prophet and Oliver were translating at Harmony, the subject of baptism was introduced, and the two young men wondered what should be done. B. H. Roberts reviews the events surrounding their decision:

The subject of Christian baptism was much discussed among the rival sects in the early decades of the 19th century. The purpose of it; the proper subjects to receive it; the effects of it; the manner in which it should be administered; by whom it could be administered, by any Christian who understood its significance, or only by ordained ministers? By pouring, or sprinkling, or by immersion only? All these questions were subjects of intense controversy in the period named.

When, therefore, in the course of translating the *Book of Mormon*, Joseph Smith and Oliver Cowdery came to a passage making reference to "baptism for the remission of sins," it is not surprising that they held divergent views upon the subject; but instead of resorting to argument on the matter they agreed to inquire of the Lord, through prayer, for the knowledge essential to a right understanding of the subject. It was while thus engaged, according to the testimony of both these men, that a heavenly messenger appeared unto them and announced himself to be John, the same that in the *New Testament* is called "the Baptist." He was now raised from the dead and had been sent to confer upon Joseph Smith and Oliver Cowdery the Aaronic priesthood, which he did in these words:

"Upon you my fellow servants, in the name of Messiah, I confer the Priesthood of Aaron, which holds the keys of the ministering of angels, and of the gospel of repentance, and of baptism by immersion for the remission of sins; and this shall never be taken again from the earth, until the sons of Levi do offer again an offering unto the Lord in righteousness."

The messenger directed that Joseph Smith should baptize Oliver Cowdery, and afterwards that Oliver should baptize Joseph; which when done Joseph proceeded to ordain Oliver to the Aaronic priesthood, and afterwards received ordination at Oliver's hands— "for so were we commanded," says the Prophet, in his narration of the circumstance. Both experienced great exaltation of spirit on this occasion. "No sooner had I baptized Oliver Cowdery," says the Prophet, "than the Holy Ghost fell upon him, and he stood up and prophesied many things which should shortly come to pass. And again, so soon as I had been baptized by him, I also had the spirit

30 of prophecy. . . I prophesied concerning the rise of this church, and many other things connected with the church and this generation of the children of men.". . .

The exact date upon which was fulfilled the promise of John the Baptist that the greater priesthood should be restored is not known. But beyond all doubt it was between the 15th of May, 1829, and the month of April, 1830; for in the revelation directing the manner of organizing the church, given early in April of the year last named, the ordination of the Prophet and of Oliver Cowdery to the "apostleship"—and consequently to the higher priesthood, since the office of an apostle is an office of that higher priesthood— is referred to as an accomplished fact. (Roberts, *A Comprehensive History of the Church,* 1:177-79, 183.)

This event naturally had a profound influence and effect upon the two young men. Oliver Cowdery recorded the glorious incidents in the following words:

After writing the account given of the Savior's ministry to the remnant of the seed of Jacob upon this continent, it was easily to be seen, that amid the great strife and noise concerning religion, none had authority from God to administer the ordinances of the gospel. For the question might be asked, have men authority to administer in the name of Christ, who deny revelations, when His testimony is no less than the spirit of prophecy and His religion based, built, and sustained by immediate revelations in all ages of the world, when He has had a people on earth! If these facts were buried and carefully concealed by men whose craft would have been in danger if once permitted to shine in the faces of men, they were no longer to us; and we only waited for the commandment to be given, "Arise and be baptized."

This was not long desired before it was realized. The Lord, who is rich in mercy, and ever willing to answer the consistent prayer of the humble, after we had called upon Him in a fervent manner, aside from the abodes of men, condescended to manifest to us His will. On a sudden, as from the midst of eternity, the voice of the Redeemer spake peace to us, while the veil was parted and the angel of God came down clothed with glory, and delivered the anxiously looked for message, and the keys of the gospel of repentance. What joy! What wonder! What amazement! While the world was racked and distracted—while millions were groping as the blind for the wall, and while all men were resting upon uncertainty, as a general mass, our eyes beheld—our ears heard. As in the "blaze of day"; yes, more—above the glitter of the May sunbeam, which then shed its brilliancy over the face of nature! Then his voice, though mild, pierced to the center, and his words, "I am thy

fellow-servant," dispelled every fear. We listened, we gazed, we ad-   31
mired! 'Twas the voice of an angel from glory—'twas a message
from the Most High, and as we heard we rejoiced, while His love
enkindled upon our souls, and we were rapt in the vision of the
Almighty! Where was room for doubt? Nowhere; uncertainty had
fled, doubt had sunk, no more to rise, while fiction and deception
had fled forever. . . .

I was present with Joseph when an holy angel from God came
down from heaven and conferred on us, or restored, the lesser or
Aaronic Priesthood, and said to us at the same time, that it should
remain upon the earth while the earth stands.

I was also present with Joseph when the higher or Melchizedek
Priesthood was conferred by the holy angel on high. This Priesthood we then conferred on each other, by the will and commandment of God. This Priesthood, as was then declared, is also to
remain upon the earth until the last remnant of time. This Holy
Priesthood, or authority, we then conferred upon many, and is just
as good, and valid as though God had done it in person. (Kirkham,
A New Witness for Christ in America, 1:82, 72.)

Completion of the translation

After receiving the priesthood from the angel of God, the
Prophet and Oliver continued their translation and writing
of the plates. However, as Joseph Fielding Smith indicates
below, the final work of the translation did not take place at
Harmony, Pennsylvania.

It was not destined that the work of translation should go on in
Harmony, without interruption. Opposition finally made itself
manifest and became so strong that even Isaac Hale—a man who
believed in justice, law and order, but who did not express much
faith in the mission of Joseph Smith—became somewhat bitter in
his feelings. The necessity of a change of residence was apparent.
Oliver Cowdery wrote to a young friend, David Whitmer of
Fayette, New York, with whom he had previously corresponded regarding the coming forth of the Book of Mormon, desiring that he
would come and take Joseph and himself to the Whitmer home in
Fayette. This David Whitmer consented to do, and the removal
was made in June, 1829.

When David was on the journey to Harmony on this mission,
he was met some distance from the town of Harmony by Joseph
and Oliver. In referring to this circumstance some years later,
David Whitmer wrote: "Oliver told me that Joseph had informed
him when I started from home, where I stopped the first night, how
I read the sign at the tavern, where I stopped the next night, etc.,
and that I would be there that day for dinner, and this is why they

32   had come out to meet me. All of which was exactly as Joseph had told Oliver, at which I was greatly astonished." (*Millennial Star,* 40:769-74; also quoted by Joseph Fielding Smith, *Essentials in Church History,* pp. 59-60.)

The translation was finally completed at the Whitmer farm in Fayette, New York. Concerning the actual date of the completion of the translation, Francis Kirkham has written:

It appears that the entire copy might have been prepared before the printing began for the reason that the original copy would be kept at a separate place to guard against loss or destruction. In any event, one month to six or seven weeks would be no more than sufficient time to prepare the manuscript, arrange for, and actually begin the printing which, from the evidence presented below, began in August, 1829.

The conclusion is this:

The translation and writing of the Book of Mormon commenced April 7, 1829, at page sixteen or a little before and were completed about July 1, 1829. . . .

The evidence appears complete, that the printing of the Book of Mormon began in August, 1829, and was completed not later than March 26, 1830, at the printing press of E. B. Grandin at Palmyra, New York.

From the above sources, it is clear that the Book of Mormon was dictated by Joseph Smith in the relatively short period of seventy-five working days. There were many witnesses both at his home at Harmony, Pennsylvania, and at Fayette, New York. Many persons knew all the facts. No one has attempted to deny them. The physical facts concerning time, place and scribes of the writing of the translation and the publishing of the Book of Mormon are attested by both believers and non-believers in the divine origin of the book. There was no incentive for deception or misrepresentation of these facts by the persons who willingly gave their time to this effort. No wealth, honor, power or influence was to come to any one of them from this achievement only the privilege to serve. The reward was joy in this life and in eternity by helping to lead "save it be but one soul" into the way of divine love and eternal progress. (*A New Witness for Christ in America,* 1:224-25, 227.)

In March and again in June of 1829 Joseph Smith received by revelation commandments of the Lord to have three witnesses view the plates of the Book of Mormon. Concerning the fulfillment of these commandments, Joseph writes:

Not many days after the above commandment [Doctrine and

Covenants 17] was given, we four, viz., Martin Harris, David 33
Whitmer, Oliver Cowdery and myself, agreed to retire into the
woods, and try to obtain, by fervent and humble prayer, the
fulfilment of the promises given in the above revelation—that they
should have a view of the plates. We accordingly made choice of a
piece of woods convenient to Mr. Whitmer's house, to which we
retired, and having knelt down, we began to pray in much faith to
Almighty God to bestow upon us a realization of these promises.

According to previous arrangement, I commenced by vocal
prayer to our Heavenly Father, and was followed by each of the
others in succession. We did not at the first trial, however, obtain
any answer or manifestation of divine favor in our behalf. We
again observed the same order of prayer, each calling on and praying fervently to God in rotation, but with the same result as before.

Upon this, our second failure, Martin Harris proposed that he
should withdraw himself from us, believing, as he expressed
himself, that his presence was the cause of our not obtaining what
we wished for. He accordingly withdrew from us, and we knelt
down again, and had not been many minutes engaged in prayer,
when presently we beheld a light above us in the air, of exceeding
brightness; and behold, an angel stood before us. In his hands he
held the plates which we had been praying for these to have a view
of. He turned over the leaves one by one, so that we could see them,
and discern the engravings thereon distinctly. He then addressed
himself to David Whitmer, and said, "David blessed is the Lord,
and he that keeps His commandments;" when, immediately afterwards, we heard a voice from out of the bright light above us,
saying, "These plates have been revealed by the power of God, and
they have been translated by the power of God. The translation of
them which you have seen is correct, and I command you to bear
record of what you now see and hear."

I now left David and Oliver, and went in pursuit of Martin
Harris, whom I found at a considerable distance, fervently engaged
in prayer. He soon told me, however, that he had not yet prevailed
with the Lord, and earnestly requested me to join him in prayer,
that he also might realize the same blessings which we had just received. We accordingly joined in prayer, and ultimately obtained
our desires, for before we had yet finished, the same vision was
opened to our view, at least it was again opened to me, and I once
more beheld and heard the same things; whilst at the same moment, Martin Harris cried out, apparently in an ecstasy of joy,
" 'Tis enough; 'tis enough; mine eyes have beheld; mine eyes have
beheld;" and jumping up, he shouted, "Hosanna," blessing God,
and otherwise rejoiced exceedingly. (Joseph Smith, *History of the
Church,* 1:54-55.)

The Prophet's mother adds the following interesting information concerning the manifestation to the special witnesses:

The next morning (i.e. following the arrival of the party from Palmyra), after attending to the usual services, namely, reading from the scriptures, singing, and praying, Joseph arose from his knees, and approaching Martin Harris with a solemnity that thrills through my veins to this day, when it occurs to my recollection, said: "Martin Harris, you have got to humble yourself before your God this day, that you may obtain a forgiveness of your sins. If you do, it is the will of God that you should look upon the plates, in company with Oliver Cowdery and David Whitmer."

Joseph, Oliver and David, repaired to a grove, a short distance from the house, where they commenced calling upon the Lord, and continued in earnest supplication, until he permitted an angel to come down from his presence and declare to them that all Joseph testified of concerning the plates was true. When they returned to the house, it was between three and four o'clock in the afternoon. Mrs. Whitmer, Mr. Smith and myself were sitting in a bedroom at the time. On coming in Joseph threw himself down beside me, and exclaimed: "Father, mother, you do not know how happy I am; the Lord has now caused the plates to be shown to three more besides myself. They have seen an angel, who has testified to them, and they will have to bear witness to the truth of what I have said, for now they know for themselves that I do not go about to deceive the people, and I feel as if I was relieved of a burden which was almost too heavy for me to bear, and it rejoices my soul, that I am not any longer to be entirely alone in the work." Upon this Martin Harris came in: He seemed almost overcome with joy, and testified boldly to what he had both seen and heard. And so did David and Oliver, adding, that no tongue could express the joy of their hearts, and the greatness of the things which they had both seen and heard. (Berrett and Burton, *Readings in L.D.S. Church History,* 1:58-59.)

None of these men ever denied their testimony of the Book of Mormon, although some of them were later separated from the Church. For example, Oliver Cowdery left the Church in 1838 but returned and was rebaptized in 1848. During the period he was away from the Church, the following incident happened to him, according to a report published by Berrett and Burton:

... a Mr. Barrington, a successful farmer of that state related to him the following incident in the career of Oliver Cowdery that happened in the state of Michigan, when Mr. Barrington was about twenty years of age. A murder trial was in progress in the town

where Mr. Barrington then lived, and walking along the main street   35
one day Mr. B. noticed a great many people walking up to the
county court house, and not knowing what was going on there, he
says, "I became inquisitive, and made up my mind to go there also,
and on entering the court room I found that the same was crowded
to overflowing, but being young and strong I soon made my way up
to the railing in front of the bench and jury box, and I then learned
from a friend that it was a murder trial on before the court, and
that the young attorney who was then addressing or making his
opening argument to the jury was the county attorney, Oliver
Cowdery; as soon as Mr. Cowdery closed his opening argument the
attorney for the prisoner arose, and, in a sneering way, said: 'May it
please the Court, and gentlemen of the jury, I challenge Mr.
Cowdery, since he seems to know so much about this poor defendant, to tell us something about his connection with Joe Smith, and
the digging out of the hill of the Mormon Bible, and how Mr.
Cowdery helped Joe Smith to defraud the American people out of
a whole lot of money by selling the Mormon Bible and telling them
that an angel appeared to them from heaven, dressed in white
clothes.' After having kept on for a while in this way, abusing Mr.
Cowdery, he (attorney for the defendant) began to argue the case
to the jury; but all interest was shifted from the prisoner and his
case and directed towards Oliver Cowdery; everybody was wonder-
ing in what manner he would reply to the accusation just made.
The people did not believe, or know before this, that they had
elected a county prosecutor who had been an associate of the
"Mormon Prophet," Joseph Smith. Finally, when the defendant's
attorney had completed his argument, Oliver Cowdery's turn came
to reply, and everybody in the court room strained their necks to
catch a glimpse of Mr. Cowdery.

He arose as calm as a summer morning, and in a low but clear
voice which gradually rose in pitch and volume as he proceeded,
said:

"If your honor please, and gentlemen of the jury, the attorney
of the opposite side has challenged me to state my connection with
Joseph Smith and the *Book of Mormon;* and as I cannot now avoid
the responsibility, I must admit to you that I am the very Oliver
Cowdery whose name is attached to the testimony, with others, as
to the appearance of the angel Moroni; and let me tell you that it is
not because of my good deeds that I am here, away from the body
of the Mormon church, but because I have broken the covenants I
once made, and I was cut off from the church; but, gentlemen of
the jury, I have never denied my testimony, which is attached to
the front page of the *Book of Mormon* and I declare to you here
that these eyes saw the angel, and these ears of mine heard the

voice of the angel, and he told us his name was Moroni; that the book was true, and contained the fulness of the gospel, and we were also told that if we ever denied what we had heard and seen that there would be no forgiveness for us, neither in this world nor in the world to come." (Berrett and Burton, *Readings in L.D.S. Church History,* 1:60-61.)

Oliver Cowdery remained true to his death to his testimony of the Book of Mormon. Concerning his death, Kirkham writes:

In the year 1878, David Whitmer said to Elders Orson Pratt and Joseph F. Smith concerning his departure: "Oliver died the happiest man I ever saw. After shaking hands with the family and kissing his wife and daughter, he said, 'Now I lay me down for the last time; I am going to my Savior'; and he died immediately, with a smile on his face." (*A New Witness for Christ in America,* 1:248.)

David Whitmer always maintained his testimony of the Book of Mormon also, even though he was excommunicated from the Church in 1838.

After his separation from the Church, David Whitmer located at Richmond, Mo., where he resided until he passed away, January 25, 1888. In that place he was honored and respected, as a citizen and a Christian gentleman. This is evident from the following statement, which appeared in the Richmond *Conservator* of March 25, 1881:

"We, the undersigned citizens of Richmond, Ray Co., Mo. where David Whitmer, Sr., has resided since the year 1838, certify that we have been long and intimately acquainted with him and know him to be a man of the highest integrity and of undoubted truth and veracity."

This public acknowledgment of the trustworthiness of Mr. Whitmer was signed by twenty-one prominent business and professional men of Richmond. Among them were judges, lawyers, a bank president, the post-master, a doctor, and many other prominent citizens. Such was his reputation in a place where he had lived for half a century.

David Whitmer, in 1881, as reported in the Richmond *Conservator,* of March 25, that year, made this statement:

"Those who know me best know well that I have always adhered to that testimony. And that no man may be misled or doubt my present views in regard to the same, I do again affirm the truth of all my statements as then made and published. . . .

"In the spirit of Christ, who hath said, 'Follow thou me, for I am the Life, the Light, and the Way,' I submit this statement to the

world; God in whom I trust being my judge as to the sincerity of   37
my motives and the faith and hope that is in me of eternal life."
  On Sept. 7, 1878, David Whitmer, in the presence of Elder Joseph F. Smith, Elder Orson Pratt, and a number of other persons, including his eldest son, a grandson, and a son, Jacob Whitmer, bore this testimony:
  "He (the angel) stood before us. Our testimony, as recorded in the Book of Mormon, is strictly and absolutely true."
  In 1886, David Whitmer said to Elder Edward Stevenson:
  "As sure as the sun shines and I live, just so sure did the angel appear unto me and Joseph Smith and I heard his voice and did see the angel standing before us." (Kirkham, *A New Witness for Christ in America*, 1:248-49.)

  Martin Harris always bore a strong testimony of the Book of Mormon, and although he left the Church for a number of years he was a member in good standing at the time of his death. Concerning the last years of Harris's life, Francis Kirkham has written:
  Martin Harris passed the last five years of his earthly career at Clarkston, Cache County, Utah. While he lived there, visitors came from far and near to see and hear him, and he was never happier than when he had an opportunity to bear his testimony.
  Among his visitors was Elder Ole Jensen, then a resident of Clarkston, but later of Fairview, Wyoming. One day in the month of July, 1875, he and others heard the venerable witness relate his wonderful story. After having stated the circumstances attending the appearance of the angel with the plates, he said:
  "The angel stood before me and said, 'Look!' When I gazed upon him, I fell to the earth, but I rose to my feet again and saw the angel turn the golden leaves over and over, and I said, 'That is enough, my Lord and my God.' Then I heard the voice of God say, 'The book translated from these plates is true and translated correctly.' "
  Martin Harris added solemnly:
  "As sure as you are standing here and see me, just as sure did I see the angel with the gold plates in his hand as he showed them to me. I have promised that I will bear witness of this both here and hereafter."
  In a letter to President George A. Smith, dated July 9, 1875, the day before the death of Martin Harris, the writer, Martin Harris, Jr., says of his father:
  "He was taken ill a week ago yesterday with some kind of a stroke. . . . He has continued to talk about and testify to the truth of the Book of Mormon, and was in his happiest mood when he could

get somebody to listen to his testimony. . . . The last audible words he has spoken were something about the three witnesses of the Book of Mormon."

Among those who heard Martin Harris bear his testimony was Elder William Waddoups, second counselor in the Benson Stake Presidency. He was introduced to Martin Harris in Salt Lake City. To him Harris said:

"Young man, I had the privilege of being with the Prophet Joseph Smith, and with these eyes of men, (pointing to his eyes) I saw the angel of the Lord, and I saw the plates and the Urim and Thummim and the sword of Laban, and with these ears (pointing to his ears), I heard the voice of the angel, and with these hands (holding out his hands), I handled the plates containing the record of the Book of Mormon, and I assisted the Prophet in the translation thereof. I bear witness that this testimony is true." (Kirkham, *A New Witness for Christ in America,* 1:249-50.)

David Whitmer was the last of the three witnesses to pass away, and in a statement published less than a year before his death he reaffirmed that all three of the special witnesses had remained true to their testimony of the Book of Mormon. His statement is as follows:

It is recorded in the American Encyclopaedia and the Encyclopaedia Brittanica, that I, David Whitmer, have denied my testimony as one of the three witnesses to the divinity of the *Book of Mormon,* and that the other two witnesses, Oliver Cowdery and Martin Harris, denied their testimony of that book. I will say once more to all mankind, that I have never at any time denied that testimony or any part thereof. I also testify to the world, that neither Oliver Cowdery nor Martin Harris ever at any time denied their testimony. They both died reaffirming the truth of the divine authenticity of the *Book of Mormon.* (Berrett and Burton, *Readings in L.D.S. Church History,* 1:62.)

Eight witnesses and their testimonies

A second group of witnesses saw the plates a few days following the manifestation to the three witnesses. B. H. Roberts reviews this important event as follows:

A few days after the three witnesses obtained their view of the *Book of Mormon* plates, said plates were shown to the eight witnesses by the Prophet himself. Lucy Smith gives the most detailed account of the attendant circumstances. The day following the one on which the three witnesses received their testimony, the Palmyra party, consisting of the Prophet's father and mother and Martin Harris returned home; and now Lucy Smith's statement:

"In a few days we were followed by Joseph, Oliver and the Whitmers, who came to make us a visit, and make some arrangements about getting the book printed. Soon after they came, all the male part of the company, with my husband, Samuel and Hyrum, retired to a place where the family were in the habit of offering up their devotions to God. They went to this place because it had been revealed to Joseph that the plates would be carried thither by one of the ancient Nephites. Here it was that those eight witnesses, whose names are recorded in the *Book of Mormon,* looked upon them and handled them . . . After these witnesses returned to the house, an angel again made his appearance to Joseph, at which time Joseph delivered up the plates into the angel's hands." . . .

In the evening of the day that the eight witnesses saw and examined the Nephite plates, according to Lucy Smith, they held meeting at the Smith residence, "in which all the witnesses bore testimony to the facts as stated above", that is, to the facts stated in their testimony as here given and which appeared in the first and in all subsequent editions of the *Book of Mormon. . . .*

. . . They saw the plates; they handled them; they turned the leaves of the old Nephite record, and saw and marveled at its curious workmanship. No brilliant light illuminated the forest or dazzled their vision; no angel was there to awe them by the splendor of his presence; no soul-piercing voice of God from the midst of a glory to make them tremble by its power. All these supernatural circumstances present at the view of the plates by the three witnesses were absent at the time when the eight witnesses saw them. In this latter event all was natural, matter-of-fact, plain. Nothing to inspire awe, or fear, or dread; nothing uncanny or overwhelming, but just a plain, straightforward proceeding that leaves men in possession of all their faculties, and self-consciousness; all of which renders such a thing as deception, or imposition entirely out of the question. They could pass the plates from hand to hand, guess at their weight—doubtless considerable, that idea being conveyed in their testimony—"we have seen and *hefted,* and know of a surety, that the said Smith has got the plates." They could look upon the engravings, and observe calmly how different they were from everything modern in the way of record-making known to them, and hence the conclusion that the workmanship was not only curious but ancient.

Of these eight witnesses five of them, *viz:* Christian Whitmer, Peter Whitmer, Jun., Joseph Smith, Sen., Hyrum Smith, and Samuel Smith, all remained true throughout their lives, not only to their testimony, but faithful to the church also, and were honorable, upright men. While the three of the eight witnesses who left the church, or were excommunicated from it, *viz:* John Whitmer,

40 Hirum Page, and Jacob Whitmer, not one of them ever denied the truth of his testimony; a circumstance of some weight in helping one to determine the value of the testimony to which, with those who remained faithful to the church, they subscribed their names when the *Book of Mormon* was first given to the world. (Roberts, *A Comprehensive History of the Church,* 1:147-49.)

Other incidents concerning the lives and testimonies of these men have been related by Francis Kirkham as follows:

The eight witnesses, as well as the three, maintained their testimonies to the last. Joseph Smith, Sr., who was the first to receive the message of his chosen son as from God, passed away Sept. 18, 1840, after having endured faithfully all trials and hardships for the sake of the gospel. He was, at the time of his death, the Patriarch to the Church.

Hyrum Smith sealed his faithful testimony with his blood, June 27, 1844, the day of the martyrdom of the prophet, his brother, and the two, united in life, were not separated in death.

In December, 1839, the Patriarch wrote:

"I had been abused and thrust into a dungeon, and confined for months on account of my faith and the testimony of Jesus Christ. However, I thank God that I felt a determination to die, rather than deny the things which my eyes had seen, which my hands had handled, and which I had borne testimony to, wherever my lot had been cast; and I car assure my beloved brethren that I was enabled to bear as strong a testimony, when nothing but death presented itself, as ever I did in my life."

Samuel Smith also passed away in 1844, faithful to the last.

Of the Whitmers, Christian died in 1835, and Peter, Jr., in 1836, both in full fellowship with the Church. Jacob Whitmer and John Whitmer were separated from the Church in 1838, but neither retracted his testimony at any time. The latter died forty years later at Far West, maintaining to the last the truth of his testimony.

Hiram Page was one of the prominent men of the Church, who fell by the wayside in 1838. But he never denied what he had testified to. He died in 1852, rejoicing that he had been privileged to see the plates of the Book of Mormon.

The facts presented . . . prove that honest men of sound mind and body were given objective evidence of the divine power manifested in Joseph Smith in the "coming forth" and the translation of the Book of Mormon. Eight witnesses, besides Joseph Smith, together and in the day time, saw and handled the plates. Three witnesses, beside Joseph Smith, also together and in the daytime, were shown the plates by Moroni, the immortal messenger from God, and heard a voice from above them declare the translation of the Book of Mormon was correct. Illusion or hallucination is impossible to two persons at the same time and place. Motives for fraud were absent. The only reward that awaited these witnesses was service to their fellow men. They realized they must meet opposition, persecution, loss of friends, and loss of opportunities for personal advancement and income. Their testimony would be admissable before a jury and the members of that jury alone would determine its credibility. (*A New Witness for Christ in America,* 1:254-56.)

Publication of the Book of Mormon

As soon as the translation was completed, the Prophet and his associates immediately started to make plans to have the translation published. Joseph Fielding Smith summarizes the major events of this period in the following pertinent words:

After the completion of the translation of the Book of Mormon in 1829, the angel again appeared to Joseph Smith and received back the plates into his keeping. Of this circumstance the Prophet wrote in 1838: "By the wisdom of God, they [the plates] remained safe in my hands, until I had accomplished by them what was required at my hand. When, according to arrangement, the messenger called for them, I delivered them up to him, and he has them in his charge until this day."

The question of printing the manuscript now confronted Joseph Smith. Not only was he without the necessary means, but printers were scarce and those who were approached were either prejudiced through bigotry, or unwilling for fear of the opposition of customers. Martin Harris, who possessed the means, came to the rescue with a promise to pay for the printing of the book. Finally a contract was entered into with Mr. Egbert B. Grandin, of Palmyra, who consented to print five thousand copies of the Book of Mormon for three thousand dollars. In the meantime the copyright to the book had been secured. The appearance of the words "Author and Proprietor," which appear on the title page of the first edition of the Book of Mormon, [had caused] some ridicule by enemies of Joseph Smith. This expression was printed in the book in accord with the law governing copyrights, and in no way detracts from the validity of the story of the translation of the record.

Soon after the completion of the translation and the securing of the copyright, the Lord commanded that Oliver Cowdery should transcribe the entire manuscript, and that in furnishing copy to the printer, the second copy should be used, and that only sheet by sheet, as the type should be set up. It was further provided that in going to and from the printing office, there should always be a guard to protect the manuscript, and that a guard should be placed

42 at the home constantly to watch and protect the translation from evil disposed persons. These precautions were necessary because of the malicious opposition which prevailed in and about Palmyra, where the work was done. At times attempts were made to get the manuscript from the possession of Joseph and those who, with him, had the work in charge.

One man, named Cole, more cunning than the others who opposed the work, devised the plan of anticipating the publication of the book. Cole, an ex-justice of the peace, was printing a paper which he called *The Reflector*. . . . He had announced to his subscribers that he would furnish them weekly installments of the Book of Mormon in his paper. Having access to the Grandin printing office, he commenced his publication by working on Sundays when the office was closed. In this manner he was able to publish a number of issues containing extracts from the printed sheets of the Book of Mormon. As the copyright was secured, he was warned and finally stopped from this method of stealing. The work of printing the book continued, but not without interruption, for great pressure was brought to bear upon the printer who was threatened by enemies of the latter-day work with a withdrawal of trade that would ruin his business. This came near breaking the contract. However, after some delays, the book was finished some time in the spring of 1830, and made ready to go forth, as the Nephite prophets had foretold, to the Gentiles and then to the house of Israel as a voice speaking out of the dust. (*Essentials in Church History*, pp. 68-71.)

Major editions of the Book of Mormon

The Book of Mormon has been translated and published in many languages since 1830. The first edition was printed in 1830 by Egbert E. Grandin at Palmyra, New York. The edition consisted of 5,000 copies and the cost was $3,000.

The second edition was published at Kirtland, Ohio, by Parley P. Pratt and John Goodson. In the preface to this edition the publishers stated that they had "obtained leave to issue 5,000 copies of the same, from those holding the copyright."

The third edition was published in Nauvoo, Illinois, in 1840 by Don Carlos Smith and Ebenezer Robinson. Another edition was printed from these plates in 1842, also in Nauvoo.

The first European edition was published in 1841 by Brigham Young and the apostles who were then in England. In this edition the testimonies of the three and the eight spe-

cial witnesses were published in the front of the book; pre- 43
vious to that edition they had been published in the back of
each copy.

The second European edition was published in 1849 by
Orson Pratt, and in 1852 the third European edition was
published by Franklin D. Richards. In this edition Brother
Richards numbered the verses in the various chapters.

Orson Pratt divided the book into further chapters and
verses and added some footnote references in the elec-
trotyped edition published in 1879.

The current edition is essentially the same as the edition
of 1920 in which the Book of Mormon was "first issued in
double-column pages, with chapter headings, chronological
data, revised foot-note references, pronouncing vocabulary,
and index." (See the copyright page in the Book of
Mormon.) These changes in format and explanatory material were the result of the recommendations of a committee
headed by Elder James E. Talmage of the Council of the
Twelve.

MAJOR PURPOSES OF
THE BOOK OF MORMON

Many purposes can be and have been listed for the coming forth of the Book of Mormon, but the ones that will be emphasized here are those that are mentioned by the original writers of the book themselves and those listed by the Lord in revelations to the Prophet Joseph Smith.

After a rather extensive analysis of all the statements in both the Book of Mormon and the Doctrine and Covenants concerning the purposes for which the Book of Mormon was written, B. H. Roberts lists the following seven major reasons:

First, to show unto the remnant of the house of Israel what great things the Lord has done for their fathers.

Second, to teach them the covenants of the Lord made with their fathers, that the remnants may know that they are not cast off forever.

Third, to convince both Jews and Gentiles that Jesus is the Christ, the Eternal God, and that he manifests himself to all nations.

Fourth, to bring the knowledge of a Savior to the remnants of the house of Israel on the western hemisphere, through the testimony of the Nephites and Lamanites as well as through the testimony of the Jews, that they might more fully believe the gospel.

Fifth, to bring to the Jews the testimony of the Nephites that Jesus is the Christ, the Son of the living God; that they might have the testimony of the Nephites as well as that of their fathers that Jesus is their Messiah.

Sixth, to be a witness for the truth of the Bible, to establish its authenticity, and its credibility by bringing other witnesses than those of the Eastern world to testify to the same great truths that are contained in the sacred pages of the Bible.

Seventh, to restore to the knowledge of mankind many plain and precious truths concerning the gospel which men have taken out of the Jewish Scriptures, or obscured by their interpretations; by the absence of which passages, or misleading interpretations, many have stumbled and fallen into unbelief. In a word, it is the mission of the Book of Mormon to be a witness for Jesus, the Christ; for the truth of the gospel is the power of God unto salvation; for that purpose it was written, preserved from destruction,

and has now come forth to the children of men through the goodness and mercy and power of God. (*New Witnesses for God*
[Deseret News Press, 1911], 2:45-46.)

Of course, other scholars of the Book of Mormon have
prepared lists of purposes for the coming forth of the Book
of Mormon in a somewhat different order than those of B.
H. Roberts, and some of them have also listed additional
reasons for the publication of this scripture, including (a) to
help the people of this dispensation to solve their problems,
(b) to convince mankind that every person must be judged of
his works, (c) to prepare the faithful for the second coming
of Jesus Christ and the millennial reign, (d) to test the faith
of this generation and to help the faithful, and (e) to provide
mankind with secrets of national survival. Although there
may be some slight overlapping between these various purposes as listed here, they will each be considered briefly with
a few pertinent quotations from the Book of Mormon and
other sources.

*A. To be a witness for the divinity of Jesus Christ and to
bring to the Jews the testimony of the Nephites that Jesus is the
Christ.*

These are undoubtedly some of the most important
reasons for the coming forth of the Book of Mormon; the
Lord has stated this himself, as have some of the original
writers of this sacred record.

In a revelation given to Joseph Smith in July 1828, the
Lord gives the following reason as to why the Book of
Mormon must be translated and published:

... My work shall go forth, for inasmuch as the knowledge of a
Savior has come unto the world, through the testimony of the Jews,
even so shall the knowledge of a Savior come unto my people ...
through the testimony of their fathers. (Doctrine and Covenants
3:16-17.)

Nephi, the first writer in our present Book of Mormon,
also lists this as a reason for his writing the record:

... as the Lord liveth, there is none other name given under
heaven save it be this Jesus Christ, of which I have spoken,
whereby man can be saved.

Wherefore, for this cause hath the Lord God promised unto me
that these things which I write shall be kept and preserved, and
handed down unto my seed, from generation to generation, that
the promise may be fulfilled unto Joseph, that his seed should

46 never perish as long as the earth should stand.

Wherefore, these things shall go from generation to generation as long as the earth shall stand. . . . (2 Nephi 25:20-22.)

The story of the Book of Mormon itself also testifies amply that Jesus is indeed the Christ, the Savior and Redeemer of the world. In 3 Nephi is found this stirring account of the appearance of the resurrected Jesus Christ to the righteous survivors of the Lehite nation (the resurrected Savior is speaking):

Arise and come forth unto me, that ye may thrust your hands into my side, and also that ye may feel the prints of the nails in my hands and in my feet, that ye may know that I am the God of Israel, and the God of the whole earth, and have been slain for the sins of the world.

And it came to pass that the multitude went forth, and thrust their hands into his side, and did feel the prints of the nails in his hands and in his feet; and this they did do, going forth one by one until they had all gone forth, and did see with their eyes and did feel with their hands, and did know of a surety and did bear record, that it was he, of whom it was written by the prophets, that should come.

And when they had all gone forth and had witnessed for themselves, they did cry out with one accord. . . . (3 Nephi 11:14-16.)

Many other scriptures could be listed to indicate that the Book of Mormon does testify of the divinity of Jesus Christ (2 Nephi 25:13, 16; 33:8-11; 3 Nephi 17:25; 29:4-6; Ether 12:38-41; Moroni 10:32-34), but the final one quoted here is from Moroni, the last writer in the Book of Mormon, and it appears on the title page of the Book of Mormon. In listing several reasons why he wrote his record Moroni states: "And also to the convincing of the Jew and Gentile that Jesus is the Christ, the Eternal God, manifesting himself unto all nations."

B. To fulfill biblical prophecy and to be a witness for the Bible.

In his farewell address to us, Mormon—the great prophet, historian, and military leader—gives this message:

Therefore repent, and be baptized in the name of Jesus, and lay hold upon the gospel of Christ, which shall be set before you, not only in this record [the Book of Mormon] but also in the record which shall come unto the Gentiles from the Jews, which record

[the Bible] shall come from the Gentiles unto you.
For behold, this [the Book of Mormon] is written for the intent that ye may believe that [the Bible]; and if ye believe that [the Bible] ye will believe this also. (Mormon 7:8-9.)

Mormon was not the only writer in the Book of Mormon who claimed that one purpose of his writing was for "the intent that ye may believe" the Bible. Nephi, the first writer in our present Book of Mormon, also testifies of these things as is indicated in the thirteenth chapter of 1 Nephi and in the following quotation:

And now, my beloved brethren, and also Jew, and all ye ends of the earth, hearken unto these words and believe in Christ; and if ye believe not in these words believe in Christ. And if ye shall believe in Christ ye will believe in these words, for they are the words of Christ, and he hath given them unto me; and they teach all men that they should do good.

And if they are not the words of Christ, judge ye—for Christ will show unto you, with power and great glory, that they are his words, at the last day; and you and I shall stand face to face before his bar; and ye shall know that I have been commanded of him to write these things. . . . (2 Nephi 33:10-11.)

The coming forth of the Book of Mormon also fulfills biblical prophecy, as is indicated in the following analysis by Eldin Ricks:

Genesis 11:1-9. People spread over "the face of all the earth" at the fall of the tower of Babel—This prophecy assumes added significance in view of the fact that one of the three groups which the Book of Mormon tells about, the Jaredites, left the Middle East and arrived in the Western world soon after the fall of the tower of Babel. (Ether 1:3-5, 33.)

Genesis 49:22-26. Joseph's branches to "run over the wall."— The obscure prophecy that the posterity of Jacob's son, Joseph, should extend beyond the garden wall becomes meaningful in the Book of Mormon. The Book deals mainly with the history of a branch of Joseph's descendants who broke away from their home ties in Jerusalem and migrated to American shores. (1 Nephi 5:14; 6:2; 2 Nephi 3:4-5; Ether 13:8.)

Isaish 29:4. "And thou shalt be brought down, and shalt speak out of the ground."—What at first looks like a prophecy about Jerusalem's downfall is seen, in the light of Book of Mormon history, to include the remnant of Jerusalem's children that settled in early America. The more highly civilized faction of this remnant met destruction in desolating wars in the fourth century A.D. Their

48 unearthed record, the Book of Mormon, is their voice speaking "out of the ground" today.

Isaiah 29:9-12. "The vision of all is become as the words of a book that is sealed."—Isaiah pursues the subject of a people speaking out of the ground and observes how in a day when men would be (spiritually) asleep, a book should come forth. The reference to its being "sealed" again points to the Book of Mormon, for a considerable number of the plates of the metal book that Joseph Smith received were sealed with some substance of a strong cement-like quality. This part he was not permitted to translate. (Ether 5:1; Pearl of Great Price, Smith 2:63-65; Orson Pratt, *Remarkable Visions*, p. 6.) In the same passage Isaiah speaks of the words of the book being delivered to a learned man who would protest he could not read a sealed book. The fulfillment of this figures prominently in the account of Joseph Smith's translation of the record.

Isaiah 29:13-14. In time of spiritual darkness a "marvellous work and a wonder" to be performed by God.—This prediction follows Isaiah's discussion of a book that should come forth in an age of apostasy. A few verses further (v. 18) he again refers to the book. Believers in the Book of Mormon point to the miraculous events attending the coming forth of this volume as part of the "marvellous work and a wonder" alluded to by Isaiah.

Ezekiel 37:15-21. The stick of Judah and the stick of Joseph to be united.—The union of Judah's scroll with Joseph's appears to be suggested by Ezekiel's prophecy. Since the Bible is the record of Judah's descendants and the Book of Mormon is a record of Joseph's, students of the latter volume see the fulfillment of Ezekiel's prophecy in the coming together of the two books.

John 10:15-16. Jesus to lay down His life and visit "other sheep . . . which are not of this fold."—The meaning of Jesus' announcement becomes clear through the Book of Mormon's thrilling story of Christ's appearance, after His resurrection, to the Josephite branch in America. He told them they were His "other sheep." (3 Nephi 15:13-24.)

Revelation 14:6-7. An angel to bring again the "everlasting gospel" and a warning that "the hour of God's judgment is come."—"Mormonism" declares that this heavenly messenger has come in fulfillment of John's prophecy, that he has given the promised warning of impending judgments, and that the Book of Mormon, which he revealed, unfolds "the everlasting gospel" to the inhabitants of the earth. (Doctrine and Covenants 133:36ff; Pearl of Great Price, Smith 2:34.) (Eldin Ricks, *Book of Mormon Commentary* [Deseret News Press, 1953], 1:10-12.)

C. To convince the Lamanites that they are of the house of Israel; to show unto the remnant of the house of Israel what

great things the Lord has done for their fathers; to teach the   49
remnant of Israel the covenants of the Lord made with their
fathers, that they may know they are not cast off forever; to
bring the knowledge of a Savior unto the remnants of the house
of Israel through the testimony of the Nephites as well as the
Jews.

Although these might well be considered separate and distinct purposes for which the Book of Mormon was written, they will all be considered together in this section inasmuch as the statements of the Lord and the original writers of the Book of Mormon generally mention them together.

For example, the Lord revealed to Joseph Smith:

Nevertheless, my work shall go forth, for inasmuch as the knowledge of a Savior has come unto the world, through the testimony of the Jews, even so shall the knowledge of a Savior come unto my people—

And to the Nephites, and the Jacobites, and the Josephites, and the Zoramites, through the testimony of their fathers—

And this testimony shall come to the knowledge of the Lamanites, and the Lemuelites, and the Ishmaelites, who dwindled in unbelief because of the iniquity of their fathers, whom the Lord has suffered to destroy their brethren the Nephites, because of their iniquities and their abominations.

And for this very purpose are these plates preserved, which contain these records—that the promises of the Lord might be fulfilled, which he made to his people;

And that the Lamanites might come to the knowledge of their fathers, and that they might know the promises of the Lord, and that they may believe the gospel and rely upon the merits of Jesus Christ, and be glorified through faith in his name, and that through their repentance they might be saved. Amen. (Doctrine and Covenants 3:16-20.)

Also, Mormon testified in these words that his writings were intended primarily for the remnant of the house of Israel:

Now these things are written unto the remnant of the house of Jacob; and they are written after this manner, because it is known of God that wickedness will not bring them forth unto them; and they are to be hid up unto the Lord that they may come forth in his own due time.

And this is the commandment which I have received; and behold, they shall come forth according to the commandment of the Lord, when he shall see fit, in his wisdom.

50   And behold, they shall go unto the unbelieving of the Jews; and for this intent shall they go—that they may be persuaded that Jesus is the Christ, the Son of the living God; that the Father may bring about, through his most Beloved, his great and eternal purpose, in restoring the Jews, or all the house of Israel, to the land of their inheritance, which the Lord their God hath given them, unto the fulfilling of his covenant;

And also that the seed of this people may more fully believe his gospel, which shall go forth unto them from the Gentiles. . . . (Mormon 5:12-15.)

This same writer, Mormon, addresses himself to the remnants of the house of Israel when he says, "Know ye that ye must come to the knowledge of your fathers, and repent of all your sins and iniquities, and believe in Jesus Christ, that he is the Son of God. . . ." (Mormon 7:5.) The remainder of his plea (Mormon 7:5-10) lists additional reasons why his record must come forth to the remnant of Israel.

Nephi, the first writer on the small plates of Nephi, also lists several reasons why these records were being preserved for the remnant of the house of Israel (1 Nephi 22:3-14; 2 Nephi 3:6-9, 15), as does the resurrected Jesus Christ in his teachings (3 Nephi 20:10-18, 22, 24-25, 29-31). And finally, Moroni lists most of these same reasons in the section that now comprises the title page of the Book of Mormon:

Wherefore, it is an abridgment of the record of the people of Nephi, and also of the Lamanites—Written to the Lamanites, who are a remnant of the house of Israel; and also to the Jew and Gentile—Written by way of commandment, and also by the spirit of prophecy and of revelation—Written and sealed up, and hid up unto the Lord, that they might not be destroyed—To come forth by the gift and power of God unto the interpretation thereof—Sealed by the hand of Moroni, and hid up unto the Lord, to come forth in due time by way of the Gentile—The interpretation thereof by the gift of God.

An abridgment taken from the Book of Ether also, which is a record of the people of Jared, who were scattered at the time the Lord confounded the language of the people, when they were building a tower to get to heaven—Which is to show unto the remnant of the House of Israel what great things the Lord hath done for their fathers; and that they may know the covenants of the Lord, that they are not cast off forever—And also to the convincing of the Jew and Gentile that JESUS is the CHRIST, the ETERNAL GOD, manifesting himself unto all nations—And now, if there are faults

they are the mistakes of men; wherefore, condemn not the things of 51
God, that ye may be found spotless at the judgment-seat of Christ.

D. To restore to the knowledge of mankind many plain and precious truths concerning the gospel of Jesus Christ.

Nephi, the first writer in our present Book of Mormon, saw in a vision nearly 600 B.C. that many parts of the gospel "which are plain and most precious" were to be taken out of the Jewish scripture—the Bible. (1 Nephi 13:2-26.) Later in his vision, he was told the words of the Lord by an angel, that "after the Gentiles do stumble exceedingly, because of the most plain and precious parts of the gospel of the Lamb which have been kept back . . . I will be merciful unto the Gentiles in that day, insomuch that I will bring forth unto them, in mine own power, much of my gospel, which shall be plain and precious, saith the Lamb." (1 Nephi 13:34.) Nephi beheld further that these precious truths would be restored through written records, including the one he was then writing, and that these records would "make known the plain and precious things which have been taken away . . . and shall make known to all kindreds, tongues, and people, that the Lamb of God is the Son of the Eternal Father, and the Savior of the world; and that all men must come unto him, or they cannot be saved." (1 Nephi 13:40.)

To illustrate how the Book of Mormon has restored some of these "plain and precious truths," consider the first ordinances of the gospel. The two most basic ordinances that are prevalent and quite widely practiced among both Protestant and Catholic groups are (1) baptism and (2) holy communion—the sacrament of the Lord's Supper. Yet, there are important and significant differences of opinions among Protestant and Catholic theologians concerning the fundamentals of these ordinances, such as the purpose of the ordinance, who should receive the ordinance, the mode or method of performing the ordinance, and whether or not priesthood authority is necessary to perform the ordinance. The Book of Mormon clearly teaches these and other principles and ordinances of the gospel; thus it is a means by which plain and precious truths have been restored.

E. To convince mankind that every person must be judged of his works; to test the faith of this generation; to help the faithful.

52 Mormon, the great prophet and historian after whom the Book of Mormon is named, listed the following major reasons for writing his record:

And these things doth the Spirit manifest unto me; therefore I write unto you all. And for this cause I write unto you, that ye may know that ye must all stand before the judgment-seat of Christ, yea, every soul who belongs to the whole human family of Adam; and ye must stand to be judged of your works, whether they be good or evil;

And also that ye may believe the gospel of Jesus Christ, which ye shall have among you; . . .

And I would that I could persuade all ye ends of the earth to repent and prepare to stand before the judgment-seat of Christ. (Mormon 3:20-22.)

Several other prophets in the Book of Mormon have also emphasized the importance that every man should realize he is to be held accountable for all of his actions, words, and even thoughts. (See particularly 1 Nephi 10:20-21; 12:8-10; 2 Nephi 9:15-16; Alma 12:14-18; 40:25-26; Mormon 9:3-5; and Moroni 10:34.)

Eldin Ricks has written the following concerning the purpose of the Book of Mormon as a test of faith.

A prominent nineteenth century Protestant churchman states: *"Were a parchment discovered in an Egyptian mound, six inches square, containing fifty words which were certainly spoken by Jesus, this utterance would count more than all the books which have been published since the first century. If a veritable picture of the Lord could be unearthed from a catacomb, and the world could see with its own eyes what like he was, it would not matter that its colors were faded, and that it was roughly drawn, that picture would have at once a solitary place amid the treasures of art."* [B. H. Roberts, *New Witness for God,* 2:18-19.]

The Book of Mormon is offered to the world as just such a "find," the actual translation of an ancient record. But instead of fifty words spoken by Jesus (through prophets and in person), it contains many thousand; and instead of being discovered by an explorer in Egypt it was found by a young man in western New York, to whom its hiding place was divinely revealed.

Since the publication of this remarkable record in 1830, tens of thousands of missionaries have carried it to the far corners of the civilized world, announcing it to be a new revelation from God; and nearly two million people, living and dead, have accepted the truth of that claim. This fact, however, does not prove the book to

be true. The discovery of its truth is made by each reader who   53
studies it in harmony with *"the inspiration of the Almighty [that]*
giveth . . . understanding." [Job 32:8.] It is the goal of the book's
adherents that in time every living soul shall have the chance of
forming his own prayerful and studied conclusion as to its divinity.

In a large sense, however, the *Book of Mormon is not on trial;*
the world is. The ancient abridger and compiler, Mormon, who
lived in the fourth century A.D., affirmed this challenging thought
when he said the Lord revealed to him that in the day of its coming
forth it would serve as a means of testing the faith of His people. [3
Nephi 26:8-11.] It is a test by virtue of the fact that from age to age
they who are "his sheep hear his voice" and recognize it, while they
who are spiritually asleep reject it and, in so doing, are rejected of
Him. This is the doctrine of the New Testament. [John 10:3-4;
26:29; Matthew 10:33.] And because His voice speaks forth anew
to the modern world through the Book of Mormon, this scripture of
ancient America keenly tests the spiritual perception and quality of
faith of the present generation. (Ricks, *Book of Mormon Com-*
mentary, 1:2-3.)

F. To help the people of this generation solve their prob-
lems; to provide mankind with secrets of national survival; to
prepare the faithful for the second coming of Jesus Christ and
the millennial reign.

Too many readers of the Book of Mormon overlook the
fact that the book was written for *them.* Although the actual
writers of the Book of Mormon lived hundreds of years ago,
they knew their writings would not be published during their
own lifetimes. Thus they did not write primarily for the
people of their own day; rather, they wrote their materials to
help those living in the last days who would read their
records.

Through the spirit of prophecy and the power of revelation, the prophet-writers of the Book of Mormon knew a
great deal concerning the people of the last days. Therefore,
they were able to include in their records those truths which
would help the people living on the earth in the last days to
solve their problems. Concerning his knowledge of the
events of the last days, Moroni, the last writer on the plates
of Mormon, wrote the following:

Behold, the Lord hath shown unto me great and marvelous
things concerning that which must shortly come, at that day when
these things shall come forth among you.

Behold, I speak unto you as if ye were present, and yet ye are not. But behold, Jesus Christ hath shown you unto me, and I know your doing. (Mormon 8:34-35.)

Then he listed some of the serious conditions that he saw would exist during and after the time his record would be published:

And I know that ye do walk in the pride of your hearts; and there are none save a few only who do not lift themselves up in the pride of their hearts, unto the wearing of very fine apparel, unto envying, and strifes, and malice, and persecutions, and all manner of iniquities; and your churches, yea, even every one, have become polluted because of the pride of your hearts.

For behold, ye do love money, and your substance, and your fine apparel, and the adorning of your churches, more than ye love the poor and the needy, the sick and the afflicted.

O ye pollutions, ye hypocrites, ye teachers, who sell yourselves for that which will canker, why have ye polluted the holy church of God? Why are ye ashamed to take upon you the name of Christ? Why do ye not think that greater is the value of an endless happiness than that misery which never dies—because of the praise of the world?

Why do ye adorn yourselves with that which hath no life, and yet suffer the hungry, and the needy, and the naked, and the sick and the afflicted to pass by you, and notice them not?

Yea, why do ye build up your secret abominations to get gain. . . . (Mormon 8:36-40.)

Speaking specifically of the secret combinations that led to the destruction of both the Jaredite and Nephite nations, and which he saw would exist among the nations of the last days, Moroni gave the following warning and explanation:

And whatsoever nation shall uphold such secret combinations, to get power and gain, until they shall spread over the nation, behold, they shall be destroyed; for the Lord will not suffer that the blood of his saints, which shall be shed by them, shall always cry unto him from the ground for vengeance upon them and yet he avenge them not.

Wherefore, O ye Gentiles, it is wisdom in God that these things should be shown unto you, that thereby ye may repent of your sins, and suffer not that these murderous combinations shall get above you, which are built up to get power and gain. . . .

Wherefore, the Lord commandeth you, when ye shall see these things come among you that ye shall awake to a sense of your awful situation, because of this secret combination which shall be among you; . . .

For it cometh to pass that whoso buildeth it up seeketh to

overthrow the freedom of all lands, nations, and countries; and it   55
bringeth to pass the destruction of all people, for it is built up by
the devil, . . .

Wherefore, I, Moroni, am commanded to write these things
that evil may be done away, and that the time may come that Satan
may have no power upon the hearts of the children of men, but
that they may be persuaded to do good continually, that they may
come unto the fountain of all righteousness and be saved. (Ether
8:22-26.)

And finally, another purpose of the Book of Mormon is
to prepare people to be worthy to live with Jesus Christ at
the time of his second coming. In fact, the Prophet Joseph
Smith has indicated that one of the major purposes of the
restoration of the gospel in the last days was to prepare
people to be worthy to live with Jesus Christ when he comes
on the earth to reign. The Book of Mormon is uniquely
constructed to help achieve this purpose of helping a people
to live with Christ inasmuch as it contains a detailed account
of the circumstances that surround the appearances of the
resurrected, glorified, celestialized Jesus Christ to the
righteous Nephites.

THE MAJOR SETS OF PLATES

Our present Book of Mormon is comprised of writings and abridgments of several sets of plates that were prepared and written at various times between about 2200 B.C. and A.D. 421. However, the five sets of plates briefly described here are those most closely connected with our present Book of Mormon.

The Brass Plates of Laban

The brass plates of Laban served as a scripture for the people of the Nephite nation. These plates were obtained from Laban in Jerusalem and were taken to the promised land by Lehi's colony. They were evidently written in Egyptian (Mosiah 1:3-4) and were kept by the descendants of Joseph who was sold into Egypt (1 Nephi 5:14-16). These two facts suggest that the brass plates were probably started in the days of Joseph.

The brass plates contained the following:

1. A "record of the Jews" and a genealogy of the forefathers of Lehi. (1 Nephi 3:3.)

2. The words of the prophets from the beginning of the world down to the time of Jeremiah (who was a contemporary of Lehi), including the prophecies of some prophets who are not even mentioned in the Old Testament such as Zenos, Zenock, Neum and Ezias. (1 Nephi 3:20; 5:12-13; 19:10, 21; Helaman 8:19-20.)

3. Additional prophecies of Jacob (Israel) and of his son Joseph, who was sold into Egypt. (2 Nephi 3:1-25; 4:1-2; Alma 46:24-25.)

4. The five books of Moses, which include an account "of the creation of the world, and also of Adam and Eve, who were our first parents." (1 Nephi 5:11.)

Thus the brass plates were similar to our Old Testament down to the time of Jeremiah except that they were more complete and comprehensive. (1 Nephi 13:23.)

Joseph Smith did not translate directly from the brass plates of Laban, but he did translate two records that contained some of the writings on the brass plates. These were (1) the small plates of Nephi, which frequently quoted directly from the brass plates, and (2) the plates of Mormon, which contained a few writings from the brass plates that Mormon included in his abridgment of the large plates of Nephi.

Therefore, through our present Book of Mormon a portion of the brass plates has already gone forth "unto all nations, kindreds, tongues, and people," just as Lehi prophesied. (1 Nephi 5:17-19.)

The Large Plates of Nephi

These plates were started by Nephi soon after Lehi's colony arrived in the promised land. They served as the official record of the Nephites from about 590 B.C. to A.D. 385. (1 Nephi 19:1-4.) During part of this period they were primarily a record of secular events among the descendants of Lehi, but later they contained the religious record as well. (1 Nephi 19:4; Jacob 3:13.) These plates contained a "full account of the history of [Nephi's] people" (1 Nephi 9:2, 4; 2 Nephi 4:14; Jacob 1:2-3), the genealogy of Lehi (1 Nephi 19:2), and the "more part" of the teachings of the resurrected Jesus Christ to the Nephite nation (3 Nephi 26:7).

The major books on the large plates of Nephi were as follows: Lehi, Mosiah, Alma, Helaman, [3] Nephi, [4] Nephi, and Mormon. After the prophet Mormon was commanded by the Lord to make an additional set of plates, he abridged the writings of the large plates of Nephi and wrote this abridgment on his own plates. (3 Nephi 5:8-11; Mormon 2:17-18; 5:9.) Joseph Smith translated Mormon's abridgment of the large plates of Nephi, although he did not translate directly from the large plates themselves. The complete writings of the large plates of Nephi may yet be published to the world. (See Enos, verse 16, and 2 Nephi 29:13.)

The Small Plates of Nephi

These plates were started by Nephi about 570 B.C. and for approximately 440 years thereafter served as the religious record of the Nephite nation. (2 Nephi 5:29-32; 1 Nephi 6:3, 5; 9:4; 19:2-3, 5-6; Jacob 1:4.) Many of the religious writings from the brass plates of Laban were also copied onto these plates. (2 Nephi 4:15;24.) Joseph Smith's translation of these plates occupies the first 133 pages of our present Book of Mormon. Thus, as Enos prophesied, the teachings of these records have been preserved. (Enos, verse 16-17.)

The Plates of Ether

These plates contained the secular and religious history of the people of Jared, who came over to the promised land at the time of "the great tower" of Babel. Also, the record contained an account of "the creation of the world" (Ether 1:3) as well as a full account of the tremendous vision of the brother of Jared in which he was shown the major events that were to occur on this earth (Ether 3:25).

Moroni abridged the writings of the plates of Ether and wrote his abridgment on the plates of Mormon. Joseph Smith translated part of Moroni's writings, and his translation appears as the book of Ether in our present Book of Mormon. (Ether 1:1-2.) However, Moroni was commanded by the Lord to seal up part of his writings that contained the "very things which the brother of Jared saw," and Joseph Smith was instructed not to translate the sealed portion. (Ether 4:1-4; 5:1.) This sealed portion will be published when the people "repent of their iniquity, and become clean before the Lord. . . . And . . . exercise faith . . . even as the brother of Jared did." (Ether 4:6-7.)

The Plates of Mormon

These plates were started by Mormon and contained his abridgment of the books that were written on the large plates of Nephi. (3 Nephi 5:8-11; Mormon 2:17-18; 5:9.) Moroni also added on these plates (1) a brief postscript to his father's record (Mormon 8-9); (2) his abridgment of the plates of Ether (see Ether 1:1-3); (3) his own book of Moroni (see Moroni 1:1-4); (4) the material that appears as the title page in our present Book of Mormon; and (5) his account of the vision of the brother of Jared, which he was commanded to "seal up" (see Ether 4:4-5).

The plates of Mormon were given to Joseph Smith by the angel Moroni on September 22, 1827. The Prophet translated all of these plates that were not sealed. However, his translation of Mormon's abridgment of the book of Lehi, comprising 116 pages of manuscript, was subsequently lost by Martin Harris. The Lord then instructed Joseph to translate the small plates of Nephi in the place of the lost manuscript. (See *History of the Church*, 1:20-22.)

Additional Information Concerning These Plates   59
The following references and sources provide additional information concerning the major sets of plates associated with the Book of Mormon:

A. *From the Book of Mormon*
1 Nephi—1:17; 3:3-4, 19-20; 4:24; 5:10-22; 6:1-6; 9:1-6; 10:1, 15; 13:19-29, 35-41; 14:25-28; 19:1-6
Second Nephi—4:1-2, 14-15; 5:12, 28-33; 26:16-17; 27:6-23; 28:29-30; 29:1-13; 33:10-15
Jacob—1:1-4; 3:12-14; 4:1-3; 7:26-27
Enos—12-17
Jarom—1-2, 15-15
Omni—1, 3-4, 8-22, 25, 30
Words of Mormon—3-11
Mosiah—1:3-6, 15-16; 8:5-19; 21:27; 22:13-14; 25:5-7; 28:10-20
Alma—37:1-4, 21-22; 44:24; 63:1, 10-13
Helaman—the superscription before chapter 1; 6:25-26
Third Nephi—1:2-3; 5:8-19; 7:17; 10:16-17; 23:6-14; 26:6-11
Mormon—1:1-4; 2:17-18; 4:23; 5:8-9; 6:6; 7:8-9; 8:1-5; 9:32-34
Ether—the superscription before chapter 1; 1:1-5; 4:1-17; 5:1-6; 6:1; 13:1, 13; 15:33
Moroni—1:1, 4; 10:1-5, 27-29

B. *From other sources:*
William E. Berrett and Alma P. Burton, *Readings in L.D.S. Church History,* 1:38
Comprehensive History of the Church, 1:167-72
Hugh Nibley, *An Approach to the Book of Mormon,* pp. 18-25
George Reynolds and Janne M. Sjodahl, *Commentary on the Book of Mormon,* pp. xiii-xiv
Eldin Ricks, *Story of the Formation of the Book of Mormon Plates,* pp. 1-15
B. H. Roberts, *New Witnesses for God,* 2:159-164
Sidney B. Sperry, *Our Book of Mormon,* pp. 39-76, with special emphasis on pages 39-46, 55-56, 65-66, 70-71
J. N. Washburn, *The Contents, Structure and Authorship of the Book of Mormon,* pp. 73-88

HISTORICAL BACKGROUND LEADING TO THE PERIOD OF THE BOOK OF MORMON

It is difficult to place the Book of Mormon in its proper historical perspective for two major reasons: (1) biblical scholars sometimes disagree as to the exact dates of the early events in the Bible, and (2) the Book of Mormon contains the accounts of two major groups of people—the Lehite colony and the Jaredites—and no date is given in the Book of Mormon for the beginning of the Jaredite journey. Therefore, the dates listed here are suggested dates only.

From Adam to Abraham

The account in the Bible from Adam to Abraham occupies only eleven chapters in the book of Genesis; yet these chapters cover a time period of approximately 2,000 years. Thus it is evident we do not know very much detail concerning the people of this period. Marginal notes of the King James Version of the Bible usually list the date of the fall of Adam and Eve as about 4000 B.C. Using the chronological data provided within the first chapters of the book of Genesis, Noah would be dated somewhere around 2400-2300 B.C. Thus the tower of Babel, which occurred after the great flood in the days of Noah, would probably date about 2200 B.C. This, then, would be a possible approximate date for the departure of the Jaredites from the Old World. However, some biblical and Book of Mormon scholars place the date of the flood back to nearly 3000 B.C. and the date of the tower of Babel to approximately 2600 B.C.

Most biblical scholars agree, however, that Abraham lived approximately 2000-1900 B.C. The story of Abraham is told in chapters 11 through 25 of Genesis.

The patriarchs Abraham, Isaac, and Jacob

Probably most members of the Church are descendants of the patriarch Abraham through the loins of his son Isaac and his grandson Jacob (Israel). Although the dates of these patriarchs are not exact, most biblical scholars believe that

Abraham lived approximately 2000-1900 B.C. This would 61
place Isaac's birth shortly after 1900 B.C. and Jacob's birth at
about 1850 B.C. Abraham became known as the first Hebrew.
Thus his descendants are frequently referred to as Hebrews.
The descendants of these three patriarchs are referred to as
the "covenant people" because of the promises the Lord
made to them.

Origin of the House of Israel

Jacob, the son of Isaac and the grandson of Abraham,
was given the name Israel. (Genesis 32:28.) He had twelve
sons: Reuben, Simeon, Levi, Judah, Zebulun, Issachar, Dan,
Gad, Asher, Naphtali, Joseph, and Benjamin. Joseph, who
was sold into Egypt, had two sons—Manasseh and Ephraim.
Although Ephraim was the younger son, he received the
greater blessing and was also given the birthright over all the
sons of Israel. (Genesis 48:18-20; 1 Chronicles 5:1-2.)
Manasseh, however, was also listed as one of the "sons" of
Israel. (Genesis 48:5.) The tribes of Israel were called after
the names of the sons of Jacob, except that Levi was not
given land as a separate tribe, and Joseph's two sons were
given land in the place of Levi and their father. (Numbers
1:5-10.)

From bondage in Egypt to the United Kingdom

The descendants of Israel were in bondage in Egypt from
approximately 1700 B.C. to 1490 B.C. During this period they
were greatly influenced by the cultural life of Egypt, and
many of them learned to speak and write Egyptian. Finally
they were delivered by the power of God through Moses.
(Exodus 13 and 14.) After 40 years in the wilderness (c. 1490-
1450 B.C.) they were governed by at least thirteen judges,
with Samuel being the last judge. (1 Samuel 8:5-10.) Then
the people demanded a king and the United Kingdom was
established, which lasted for approximately 120 years (c.
1095-975 B.C.). Three kings reigned during this period—Saul,
David, and Solomon.

The divided kingdom and the conquest of Israel

Dissension developed in the kingdom, and about 975
B.C. the kingdom was divided. The northern kingdom
(kingdom of Israel), led by descendants of Ephraim,
consisted of most of the tribes of Israel. The southern

62   kingdom of Judah, ruled over by descendants of Judah, consisted of the tribe of Judah and most of the tribe of Benjamin, plus many descendants of Levi and a few individuals from most or all of the other tribes. (Note: Judah controlled the southern part of the land, including the city of Jerusalem; thus individuals from all of the tribes undoubtedly lived in Jerusalem among the tribe of Judah, particularly if they were merchants, temple workers, traders, etc. See also 2 Chronicles 15:9.)

Events in Judah immediately before 600 B.C.

For more than a century the southern kingdom continued a troubled and uncertain existence. Then in the year 608 B.C. —which marks the era immediately preceding the opening of the Book of Mormon—Judah faced its crucial hour. Necho, Pharaoh of Egypt, had dispatched an army against Assyria, and the path of the Egyptian advance lay through Palestine. Josiah, king of Judah, resolved to resist the approaching army and went out to meet it at the head of a plucky little Judean force. In the battle that followed, the Hebrews were beaten and King Josiah was slain. The Jews then chose one of Josiah's sons, Jehoahaz, for their king; but after a three-month term of office the Egyptians replaced him with another of Josiah's sons, whose name was Jehoiakim. For three years the Pharaoh of Egypt exercised political control of the kingdom of Judah through the puppet Jehoiakim. Then in the memorable year 605 B.C. the Babylonians marshalled a mighty army and crushed the Pharaoh's cohorts in the battle of Carchemish and, in so doing, took the Jewish nation out of Egypt's grasp. (The biblical account of this era is found in 2 Kings, chaps. 23-25; 2 Chronicles, chap. 36; Jeremiah, chaps. 26-39.)

But the Jewish people did not gain their freedom. Instead of Egyptian foreigners ruling their country, Babylonian foreigners took their place. Southern Palestine became a Babylonian vassal state. Unfortunately for all concerned, they allowed the quisling Jehoiakim, Jewish appointee of Egypt, to retain his throne. Before long the new monarch and his subjects were in revolt. In response, King Nebuchadnezzar moved an army to Jerusalem and laid siege against the rebellious city. About this time Jehoiakim either died or was taken captive by the enemy, for Jehoiachin, his

son, is spoken of in the biblical account as surrendering to   63
the Babylonians.

The period at the time of the departure of Lehi from
Jerusalem

These struggles between Assyria, Babylonia, and Egypt
took place before the Book of Mormon record opens but
during the lifetime of its early leading characters. When the
account commences, twenty-one-year-old Zedekiah, the
well-meaning but utterly weak uncle of the ill-fated King
Jehoiachin, is spoken of as being in the first year of his reign.
According to the book of 2 Kings, he was appointed to the
throne by Nebuchadnezzar of Babylon. It was a time of great
wickedness. Immorality and corruption were rampant.
Dishonesty, false swearing, and idolatry were common vices
of the day. As if the sins of the people were not already
enough to invite God's judgments, Zedekiah chose to follow
the disastrous course of Jehoiakim in seeking an alliance
with Egypt and scheming a break from Babylonia. It was at
this point that the prophet Jeremiah, whose gloomy prophecies had already brought him notoriety in Jehoiakim's day,
thundered forth anew the ominous pronouncement that
Jerusalem and its temple were doomed for destruction and
the entire nation would be led into captivity if they did not
repent and heed the admonitions of the Lord. But the declaration that God would turn against his chosen people and
allow his sacred temple and his holy city to be destroyed was
considered an outrage. To the incensed priests and princes
the prophecy was traitorous and bordered on blasphemy.
Jeremiah's arrest and imprisonment were ordered.

Postscript to subsequent history of the house of Israel

Although the following events took place after Lehi's departure from Jerusalem, they are listed here to complete this
brief summary of the origin and scattering of the house of Israel.

At length, on the promise of support from Egypt, Zedekiah revolted; but before Egyptian help materialized, Nebuchadnezzar's army invaded Jerusalem. Ruthlessly the
Babylonians burned out Zedekiah's eyes and enslaved his
people. Nebuchadnezzar also removed the treasures of the
temple and the palace and carried them to his own capital,
and thus the words of the prophets of God were fulfilled.

64   However, the prophets had also prophesied concerning the restoration of the people of Judah, and some fifty years later (c. 538 B.C.), after Babylonia had been conquered by Persia, they were allowed to return to their lands by Cyrus, king of Persia. They rebuilt the temple and lived in the Holy Land for over five hundred years under the rule of four separate groups: Persians, Greeks, Asmonaeans, and Romans. Finally, about A.D. 71 the Romans destroyed the city of Jerusalem, tore down the temple, and took the people of the kingdom of Judah to Rome. These people were later scattered among the nations of the world.

A SECULAR HISTORY
OF THE BOOK OF MORMON
PEOPLES

The Book of First Nephi

The Book of Mormon story commences in the city of Jerusalem in the year 600 B.C. Many prophets were called of God to warn the wicked that if they did not speedily repent, the capital city, Jerusalem, would be destroyed. Among the numerous prophets called to warn the people was Lehi. He saw in vision that Jerusalem would be destroyed, so he emphatically warned the wicked of the pending calamity. The people, who were hardened in iniquity and spiritually deaf, sought to kill him. Then God commanded Lehi to take his family and depart into the wilderness. His family consisted of Sariah, his wife; four sons, Laman, Lemuel, Sam, and Nephi; and some daughters who are unnamed in the Book of Mormon. (2 Nephi 5:6.)

The group traveled south into the wilderness adjacent to the Red Sea. Lehi was told that if he and his family remained obedient they would be led to a land "choice above all lands" for their inheritance. Lehi, under inspiration, sent his sons back to Jerusalem to obtain from Laban some valuable records written on brass plates, which contained both the sacred scriptures and the genealogy of Lehi and his ancestors. After a great deal of trouble the plates were obtained; Laban's servant, Zoram, joined with the Nephites; and the sword of Laban, a weapon of superior craftsmanship, was brought back to Lehi.

The Lord counseled Lehi that Ishmael and his family, still living in Jerusalem, should also accompany them to the "promised land" so that the sons of Lehi might marry the daughters of Ishmael to "raise up seed unto the Lord." Ishmael and his family consented to join Lehi and his family in the wilderness.

The people of Lehi were directed in the wilderness by a "ball of curious workmanship" called the Liahona, which worked according to the faith of the people. One of the two

66   spindles acted as a director and pointed the way the group should travel in the wilderness.

Nephi was commanded to keep accurate records of the events he would witness. Obedient to this command, he formed some plates that he called the plates of Nephi (later called the large plates of Nephi), upon which he engraved the history of this people.

The company had some serious internal contentions basically prompted by Laman and Lemuel. These two oldest sons were rebellious against both their father, Lehi, and their righteous younger brother, Nephi. Divine intervention was necessary on several occasions to keep these sons from thwarting the plans of their prophet father. The colony spent a total of eight years in the wilderness.

Traveling south-southeast from their first encampment, the group was then led eastward to the seashore, where the Lord commanded Nephi to build a seaworthy ship. The rebellious Laman and Lemuel vigorously opposed Nephi, and again God intervened to see that His commands were obeyed. The ship was completed and preparations were concluded for the journey.

The family now consisted of Lehi, Sariah, Laman, Lemuel, Sam, Nephi, the daughters, and two sons, Jacob and Joseph, born while the family was traveling in the wilderness. In addition there were Zoram, Laban's former servant; Ishmael; his wife; their five daughters; and their two sons "and their families." After a near tragic journey where rebellion was again obvious, the vessel arrived in the "promised land" at a location unknown to us today. The people of Lehi were soon blessed in abundance with bounteous harvests, and they recorded that their land had "beasts . . . of every kind" and "all manner of wild animals" in addition to "all manner of ores."

The Book of Second Nephi

Lehi, realizing that he would soon die, called his people together and blessed them and prophesied of their choice futures in the "land of promise" if they would live the gospel principles. Shortly after Lehi's death, Laman and Lemuel and the sons of Ishmael openly rebelled against Nephi, the spiritual successor of their father, insomuch that they sought to kill him. The Lord warned Nephi to leave them and depart into the wilderness and take all who would accompany him. The people who left with Nephi and his family were Zoram and his family; Sam, Nephi's older brother, and his family; Jacob; Joseph; and at least some of Nephi's sisters and "all those who would go with him."

The people who followed Nephi began to call themselves by the term "Nephites"; those who remained with Laman and Lemuel took upon themselves the name "Lamanites." The Nephites retained the brass plates, the ball or director known as the Liahona, the sword of Laban, and the plates of Nephi.

The Nephites began to construct buildings, using wood and the ores and metals that were so plentiful. They also built a temple patterned after Solomon's temple. They became an industrious people. Priests and teachers were consecrated among them by Nephi the prophet.

The Lamanites had turned from righteousness, and "so they would not be enticing to the Nephites," the Lord caused a dark skin to come upon them. They became an idle people "full of mischief and subtlety."

Thirty years after leaving Jerusalem, Nephi was commanded to make another set of plates, which became known as the small plates of Nephi, for the purpose of keeping the sacred records of the Nephites. The first plates, or large plates, would now be particularly devoted to the secular history.

The Book of Jacob

In his old age Nephi anointed a man to be a king and ruler over his people. In deference to the name of Nephi, the kings were called second Nephi, third Nephi, etc. Nephi passed away and the Nephites now had second Nephi as their king and Jacob, the younger brother of Nephi, as their prophet.

Jacob engraved his record on the small plates, which had been started by Nephi. Among other things he recorded that the Lamanites perpetuated a bitter hatred for the Nephites; this enmity predominates as a central theme throughout most of the Book of Mormon. Jacob, realizing that he would die soon, entrusted the sacred plates to his son Enos.

68

The Book of Enos

The prophet Enos wrote a brief but spiritually stirring account of his ministry in the three-page record that bears his name in our present Book of Mormon. He summarized his ministry by stating that

there was nothing save it was exceeding harshness, preaching and prophesying of wars, and contentions, and destructions, and continually reminding them of death, and the duration of eternity, and the judgments and the power of God, and all these things—stirring them up continually to keep them in the fear of the Lord. I say there was nothing short of these things, and exceeding great plainness of speech, would keep them from going down speedily to destruction. And after this manner do I write concerning them. (Enos 23.)

Enos also referred to the wars between the Nephites and Lamanites in his lifetime. Realizing that he would die soon, he turned the records over to his son Jarom, in about the year 420 B.C., or 179 years after Lehi's colony left Jerusalem.

The Book of Jarom

Jarom kept the plates 59 years, until the year 361 B.C. (or 238 years since Lehi had left Jerusalem). Jarom recorded in his abbreviated account (1) that the Nephites kept the law of Moses and looked forward to the Messiah and (2) that the Lamanites and the Nephites were scattered on much of the face of the land and had had many battles during his ministry. Within his writings he emphasized the great wealth of the people and their proficiency in the use of woods, buildings, machinery, weapons, and farm implements.

The Book of Omni

Omni received the plates from his father, Jarom, in about 361 B.C. The book that bears his name is only three pages long, and it also contains the writings of four other writers: Aaron, Chemish, Abinadom, and Amaleki. The small book of Omni, which covers over 230 years of history, contains evidence of apostasy and of the continued bitterness of the Lamanites toward the Nephites.

During the leadership of Amaleki, Mosiah led a group of righteous people into the wilderness away from the land of Nephi. They discovered a people known as the people of Zarahemla, who had been led to this continent from

Jerusalem just a few years after Lehi and his colony had left. Among the members of the colony, which had left Jerusalem in about 587 B.C., was Mulek, a son of Zedekiah, the king of Judah. The people of Zarahemla (sometimes referred to by members of the Church as Mulekites) were very numerous by the time Mosiah discovered them. However, they had failed to bring written records with them; hence their language had become corrupted as well as their theology, even to the point of denying their Creator. Mosiah could not communicate with them because of their corrupt language.

The people of Zarahemla united under Mosiah's leadership and were taught his language. Also, they brought to Mosiah a large stone with engravings on it, which told part of the history of another group of people who had been led to this continent from the Middle East at the time of the tower of Babel (approximately 2600-2300 B.C.). These people, known as the Jaredites, had annihilated themselves through internal strife.

Therefore, the brief book of Omni mentions the Nephites, who left Jerusalem in 600 B.C.; the Mulekites, who departed in about 589-587 B.C.; and the ancient Jaredites, who left the Middle East in 2600-2300 B.C.

The last writer in the book of Omni had no children so he delivered the religious records to King Benjamin, a "just man before the Lord."

The Words of Mormon

This small two-page insertion by Mormon serves as a bridge between the history on the small plates of Nephi and Mormon's abridgment of the large plates of Nephi. The time period covered by the insertion includes part of the life of Benjamin. The reign of King Benjamin witnessed a serious war between the two archenemies. Many thousands of Lamanites were slain and were driven out of the Nephite lands. Following the conflict, King Benjamin, with the assistance of many holy prophets, once again established peace in the land.

The Book of Mosiah

Toward the end of his life King Benjamin chose his son Mosiah (named after his grandfather) to succeed him both in the ministry and in the kingship. Mosiah was entrusted with

70   the brass plates, the large plates of Nephi, the Liahona, and the sword of Laban. Apparently the small plates of Nephi were discontinued in the days of Benjamin.

King Benjamin delivered a powerfully spiritual address to the Nephites in Zarahemla. As a result, they covenanted to take upon themselves the name of Christ and promised to live his commandments, even though they continued to live the law of Moses.

Mosiah began his reign at age thirty, approximately 476 years after Lehi left Jerusalem, or in the year 124 B.C. The main body of Nephites was apparently still in the land of Lehi-Nephi, while King Mosiah ruled in Zarahemla over (1) the people who accompanied his grandfather, Mosiah, and (2) the people of Zarahemla whom they discovered and with whom they joined.

The people of Mosiah were desirous to know of the people in the land of Lehi-Nephi and particularly of an expedition that had left from Zarahemla a few years earlier and had not been heard of since. Mosiah selected sixteen men to scout the land of Lehi-Nephi and bring back a report of conditions there. Ammon, a Mulekite, was selected as the leader.

When they arrived in Lehi-Nephi, Ammon and his men were captured by King Limhi, a grandson of Zeniff, who had come from Zarahemla. Limhi and his people were in servitude to the Lamanites to the extent of one-half of all they possessed in exchange for their lives. The entire land of Lehi-Nephi was ruled by the Lamanites. Limhi told Ammon of an expedition they had sent consisting of forty-three people who had been searching for the land of Zarahemla to appeal for help. These people became lost and discovered a land "among many waters" that was covered with bones of men and beasts and which also contained numerous ruins of buildings, indicating a once populous civilization. They brought back twenty-four plates of gold filled with engravings, as well as breastplates and other artifacts. Limhi inquired whether Ammon could translate the old engravings on the plates of gold. Admitting that he could not, Ammon told Limhi that King Mosiah could translate them with the aid of the sacred interpreters, the Urim and Thummim, which he had in his possession as the prophet of God.

The people of Zeniff had kept a detailed record of their travels in search of the land of Lehi-Nephi. Part of this record is found in Mosiah, chapters 9 through 22. The people of Zeniff were in the land of Lehi-Nephi under three generations of leaders: Zeniff, Noah, and Limhi. However, all three had been in servitude to the Lamanites. Two great prophets had been among these Nephites at the time: Abinadi, who was martyred for his strong testimony against wicked King Noah, and Alma, a former priest of Noah who was converted to the gospel.

Ammon and King Limhi adopted a plan suggested by Gideon, a soldier, by which they might escape from the Lamanites. The plan was to give a tribute of wine to the Lamanite guards, who were known to drink on duty. The Nephites planned to escape with their families and flocks through a particular pass into the wilderness while the guards were. drunken. This they successfully did, traveling many days in the wilderness and finally arriving in Zarahemla, where they became subjects of King Mosiah.

Chapters 23 and 24 of the book of Mosiah contain the account of Alma and his people who escaped from Lehi-Nephi and eventually, with many near mishaps, arrived in Zarahemla and united with Mosiah and his people.

King Mosiah, in his prophetic role, authorized Alma to establish churches throughout all the land of Zarahemla and gave him authority to ordain priests and teachers over every congregation. Later, King Mosiah also translated the twenty-four gold plates that contained the account of the Jaredites, including their entire destruction as a people.

Unfortunately, this was also a period of severe persecution of the members of the church by the unbelievers, and four "sons of Mosiah were numbered among the unbelievers; and also one of the sons of Alma was numbered among them, he being called Alma, after his father." (Mosiah 27:8.) These five rebellious young men were converted by the appearance of an angel to them, and subsequently they all became faithful missionaries and members of the church. Indeed, the four sons of Mosiah spent about fourteen years traveling among the Lamanites as missionaries, a significant step in attempting to unite these two peoples who had been embittered for approximately five

72 hundred years. Also, Alma, the son of Alma (known also as Alma the younger to distinguish him from his illustrious father), had the sacred writings and other artifacts conferred upon him by Mosiah.

King Mosiah counseled the Nephites against perpetuating the kingly line and advocated that the people should be ruled by judges appointed by the voice of the people. Mosiah was successfully persuasive; therefore the kingly line that began with Nephi nearly five hundred years before ended with Mosiah.

Alma the younger, the newly ordained prophet, was appointed to be the first chief judge of the Nephites in the year 91 B.C.

The Book of Alma

Alma the younger witnessed some early problems in his reign as chief judge. Nehor, who was desirous of introducing priestcraft among the Nephites, had considerable success until he was punished by Alma. Amlici, a very cunning man similar in nature to Nehor, desired to reintroduce a kingly line among the Nephites with his less than modest self as monarch. The Nephites and Amlicites warred over this basic governmental difference, with thousands recorded as having been slain on both sides. Amlici was killed in battle after having joined with the Lamanites against their common enemy, the Nephites. The Amlicites who joined the Lamanites marked themselves with red on their foreheads, thus distinguishing themselves from the Nephites. The battles ended with the Nephites as victors.

Alma the younger was extremely concerned about the afflictions of the church members and the persecutions heaped upon them by the residue of the people; therefore, so that he might devote his full attention to the ministry, he relinquished the judgment seat to Nephihah. Alma had considerable success as a missionary in establishing the church in many lands in and around Zarahemla.

The account of the four sons of Mosiah who served as missionaries among the Lamanites for fourteen years is inserted in Alma, chapters 17 through 26. They had suffered a great deal but had been instrumental in the conversion of many of the Lamanites, including King Lamoni and his father, who was king over all the Lamanites. The missionaries then ordained priests and teachers among the Lamanites.

The converted Lamanites desired to be distinguished from the other Lamanites; therefore, they called themselves Anti-Nephi-Lehies. In a few years the Anti-Nephi-Lehies sought safety in the land of Zarahemla. The land of Jershon was given to them, and they were then called the people of Ammon, or the Ammonites.

A tremendous battle took place between the Lamanites and Nephites in the fifteenth year of the reign of the judges (about 77 B.C.). This was the most devastating battle in the entire history of the two peoples up to that time. "Tens of thousands of Lamanites" were destroyed and a tremendous slaughter "was seen among the Nephites." The Nephites were finally successful in this great war.

In the eighteenth year of the reign of the judges another war began. By now those who were called Lamanites were a conglomeration of descendants of Laman and Lemuel, the sons of Ishmael and all Nephite dissenters, including Amalekites, Zoramites, and descendants of the priests of Noah. The Nephites also included some converted Lamanites—the Ammonites—although they had covenanted not to take up arms, and so they did not participate in the wars.

A most dynamic military leader, Moroni, was the chief captain of the Nephites during this period of time. He was a man blessed of the spirit whose great hope was to "defend his rights, his country, and his religion, even to the loss of his blood." Alma, as the high priest, gave Moroni inspired instructions on occasion, which gave Moroni a decided advantage in his military campaigns.

In the end of the eighteenth year of the reign of the judges (or about 73 B.C.), Alma gave some inspiring patriarchal blessings to his three sons. He then ended his record on the plates of Nephi and turned them over to Helaman, his eldest son. Helaman continued to record his account in the book of Alma (Alma 45-62).

Helaman and his brothers went forth to establish the church throughout all the land. They appointed priests and teachers over all the church but not without some major opposition. Amalickiah, a man desirous to be king, led many people away from the church by his flattery.

Moroni, hearing of Amalickiah's success, tore his coat, wrote on a piece of it "In memory of our God, our religion, and freedom, and our peace, our wives, and our children," and fastened it upon a pole. He used this "title of liberty" as a patriotic banner that aroused men of faith and good will to their senses. He caused all freedom-loving people to stand against Amalickiah; hence Amalickiah took his people and departed from the Lamanite-controlled land of Nephi. Moroni overtook them and captured them with the exception of Amalickiah and a few who escaped and joined the Lamanites. Then he had the captured Amalickiahites take an oath to support the cause of freedom or be put to death.

Amalickiah, seasoned in his flattery and gross wickedness, eventually became king of the Lamanites and even married the former king's wife. Drunk with power, he then persuaded the Lamanites to war with the Nephites, but they were badly beaten by the superior preparations of the Nephites. The Nephites had dug ridges of earth around their cities to shield their cities from the arrows and stones of the Lamanites. They also wore shields, breastplates, and thick garments of skins to further protect themselves. This was a new manner of preparation for the Nephites, never employed by them before the days of Moroni.

When Nephihah, the second chief judge, died, his son Pahoran was appointed to that office. Pahoran was pressured by some who desired changes in the law, but he refused to alter their basic law. Consequently, the dissenters desired that he be removed from office. Those who wished Pahoran's removal were called king-men because they desired the law altered so that free government would be abolished and a king once again would be reestablished in the land. Those who sustained Pahoran in office called themselves free-men.

Moroni quelled the rebellious king-men after having to slay 4,000 of them. While this intense strife was commanding the attention of the Nephites, the Lamanites began to invade the land of the Nephites with great success, capturing many Nephite strongholds.

Amalickiah was killed by a Nephite leader, Teancum, while he slept in his tent. This frustrated the Lamanite plan of marching more deeply into Nephite territory. The

Lamanites prepared to maintain the Nephite cities they had captured, and the Nephites did not attempt to recapture them at once (1) because of the numerical superiority of the Lamanites and (2) because the well-fortified cities now acted as a hindrance to the Nephites, who had fortified them.

The prophet Helaman was concerned because the Ammonites, who had covenanted with God not to take up arms, were about to break their oath in order to help the Nephite cause. Helaman dissuaded them. Many of their sons, however, had not taken such an oath, and they entered into a covenant to fight under Helaman's leadership for the liberty of the Nephites. These 2,000 "stripling warriors" engaged in numerous battles in vicious hand-to-hand combat, but none of them ever lost their lives.

The bitter battles between the Nephites and the Lamanites raged on, as the Nephites tried to regain territory they had lost to the Lamanites because of their civil strife.

Moroni, in need of reinforcements, contacted Pahoran for assistance. He was not answered, so he sent a second, very caustic, epistle to Pahoran demanding help. Pahoran replied that intense strife was the reason for his delayed letter. The king-men had flattered away a powerful nucleus of Nephites, had driven Pahoran and the free-men from the capital, Zarahemla, and had allied themselves with the Lamanites. Pahoran pleaded for Moroni's help in that dark hour.

Moroni, dynamic leader that he was, recruited a large army and went to the support of Pahoran in the land of Gideon, leaving Lehi and Teancum in charge of the other Nephite armies on the war front near the east sea. The combined armies of Moroni and Pahoran recaptured Zarahemla, Pahoran was restored to the judgment seat, and soon order once more prevailed in the land. Many of the captured Lamanites were desirous of joining the people of Ammon and becoming a free people. This they were allowed to do. The church was strengthened after the exceedingly long war by the Lord's working through Helaman and his brethren.

Helaman died in 57 B.C., and Moroni died a year later. Shiblon, Helaman's brother, took possession of the sacred things.

In 55 B.C. a large company of men (5,400) and their families left Zarahemla for the land northward. About this same time, Hagoth built an "exceedingly large ship" and set sail with many Nephites and their provisions to the land northward. He built other ships, and other Nephites set sail northward. The first ship returned and sailed again, and "they were never heard of more."

Shiblon died in 53 B.C. after conferring "those sacred things" upon Helaman, son of Helaman the prophet.

The Book of Helaman

At the death of Pahoran a serious contention arose as to who should be his successor. Three of his sons contended for the honor: Pahoran, Paanchi, and Pacumeni. Pahoran was elected. Pacumeni adhered to the voice of the people and supported Pahoran, but Paanchi united the disgruntled factions and planned a rebellion against his brother. He was captured in his attempt and was condemned to death. Others of similar persuasion sent a man named Kishkumen to the judgment seat, and Kishkumen murdered Pahoran. Kishkumen escaped and returned to those who had sent him; they entered into a covenant that they would tell no one who had murdered Pahoran.

Pacumeni was elected to replace Pahoran in the very same year, 51 B.C. In that year the Lamanites daringly marched into the heart of the Nephite stronghold, captured the capital city of Zarahemla, and killed Pacumeni, the chief judge. The city was recaptured by the Nephites that same year, as they finally defeated the Lamanite armies.

Helaman, the son of Helaman, was appointed chief judge to replace Pacumeni. Early in Helaman's leadership Gadianton, a man "expert in many words" and also a powerful force in Kishkumen's secret society, became the leader of the secret combination. Kishkumen was killed in an attempt to assassinate Helaman, the chief judge; therefore, Gadianton had the secret band flee into the wilderness.

In the year 46 B.C. there were many dissensions in the land; hence "an exceeding great many" left the land of Zarahemla and went to settle in the land northward, traveling an exceeding great distance. The settlers became experts in the use of cement (out of necessity, due to the lack of timber in the land) to build their cities, temples, synagogues, and other buildings.

When Helaman died, his eldest son, Nephi, reigned in his stead. Nephi reigned nine years and then gave up the judgment seat to Cezoram so he would be able to devote full time to the ministry. About this time (29 B.C.), the Lamanites sent missionaries to the Nephites, a very interesting turn of events.

In 26 B.C. Cezoram was murdered by members of Gadianton's band as he sat upon the judgment seat, as was his son who succeeded him. The Nephites at this time in history were so wicked that they supported the secret combinations in their practices and even joined with them; on the other hand, the Lamanites sought the wicked out from among them and destroyed them. Thus, in the year 24 B.C. the Gadianton band overthrew the Nephite government.

Nephi was sent to warn the Nephites of their pending destruction unless they repented. He told them that their evil chief judge had just been murdered by his brother. Nephi was accused of having the judge killed, but when he declared the murderer, who finally confessed, Nephi was finally exonerated.

Samuel, a Lamanite prophet, appeared among the Nephites about 6 B.C. and prophesied of two great events: the signs to testify of the birth of Christ in Bethlehem and the great and terrible destruction to accompany his crucifixion. Samuel warned the Nephites that they would be utterly destroyed if they did not repent. The majority rejected Samuel and sought to take his life, so he returned to his own land.

The Book of Third Nephi

In the ninety-second year of the reign of the judges, or approximately 1 B.C., the sign of Christ's birth was given; that is, there was a day, a night, and a day without darkness. The people soon began to reckon their time from the sign of the birth of the Savior. The Nephites did not repent fully of their sins; therefore the sign did not have a lasting effect upon them. Soon the Gadianton band again gained strength, and the Nephites retrogressed to their evil ways.

Continual chaos and unrest marked the years following the sign of Christ's birth. There were brief periods of peace

78   interspersed between bloodshed, but in general the times were trying. There was a period of prosperity between A.D. 26 and A.D. 29, when peace was restored and the people began to "prosper and wax great." Many cities were rebuilt and many highways were constructed. In A.D. 29, however, pride overtook many people and class distinctions developed. The great concern of Nephi the prophet was that "they did not sin ignorantly, for they knew the will of God concerning them, for it had been taught unto them; therefore they did willfully rebel against God." (3 Nephi 6:18.) In A.D. 30 their system of government collapsed; the chief judge was murdered; and the Nephites divided themselves into tribes.

In the first month of A.D. 34 the predicted signs of Christ's crucifixion became a stark reality. Great storms, thunder and lightning, earthquakes, fires, and then darkness enveloped the land. The entire face of the land was altered, and multitudes of people were destroyed. During the period of darkness, the voice of God proclaimed the extent of the disaster. The darkness dispersed after three days. One of the most awesome, frightening "acts of nature" ever recorded ended with only the righteous being spared.

At the end of A.D. 34, Jesus the Christ personally appeared to the survivors as a resurrected being and began a three-day ministry among them. He was introduced by the Father's powerful introduction, "Behold my Beloved Son, in whom I am well pleased, in whom I have glorified my name—hear ye him." (3 Nephi 11:7.)

The Savior first appeared to 2500 people gathered at the temple in the land of Bountiful. He invited the multitude to come forth and feel the prints of the nails in his hands and feet so they would be assured that he was the "God of Israel, and the God of the whole earth, and [had] been slain for the sins of the world." (3 Nephi 11:14.)

This the congregation did. He then called forth Nephi the prophet and then eleven other disciples and gave them power to baptize. He counseled the multitude, "Blessed are ye if ye shall give heed unto the words of these twelve whom I have chosen from among you to minister unto you, and to be your servants; and unto them I have given power that they may baptize you with water. . . . " (3 Nephi 12:1.)

The Savior then gave the "Great Sermon" that he had

given upon the mount to the Jews in Palestine, laying the 79
foundation for Christian living. He stressed the relationship
of his gospel to the law of Moses. (3 Nephi 15.) He told the
Nephites that he had them in mind when he told his Jewish
disciples that there were "other sheep . . . not of this fold;
them also I must bring, and they shall hear my voice; and
there shall be one fold, and one shepherd." (3 Nephi 15:21.)
After considerable instruction, he declared that he must
leave but that he would return on the morrow. He informed
them that he must report to the Father and that he would
also introduce the gospel to the lost tribes of Israel. He had
great compassion on the multitude who bade him stay, and a
great scene of healing, prayer, and blessing of the little
children followed. (3 Nephi 17.) The sacrament of bread and
wine was instituted among the Nephites, accompanied by
appropriate instruction.

The next day the Savior spoke of future events prior to
his second coming and then quoted Isaiah 54. Following the
quotations he gave "a commandment" that the people
search the book of Isaiah diligently, "For great are the words
of Isaiah." He also quoted Malachi 3 and 4 so that the Nephites might benefit from these truths given to the Jews after
Lehi had left Jerusalem. He named his church, declaring
that "if it [the church] be called in my name then it is my
church, if it so be that they are built upon my gospel." (3
Nephi 27:8.) He counseled his disciples to be "even as I am."

The disciples were given the wishes of their hearts. Nine
desired to live with the Savior as soon as their lives were
ended, whereas three desired to live upon the earth to bring
more souls unto Christ until Christ came in glory the second
time. This was the same request that John the Beloved had
desired, and the three Nephites were granted their desire, as
was John.

The ministry of Christ to the Nephites is recorded in 3
Nephi 11-28.

The Book of Fourth Nephi

Following Christ's ascension, the Nephites had a golden
age. Within two years all the people had joined the church
and peace prevailed for nearly 170 years. It is recorded that
during this abbreviated millennium "there could not be a
happier people among all the people who had been created

80   by the hand of God. . . . they were in one, the children of Christ, and heirs to the kingdom of God." (4 Nephi 16-17.)

In the year A.D. 201 pride again entered among the people, and from then on they no longer had all things common among them. They divided into classes; they built up churches to get gain; and they began to deny the true church of Christ. By the year A.D. 211 there were many denominations in the land that professed to know Christ and yet denied most of the fundamentals of the gospel.

By A.D. 231 there was a great division among the people. Those who were called Nephites were the true believers in Christ, and those who rejected the gospel were called Lamanites. The secret oaths of Gadianton's band also reappeared among the wicked in A.D. 260.

The Book of Mormon

In the year A.D. 321 the prophet Ammaron, under inspiration, hid all the sacred records that had been handed down from generation to generation. He told Mormon, a ten-year-old boy, to observe carefully the current events of his day, and when he was about twenty-four years old, he was to go to the land Antum, to a hill called Shim, and engrave on the plates of Nephi all the events he had observed. The Lord appeared to Mormon when he was fifteen years old, but he was forbidden to share with the Nephites all the truths he knew because the Nephites had willfully rebelled against God.

Mormon, who was young, but large in stature, was also selected as the military leader of the Nephites while he was but sixteen years old. He saw much bloodshed. Both the Nephites and the Lamanites were bloodthirsty, having forfeited the Spirit because of their gross wickedness. Finally in the year A.D. 350 a treaty was effected wherein the Lamanites took the land southward and the Nephites took the land northward, the narrow neck of land being the dividing line.

In A.D. 363 the Nephites, against the advice of Mormon and without his leadership, began a war of revenge against the Lamanites. The prophet Mormon recorded that "there never had been so great wickedness among all the children of Lehi, nor even among all the house of Israel, according to the words of the Lord, as was among this people." (Mormon 4:12.)

Mormon, seeing that the Lamanites were about to   81
overthrow the land, went to the hill Shim and removed all
the records Ammaron had hidden up unto the Lord. Later
he again led the Nephite armies, but he "was without hope"
for their success because the Nephites were still wicked and
unrepentant. In the year A.D. 385 he sent an epistle to the
king of the Lamanites requesting that he gather his armies in
the land of Cumorah by the hill Cumorah to give battle. The
wish was granted.

Realizing that he was old, and knowing this was the last
battle, Mormon abridged the plates of Nephi onto some
plates he had made himself and then hid up the plates in the
hill Cumorah. All of the Nephite plates were buried with the
exception of the small abridgment, which he gave to his son
Moroni.

The battle commenced, and after at least 230,000 Nephite men were slain, in addition to their women and
children, the Nephites were destroyed as a nation and people
from the face of the earth. Mormon's parting words were directed to the Lamanites, affirming to them that they were of
Israel and had great hope if they would but embrace the
gospel.

Moroni, despondent and lonesome, added his own
thoughts to the abridgment his father had made of the plates
of Nephi (chapters 8 and 9). He related the death of his
father and the continual hunt by the Lamanites to kill the
Nephites who had escaped. He then prophesied of conditions in the last days and recorded these on the plates.

Moroni lived for over thirty-five years after the final Nephite-Lamanite battle at Cumorah. The Book of Mormon is
largely silent on his major activities during that long period
of time. However, we can detect from his writings that he
was discouraged and lonesome, having to take great precautions so as not to be detected by the Lamanites.

The Book of Ether

One major contribution during this period was that of
Moroni's abridgment of the account of the Jaredites onto the
plates of Mormon. The Jaredites settled on this hemisphere
at the time of the tower of Babel approximately 2600-2300
B.C. Their writings were engraved on twenty-four plates of

82   gold covering a history from 2600-2300 B.C. to c. 200 B.C.
These records were first discovered by King Limhi, who gave
them to the prophet-king Mosiah to translate. (Mosiah
28:10-19.) Moroni did not record information from the first
part of the Jaredite records, which discussed the creation of
the world and events up to the tower of Babel, since he was
aware it would be available from the Jewish records to the
future readers to whom he was directing his message.

The book of Ether bears the name of Ether, the last of
the Jaredite prophets who wrote the record. The record
begins by tracing the genealogy of Ether to Jared, one of the
original settlers. In time sequence, the Jaredite story begins
in the Middle East at the time the Lord confounded the language of the people and before they were scattered
throughout the world. Jared went to his brother, "a large and
mighty man and a man highly favored of the Lord," to have
him ask the Lord if he would favor their family and friends
in that their language might not be confounded. (In the Book
of Mormon account, Jared's brother is never called by name,
but is identified only as the "brother of Jared.") The request
was granted, and in response to the query as to where they
were to be driven, the Lord told the brother of Jared to
gather flocks and seeds of every kind and, with his relatives
and friends, to go to the valley northward. There God
promised to meet them and further direct them to a land
"choice above all the lands of the earth." The Lord further
promised that their people would become a great nation; in
fact, the Lord stated that "there shall be none greater than
the nation which I will raise up unto me of thy seed, upon all
the face of the earth." (Ether 1:43.)

The Jaredites were obedient and began their preparations, gathering the animals and supplies, and with their
loved ones they started their journey. They went to the valley
northward, which they called Nimrod; there the Lord appeared to the prophet and gave further directions. After
traveling in an area never before traveled by man, they arrived at the ocean, where the Lord commanded them to
build eight barges so as to set sail to their promised land.
The barges were of a singular construction previously unknown to the Jaredites. They completed the construction
after four years and then began their voyage to the

"promised land," having been warned of the Lord that 83
"whoso should possess this land of promise, from that time
henceforth and forever, should serve him, the true and only
God, or they would be swept off when the fulness of his
wrath should come upon them." (Ether 2:8.)

The Jaredites arrived in the promised land (somewhere
on the land mass now known as the American continent)
after being driven by the winds in their curious barges for
344 days. The people of Jared desired a king to rule over
them against the counsel of the brother of Jared, but Jared
encouraged them to select a king, which they did. The first
king selected, after many refusals, was Orihah, the son of
Jared. Orihah was a righteous king, but soon after his reign
turmoil began, and from then on the history of the kingly
line of the Jaredites was typical of the kingly lines of so
many nations—periods of peace interspersed with great and
terrible wars. Secret combinations, similar in intent and motives to Gadianton's band among the Nephites, were introduced within the first few generations of Jaredite history.
These proved their destruction, as they did in Nephite history.

The Savior appeared to some of the Jaredite prophets,
and great spiritual blessings were enjoyed when the people
adhered to the gospel. They also achieved a very high degree
of cultural attainment. They worked all manner of ore, gold,
silver, iron, and copper and had silks, fine twined linen, farm
tools, and weapons of war.

The Jaredites, as did the Nephites toward the end of
their history, became proud and haughty, willfully rebelling
against spiritual things. Eventually many prophets
prophesied of their destruction "except they repent and turn
to the Lord and forsake their murders and wickedness." But
the Jaredites were past feeling.

The last king in a line of about thirty kings was Coriantumr, who lived at the same time as Ether, the prophet. The
Lord told Ether to go to Coriantumr and prophesy unto him
that

if he would repent, and all his household, the Lord would give unto
him his kingdom and spare the people.

Otherwise they should be destroyed, and all his household save
it were himself. And he should only live to see the fulfilling of the
prophecies which had been spoken concerning another people

84 receiving the land for their inheritance; and Coriantumr should receive a burial by them; and every soul should be destroyed save it were Coriantumr. (Ether 13:20-21.)

Unfortunately, Coriantumr and his household did not repent and the wars continued. After great wickedness and sorrow the Jaredites, "drunken with anger," gathered for what became their final wars. These wars were centered around the hill Ramah (the same hill that the Nephites later called Cumorah). Over two million soldiers were killed, in addition to their wives and children who had also been armed with weapons of war in order to enter the battle. Coriantumr was the sole survivor. He was found by the people of Zarahemla and lived with them for nine months prior to his death.

Moroni surely saw some striking parallels between the histories of the Jaredites and his own people.

The Book of Moroni

After abridging the records of the Jaredites, Moroni stated he had not intended to write more, but he almost apologetically stated that "I have not as yet perished; and I make not myself known to the Lamanites lest they should destroy me. . . . Wherefore, I write a few more things. . . . " (Moroni 1:1, 4)

Moroni reported fierce civil wars among the Lamanites, who, because of their unquenchable thirst for blood, also killed every Nephite who would not deny the Christ. Even with this picture before him Moroni wrote, "I write a few more things, that perhaps they may be of worth unto my brethren the Lamanites, in some future day, according to the will of the Lord." (Moroni 1:4.) Then he recorded several significant prayers and explained some ordinances of the gospel, including the two sacramental prayers, the manner of authorization of the Holy Ghost, the manner of ordaining priesthood bearers, and an excellent clarification and emphasis on baptism.

Moroni also included some excellent teachings of his father on faith, hope, and charity; an epistle from Mormon that clarifies the evil of baptizing infants (chapters 7 and 8); and a letter from Mormon that contained an admonition to his son and also mentioned the great extent of the wickedness of the Nephites, who had debased themselves by resorting to rape, torture, murder, and cannibalism. Mormon described the Nephites as "without order and without mercy"; having become "strong in their perversion . . . they delight in everything save that which is good." (Moroni 9:18-19.) They were further described as "without principle, and past feeling." (Moroni 9:20.)

After mentioning the decadence of the Nephites, Mormon encouraged Moroni to dwell on the positive blessings that were his—the hope of eternal glory and life through Jesus Christ.

Moroni then concluded the sacred records with an exhortation to the future readers of his record, encouraging them to test the validity of the Book of Mormon by reading it with "a sincere heart, with real intent, having faith in Christ . . . "; the promise was given that affirmation of the book's truthfulness would come from the Holy Ghost. (Moroni 10:4-5.)

Moroni bore strong testimony of the importance of spiritual gifts, of the record itself, and of man's need to order his life in harmony with the scriptures. He then sealed his record with his testimony and buried the plates in A.D. 421.

The postscript to this fascinating true story is that the resurrected Moroni was privileged in 1823 to direct a latter-day prophet, Joseph Smith, to the sacred depository in the Hill Cumorah. By the gift and power of God, Joseph Smith subsequently brought forth and translated the part of the records that comprises our present Book of Mormon. Thus, thanks to the mercies of the Lord and the efforts of a long line of righteous prophets, we are now privileged to read the Book of Mormon, which is the second witness—the American witness—to the divinity of Jesus Christ.

PART II

A COMPANION
TO YOUR STUDY OF THE
BOOK OF MORMON

FIRST NEPHI

1 NEPHI 1:2-3   *The language of the plates translated by Joseph Smith*

In considering the problem of the language of the plates translated by Joseph Smith it is well to keep these facts in mind: (1) the word *language* has several different meanings and includes both spoken and written concepts, such as grammatical constructions, thought patterns, and exact phraseology; (2) Joseph Smith translated from two different records (the small plates of Nephi and the plates of Mormon); these plates were prepared and written nearly 1,000 years apart, and the language of one well might not be the language of the other.

Thus several possible interpretations exist of Nephi's statement, "I make a record in the language of my father, which consists of the learning of the Jews and the language of the Egyptians." First of all, what is the antecedent of the pronoun *which:* record or language? Then what do the terms "language of my father" and "language of the Egyptians" mean? Is Nephi referring to the spoken words, the written script, the grammatical constructions, the thought patterns, the exact phraseology, or what?

One scholar of the Book of Mormon concludes from this quotation that "Nephi wrote in the Hebrew language but used Egyptian characters or script in the same sense that a stenographer uses Gregg characters to express English words" (Sidney B. Sperry, *Our Book of Mormon* [Bookcraft, 1950], p. 31), whereas another scholar believes that Nephi "is not telling us what language his father spoke, but giving notice that he is . . . going to quote or paraphrase a record actually written by his father" (Hugh Nibley, *Lehi in the Desert* [Bookcraft, 1952], p. 14). The fact that the experts honestly disagree on the interpretation of these verses should not concern us unduly; their interpretations are given here primarily to illustrate the complexity of the problem.

If this statement by Nephi does not give us a hint as to the actual language (or script) characters written on the small plates of Nephi, then we are left almost completely in the dark concerning this question, as the matter is not mentioned again by Nephi or the other writers on the small plates of Nephi. However, we are given some help as to the written script of characters of the plates of Mormon by the following statement made by Moroni about A.D. 400.

And now, behold, we have written this record according to our knowledge, in the characters which are called among us the reformed Egyptian, being handed down and altered by us, according to our manner of speech.

And if our plates had been sufficiently large we should have written in Hebrew; but the Hebrew hath been altered by us also; and if we could have written in Hebrew, behold, ye would have had no imperfection in our record.

But the Lord knoweth the things which we have written, and also that none other people knoweth our language. . . . (Mormon 9:32-34.)

Moroni, writing approximately 1,000 years later than Nephi but having access to the small plates of Nephi, can see that their written characters have been altered during the 1,000-year period; thus the written characters on the plates of Mormon are called "reformed" Egyptian because they have been "altered" by the Nephites.

1 NEPHI 1:4 *The date of "The first year of the reign of Zedekiah, King of Judah"*

Lehi and his family apparently fled from Jerusalem in "the first year of the reign of Zedekiah, king of Judah" (1 Nephi 1:4, 2:1-4). According to the Bible (2 Chronicles 36:11), Zedekiah was twenty-one years old when he was made king over the kingdom of Judah by Nebuchadnezzar, the leader of the Babylonian empire. However, the exact date of Zedekiah's ascension to the throne is not mentioned in the Bible, although nearly all of the scholars agree it must have been within a few years of 600 B.C. The Book of Mormon seems to indicate that the year 600 B.C. is correct for the departure of Lehi from Jerusalem. (See 1 Nephi 10:4 and 19:8.)

1 NEPHI 1:4 *"There came many prophets, prophesying unto the people"*

Several prophets are mentioned in the biblical account, which covers approximately the same time period as the beginning of the Book of Mormon (2 Kings 23-25; Jeremiah 1-52; and the Lamentations of Jeremiah 1-5). Among these

90   prophets is Jeremiah. The Book of Mormon would indicate that another prophet in Jerusalem during this period was Lehi. Jeremiah was evidently a descendant of Judah, and his writings are found in the Bible—the "stick of Judah." Lehi was a descendant of Joseph who was sold into Egypt (see 1 Nephi 5:14), and the writings of Lehi are contained in the Book of Mormon—the "stick of Joseph."

1 NEPHI 1:15   *The lack of quotation marks in the Book of Mormon*

No quotation marks are used in the Book of Mormon; apparently the original writers of these records were not acquainted with these marks of punctuation. Frequently, however, the writers indicate they are quoting directly by the use of such terms as "after this manner was the language of my father" (1 Nephi 1:15), or "my father . . . spake . . . saying . . . " (1 Nephi 2:9).

1 NEPHI 1:16-17   *Nephi's abridgment of his father's record*

In verse 17 Nephi states that he is going to make an abridgment of his father's record upon his own plates (apparently the small plates of Nephi), and "then will I make an account of mine own life." Chapters 1 through 8 of 1 Nephi seem to be a synopsis by Nephi of the record of Lehi; chapter 9 is an explanatory and transitional chapter; and finally at the beginning of chapter 10 Nephi states that he is now going "to give an account upon these plates of my proceedings" (1 Nephi 10:1).

1 NEPHI 1:20   *The life of Lehi is threatened*

In order to understand why the people threatened the life of Lehi when he prophesied concerning the impending destruction of Jerusalem, it might be necessary to review briefly the historical situation in the Near East about 600 B.C. When the Book of Mormon record begins in Jerusalem about 600 B.C., the kingdom of Judah is a vassal state of Babylonia and is ruled by a twenty-one-year-old puppet king, Zedekiah. The great military and economic powers in the Near East at this time are: (1) Babylonia, which just a few years before had defeated the Egyptians at the Battle of Carchemish and had thus "earned" the right to control the small kingdom of Judah ("southern" kingdom), which is located between these two great powers; (2) Egypt, which had passed the peak of her military power but still had great cultural and economic influence; and (3) Assyria, which had conquered the kingdom of Israel ("northern" kingdom) about 722 B.C. and was awaiting further opportunities for conquest.

Zedekiah does not want his kingdom to be under the control of Babylonia, however, and he and some of his advisers are considering forming an alliance with Egypt in an attempt to throw off the Babylonian yoke. Jeremiah and the other prophets of the Lord are warning against such an alliance. The position of the prophets is not a popular one with the political and economic leaders of Judah, however. Hence the prophet Jeremiah is persecuted and frequently thrown into prison (the references in the Bible that refer to this period are 2 Kings 23-25; 2 Chronicles 36; Jeremiah 26-39). Lehi, another prophet, is warned by the Lord to flee from Jerusalem to escape the destruction that the prophets state will surely result from an alliance with Egypt (1 Nephi 1:12; 2 Nephi 2:1-4). The Book of Mormon opens with the flight of Lehi and his colony from Jerusalem, and thereafter it is primarily concerned with their trip to a promised land and with the history of their descendants over a 1,000-year period.

1 NEPHI 2:2-6; 9:1   *The distance between Jerusalem and the Valley of Lemuel*

The exact distance of the Valley of Lemuel from Jerusalem is not made clear in the Book of Mormon. The superscription to 1 Nephi (wherein Nephi states that Lehi "taketh three days' journey into the wilderness with his family" from the *land* of Jerusalem) seems to indicate a distance between the two locations that can be covered in a three-day journey. However, some students of the Book of Mormon interpret 1 Nephi 2:4-6 to mean that Lehi and his group traveled an indefinite number of days until they arrived "in the wilderness in the borders which are nearer the Red Sea"; then they traveled through that wilderness for three days to the Valley of Lemuel.

1 NEPHI 2:4   *Possible meaning of the word "wilderness"*

The word *wilderness* seems to be used in the Book of

92   Mormon to refer to an uninhabited area or at least to an area only sparsely settled. Thus *wilderness* could either refer to a desert area (as it apparently does in 1 Nephi 2:4) or to a fertile area but one that is relatively uninhabited (as in 1 Nephi 18:6, 24-25; 2 Nephi 5:7).

1 NEPHI 2:4-6; 16:9-14, 33-34; 17:1-6   *The travels of Lehi's colony in the wilderness*

The exact route followed by Lehi and his colony as they fled from Jerusalem is not given in the Book of Mormon. However, the general direction of their travel is given in the references listed above. Evidently Lehi's colony first traveled south from Jerusalem until they met the Red Sea (1 Nephi 2:4-6), then south-southeast until after they had stayed at Shazer and Nahom (1 Nephi 16:9-14, 33-34), and then "nearly eastward from that time forth" until they arrived at the sea (1 Nephi 17:1-6). The following statement, if true, would throw additional light on the possible route of Lehi's colony, but the authenticity of this statement has not been completely substantiated:

> Lehi Travels.—Revelation to Joseph the Seer. The course that Lehi and his company traveled from Jerusalem to the place of their destination:
>
> They traveled nearly a south-southeast direction until they came to the nineteenth degree of north latitude; then, nearly east to the Sea of Arabia. . . . (Franklin D. Richards and James A. Little, *A Compendium of the Doctrines of the Gospel,* 1925, p. 272.)

1 NEPHI 2:5   *A possible meaning of the name "Sariah"*

According to George Reynolds and Janne Sjodahl, the name of Lehi's wife, Sariah, is probably a compound of two Hebrew words: "Sarah-Jah" meaning literally "Princess of the Lord." (*Commentary on the Book of Mormon* [Deseret News, 1955], 1:25.) The "Jah" suffix often appears as "iah" and was frequently used by the Hebrews to refer to the name of God. This suffix is found in such biblical names as Isa*iah,* Jerem*iah,* and Zedek*iah.*

1 NEPHI 2:6   *"River of water"*

Although the term "river of water" probably seemed foreign to Joseph Smith (who was born in Vermont and reared in New York, where rivers are naturally composed of water), the use of the term in the Book of Mormon is consistent with both modern and ancient Hebrew and with other Semitic languages of the Middle East. Different words are used in these languages to differentiate between (1) a riverbed that has water flowing in it and (2) a dry riverbed.

This is one of many examples that prove the Book of Mormon is translation literature. It was not *written* by Joseph Smith; rather it was *translated* by him from ancient records.

1 NEPHI 2:7   *"Altar of stones"*

The Book of Mormon uses the term "altar of stones" to refer to the sacrificial altar prepared by Lehi rather than the term "stone altar." There could be considerable difference between the two. An altar of stones could consist of a pile of uncut, separate, individual stones, whereas a stone altar could denote the use of cut rock, mortar, etc. In this connection it is of interest to note that in Exodus 20:25 the Lord said to Moses: "And if thou wilt make me an altar of stone, thou shalt not build it of hewn stone: for if thou lift up thy tool upon it, thou hast polluted it."

1 NEPHI 2:8, 10   *Why different names for the valley and the river?*

In the background of Joseph Smith it was customary for the river and the valley through which the river flowed to carry the same name; hence, the Mississippi River and the Mississippi Valley, the Missouri River and the Missouri Valley. However, this is not necessarily the practice in the Middle East, and it evidently was not the practice there 600 years B.C., as is indicated by the fact that Lehi named the river after his son Laman and the valley through which the river flowed after his son Lemuel. Concerning this practice of giving different names to valleys and rivers in the Middle East, Dr. Hugh Nibley has written:

By what right do these people rename streams and valleys to suit themselves? By the immemorial custom of the desert, to be sure. Among the laws "which no Bedouin would dream of transgressing" the first, according to Jennings-Bramley, is that "any water you may discover, either in your own territory or in the territory of another tribe is named after you." So it happens that in Arabia a great *wady* (valley) will have different names at different points along its course. . . .

This confusing custom of renaming everything on the spot seems to go back to the earliest times. . . . Yet in spite of its un-

94   doubted antiquity, only the most recent explorers have commented on this strange practice, which seems to have escaped the notice of travelers until explorers in our own times started to make official maps.

Even more whimsical and senseless to a westerner must appear the behavior of Lehi in naming a river after one son and its valley after another. But the Arabs don't think that way, for Thomas reports from the south country that "as is commonly the case in these mountains, the water bears a different name from the wadi." Likewise the Book of Mormon follows the Arabic system of designating Lehi's camp not by the name of the river by which it stood (for rivers may easily dry up), but rather by the name of the valley. (*An Approach to the Book of Mormon* [Deseret Book Co., 1964], pp. 65-66.)

1 NEPHI 2:10   *A "firm and steadfast, and immovable" valley*

Another expression that must have seemed strange to Joseph Smith as he translated the Book of Mormon was Lehi's statement to Lemuel, "O that thou mightest be like unto this valley, firm and steadfast, and immovable in keeping the commandments of the Lord." (1 Nephi 2:10.) Surely everything in the background of Joseph Smith would have caused him to think of a mountain, not a valley, as being "firm and steadfast, and immovable." Yet, as Dr. Nibley has indicated, the use of this construction in referring to a valley is authentic to the Middle East, in which this event is supposed to have occurred:

As to this valley, firm and steadfast, who, west of Suez, would ever think of such an image? We, of course, know all about everlasting hills and immovable mountains . . . but who ever heard of a steadfast valley? The Arabs to be sure. For them the valley, and not the mountain, is the symbol of permanence. It is not the mountain of refuge to which they flee, but the valley of refuge. The great depressions that run for hundreds of miles across the Arabian peninsula pass for the most part through plains devoid of mountains. It is in these ancient riverbeds alone that water, vegetation, and animal life are to be found when all else is desolation. They alone offer men and animals escape from their enemies and deliverance from death by hunger and thirst. The qualities of firmness and steadfastness, of reliable protection, refreshment, and sure refuge when all else fails, which other nations attribute naturally to mountains, the Arabs attribute to valleys. (Ibid., pp. 223-24.)

1 NEPHI 2:13 *Who were the "Jews" of 600 B.C.?*

The term "Jew" is used in the Book of Mormon with two possible meanings: (1) a descendant of Judah, the son of Jacob (or, perhaps in a more general vein, a member of the house of Israel), and (2) a citizen of the kingdom of Judah of this particular period.

Lehi and his descendants are definitely not descendants of Judah (see 1 Nephi 5:14), but they might be considered Jews in the sense that they were citizens of the kingdom of Judah. Thus Nephi states, "I have charity for the Jew—I say Jew, because I mean them from whence I came" (2 Nephi 33:8). Also, the Lord refers to the Lamanites of our day as "a remnant" of the Jews. (D&C 19:27.)

1 NEPHI 3:3 *The plates of brass*

In many of the Semitic languages (from which we get the thought patterns contained in the Book of Mormon) it is not customary to have the adjective precede the noun. Thus the Book of Mormon mentions the "plates of brass" of Laban but never refers to the "brass plates of Laban."

1 NEPHI 3:11 *Casting of lots*

The "casting of lots" was practiced extensively by the Hebrews of Old Testament times. This authentic and typical use of the custom in the Book of Mormon would indicate again that this part of the story in the Book of Mormon is concerned with a group of people with a Hebrew background and that the Book of Mormon is a translation of an ancient record. (If you want to review some of the examples in the Bible where the casting of lots was used, see Leviticus 16:8; 1 Samuel 14:42; 1 Chronicles 26:13; Psalms 22:18; Isaiah 34:17; Joel 3:3; Obadiah 11; Jonah 1:7; Nahum 3:10; Matthew 27:35; Mark 15:24; John 19:24; Acts 1:26.)

1 NEPHI 3:15 *"As the Lord liveth"*

Another Hebrew custom illustrated in the Book of Mormon is the importance and binding effect of "taking of an oath." When Nephi said, "As the Lord liveth, and as we live" (1 Nephi 3:15), he was making a promise before the Lord that he would fulfill the other part of the oath that was to follow. That the taking of an oath was binding upon all the parties concerned is indicated later in the Book of

96   Mormon when Nephi and Zoram give their promises or oaths to each other. (See 1 Nephi 4:32-37.)

1 NEPHI 4:6-18   *A brief thought concerning the killing of Laban by Nephi*

The Lord protects the free agency of his children and the rights of the righteous. Thus, when the wicked (either an individual or a nation) become so "steeped in iniquity" that they obstruct the righteous purposes of God, he removes them from the earth. Such was apparently the case at the time of the flood, and several times since then the Lord has commanded that the wicked should be destroyed. (See Deuteronomy 7:2, 9:4; Joshua 6:21.)

Laban had already attempted murder for his private gain (1 Nephi 3:13, 24-26) and was evidently a very wicked person; thus he apparently fully deserved the fate that befell him. Also, as we shall discover later in the Book of Mormon (Omni, verses 15-19), the brass plates did keep part of the Lehite nation from dwindling and perishing "in unbelief" for many hundreds of years, just as the Spirit had prophesied.

1 NEPHI 4:32-37   *The importance of an oath*

Notice again the importance of an oath among these people; when they give their word to do something, they do it! Concerning the binding effect of an oath upon the desert people and their descendants, Dr. Hugh Nibley has written:

... when he [Zoram] saw the brethren and heard Nephi's real voice he got the shock of his life and in a panic made a break for the city. In such a situation there was only one thing Nephi could possibly have done, both to spare Zoram and to avoid giving alarm—and no westerner could have guessed what it was. Nephi, a powerful fellow, held the terrified Zoram in a vice-like grip long enough to swear a solemn oath in his ear, "as the Lord liveth, and as I live", that he would not harm him if he would listen. Zoram immediately relaxed, and Nephi swore another oath to him that he would be a free man if he would join the party: "Therefore, if thou wilt go down into the wilderness to my father thou shalt have place with us."

The Oath of Power: What astonishes the western reader is the miraculous effect of Nephi's oath on Zoram, who upon hearing a few conventional words promptly becomes tractable, while as for the brothers, as soon as Zoram "made an oath unto us that he would tarry with us from that time forth . . . our fears did cease concerning him."

The reaction of both parties makes sense when one realizes that the oath is the one thing that is most sacred and inviolable among the desert people and their descendants: "Hardly will an Arab break his oath, even if his life be in jeopardy," for "there is nothing stronger, and nothing more sacred than the oath among the nomads," and even the city Arabs, if it be exacted under special conditions. "The taking of an oath is a holy thing with the Bedouins," says one authority, "Wo to him who swears falsely; his social standing will be damaged and his reputation ruined. No one will receive his testimony, and he must also pay a money fine."

But not every oath will do. To be most binding and solemn an oath should be by the life of something, even if it be but a blade of grass. The only oath more awful than that "by my life" or (less commonly) "by the life of my head," is the *wa hayat Allah* "by the life of God," or "as the Lord Liveth," the exact Arabic equivalent of the ancient Hebrew *hai Elohim.* . . .

So we see that the only way that Nephi could possibly have pacified the struggling Zoram in an instant was to utter the one oath that no man would dream of breaking, the most solemn of all oaths to the Semite: "As the Lord liveth, and as I live!" (*An Approach to the Book of Mormon,* pp. 103-5.)

1 NEPHI 5:9   *Hebrew elements in the Book of Mormon*

Lehi and his colony were "Hebrews" in the sense that they were descendants of Abraham, the father of the Hebrews, through his son Isaac, his grandson Jacob (Israel), and his great-grandson Joseph. (1 Nephi 5:14; 15:18.)

Several characteristics and customs of the Hebrews are found in the Book of Mormon, including the following mentioned in the first seven chapters of 1 Nephi:

1. Lehi offered "sacrifice and burnt offerings unto the Lord" (5:9).

2. He also built "an altar of stones" (2:7)—not a "stone altar," which could denote cut rock and mortar, but an "altar of stones." (This is of particular interest in light of Exodus 20:25 wherein the Lord said to Moses: "And if thou wilt make me an altar of stone, thou shalt not build it of hewn stone: for if thou lift up thy tool upon it, thou hast polluted it.")

3. The patriarchal order (including the law of primogeniture) was apparently observed by the group (3:28-29),

and family ties were very important (2:4).

4. An oath or vow was considered to be sacred and binding (3:15; 4:31-37).

5. The sons of Lehi "cast lots" to determine who should visit Laban (3:11).

6. Numerous references are made to Moses, to the miracles of Exodus, and to other historical events of the Israelites (4:2-3).

1 NEPHI 5:10-16 *A record for the descendants of Joseph*

In Ezekiel 37 the word of the Lord came unto Ezekiel, saying:

Moreover, thou son of man, take thee one stick, and write upon it, For Judah, and for the children of Israel his companions: then take another stick, and write upon it, For Joseph, the stick of Ephraim, and for all the house of Israel his companions:

And join them one to another into one stick; and they shall become one in thine hand. (Ezekiel 37:16-17.)

The "sticks" mentioned here evidently refer to books, since in those days books were written on long scrolls of parchment, which were then rolled on a stick.

The Bible is commonly understood to be the "stick of Judah" referred to by the Lord in his promise to Ezekiel. Latter-day Saints believe the Book of Mormon is part of the "stick of Joseph" mentioned by the Lord. It is possible that a portion of the original stick of Joseph was the brass plates of Laban, and still other portions might be the records of the Nephites as contained on the large and the small plates of Nephi. In this sense, then, our present Book of Mormon would be only an abridgment or condensation of the parts making up the original "stick of Joseph."

Lehi and Laban were both descendants of Joseph who was sold into Egypt. Thus, they had the right to include their writings on the "stick of Joseph."

1 NEPHI 5:11-13 *How could the American Indians have known of biblical teachings before the coming of the Spaniards?*

The brass plates obtained from Laban contained the five books of Moses (apparently similar to the first five books of the Bible—the Pentateuch: Genesis, Exodus, Leviticus, Numbers, and Deuteronomy), a record of the Jews from the beginning down to Zedekiah, and the prophecies of the prophets from the beginning down to Jeremiah. (1 Nephi 3:3-20, 5:11-13.) This would explain how the biblical stories were known by the American Indian groups even before the arrival of the Catholic fathers and their Bibles after the time of Columbus. Historians have concluded the American Indians knew of the story of the creation, the flood, etc., before the time of Columbus, although they have not been able to explain how the Indians came into possession of this knowledge.

In volume 4 of his *Antiquities of Mexico,* Lord Kingsborough found so many evidences of biblical stories among the Indians that he concluded:

It is unnecessary to attempt in this place to trace out any further scriptural analogies in the traditions and mythology of the New World, since the coincidences which have already been mentioned are sufficiently strong to warrant the conclusion that the Indians, at a period long antecedent to the arrival of the Spaniards in America, were acquainted with a portion at least of the Old Testament. (London: Robert Havell, 1831-1848, p. 409.)

1 NEPHI 5:14   *The genealogy of Lehi*

Although the complete genealogy of Lehi is not included in our present Book of Mormon, it is clear that Lehi was a descendant of Jacob (Israel) through his son Joseph who was sold into Egypt. (1 Nephi 5:14; 6:1-2.) A later prophet in the Book of Mormon tells us that Lehi was a descendant of Joseph through Joseph's son Manasseh. (Alma 10:3.)

1 NEPHI 7:1-5   *Possible relationship of the family of Lehi to the family of Ishmael*

After the Lord counseled Lehi "that his sons should take daughters to wife, that they might raise up seed unto the Lord in the land of promise" (1 Nephi 7:1), Lehi immediately sent back to Jerusalem for Ishmael and his family. Our present Book of Mormon does not indicate exactly why Ishmael's family was selected (except that it included at least five unmarried women!), but perhaps the following statement provides additional important reasons for this selection:

Whoever has read the Book of Mormon carefully will have learned that the remnants of the house of Joseph dwelt upon the American continent; and that Lehi learned by searching the records of his

100 fathers that were written upon the plates of brass, that he was of the lineage of Manasseh. The Prophet Joseph informed us that the record of Lehi, was contained on the 116 pages that were first translated and subsequently stolen, and of which an abridgment is given us in the first Book of Nephi, which is the record of Nephi individually, he himself being of the lineage of Manasseh; but that Ishmael was of the lineage of Ephraim, and *that his sons married into Lehi's family,* and Lehi's sons married Ishmael's daughters, thus fulfilling the words of Jacob upon Ephraim and Manasseh in the 48th chapter of Genesis, which says: "And let my name be named on them, and the name of my fathers Abraham and Isaac; and let them grow into a multitude in the midst of the land." Thus these descendants of Manasseh and Ephraim grew together upon this American continent. . . . (Erastus Snow, *Journal of Discourses,* 23:184-85. Italics added.)

1 NEPHI 8:8   *The dream of Lehi was in answer to prayer*

In several places in the scriptures the Lord has indicated that if we want an answer to our prayers we should first of all ask him. In 3 Nephi 18:20, the Lord has said: "And whatsoever ye shall ask the Father in my name, which is right, believing that ye shall receive, behold it shall be given unto you." The Lord evidently wanted to reveal some great spiritual truths to Lehi in this dream, but first of all he wanted Lehi to get into an inquiring (and thus a learning) attitude. Finally, after traveling "for the space of many hours in darkness," Lehi began to pray unto the Lord; then the remainder of the dream or vision was unfolded unto him.

1 NEPHI chapters 8-15   *The dream or vision of Lehi and its interpretation*

The dream of Lehi (1 Nephi 8) and the subsequent vision of Nephi in which he is given the interpretation of his father's dream comprise one of the most remarkable spiritual experiences recorded in all scripture. As you read this material, watch for the interpretation of the major symbols in the dream and also for the examples shown to Nephi to illustrate and clarify the interpretation. Most of these examples relate to the future events of the Lehite colony and to the scattering and gathering of other remnants of the house of Israel.

The following brief and incomplete outline might help you to understand better some of the symbols, interpreta-

tions, and examples.

Symbol	Interpretation	Examples Given
dark and dreary waste (8:7)		
large and spacious field (8:9, 20)		
tree (8:10); also called "tree of life" (11:25; 15:21-22)	love of God (11:21-22)	the coming of the Son of God (11:13-22)
the fruit of the tree (8:11-12)		
river of water (8:13); also called "fountain of filthy water" (12:16)	hell and the depths thereof (12:16; 15:26-36)	wickedness and war
rod of iron (8:19)	the word of God (11:25; 15:23-25)	the ministry of the Son of God (11:24-25)
mist of darkness	temptations of the devil (12:17)	apostasy, wickedness, war, the great abominable church, plain and precious things removed from the scriptures (12:19-23; 13:1-9, 20-29)
great and spacious building (8:26)	the pride, wisdom, and vain imaginations of the world (11:35-36; 12:18)	the persecution of the Son of God and those who followed him (11:26-36)

1 NEPHI 9:2 *The plates of Nephi*

Evidently Nephi made two sets of plates upon which he wrote the history of his people. During his lifetime and for several generations following, the religious history of the people was written upon the small plates of Nephi and the secular or nonreligious history was written upon the large plates of Nephi. After approximately 130 B.C., however, the small plates of Nephi were discontinued; then both the religious and secular histories were recorded on the large plates of Nephi. Nephi evidently made the large plates of Nephi soon after his arrival in the promised land. (See 1 Nephi 19:1-5.) However, he did not make the small plates of Nephi until approximately 570 B.C., some thirty years after his father had left Jerusalem. (See 2 Nephi 5:28-33.)

1 NEPHI 10-15 *The foretelling of events and the foreknowledge of God*

The teachings in the chapters listed above clearly mark

102   the Book of Mormon first and foremost as a book concerned with the "foretelling" aspect of prophecy. Several hundred years before the events actually occurred, Lehi and Nephi knew (and saw in vision) major events that were going to happen to their descendants. This foretelling aspect of prophecy is, of course, impossible without the foreknowledge of God—that is, God must know essentially what is going to happen before it happens; otherwise he cannot tell his servants of these things. The crucial question is: Does the fact that God knows something is going to happen *cause* it to happen? If God's foreknowledge *causes* something to happen, this is essentially predestination inasmuch as the free agency of man is destroyed.

Concerning this question, James E. Talmage has written the following:

Respecting the foreknowledge of God, let it not be said that divine omniscience is of itself a determining cause whereby events are inevitably brought to pass. A mortal father, who knows the weaknesses and frailties of his son, may by reason of that knowledge sorrowfully predict the calamities and sufferings awaiting his wayward boy. He may foresee in that son's future a forfeiture of blessings that could have been won, loss of position, self-respect, reputation and honor; even the dark shadows of a felon's cell and the night of a drunkard's grave may appear in the saddening visions of that fond father's soul; yet, convinced by experience of the impossibility of bringing about that son's reform, he foresees the dread developments of the future, and he finds but sorrow and anguish in his knowledge. Can it be said that the father's foreknowledge is a cause of the son's sinful life? The son, perchance, has reached his maturity; he is the master of his own destiny; a free agent unto himself. The father is powerless to control by force or to direct by arbitrary command; and, while he would gladly make any effort or sacrifice to save his son from the fate impending, he fears for what seems to be an awful certainty. But surely that thoughtful, prayerful, loving parent does not, because of his knowledge, contribute to the son's waywardness. To reason otherwise would be to say that a neglectful father, who takes not the trouble to study the nature and character of his son, who shuts his eyes to sinful tendencies, and rests in careless indifference as to the probable future, will by his very heartlessness be benefiting his child, because his lack of forethought cannot operate as a contributory cause to dereliction.

Our Heavenly Father has a full knowledge of the nature and disposition of each of His children, a knowledge gained by long observation and experience in the past eternity of our primeval childhood; a knowledge compared with which that gained by earthly parents through mortal experience with their children is infinitesimally small. By reason of that surpassing knowledge, God reads the future of child and children, of men individually and of men collectively as communities and nations; He knows what each will do under given conditions, and sees the end from the beginning. His foreknowledge is based on intelligence and reason. He foresees the future as a state which naturally and surely will be; not as one which must be because He has arbitrarily willed that it shall be. . . .

The Father of souls has endowed His children with the divine birthright of free agency; He does not and will not control them by arbitrary force; He impels no man toward sin; He compels none to righteousness. Unto man has been given freedom to act for himself; and, associated with this independence, is the fact of strict responsibility and the assurance of individual accountability. (*Jesus the Christ* [Deseret Book, 1976], pp. 28-29.)

1 NEPHI 10:4 *The date of Lehi's departure from Jerusalem in relationship to the birth of Jesus Christ*

It had been revealed to Nephi in a vision that the Savior or Messiah was to be born among the Jewish people, and 1 Nephi 10:4 indicates that even the exact year in which the Savior was to be born was revealed to him. If Nephi is talking in specific rather than general terms, then Lehi left Jerusalem in 600 B.C. on the Christian calendar. That Nephi intends his time reference to be taken literally is indicated by the information contained in the following references: (1) 1 Nephi 19:8: "according to the words of the angel" the Messiah cometh "in six hundred years from the time my father left Jerusalem"; (2) 2 Nephi 25:19: "according to the words of the prophets, the Messiah cometh in six hundred years from the time that my father left Jerusalem"; and (3) 3 Nephi 1:1, 13: "it was six hundred years from the time that Lehi left Jerusalem" and the Savior said "on the morrow come I into the world."

1 NEPHI 11:1 *Nephi's vision on "an exceeding high mountain"*

Although it is not absolutely clear exactly what happened to Nephi when he was "caught away in the Spirit of the Lord, yea, into an exceeding high mountain" (1 Nephi 11:1), other prophets have referred to their visions and heavenly manifestations in a similar manner. Ezekiel states that the Spirit "lifted" him up "between the earth and the heaven, and brought me in the visions of God to Jerusalem." (Ezekiel 8:3; see also Ezekiel 3:12-27 and 37:1.) Also, Moses was "caught up into an exceedingly high mountain" (Moses 1:1); the Savior was shown the glory of the world from the heights of a mountain (Matthew 4:8); Paul was caught up "to the third heaven" (2 Corinthians 12:2-4); and the apostle John was "in the Spirit" when he saw and heard the great visions he recorded in Revelation (Revelation 1:10).

1 NEPHI 11:27   *Use of the term "form of a dove"*

Biblical scholars disagree as to whether or not the Holy Ghost really descended in the "form of a dove" at the time of the baptism of Jesus Christ. In the accounts in Matthew, Mark, and John, the translators have used the construction "like a dove," which could mean that the Holy Ghost descended in the manner of a dove or a bird; however, the account in Luke reads, "And the Holy Ghost descended in a bodily shape like a dove upon him." (Luke 3:22.)

The Prophet Joseph Smith has explained that these terms all mean that the Spirit descended "in the sign of the dove." His inspired statement is as follows:

The sign of the dove was instituted before the creation of the world, a witness for the Holy Ghost, and the devil cannot come in the sign of a dove. The Holy Ghost is a personage, and is in the form of a personage. It does not confine itself to the *form* of a dove, but in *sign* of the dove. The Holy Ghost cannot be transformed into a dove; but the sign of a dove was given to John to signify the truth of the deed, as the dove is an emblem or token of truth and innocence. (*History of the Church,* 5:261.)

1 NEPHI 11:29; 12:8-10   *Two groups of church leaders to be on the earth at the same time*

Nephi saw in his vision that there were to be two sets of church leaders on the earth at the same time shortly after the death and resurrection of the Savior. (1 Nephi 11:29, 33; 12:1, 8-10.) However, the Lord had already provided that the apostles on the eastern continent (headed by Peter, James, and John) were to preside over the twelve Nephite disciples in the day of judgment. (1 Nephi 12:9.) Concerning this prophecy by Nephi outlining the relationship between these two groups of church leaders, President Joseph Fielding

Smith has written:

In fulfillment of this prophecy [3 Nephi 12:8-10], when the Savior came to the Nephites, he chose twelve men and gave them authority to minister in his name among the Nephites on this American continent in all the ordinances essential to their salvation. These twelve went forth healing the sick, performing many miracles, and administering the ordinances as they had been commanded to do. The fulness of the gospel, with the power and the authority of the Melchizedek Priesthood, was given to the Nephites the same as it was to the Church on the Eastern Hemisphere. Moreover, the Lord informed the Nephites that the law that had been given to Moses, including the offering of sacrifices by the shedding of blood, had been done away in him.

While in every instance the Nephite Twelve are spoken of as disciples, the fact remains that they had been endowed with divine authority to be special witnesses for Christ among their own people. Therefore, they were virtually apostles to the Nephite race, although their jurisdiction was, as revealed to Nephi, eventually to be subject to the authority and jurisdiction of Peter and the Twelve chosen in Palestine.

According to the definition prevailing in the world, an apostle is a witness for Christ, or one who evangelizes a certain nation or people, "a zealous advocate of a doctrine or cause." Therefore, in this sense the Nephite Twelve became apostles, as special witnesses, just as did Joseph Smith and Oliver Cowdery in the dispensation of the fulness of times. (*Doctrines of Salvation* [Bookcraft, 1954], 3:158-59.)

1 NEPHI 13:4-9, 28; 14:9-17 *Possible meanings of the terms "church of the devil" and "great and abominable church"*

The terms "church of the devil" and "great and abominable church" are apparently used with two senses in the Book of Mormon.

1. All churches that are not the true church of Christ are false churches, and they thus represent the "church of the devil" to the extent that they contain error and lead people away from the true church and its saving principles and ordinances. As the Lord stated in the New Testament: "He that is not with me is against me." (Matthew 12:30.)

2. The "mother of abominations" (1 Nephi 14:9) that is "most abominable above all other churches" (1 Nephi 13:5) and is described in detail (1 Nephi 13:1-9, 26-29; 14:10-17; 22:13-14) as being the source of religious persecution and

106   bigotry after the ministry of Christ (1 Nephi 13:26-28) might refer to the "mother" church from which other so-called Christian churches have protested or rebelled.

Elder Bruce R. McConkie has defined these terms:

The titles *church of the devil* and *great and abominable church* are used to identify all churches or organizations of whatever name or nature—whether political, philosophical, educational, economic, social, fraternal, civic, or religious—which are designed to take men on a course that leads away from God and his laws and thus from salvation in the kingdom of God.

Salvation is in Christ, is revealed by him from age to age, and is available only to those who keep his commandments and obey his ordinances. These commandments are taught in, and these ordinances are administered by, his Church. There is no salvation outside this one true Church, the Church of Jesus Christ. There is one Christ, one Church, one gospel, one plan of salvation, one set of saving ordinances, one group of legal administrators, "One Lord, one faith, one baptism." (Eph. 4:5.)

Any church or organization of any kind whatever which satisfies the innate religious longings of man and keeps him from coming to the saving truths of Christ and his gospel is therefore not of God.

Hence we find our Lord saying, "He that is not with me is against me; and he that gathereth not with me scattereth abroad." (Matt. 12:30.) And hence we find Alma inviting the wicked to repent and join the true Church of Christ and become the sheep of the Good Shepherd. "And now if ye are not the sheep of the good shepherd, of what fold are ye?" he asks. "Behold, I say unto you, that the devil is your shepherd, and ye are of his fold; and now, who can deny this? Behold, I say unto you, whosoever denieth this is a liar and a child of the devil." (Alma 5:39; Jos. Smith 2:19.)

Iniquitous conditions in the various branches of the great and abominable church in the last days are powerfully described in the Book of Mormon. (2 Ne. 28; Morm. 8:28, 32-33, 36-38; D. & C. 10:56.) Nephi saw the "church which is most abominable above all other churches" in vision. He "saw the devil that he was the foundation of it"; and also the murders, wealth, harlotry, persecutions, and evil desires that are part of this organization. (1 Ne. 13:1-10.)

He saw that this church took away from the gospel of the Lamb many covenants and many plain and precious parts; that it perverted the right ways of the Lord; that it deleted many teachings from the Bible; that it was "the mother of harlots"; and finally that the Lord would again restore the gospel of salvation. (1 Ne. 13:24-42.)

Similar visions were given to John as recorded in the 17th and 18th chapters of Revelation. He saw this evil church as a whore ruling over peoples, multitudes, nations and tongues; as being full of blasphemy, abominations, filthiness, and fornication; as having the name, "MYSTERY, BABYLON THE GREAT. THE MOTHER OF HARLOTS AND ABOMINATIONS OF THE EARTH"; as drunken with the blood of the saints; as revelling in wealth and the delicacies of the earth; as making merchandise of all costly items and of "slaves, and souls of men." And then John, as did Nephi, saw the fall and utter destruction of this great church whose foundation is the devil.

In this world of carnality and sensuousness, the great and abominable church will continue its destructive course. But there will be an eventual future day when evil shall end, "and the great and abominable church, which is the whore of all the earth, shall be cast down by devouring fire." (D. & C. 29:21; Ezek. 38; 39; 1 Ne. 22:23; Rev. 18.) Before that day, however, desolations will sweep through the earth and the various branches of the great and abominable church "shall war among themselves, and the sword of their own hands shall fall upon their own heads, and they shall be drunken with their own blood." (1 Ne. 22:13-14; 14:3.)

The resurrected Christ gave to the Nephites this test whereby they might distinguish the true Church from any other: 1. It would be called in his name, for "how be it my church save it be called in my name?" he said. 2. It would be built upon his gospel, that is, the eternal plan of salvation with all its saving powers and graces would be had in it. 3. The Father would show forth his works in it, meaning that miracles, righteousness, and every good fruit would abound in it. 4. It would not be hewn down and cast into the fire as must surely come to pass with the great and abominable church. "If it be not built upon my gospel, and is built upon the works of men, or upon the works of the devil, verily I say unto you they have joy in their works for a season, and by and by the end cometh, and they are hewn down and cast into the fire, from whence there is no return." (3 Ne. 27:4-12.) (*Mormon Doctrine* [Bookcraft, 1966], pp. 137-39.)

1 NEPHI 13:12 *The man "wrought upon" by the Spirit of God*

This prophecy apparently refers to the coming of Christopher Columbus to the continent that was later called the American continent. Abundant evidences exist that indicate Columbus was "wrought upon" by the Spirit of God as was shown unto Nephi. In his book *Columbus, Don Quixote of the Seas,* Jacob Wasserman quotes directly from the writings of Columbus as follows:

108

From my first youth onward, I was a seaman, and have so continued until this day. . . . The Lord was well disposed to my desire, and he bestowed upon me courage and understanding. . . . Our Lord with provident hand unlocked my mind, sent me upon seas, and gave me fire for the deed. Those who heard of my emprise called it foolish, mocked me, and laughed. But who can doubt but that the Holy Ghost inspired me? (Boston: Little, Brown, and Co., 1930, p. 18.)

Later in his book, Wasserman quotes from a letter written to King Ferdinand by Columbus wherein he said, "I came to your majesty as the emissary of the Holy Ghost." (Page 46.)

1 NEPHI 13:20-23   The record of the Jews

The book that Nephi beheld in vision and which "proceedeth out of the mouth of a Jew" and contained "a record of the Jews" (1 Nephi 13:23) is evidently our present Old Testament. Reynolds and Sjodahl indicate in the following statement the appropriateness of these terms in referring to the Old Testament.

The prophet is here speaking of the Old Testament, as it was to appear through the labors of Ezra and his associates and successors.

When Lehi left Jerusalem, the so-called canon of the Old Testament, as we know it, was not yet completed. The five books of Moses, undoubtedly, had been collected and written on one roll, numerous copies of which must have been in existence. The writings of the prophets, such as Joshua, the Judges, Samuel, Kings down to the reign of Zedekiah, and the prophecies of Isaiah, Hosea, Amos, Micah, and parts of Jeremiah, and their contemporaries, Joel, Amos and Jonah, must have existed in separate volumes, and individual collectors may have owned more or less complete sets. The Book of Job, some of the Psalms, the Proverbs, the Song of Solomon, and Ecclesiastes were also known, even if not generally accepted as sacred scripture. There were also books by authors whose names are mentioned in the Bible, but whose writings have not come down to us. The collection of Laban, known in the Book of Mormon as the Brass Plates, must have been unusually complete, judging from the contents. It must have been a very valuable library. Such libraries must have been owned by prominent individuals.

Ezra undertook the work of collecting all the sacred writings that existed at his time. This work included not only the discovery of copies in various places, the rejection of those that were not authentic and the copying of manuscripts the contents of which could not otherwise be secured, but also the correction of the text, after careful examination of the variations that must have been found. It was this work that was shown to Nephi in his vision of the Old Testament, and therefore, he, very properly, says he beheld it coming "out of the mouth of a Jew."

This expression appears still more significant when we recall the fact that Ezra, after the completion of the Pentateuch, gathered the people and read it to them and expounded it for seven days, and submitted it to them for their acceptance (Nehemiah 8:1-18; 9:3). Then it, literally, proceeded out of the mouth of a Jew. This took place about 445 B.C., about 150 years after the exodus of Lehi.

The canon was gradually completed by the addition of the writings of Ezra, Nehemiah, and the prophets who lived during and after the exile, Ezekiel, Daniel, Obadiah, Habakkuk, Zephaniah, Haggai, Zechariah, and Malachi. The canon as thus completed was accepted by our Lord Himself, and it is, in this remarkable vision, called, on that account, "The Book of the Lamb of God" (1 Nephi 13:38). (*Commentary on the Book of Mormon*, 4:262-63.)

1 NEPHI 13:23   *The Old Testament is not complete*

Nephi, who was acquainted with the writings contained on the brass plates of Laban, was permitted to see the contents of the latter-day Old Testament, and he concluded that it did not contain as many promises and covenants as were contained on the brass plates. Thus it should not be surprising to hear of prophets whose writings appeared on the brass plates (such as Zenos, Zenock, Neum and Ezias— see 1 Nephi 19:10 and Helaman 8:19-20) but which are not found in our Old Testament.

Scholars of the Bible have long been aware that the Bible was not a complete book in and of itself. Concerning the incompleteness of the Bible, Elder Mark E. Petersen has said:

. . . the Bible itself admits that it is an incomplete record and does not contain all of God's word. It mentions other books of scripture which are not within its covers and therefore are not available for study by anyone seeking the full truth of the gospel.

Moses spoke of the "Book of the Covenant," which we do not have. He also mentions the "Book of the Wars of Israel," which has never been found. . . .

The "Book of Jasher," referred to by Joshua, is not in the Bible. The same is true of the "Book of the Acts of Solomon," referred to in First Kings.

110   The books of Nathan and Gad, both of whom were prophets
and seers, are missing. . . .
Ahijah and Iddo were prophets and seers likewise. Would their
works not inspire modern people if they were available? But where
are they? Can we say that our Bible is actually complete without
them?

The "Book of Jehu" is mentioned in the Old Testament but is
not included in it. Isaiah wrote a second book known as the "Acts
of Uzziah," but where is it? . . .

"The Sayings of the Seers," another book of sacred writings, is
referred to in the Bible. Where is it now? . . .

Paul wrote letters, in addition to those we have in our Bible,
and speaks of them. He wrote a third letter to the Corinthians, and
at least another one to the Ephesians. Where are they? He also
wrote an Epistle to the Laodiceans, but it is not in our possession. Is
the Bible then complete? Does it contain all of God's word?

Jude wrote another Epistle in addition to the one in the New
Testament. He also mentions a volume of scripture known as the
"Prophecies of Enoch" to which he evidently had access, but which
we do not have today.

Then there is the matter of the Savior's teachings. He lived an
intensive and full life during the three years of his public ministry.
He preached to multitudes repeatedly. He conversed with individuals almost constantly, and gave many intimate instructions to
the Twelve.

Can anyone say that his three years of instruction are
contained in the Bible? May they be read in the few hours it takes
to peruse what he said in the four Gospels? Can three years of the
Savior's eloquent teachings be condensed into three hours of reading material? The Apostle John says twice in his Gospel that not a
fraction of the Savior's ministry is recorded.

Much as we love it, sincerely as we believe it, can we in all
truth say that the Bible is complete, that it contains all of God's
word, or even the full text of the Savior's instructions? (*Conference
Report*, April 1964, pp. 18-19.)

1 NEPHI 13:24-28   *Plain and precious truths taken from
the Bible*

The angel clearly teaches Nephi that the book that
"proceedeth out of the mouth of a Jew" (the Bible)
contained the plainness of the gospel until after it came into
the hands of a great and abominable church. In fact, the
angel seems to indicate that this church is called an
abominable church *because* it has taken away "from the

gospel of the Lamb many parts which are plain and most precious." (1 Nephi 13:26.)

Thus, apparently the first part of our present Bible (the Old Testament) is incomplete because of deletions and changes made by some of the wicked "pastors" of the house of Israel (see 1 Nephi 21:1), and the second part of our Bible (the New Testament) has been altered and changed because of the influence of "a great and abominable church." One purpose for the coming forth of the Book of Mormon is to restore these plain and precious truths that have been deleted or altered in the "stick of Judah."

1 NEPHI 13:40 Definition of "gentiles"

The word *gentile* has been used with varying meanings, as indicated in this statement by Elder Bruce R. McConkie:

In the days of Abraham, the term [gentile] was used to refer to those nations and peoples who had not descended from him, with the added assurance that all Gentiles who should receive the gospel would be adopted into the lineage of Abraham and be accounted his seed. (Abra. 2:9-11.) The Prophet taught that those so adopted became literally of the blood of Abraham. (*Teachings*, pp. 149-150.) In the days of ancient Israel, those not of the lineage of Jacob were considered to be Gentiles, although the Arabs and other races of Semitic origin who traced their lineage back to Abraham would not have been Gentiles in the strict Abrahamic use of the word.

After the Kingdom of Israel was destroyed and the Ten Tribes were led away into Assyrian captivity, those of the Kingdom of Judah called themselves Jews and designated all others as Gentiles. It is this concept that would have been taught to Lehi, Mulek and the other Jews who came to the Western Hemisphere to found the great Nephite and Lamanite civilizations. It is not surprising, therefore, to find the Book of Mormon repeatedly speaking of Jew and Gentile as though this phrase marked a division between all men; to find the United States described as a Gentile Nation (1 Ne. 13; 3 Ne. 21); and to find the promise that the Book of Mormon would come forth "by way of the Gentile." (Title page of Book of Mormon; D. & C. 20:9.)

Actually, of course, the house of Israel has been scattered among all nations, and Joseph Smith (through whom the Book of Mormon was revealed) was of the Tribe of Ephraim. At the same time the Prophet was of the Gentiles, meaning that he was a citizen of a Gentile nation and also that he was not a Jew. Members of the Church in general are both of Israel and of the Gentiles. Indeed, the gospel has come forth in the last days in the *times of the Gentiles*

112   and, in large measure, will not go to the Jews until the *Gentile fulness* comes in. (D. & C. 45:28-30.)

Having in mind the principle that Gentiles are adopted into the lineage of Israel when they accept the gospel, and that those who fail to believe the truths of salvation (no matter what their lineage) lose any preferential status they may have had, it is not inappropriate in our day to speak of members of the Church as Israelites and unbelievers as Gentiles. (*Mormon Doctrine,* pp. 310-11.)

1 NEPHI 13:40   *The "last records"*

The "last records" referred to in 1 Nephi 13:40 would include the Book of Mormon, the Doctrine and Covenants, the Pearl of Great Price, and any future scriptures that are yet to come forth from the true church of Jesus Christ. One purpose of the coming forth of these latter-day scriptures is to "establish the truth of the first" records referred to by the angel—our present Bible. This is one reason why Latter-day Saints refer to the Book of Mormon as a "second witness of the Bible" that helps to restore many of the essential doctrines and ordinances of the gospel.

1 NEPHI 14:20-22, 27   *The apostle John seen by Nephi*

The apostle John referred to here is the same apostle in the New Testament who is also known as John the Beloved (John 21:20) and John the Revelator. He is the author of the Gospel of John (John 21:24), the book of Revelation (Revelation 1:19), and the three epistles of John, which appear shortly before Revelation in the New Testament.

1 NEPHI 15:8   *"Have ye inquired of the Lord?"*

Nephi gives a clue here as to how we can arrive at a knowledge of spiritual things. Lehi had told Nephi, Laman, and Lemuel of his dream. All three of them were evidently intrigued and interested in the possible interpretation of the symbols in their father's dream. Laman and Lemuel attempted to find their answers through the power of their own reasoning. Nephi, however, asked the Lord for the interpretation of these symbols, and as a result he received the great vision recorded in 1 Nephi 11-14. Nephi's question "Have ye inquired of the Lord?" teaches the same principle as that taught later by the resurrected Jesus Christ to the righteous Nephites of about A.D. 34: ". . . whatsoever ye shall ask the Father in my name, which is right, believing that ye shall receive, behold it shall be given unto you." (3 Nephi 18:20.)

1 NEPHI 15:12-17   *The house of Israel is compared to an olive tree*

In several places in the Book of Mormon the house of Israel is likened to an olive tree. In this analogy, some of the natural branches of the olive tree (the direct descendants of the house of Israel) are grafted or planted in other parts of the vineyard (in other words, they are led to other parts of the earth). However, Nephi prophesies that in the last days these natural branches of the house of Israel "shall be grafted *in,* being a natural branch of the olive-tree, into the true olive-tree." (1 Nephi 15:16. Italics added.) This evidently means that the direct descendants of Israel are going to be brought to a knowledge of the true covenants that the Lord made anciently with the house of Israel.

Essentially this same idea is expressed in 1 Nephi 10:14, where Nephi says that in the last days "the natural branches of the olive-tree, or the remnants of the house of Israel, should be grafted in, or come to the knowledge of the true Messiah, their Lord and their Redeemer." (1 Nephi 10:14.)

1 NEPHI 16:10   *The "Liahona"—a round brass ball*

The "round ball of curious workmanship" that was made of "fine brass" is later known in the Book of Mormon as the Liahona. (Alma 37:38.) This name is evidently a transliteration from the original language of Lehi, and Reynolds and Sjodahl have suggested the following meaning for it:

LIAHONA. This interesting word is Hebrew with an Egyptian ending. It is the name which Lehi gave to the ball or director he found outside his tent the very day he began his long journey through the "wilderness," after his little company had rested for some time in the Valley of Lemuel. (1 Nephi 16:10; Alma 37:88)

L is a Hebrew preposition meaning "to," and sometimes used to express the possessive case. *Iah* is a Hebrew abbreviated form of "Jehovah," common in Hebrew names. *On* is the Hebrew name of the Egyptian "City of the Sun." . . . *L-iah-on* means, therefore, literally, "To God is Light"; or, "of God is Light." That is to say, God gives light, as does the Sun. The final *a* reminds us that the Egyptian form of the Hebrew name *On* is *Annu,* and that seems to be the form Lehi used. . . .

114

Lehi gave the metal ball a name commemorative of one of the great experiences of his life. . . . And, furthermore, he gave it a name that no one but a devout Hebrew influenced by Egyptian culture would have thought of. (*Commentary on the Book of Mormon,* 4:178-79.)

1 NEPHI 16:13 *Possible meaning of the word "Shazer"*

The place name "Shazer," referring to the location where Lehi and his group rested for a while, is another possible transliteration of an original term used by Lehi and his group. Dr. Hugh Nibley has suggested the following possible meaning of this word:

The first important stop after Lehi's party had left their base camp was at a place they called *Shazer.* The name is intriguing. The combination *shajer* is quite common in Palestinian place names; it is a collective meaning "trees," and many Arabs (especially in Egypt) pronounce it *shazher.* It appears in *Thoghret-as-Sajur* (the Pass of Trees), which is the ancient *Shaghur,* written *Segor* in the sixth century. It may be confused with *Shaghur* "seepage," which is held to be identical with *Shihor,* the "black water" of Joshua 19:36. This last takes in western Palestine the form *Sozura,* suggesting the name of a famous water hole in South Arabia, called *Shisur* by Thomas and *Shisar* by Philby. . . . So we have *Shihor, Shaghur, Sajur, Saghir, Segor* (even *Zoar*), *Shajar, Sozura, Shisur,* and *Shisar,* all connected somehow or other and denoting either seepage—a weak but reliable water supply—or a clump of trees. Whichever one prefers, Lehi's people could hardly have picked a better name for their first suitable stopping place than *Shazer.* (*Lehi in the Desert* [Bookcraft, 1952], p. 90.)

1 NEPHI 16:34-35 *Possible meaning of the word "Nahom"*

The place names used by Lehi and his group provide readers of the Book of Mormon with some of the best means of testing the authenticity of the Book of Mormon from a linguistic viewpoint. Apparently most of these names were transliterated by Joseph Smith, and it should be remembered that the Prophet had not studied Semitic languages before his translation of the Book of Mormon. Yet, as Dr. Nibley indicates in the following quotation, the place names given by Lehi evidently came from a Semitic source:

When Ishmael died on the journey, he "was buried in the place which was called Nahom." (1 Nephi 16:34.) Note that this is not "*a* place which *we* called Nahom," but *the* place which *was* so called, a desert burial ground. Jaussen reports (*Rev. Biblique* X, 607) that though Bedouins sometimes bury the dead where they die, many carry the remains great distances to bury them. The Arabic root NHM has the basic meaning of "to sigh or moan," and occurs nearly always in the third form, "to sigh or moan with another." The Heb. *Nahum,* "comfort," is related, but that is not the form given in the Book of Mormon. At this place, we are told, "the daughters of Ishmael did mourn exceedingly," and are reminded that among the desert Arabs mourning rites are a monopoly of the women. (Ibid., pp. 90-91.)

1 NEPHI 17 *The miracles of the exodus of Israel under Moses*

The so-called higher critics of the Bible have raised the question as to whether or not the miracles of the exodus of Israel under Moses actually happened as they are recorded in the Old Testament. (See Exodus 14:19-20, 26-31; 16:4, 15; 17:5-6; Numbers 21:6-9.) However, the Book of Mormon substantiates the actuality of these miraculous events. (1 Nephi 17:23, 26, 28, 29, 30, 41.) Inasmuch as Nephi's knowledge of these miracles came from the authentic account on the brass plates of Laban (1 Nephi 5:11), Latter-day Saints should have no question concerning the reliability of the biblical account. Once again the Book of Mormon serves as a witness to its companion scripture, the Bible.

1 NEPHI 18:9 *Did the progenitors of the American Indians come "dancing" in their ships?*

Brother Eldin Ricks has the following interesting statement in his *Book of Mormon Commentary,* vol. 1, pp. 218-19:

There is a French translation by Brasseur de Bourbourg of a Mexican tradition that runs as follows: "Here is the beginning of the accounts of the arrival of the Mexicans from the place named Aztlan. It was through the midst of the water that they made their way to this locality, being four tribes. And in coming they were *rowing* in their ships." Bourbourg, who records this tradition in his *Ancient Monuments of Mexico,* explains that the word in the original language that he translated "rowing" actually is the native word for "dancing." But because he could make no sense out of "dancing" in reference to ships, he had translated it "rowing"!

Is it possible that the originators of this tradition knew more than the French scholar concerning the coming of the Mexicans to this continent? The Book of Mormon says

116 absolutely nothing concerning the coming of the people *rowing* in their ships (apparently they were driven by the winds and currents—1 Nephi 18:8, 13, 21-23), but it does say something concerning their *dancing* in their ships.

1 NEPHI 18:10 *The law of primogeniture*

Several experiences in the Book of Mormon indicate that the law of primogeniture (where the first-born son has special rights and privileges) was part of the belief and tradition of Lehi and his colony. Note particularly the following references in this regard: 1 Nephi 18:10; 2 Nephi 5:3; Mosiah 10:11-15. In only one chapter of 1 Nephi 18, we find at least three examples of the practice of this law.

1. Nephi's position of leadership was objected to by Laman and Lemuel, who were his elder brothers. (1 Nephi 18:10; see also 16:37.)

2. Despite the strong faith and numerous religious experiences of Nephi, most of the revelations from the Lord concerning the colony continued to come through his father, Lehi. (1 Nephi 18:5; see also 16:9, 23-26.)

3. Lehi and his group entered the ship "every one according to his age." (1 Nephi 18:6.)

1 NEPHI 18:21 *Use of the word "compass"*

The word *compass* as used here does not refer to the magnetic instrument of the mariner (the magnetic compass was apparently not known in the western world until about the twelfth century A.D.), but refers to the Liahona or "director ball" given to Lehi by the Lord to show him the way whither they should travel. (1 Nephi 16:9-10; Alma 37:38.)

George Reynolds has explained the differences between these two "compasses":

In the days of Moses, when he led the children of Israel out of Egypt a pillar of cloud by day and of fire by night moved in front of them. This the Hebrews followed. But to Lehi he gave this Liahona, or compass, as the ball was called and it pointed the way they should travel. It had one strange peculiarity, which was that it worked according to their faith and diligence. When they kept God's law it showed them much more clearly the way they should go than when they were careless or rebellious. Some people have confused this ball, because it is called a compass, with a mariner's compass, that sailors use at sea to direct the course of their ships. But there is a great difference between the two. The Liahona pointed the way that Lehi's company should travel while the needle in the mariner's compass points to the north. The one showed the way Lehi should go, the other informs the traveler which way he is going. The one was especially prepared by the Lord for Lehi and his companions and was used through faith only; the other can be used by all men, whether believers in the true God, pagans or infidels. (*A Dictionary of the Book of Mormon* [Salt Lake City: Hyrum Parry, 1891], p. 170.)

1 NEPHI 18:25   *The "horse" on the American continent*

If Joseph Smith had been writing the Book of Mormon instead of translating it from ancient records, he would have been very foolish to have included references to horses on the American continent in Book of Mormon times. (1 Nephi 18:25; Enos 21.) In 1830, nearly all the historians and scholars were convinced there had been no horses on the American continent before the coming of Columbus. After the Book of Mormon was published, however, archaeological discoveries were made that clearly indicate that horses were in the Americas before Columbus arrived. In the asphalt deposits of Rancho LaBrea in southern California, numerous fossil remains of horses have been found that antedate Book of Mormon times. Although these discoveries do not absolutely prove horses were in the Americas in the time period covered by the Book of Mormon (about 2600 B.C. to A.D. 421), they do prove horses were there before the coming of Columbus.

Some scientists have now accepted the possibility that horses and men lived concurrently in the Americas before the coming of Columbus. Franklin S. Harris, Jr., quotes the zoologist Ivan T. Sanderson as saying: "There is a body of evidence both from the mainland of Central America and even from rock drawings in Haiti itself tending to show that the horse may have been known to man in the Americas before the coming of the Spaniards." (*The Book of Mormon Message and Evidences* [Salt Lake City: Deseret News Press, 1953], pp. 88-89.)

1 NEPHI 19:22   *A brief history of the house of Israel*

In a sense, the Book of Mormon is of, by, and for the house of Israel. The book was written *by* the descendants of Israel (Jacob), "*to* the Lamanites, who are a remnant of the

118   house of Israel," and *for* the purpose of showing "unto the remnant of the House of Israel what great things the Lord hath done for their fathers; and that they may know the covenants of the Lord, that they are not cast off forever." (Title page of the Book of Mormon.)

Thus it is only natural that the writers in the Book of Mormon should be vitally concerned with the origin, scattering, and gathering of the house of Israel. Although the story of the origin of the house of Israel is told primarily in the Bible (the stick of Judah), a great deal of information on the *scattering* and *gathering* of Israel is contained in the Book of Mormon (the stick of Joseph). The following references are concerned almost entirely with these topics: 1 Nephi 10:12-14; 12:15; 19:14-17; 22:3-4, 7-14; 2 Nephi 10:7-8; 25:30; 30:7; Jacob 5 and 6; 3 Nephi 16:1-5; 20:20-46.

A brief history of the house of Israel is found in the chapter "Historical Background Leading to the period of the Book of Mormon." It is presented to help in the interpretation of statements in the Book of Mormon concerning the various scatterings and gatherings of Israel. For example, Isaiah lived about 700 B.C. while Nephi lived in 600 B.C.; thus, when Nephi says in interpreting the writings of Isaiah, "And the Lord will set his hand again the second time to restore his people from their lost and fallen state" (2 Nephi 25:17), it is quite clear that he is talking about the gathering of Israel in the dispensation of the fulness of times, because this is the *second* major gathering of Israel since the times of Nephi and Isaiah.

The scattering of the house of Israel: About 721 B.C. the kingdom of Israel was conquered by Shalmaneser of Assyria, and the ten tribes of the kingdom of Israel were led away into captivity (2 Kings 17). According to tradition, about a year after this these tribes mysteriously escaped and fled toward the north. Since then, they have been referred to as the "Ten Lost Tribes" of Israel. The kingdom of Judah was preserved until about 587 B.C. when it was conquered by Nebuchadnezzar of Babylonia. (The Lord warned Lehi about 600 B.C. to flee from Jerusalem so that he would escape before the war took place—1 Nephi 1:4, 13; 2 Nephi 1:4.) The people were taken away captive into the land of Babylonia (2 Kings 25), but some fifty years later (about 538

B.C.), after Babylonia had been conquered by Persia, they were allowed to return to their land by Cyrus, king of Persia. They rebuilt the temple and lived in the Holy Land for over five hundred years under the rule of four separate groups: Persians, Greeks, Asmonaeans, and Romans. Finally about A.D. 70 the Roman legions destroyed the city of Jerusalem and the temple. The people of the kingdom of Judah were later scattered among the nations of the world.

The gathering of the house of Israel: On September 21, 1823, the angel Moroni appeared to Joseph Smith and quoted the eleventh chapter of Isaiah to him and emphasized that it was soon to be fulfilled. (See Isaiah 11:10-12.) On April 6, 1830, the church of Jesus Christ was restored to the earth, and soon missionaries were sent to proclaim the glad tidings. On April 3, 1836, Moses appeared in the Kirtland Temple and restored the "keys of the gathering of Israel." (See Doctrine and Covenants 110:11.) On October 24, 1841, Elder Orson Hyde dedicated the Holy Land for the return of the Jews. In May 1948 the state of Israel was created and was officially recognized by the leading countries of the world.

The scriptures indicate there are to be three main aspects of the gathering: (1) the gathering of the dispersed of Israel from the nations of the earth to Zion; (2) the return of the Jews (tribe of Judah) to Jerusalem and the ancient promised land; and (3) the restoration of the lost tribes of Israel to the true fold of the Shepherd.

The following references in the Book of Mormon discuss the various aspects of the gathering of Israel and of the building of the New Jerusalem on the American continent: 1 Nephi 19:14-17; 2 Nephi 10:7-8; 2 Nephi 25; 3 Nephi 20:20-33, 46 (these verses are now in the process of fulfillment); 3 Nephi 21:20-25; 3 Nephi 29:8-9; Ether 3:1-12.

1 NEPHI 19:1   *The origin of the "large" and the "small" plates of Nephi*

The part of our present Book of Mormon that is found in the books of 1 Nephi, 2 Nephi, Jacob, Enos, Jarom, and Omni came from the small plates of Nephi. Much of the remainder of the Book of Mormon (the books of Mosiah, Alma, Helaman, 3 Nephi, 4 Nephi, and Mormon) came from Mormon's abridgment of the large plates of Nephi.

120 The large plates of Nephi were evidently made first. First Nephi 10:1-2 would seem to indicate that Nephi made the large plates of Nephi soon after his arrival in the promised land (about 588 B.C.). However, Nephi did not make the small plates of Nephi until approximately 570 B.C. (2 Nephi 5:28-33.)

1 NEPHI 19:10, 13 *The "three days of darkness" as a sign of the crucifixion of Jesus Christ*

A careful reading of these words of Zenos seems to indicate that the "three days of darkness" that were to accompany the crucifixion of Christ were not to be a sign to those of the house of Israel around Jerusalem but only to those who lived away from Jerusalem or on "the isles of the sea." (1 Nephi 19:10.) The sign to be given to those at Jerusalem is listed later by Zenos wherein he states, "And as for those who are at Jerusalem . . . they shall be scourged by all people, because they crucify the God of Israel." (1 Nephi 19:13.)

1 NEPHI 20:1 *Origin of the term "or out of the waters of baptism"*

The term "or out of the waters of baptism" did not appear in the first edition of the Book of Mormon. It first appeared in the edition of 1840 on page 53, and the sentence in which it appeared was punctuated as follows: "Hearken and hear this, O house of Jacob, who are called by the name of Israel, and are come forth out of the waters of Judah, (or out of the waters of baptism,) who swear by the name of the Lord," etc. It is not absolutely clear who was responsible for the insertion of this phrase, although the title page of this edition indicates that it was the "Third Edition, Carefully Revised by the Translator" and was published in Nauvoo, Illinois.

In the "Committee Copy" of the Book of Mormon that was used by Elder James E. Talmage and his committee in making the changes for the 1920 edition, the words "or out of the waters of baptism" were not printed in the text although they had been inserted in red ink in parentheses. However, the parentheses were crossed out by red pencil. These words are printed in the current edition of the Book of Mormon without the parentheses.

1 NEPHI 21:1 *An addition of the Book of Mormon to the Isaiah text of the Bible*

The following part of 1 Nephi 21:1 has been entirely left out of the Old Testament account: "And again: Hearken, O ye house of Israel, all ye that are broken off and are driven out, because of the wickedness of the pastors of my people; yea, all ye that are broken off, that are scattered abroad, who are of my people, O house of Israel." It is entirely possible that one of the "wicked pastors" of Israel objected to this statement and deleted it from the record of the scriptures that remained in Jerusalem.

1 NEPHI 21:1, 8; 22:4 *The term "isles of the sea" as used by the Hebrews*

According to a quotation by Reynolds and Sjodahl, "Sir Isaac Newton observes that to the Hebrews the continents of Asia and Africa were 'the earth,' because they had access to them by land, while the parts of the earth to which they sailed over the sea were 'the isles of the sea.' " (*Commentary on the Book of Mormon,* 1:214.)

Thus, Nephi not only refers to the isles of the sea as the location of other remnants of the house of Israel, but he also indicates that he and his people were then living upon an "isle of the sea" when he quite clearly is referring to the great land mass known as the American continent. (2 Nephi 10:20-21.) The following quotation is of interest:

> The Indians almost universally believed the dry land they knew, to be part of a great island, everywhere surrounded by wide waters whose limits were unknown. Many tribes had vague myths of a journey from beyond this sea; many placed beyond it the home of the sun and of light, and the happy hunting grounds of the departed souls. (Quoted from "Library of Aboriginal American Literature," 5:134, in Reynolds and Sjodahl, *Commentary on the Book of Mormon,* 1:319.)

1 NEPHI 22:7 *The gentile nation to be raised up on "this land"*

The "mighty nation among the Gentiles" which the Lord was to raise up "even upon the face of this land" evidently refers to the great nation of the United States of America. The early pilgrims and other colonizers of the U.S. were largely those who scattered the seed of Nephi, as he prophesied.

1 NEPHI 22:8 "... *being nourished by the Gentiles*"

President Spencer W. Kimball has indicated that the taking of the Book of Mormon to the modern Lamanites is in partial fulfillment of 1 Nephi 21:8:

My Lamanite brothers and sisters, we love you. Our bringing the gospel to you is "likened unto their being nourished by the Gentiles and being carried in their arms and upon their shoulders. . . . " (1 Nephi 22:8.) Your God has performed many miracles to get the story written by his prophets, to preserve the records against threats of enemies and the ravages of nature, and to get them translated into a language you can understand, and bring to you this second witness of Christ. Your Book of Mormon record is as a voice from the dust, messages from the dead, warnings from the Lord:

"Return unto me and I will return unto you, saith the Lord of Hosts." (3 Nephi 24:7.)

Our Lord cries, "Wo unto him that spurneth at the doings of the Lord; yea, wo unto him that shall deny the Christ and his works!" (*Ibid.,* 29:5.)

You have been preserved to this epochal day, and the gospel is available to you now. Wash your souls in the blood of the Lamb. Cleanse your lives, study the scriptures, accept the gospel and ordinances.

These predictions can be fulfilled and come to you through one channel only, the path of righteousness and faith; else all these promises are but empty, unfulfilled dreams.

May God bless you that you may accept the truths now revealed to you. (*Conference Report,* October 1959, pp. 61-62.)

1 NEPHI 22:16-17 *Conditions in the last days*

Elder Mark E. Petersen has offered the following explanation on conditions in the world as outlined in 1 Nephi 22:16-17:

. . . in these, the last days, the Lord has predicted that there shall be two simultaneous movements. One of these movements is the great tribulation that shall come upon the world. The wicked will destroy the wicked.

The other great movement which will be going forward simultaneously is that there shall be a stone cut out of the mountain without hands, and it shall roll forth and eventually fill the whole earth. The Church to which you and I belong is that stone. It has been cut out of the mountain without hands, and your destiny and mine is to help roll it forth. (D&C 65:2.)

Now do you suppose for one moment that the judgments of God are going to interfere with the progress of his work? He is consistent, isn't he? Although he will pour out his tribulations upon the wicked, he nevertheless will carry forward his work, and his people, under divine protection, will roll forth that stone until eventually it fills the whole earth.

And so says the Book of Mormon:

"For the time soon cometh that the fulness of the wrath of God shall be poured out upon all the children of men; for he will not suffer that the wicked shall destroy the righteous.

"Wherefore, he will preserve the righteous by his power, even if it so be that the fulness of his wrath must come, and the righteous be preserved, even unto the destruction of their enemies by fire. Wherefore, the righteous need not fear; for thus saith the prophet, they shall be saved, even if it so be as by fire." (1 Nephi 22:16-17.)

I believe that. In the midst of all these tribulations God will send fire from heaven, if necessary, to destroy our enemies while we carry forward our work and push that stone until it fills the whole earth!

Your destiny is to do that very thing, and this is the kind of protection you will have. You do not need to fear about world conditions. You do not need to fear about anybody. Just serve the Lord and keep his commandments and build the kingdom, and as you do so you will be protected in these last days. God will have his hand over you, and you can plan your lives in confidence. (*Conference Report,* October 1960, pp. 81-83.)

1 NEPHI 22:31 *Nephi's closing signature to his first book*

It is quite evident that Nephi intended that the concluding verse of 1 Nephi should close a major part of his literary efforts. Thus, he concludes this section with the construction "And thus it is. Amen." Dr. Hugh Nibley has indicated that Nephi frequently closed the major sections of his writing with such a phrase; he also indicates that Nephi may have gotten this idea from the Egyptians: "Egyptian literary writings regularly close with the formula *iw-f-pw,* 'Thus it is,' 'and so it is.' Nephi ends the main sections of his book with the phrase, 'And thus it is. Amen.' (9:6; 14:30; 22:31.)" (*Lehi in the Desert,* p. 18.)

2 NEPHI 1:4 *Lehi's vision that Jerusalem had been destroyed*

The destruction of Jerusalem referred to in 2 Nephi 1:4 is recorded in the Bible in 2 Kings 25. Lehi and his group had been warned by the Lord to flee from the land of Jerusalem so that they would escape this destruction. Most biblical scholars date the destruction of Jerusalem by the Babylonians somewhere between 586 B.C. and 590 B.C. Thus in his chronological footnotes in this section of the Book of Mormon, Brother Talmage suggests that the events following Lehi's vision of the destruction of Jerusalem took place sometime after about 588 B.C.

2 NEPHI 1:8 *Other nations kept from a knowledge of the promised land*

One of the great mysteries of history is how the existence of the great north and south American continents could be kept from the knowledge of the inhabitants of the Old World (Europe, Asia, and Africa). However, with the Lord all things are possible, and the Lord revealed to Lehi that it was wisdom in Him that the existence of this land should be kept from the knowledge of other nations; otherwise "many nations would overrun the land, that there would be no place for an inheritance" for Lehi and his descendants. (2 Nephi 1:8.)

2 NEPHI 1:14 *Did Joseph Smith quote from Shakespeare?*

Anti-Mormon critics claim that Joseph Smith received from Shakespeare the idea of referring to death as "the cold and silent grave, from whence no traveler can return." (2 Nephi 1:14.) Shakespeare's quotation, which critics say is too similar to the statement by Lehi, reads as follows: "But that the dread of something after death, The undiscovered country from whose bourn no traveller returns." (*Hamlet,* Act 3, scene 1.) Such critics overlook other possibilities for the explanation of the similarity between this statement by Joseph Smith and the one by Shakespeare. In the first place, the idea of referring to death in such a manner is not unique to either of these men. In the book of Job in the Old Testament, we find such statements as: "Before I go whence I shall not return, even to the land of darkness and the shadow of death" (Job 10:21), and "When a few years are come, then I shall go the way whence I shall not return" (Job 16:22). Also, the Roman poet Catulus (who lived in the first century B.C.) included a similar thought in his "Elegy on a Sparrow": "Now having passed the gloomy bourne/From whence he never can return."

Also, Joseph Smith, as the translator of the Nephite record, naturally had to include in his translation those words and expressions with which he was familiar. Therefore, if he had ever heard the grave referred to as a place "from whence no traveler can return" it would be logical for him to translate the similar statement by Lehi in essentially these same words.

2 NEPHI 2:4   *Jacob saw the Redeemer*

Apparently Jacob, the son of Lehi and the brother of Nephi, is one of the select few persons who was visited by the pre-earthly Savior. In 2 Nephi 2:4 Nephi says concerning Jacob, "Thou hast beheld in thy youth" the glory of the Redeemer. In a later statement Nephi mentioned that Isaiah had seen "my Redeemer, even as I have seen him. And my brother, Jacob, also has seen him as I have seen him." (2 Nephi 11:2-3.)

2 NEPHI 2:11-27   *The necessity of an "opposition in all things"*

Notice the major points in Lehi's argument as to why there must be opposition before a man can be truly free and before he can experience real joy: (1) Every law has both a punishment and a blessing attached to it. (2) Disobedience to law requires a punishment which results in misery. (3) Obedience to law provides a blessing which results in happiness (joy). (4) Without law there can be neither punishment nor blessing, neither misery nor happiness—only innocence. (5) Thus happiness (or joy) can exist only where the possibility of the opposite (unhappiness or misery) also exists. (6) In order to exercise free agency a person must have the possibility (and the freedom) of choice; in a world without law—and thus without choice—there could be no freedom of choice and thus no true exercise of free agency. (2 Nephi 2:15-16; see also Alma 12:31-32 and Alma 42:17-25.)

Lehi does not say it is necessary to choose evil in order to recognize good from evil, but he does make it quite clear that a choice of opposites is necessary for growth.

The major points in Lehi's explanation of the necessity of opposition might be diagramed as follows:

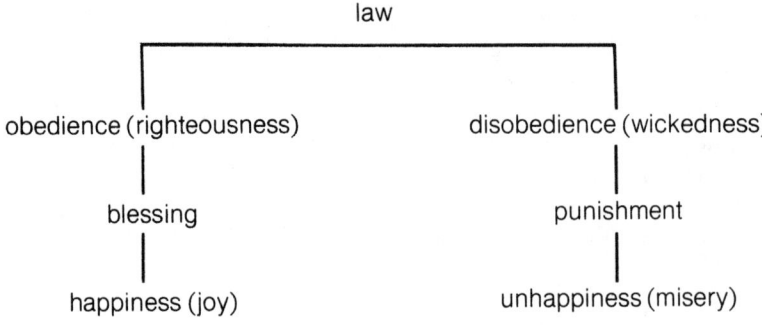

The teachings of Lehi are consistent with statements of the Lord in the Doctrine and Covenants:

There is a law, irrevocably decreed in heaven before the foundations of this world, upon which all blessings are predicated—

And when we obtain any blessing from God, it is by obedience to that law upon which it is predicated. (D&C 130:20-21.)

For all who will have a blessing at my hands shall abide the law which was appointed for that blessing, and the conditions thereof, as were instituted from before the foundation of the world. (D&C 132:5.)

2 NEPHI 2:22-25   *The Book of Mormon concept of the "fall" of Adam*

A correct concept of the fall of Adam is necessary to an understanding of the basic claims of Christianity. The churches of the world, however, have largely lost sight of the essential differences in the status of Adam and Eve before and after the fall. Lehi provides a wealth of information on this important subject in 2 Nephi 2:14-27. The general conditions of Adam and Eve before the fall are listed on the left side of the chart which follows; the corresponding general conditions of Adam and Eve after the fall are listed on the right side of the chart.

Status of Adam and Eve before the fall

1. They were in the presence of God.

2. They were not mortal—that is, they were not subject to physical death. (2 Nephi 2:22.)

3. They were in a state of innocence—that is, they did not know the difference between good and evil. (2 Nephi 2:23.)

4. They "would have had no children." (2 Nephi 2:23.)

Status of Adam and Eve after the fall

1. They were cast out of the presence of God—that is, they suffered a spiritual death.

2. They became mortal (subject to physical death).

3. They knew good from evil.

4. They had children.

Thus, Lehi makes two major conclusions from these teachings: (1) the fall was necessary in order for "men to be"—that is, in order for Adam and Eve to have children. (2) A major purpose of man's existence is for him to have "joy." True joy was not possible for Adam and Eve before the fall.

These truths are stated clearly by Lehi in 2 Nephi 2:22-23: "And now, behold, if Adam had not transgressed he would not have fallen . . . and they (Adam and Eve) *would have had no children;* wherefore they would have remained in a state of innocence, *having no joy,* for they knew no misery; doing no good, for they knew no sin." (Italics added.)

Once Adam and Eve knew the difference between good and evil and had been taught the gospel by an angel, they realized the necessity of the fall in order for them to have joy and to have increase (children). Adam then said: "Blessed be the name of God, for *because of my transgression* my eyes are opened, and in this life *I shall have joy,* and again in the flesh I shall see God. And Eve, his wife, heard all these things and was glad, saying: *Were it not for our transgression we never should have had seed,* and never should have known

128   good and evil, and the joy of our redemption, and the eternal life which God giveth unto all the obedient." (Moses 5:10-11. Italics added.)

A careful examination of the status of Adam and Eve after the fall indicates there were two desirable effects of the fall (they knew good from evil and they had children), but also two undesirable effects so far as eternity is concerned (they suffered spiritual death because of their disobedience and they also became subject to physical death). The atonement of Jesus Christ, however, makes it possible to overcome both of the undesirable effects: spiritual death of an individual can be overcome through sincere repentance and obedience to God's commandments, and physical death has been overcome through the breaking of the bands of death by Jesus Christ through the resurrection. Thus, when the fall of Adam and the atonement of Jesus Christ are considered together, it is seen that both are part of God's plan of eternal progression for man.

2 NEPHI 2:26-27   *The freedom of choice*

As Lehi indicates, it is only through the atonement of Jesus Christ that men are made free. Because the atonement redeems men from the fall of Adam, they "become free forever, knowing good from evil; to act for themselves and not to be acted upon, save it be by the punishment of the law." (2 Nephi 2:26.) Although the Savior freed us from the effects of the fall and thus gave us the freedom to choose either good or evil, we remain free only as we keep the commandments and "choose liberty and eternal life"; if we choose "captivity and death," then we become "miserable like unto" the devil. (2 Nephi 2:27.)

2 NEPHI 3:1-25   *The four "Josephs"*

Four different men named Joseph are referred to in 2 Nephi 3 as follows: (1) Joseph who was sold into Egypt; he is also known as Joseph the son of Jacob (Israel)—verses 4-22; (2) Joseph the son of Lehi—verses 1-3, 22-25; (3) Joseph Smith, Sr., the father of the Prophet—verse 15, and (4) Joseph Smith, Jr., the Prophet—verses 7-9, 11, 14-15, 18-19.

2 NEPHI 3:3   The seed of Joseph to be preserved

The descendants of Joseph, the son of Lehi, were known as Nephites during much of the period covered by the Book of Mormon. However, when the Book of Mormon records the destruction of the Nephite nation (Mormon 6-8), this does not mean that all of the descendants of Joseph were destroyed. Joseph is specifically promised in this patriarchal blessing that his "seed shall not utterly be destroyed." (2 Nephi 3:3.) That this promise was literally fulfilled is indicated by the Lord when he said to Joseph Smith in 1828 that the Book of Mormon had to be translated and published so that it might go forth unto the "Josephites." (See D&C 3:17.)

2 NEPHI 3:12   *The records of Judah and Joseph*

The statement of the Lord to Joseph who was sold into Egypt concerning the writings of Judah and "the fruit of thy loins" (2 Nephi 3:12) is very similar to the statement of the Lord to Ezekiel concerning the "sticks" of Judah and Joseph (Ezekiel 37:15-22). When these two references are read together, it is clear that the "stick of Judah" is the Bible, whereas the "stick of Joseph" is the Book of Mormon.

In connection with the Book of Mormon's being the stick of Joseph, it is important to note that Lehi was a direct descendant of Joseph through Manasseh, Joseph's son. (Alma 10:3.) It is also reported by Erastus Snow that Joseph Smith said Ishmael was a descendant of Joseph through his other son, Ephraim. (*Journal of Discourses,* 23:184-85.) Thus the people of Lehi's colony were pure Josephites, and their record rightfully qualifies as part of the "stick of Joseph."

2 NEPHI 3:18   *The "spokesman" to be raised up by the Lord*

Many members of the Church believe that Sidney Rigdon is the "spokesman" referred to in this prophecy. (2 Nephi 3:18.) It appears that Joseph Smith is the prophet mentioned in this verse, and the Lord promised Sidney Rigdon that he should "be a spokesman to my servant Joseph." (D&C 100:9.) Elder George Q. Cannon explained as follows why he believed the calling of Sidney Rigdon as a spokesman for Joseph Smith was in direct fulfillment of this prophecy:

He [Sidney Rigdon] was baptized in the town of Kirtland, and the foundation of a great work was laid there. God afterwards revealed that this man was to be a spokesman, and he became the spokesman to this people and to the world for the prophet Joseph.

130 Those who knew Sidney Rigdon, know how wonderfully God inspired him, and with what wonderful eloquence he declared the word of God to the people. He was a mighty man in the hands of God, as a spokesman, as long as the prophet lived, or up to a short time before his death. Thus you see that even this which many might look upon as a small matter, was predicted about 1,700 years before the birth of the Savior, and was quoted by Lehi 600 years before the same event, and about 2,400 years before its fulfillment, and was translated by the power of God, through his servant Joseph, as was predicted should be the case, and at a time, as I have said, when there was not a man upon the earth who was a member of The Church of Jesus Christ of Latter-day Saints. The church had not yet been organized, and Joseph did not know, unless he knew by the spirit of revelation, whether any man would receive the Gospel. (*Journal of Discourses,* 25:126-27.)

2 NEPHI 4:2 *The prophecies of Joseph who was sold into Egypt*

Nephi mentions the prophecies of Joseph that were written on the brass plates of Laban, and, he concludes, "there are not many greater." (2 Nephi 4:2.) But where are these great prophecies of Joseph? Why do they not appear in the Old Testament? We do not know the answers to these questions, but the following observations might give some clues as to possible answers.

In the first place, Joseph's prophecies would logically be written most completely on the "stick" or record of Joseph; thus, they were probably included in detail on the brass plates of Laban. However, Joseph's prophecies are not found presently in the "stick" or record of Judah—the Bible. Again, this would indicate that the records on the brass plates of Laban were more comprehensive and complete than the records from which we get our Old Testament.

In the second place, evidently some of the writings of Joseph are still in existence but have not been published to the world. Joseph Smith said that he received some papyri scrolls that contained the record of Abraham and Joseph at the same time he obtained the Egyptian mummies from Michael Chandler. Concerning this record, Joseph Smith has written: "The record of Abraham and Joseph, found with the mummies, is beautifully written on papyrus, with black, and a small part red, ink or paint, in perfect preservation." (*History of the Church,* 2:348.) The Prophet next describes how the mummies and the record came into his possession and then concludes: "Thus I have given a brief history of the manner in which the writings of the fathers, Abraham and Joseph, have been preserved, and how I came in possession of the same—a correct translation of which I shall give in its proper place." (Ibid., 2:350-51.)

The record of Abraham translated by the Prophet was subsequently printed, and it is now known as the book of Abraham in the Pearl of Great Price. However, the translation of the book of Joseph has not yet been published. Evidently the record of Joseph was translated by the Prophet, but perhaps the reason it was not published was because the great prophecies therein were "too great" for the people of this day.

2 NEPHI 4:11 *The descendants of Sam to be numbered with the seed of Nephi*

Although Nephi's brother Sam evidently had children (2 Nephi 4:11), there are no "Samites" mentioned in the Book of Mormon. Perhaps Lehi's promise to Sam that his seed would be numbered with the seed of Nephi (2 Nephi 4:11) helps to explain why the record does not refer to "Samites," whereas the descendants of the other sons of Lehi are referred to as Lamanites, Lemuelites, Nephites, Jacobites, and Josephites (Jacob 1:13).

2 NEPHI 5:6 *The sisters of Nephi*

This is the only specific reference in the Book of Mormon that Nephi had sisters as well as brothers. How many sisters there were, whether they were older or younger than Nephi, or what their names may have been are questions not answered in our present Book of Mormon. However, the following statement by Erastus Snow may provide information on some of the sisters of Nephi:

The Prophet Joseph informed us that the record of Lehi, was contained on the 116 pages that were first translated and subsequently stolen, and of which an abridgment is given us in the first Book of Nephi, which is the record of Nephi individually, he himself being of the lineage of Manasseh; but that Ishmael was of the lineage of Ephraim, and that his sons married into Lehi's family, and Lehi's sons married Ishmael's daughters. . . . " (*Journal of Discourses*, 23:184.)

132   The words that Ishmael's sons "married into Lehi's
family" would seem to indicate that the two sons of Ishmael
(see 1 Nephi 7:6) were married to Lehi's daughters (and thus
to two of the sisters of Nephi). However, the sisters referred
to in 2 Nephi 5:6 are evidently still other sisters, because the
sisters mentioned here follow Nephi when the schism with
Laman occurs, whereas the sisters of Nephi who were married to the sons of Ishmael evidently stayed with their husbands and joined with Laman. (See Alma 3:7 and 47:35.)

2 NEPHI 5:21-23   *The "mark of the curse" of the
Lamanites*

The mark of the curse that came upon the Lamanites
was that "a skin of blackness" came upon them. A major
purpose of this mark was that the Lamanites "might not be
enticing" unto the Nephites. (2 Nephi 5:21.) The Lord stated
further that the "seed of him that mixeth" with the un-
righteous Lamanites "shall be cursed even with the same
cursing." (2 Nephi 5:23.)

This is the only reference in the entire Book of Mormon
where a definite color adjective is used to refer to this mark.
All other references call it a "skin of darkness" or a "dark
skin." It is of interest to note that the terms "blackness" and
"darkness" are interchangeable in the Hebrew. Even in
modern Hebrew it is not unusual for some skilled translator
to render a word *black* whereas other equally skilled translators select *dark* as the best translation.

2 NEPHI 5:26; 6:2   *The priesthood of the Nephites*

Many references in the Book of Mormon indicate that
the Nephites held the priesthood—that is, they had the
power and authority to act in the name of God. However,
the Book of Mormon does not refer specifically to the two
major divisions in the priesthood, the Aaronic Priesthood
and the Melchizedek Priesthood. Thus the question has
frequently arisen as to exactly what priesthood was held by
the Nephites. Joseph Fielding Smith gives his answer in the
following comprehensive statement:

The Nephites were descendants of Joseph. Lehi discovered this
when reading the brass plates. He was a descendant of Manasseh,
and Ishmael, who accompanied him with his family, was of the
tribe of Ephraim. Therefore there were no Levites who accompanied Lehi to the Western Hemisphere. Under these conditions

the Nephites officiated by virtue of the Melchizedek Priesthood from the days of Lehi to the days of the appearance of our Savior among them. It is true that Nephi "consecrated Jacob and Joseph" that they should be priests and teachers over the land of the Nephites, but the fact that plural terms *priests* and *teachers* were used indicates that this was not a reference to the definite office in the priesthood in either case, but it was a general assignment to teach, direct, and admonish the people. Otherwise the terms *priest* and *teacher* would have been given, in the singular. Additional light is thrown on this appointment showing that these two brothers of Nephi held the Melchizedek Priesthood, in the sixth chapter, second verse of II Nephi, where Jacob makes this explanation regarding the priesthood which he and Joseph held: "Behold, my beloved brethren, I, Jacob, having been called of God, and ordained *after the manner of his holy order,* and having been consecrated by my brother Nephi, unto whom ye look as a king or a protector, and on whom ye depend for safety, behold ye know that I have spoken unto you exceeding many things."

This seems to be a confirmation of the ordinations that he and his brother Joseph received in the Melchizedek Priesthood. All through the Book of Mormon we find references to the Nephites officiating by virtue of the Higher Priesthood after the holy order. Alma, discoursing on the subject before the people of the city of Ammonihah, said: "And again, my brethren, I would cite your minds forward to the time when the Lord God gave these commandments unto his children; and I would that ye should remember that the Lord God ordained priests, after his holy order, which was after the order of his Son, to teach these things unto the people." (Alma 13:1. See also D&C 107:1-4.)

In the opening verses of Alma, Chapter 43, Mormon records the following: "And now it came to pass that the sons of Alma did go forth among the people . . . and . . . they preached the word, and the truth, according to the spirit of prophecy and revelation; and they preached after the holy order of God by which they were called."

From these and numerous other passages we learn that it was by the authority of the Melchizedek Priesthood that the Nephites administered from the time they left Jerusalem until the time of the coming of Jesus Christ. By the power of this priesthood they baptized, confirmed, and ordained. During these years they also observed the law of Moses. They offered sacrifice and performed the duties which in Israel had been assigned to the priests and Levites. They observed in every detail the requirements of the law. When the Savior came to them, he fulfilled the carnal law and did away with the sacrifice by the shedding of blood of animals. He in-

134 formed the Nephites that in him the law of Moses was fulfilled.

When the Savior came to the Nephites, he established the Church in its fulness among them, and he informed them that former things had passed away, for they were all fulfilled in him. He gave the Nephites all the authority of the priesthood which we exercise today. Therefore we are justified in the belief that not only was the fulness of the Melchizedek Priesthood conferred, but also the Aaronic, just as we have it in the Church today; and this Aaronic Priesthood remained with them from this time until, through wickedness, all priesthood ceased. We may be assured that in the days of Moroni the Nephites did ordain teachers and priests in the Aaronic Priesthood; but before the visit of the Savior they officiated in the Melchizedek Priesthood. (*Answers to Gospel Questions,* 1:124-26.)

2 NEPHI 5:28-31   *Beginning of the small plates of Nephi*

All of the material so far in the Book of Mormon has come from the small plates of Nephi. Although the account in First Nephi evidently begins around 600 B.C., it is quite clear from 2 Nephi 5:28-33 that the small plates were not prepared until thirty years after Lehi left Jerusalem, or approximately 570 B.C. Thus, when Nephi started to write on the small plates in 570 B.C., he evidently started listing events in his earlier life, dating from the time his father left Jerusalem. This might be somewhat analagous to your starting this year a life history but writing first in your history some of the events of your childhood.

2 NEPHI 6-9   *Jacob's quotation of Isaiah*

The prophet Isaiah lived near Jerusalem and was one of the leading prophets of Israel during approximately 760-700 B.C. His present writings occupy sixty-six chapters in the Old Testament, and they also appear on the brass plates of Laban. The words of Isaiah that are quoted here were taken from the account on the brass plates. In 2 Nephi, chapter 6, Jacob quotes a few verses from the material contained in chapter 49 of Isaiah (Isaiah 49:22-26); then Jacob explains what these scriptures mean concerning his descendants and the future of his people. He next quotes the material found in Isaiah chapters 50 and 51 (2 Nephi 7-8); and then, beginning with chapter 9, he provides us with his commentary on these writings of Isaiah.

2 NEPHI 6:6   *The "standard" to be raised up by the Lord*
in the last days

The Lord prophesied through Isaiah that in the last days
he would set up his standard to the people of the earth. This
"standard" evidently refers to The Church of Jesus Christ of
Latter-day Saints, as is indicated in this statement by
President Marion G. Romney:

This Church is the standard which Isaiah said the Lord would
set up for the people in the latter days. This Church was given to be
a light to the world and to be a standard for God's people and for
the Gentiles to seek to. This Church is the ensign on the mountain
spoken of by the Old Testament prophets. It is the way, the truth,
and the life. (*Conference Report,* April 1961, p. 119.)

2 NEPHI 8:24-25   *Interpretation of some of Isaiah's writings*

In his concluding quotation from Isaiah, Jacob includes
the two verses that now appear as Isaiah 52:1-2. These verses
include several idiomatic expressions, and their meaning has
been widely disputed by biblical scholars. In March 1838 the
Prophet Joseph Smith was asked questions concerning these
two verses, and his answers follow:

Questions by Elias Higbee: What is meant by the command in
Isaiah, 52d chapter, 1st verse, which saith: Put on thy strength, O
Zion—and what people had Isaiah reference to?

He had reference to those whom God should call in the last
days, who should hold the power of priesthood to bring again Zion,
and the redemption of Israel; and to put on her strength is to put
on the authority of the priesthood, which she, Zion, has a right to
by lineage; also to return to that power which she had lost.

What are we to understand by Zion loosing herself from the
bands of her neck; 2d verse?

We are to understand that the scattered remnants are exhorted
to return to the Lord from whence they have fallen; which if they
do, the promise of the Lord is that he will speak to them, or give
them revelation. See the 6th, 7th, and 8th verses. The bands of her
neck are the curses of God upon her, or the remnants of Israel in
their scattered condition among the Gentiles. (D&C 113:7-10.)

2 NEPHI 9:6-9   *The "infinite" atonement of Jesus Christ*

The atonement of Jesus Christ met fully the demands of
justice in regard to the original transgression of Adam. Thus,
the atonement is "infinite" because it applies to everyone in
(1) removing the permanent effects of physical death for

136 everyone by providing for the resurrection, and (2) giving every person the opportunity of having the effects of spiritual death (alienation from the Spirit of God through sin) removed through the repentance of individual sins.

2 NEPHI 9:6-12 *The nature of "spiritual death"*

The term "spiritual death" is used in the Book of Mormon to refer to a spiritual alienation from God; according to Alma, it occurs when one dies "as to things pertaining unto righteousness." (Alma 12:16.) One definition of the word *spiritual* is "of or pertaining to the spirit or things of the spirit"; the definition of *death* includes the idea of separation. Thus spiritual death rightfully refers to a state of spiritual separation from God; it may or may not have anything to do with a physical separation from God.

The very first spiritual death on this earth occurred when Adam and Eve transgressed one of the commandments of God. By becoming subject to sin, they were cast out of God's presence because no sinful or unclean thing can dwell with God. Inasmuch as Adam and Eve were in the physical presence of God when they transgressed, they had to be expelled from his presence physically as well as spiritually.

The first spiritual death of Adam and Eve was fully atoned for by the Savior and Redeemer of mankind. Because of the atonement of Jesus Christ, a newborn child on this earth is not spiritually dead but is alive "in Christ, even from the foundation of the world." (Moroni 8:12.) However, when a person arrives at the age of accountability, learns the difference between good and evil, and then commits sin, he suffers his first individual spiritual death. He becomes spiritually dead because he alienates himself from the Spirit of God. This type of spiritual death is referred to in the scripture as the *first* spiritual death. If a person fully repents of his sins, accepts the atonement of the Savior, and is baptized of water and of the Spirit, he can be spiritually born again through the cleansing action of the Holy Ghost and thus can regain God's presence. If he does not meet the requirements of this rebirth, he cannot regain the presence of God. (John 3:5.)

President Joseph F. Smith has explained the first spiritual death and related it to the people in the world today in the following words:

When Adam, our first parent, partook of the forbidden fruit, transgressed the law of God, and became subject unto Satan, he was banished from the presence of God and was thrust out into outer spiritual darkness. This was the first death. Yet living, he was dead—dead to God, dead to light and truth, dead spiritually; cast out from the presence of God; communication between the Father and the son cut off. He was as absolutely thrust out from the presence of God as was Satan and the hosts that followed him. That was spiritual death. But the Lord said that He would not suffer Adam nor his posterity to come to the temporal death until they should have the means by which they might be redeemed from the first death, which is spiritual. Therefore angels were sent unto Adam, who taught him the Gospel, and revealed to him the principle by which he could be redeemed from the first death, and be brought back from banishment and outer darkness into the marvelous light of the Gospel. He was taught faith, repentance and baptism for the remission of sins, in the name of Jesus Christ, who should come in the meridian of time and take away the sin of the world, and was thus given a chance to be redeemed from the spiritual death before he should die the temporal death. Now, all the world today, I am sorry to say, with the exception of a handful of people who have obeyed the new and everlasting covenant, are suffering this spiritual death. They are cast out from the presence of God. They are without God, without Gospel truth, and without the power of redemption; for they know not God nor His Gospel. In order that they may be redeemed and saved from the spiritual death which has spread over the world like a pall, they must repent of their sins, and be baptized by one having authority, for the remission of their sins, that they may be born of God. (*Conference Report,* October 1899, p. 72.)

Another type of spiritual death mentioned in the scriptures is the *"second* spiritual death." This more serious spiritual death occurs when a person commits the sin against the Holy Ghost—"Having denied the Holy Spirit after having received it, and having denied the Only Begotten Son of the Father, having crucified him unto themselves and put him to an open shame. . . . And the only ones on whom the second death shall have any power." (D&C 76:35, 37.) The effects of this sin are eternal, for the sinner never can make full payment for the law he has broken. Indeed, by denying the atonement of Jesus Christ and the cleansing power of the Holy Ghost, the sinner has denied the very power upon which forgiveness and redemption are based. These sinners

138   become sons of perdition, and they "shall be chained down to an everlasting destruction" (Alma 12:17) and become "the only ones who shall not be redeemed in the due time of the Lord" (D&C 76:38).

2 NEPHI 9:20   God "knoweth all things"

The prophets, both ancient and modern, have clearly taught that God knows everything. Psalm 147:5 reads: "Great is our Lord, and of great power: his understanding is infinite." In Doctrine and Covenants 38:1-2, Jesus Christ introduces himself in these words: "Thus saith the Lord your God, even Jesus Christ, the Great I AM . . . The same which knoweth all things." (See also Alma 26:35.) The Prophet Joseph Smith also clearly taught this doctrine, as is indicated in his "Lectures on Faith" which appeared in the early editions of the Doctrine and Covenants:

. . . God is the only supreme governor and independent being in whom all fulness and perfection dwell; who *is* omnipotent [all-powerful], omnipresent [everywhere present] and omniscient [all knowing]; without beginning of days or end of life; and that in him every good gift and every good principle dwell. . . .

. . . Without the knowledge of all things, God would not be able to save any portion of his creatures; for it is by reason of the knowledge which he has of all things, from the beginning to the end, that enables him to give the understanding to his creatures by which they are made partakers of eternal life; and if it were not for the idea existing in the minds of men that God had all knowledge it would be impossible for them to exercise faith in him. ("Lectures on Faith," Lecture 2, paragraph 2; Lecture 4, paragraph 11.)

Joseph Fielding Smith quotes his grandfather, Hyrum Smith, as having said: "I would not serve a God that had not all wisdom and all power." Then Joseph Fielding Smith continues, "Do we believe that God has all 'wisdom'? If so, in that, he is absolute. If there is something he does not know, then he is not absolute in 'wisdom,' and to think such a thing is absurd." (*Doctrines of Salvation, 1:5.*) President Smith indicates possible areas in which God is progressing (glory, honor, etc.), and then concludes, "Do you not see that it is in this manner that our Eternal Father is progressing? Not by seeking knowledge which he does not have, for such a thought cannot be maintained in the light of scripture. It is not through ignorance and learning hidden truth that he progresses, for if there are truths which he does not know, then these things are greater than he, and this cannot be." (*Doctrines of Salvation,* 1:7).

2 NEPHI 9:23-24   *Baptism among the Nephites*

The teachings of Jacob clearly indicate that the early Nephites considered baptism an essential ordinance of the gospel. (2 Nephi 9:23-24.) Nephi also taught the necessity of baptism (2 Nephi 31:5-13), and then, referring to the baptism of the Savior, he counseled his followers to "do the things which I have told you I have seen that your Lord and your Redeemer should do; for, for this cause have they been shown unto me, that ye might know the gate by which ye should enter. For the gate by which ye should enter is repentance and baptism by water" (2 Nephi 31:17).

Concerning baptisms by the early Nephites, Joseph Fielding Smith has written:

The Book of Mormon teaches us that baptism for the remission of sins was a fundamental principle of the gospel among the Nephites from the time of Lehi all through their history. . . .

All through the Book of Mormon there are references to baptism as an ordinance for the remission of sins. What their word for baptism was is not revealed, but in the translation the Prophet Joseph Smith used the familiar expression of our time. (*Answers to Gospel Questions,* 2:66.)

The Lord indicates in the Pearl of Great Price that baptism has been practiced as an ordinance of the gospel since the fall of Adam (Moses 5:58; 6:52), with Adam himself being baptized (Moses 6:64-65). The purpose and necessity of baptism is clearly and beautifully explained by the Lord in this scripture. (Moses 6:52-63.)

The following statement provides additional information on the baptisms performed before the birth of Christ:

In the former ages of the world, before the Saviour came in the flesh, "the saints" were baptized in the name of Jesus Christ to come, because there never was any other name whereby men could be saved; and after he came in the flesh and was crucified, then *the saints* were baptized in the name of Jesus Christ, crucified, risen from the dead and ascended into heaven, that they might be buried in baptism like him, and be raised in glory like him, that as there was but *one* Lord, *one* faith, *one* baptism, and *one* God and father of us all, even so there was but *one* door to the mansions of bliss. Amen. (*Times and Seasons,* 3:905.)

2 NEPHI 9:41   *The "keeper of the gate"*

The inspired prophet Jacob maintains that the "keeper of the gate" of heaven is "the Holy One of Israel; and he employeth no servant there." (2 Nephi 9:41.) The "Holy One of Israel" is Jesus Christ; thus the tradition in Christianity that Peter is the keeper of the gate of heaven is apparently false and without scriptural foundation.

2 NEPHI 9:53   *The "covenants of the Lord"*

A covenant is sometimes defined as "a solemn contract between two parties who agree to bind themselves to certain requirements"; thus a covenant is sort of a two-way promise. The "covenants of the Lord" refer to certain conditions or requirements that the Lord has set down; if the person keeps these requirements, certain blessings must follow, but if he does not meet the specified conditions, the Lord is no longer bound by the covenant. The Lord has described his role in the covenant as follows: "I, the Lord, am bound when ye do what I say; but when ye do not what I say, ye have no promise." (D&C 82:10.)

2 NEPHI 10:3   *The crucifixion of Jesus Christ*

In order for Jesus Christ fully to atone or pay for the transgression of Adam, it was evidently necessary for his life to be taken so that the demands of justice could be fully met. Thus it was necessary for him to live upon the earth at a time when the people would be wicked enough to take his life. Jacob mentions it was necessary that the Savior come "among those who are the more wicked part of the world" as "there is none other nation on earth that would crucify their God." (2 Nephi 10:3.)

2 NEPHI 11:2-3   *Witnesses of the Redeemer*

God has said through his prophets, "In the mouth of two or three witnesses shall every word be established." (2 Corinthians 13:1.) Nephi was apparently aware of this system of witnesses when he introduced three great pre-Christian witnesses of the coming of Jesus Christ: Isaiah, Nephi himself, and Nephi's brother Jacob. Nephi then continues: "Wherefore, by the words of three, God hath said, I will establish my word." (2 Nephi 11:3.)

2 NEPHI chapters 12-24   *The so-called "Isaiah problem"*
of the Book of Mormon

The early prophets of the Book of Mormon frequently quoted from the writings of Isaiah that appeared on the brass plates of Laban. (1 Nephi 5:11-13; 19:21-23.) Of the 433 verses of Isaiah quoted in the Book of Mormon, 199 verses are word-for-word the same as the corresponding verses in the King James Version of the Old Testament. The so-called Isaiah problem is this: How do Latter-day Saints account for this striking similarity in nearly half of the verses and the differences in the remainder of the verses?

In order to attempt an explanation of this problem, a person should consider the following points. Joseph Smith did not explain in great detail the process used in translating the Book of Mormon; he merely stated, "through the medium of the Urim and Thummim I translated the record by the gift and power of God." (*Millennial Star,* 18:118.) However, it is quite evident that the process of translation was not automatic; Joseph Smith not only had to exercise faith in the translation procedure, but he also had to put forth mental and spiritual effort. Oliver Cowdery's unsuccessful attempt to translate indicates clearly that the translation of the Book of Mormon was more than a mechanical process. (See D&C 8:1-3, 10-11; 9:7-9.)

Also, translation is frequently concerned with general ideas rather than specific words; even the best translators do not translate the same material from one language into another word-for-word the same. There appears to be only one answer to explain the word-for-word similarities between the verses of Isaiah in the Bible and the same verses in the Book of Mormon. When Joseph Smith translated the Isaiah references from the small plates of Nephi, he evidently opened his King James Version of the Bible and compared the impression he had received in translating with the words of the King James scholars. If his translation was essentially the same as that of the King James Version, he apparently quoted the verse from the Bible; then his scribe, Oliver Cowdery, copied it down. However, if Joseph Smith's translation did not agree precisely with that of the King James scholars, he would dictate his own translation to the scribe. This procedure in translation would account for both

142   the 234 verses of Isaiah that were changed or modified by the Prophet Joseph and the 199 verses that were translated word-for-word the same. Although some critics might question this procedure of translation, scholars today frequently use this same procedure in translating the biblical manuscripts among the Dead Sea Scrolls.

2 NEPHI 15:26-29 *Possible interpretation of Isaiah 5:26-29*

In Isaiah 2:2 (also 2 Nephi 12:2) the prophet Isaiah indicates that he is going to talk about those things which are to "come to pass in the last days." The material Isaiah gives us in Isaiah 5 (2 Nephi 15) evidently pertains to this same time period; thus the events enumerated here are to take place primarily in the dispensation of the fulness of times. Concerning the possible fulfillment of this prophecy by Isaiah, Elder LeGrand Richards has written:

In fixing the time of the great gathering, Isaiah seemed to indicate that it would take place in the day of the railroad train and the airplane:

"And he will lift up an ensign to the nations from far, and will hiss unto them from the end of the earth: and, behold, *they shall come with speed swiftly:*

"None shall be weary nor stumble among them; none shall slumber nor sleep; neither shall the girdle of their loins be loosed, nor the latchet of their shoes be broken:

"Whose arrows are sharp, and all their bows bent, their horses' hoofs shall be counted like flint, and their wheels like a whirlwind:

"Their roaring shall be like a lion, they shall roar like young lions: yea, they shall roar, and lay hold of the prey, and shall carry it away safe, and none shall deliver it." (Isaiah 5:26-29.)

Since there were neither trains nor airplanes in that day, Isaiah could hardly have mentioned them by name. However, he seems to have described them in unmistakable words. How better could "their horses' hoofs be counted like flint, and their wheels like a whirlwind" than in the modern train? How better could "their roaring . . . be like a lion" than in the roar of the airplane? Trains and airplanes do not stop for night. Therefore, was not Isaiah justified in saying: "none shall slumber nor sleep; neither shall the girdle of their loins be loosed, nor the latchet of their shoes be broken"? With this manner of transportation the Lord can really "hiss unto them from the end of the earth," that "they shall come with speed swiftly." Indicating that Isaiah must have foreseen the airplane, he stated: "Who are these that fly as a cloud, and as the doves to their

windows?" (Isaiah 60:8) (*Israel! Do You Know?* [Deseret Book Co.,
1954], p. 182.)

2 NEPHI 16:9-11 *Help in understanding Isaiah 6*

The prophet Isaiah was quoted extensively not only by the Book of Mormon prophets but also by the writers of the New Testament and by the Savior himself. In fact, in our present New Testament the Savior quoted Isaiah more than all the other Old Testament prophets combined. Concerning the essential idea expressed in Isaiah 6:9-11 (and also in 2 Nephi 16:9-11), the Savior said the following concerning the people of his day:

Therefore speak I to them in parables: because they seeing see not; and hearing they hear not, neither do they understand.

And in them is fulfilled the prophecy of Esaias, which saith, By hearing ye shall hear, and shall not understand; and seeing ye shall see, and shall not perceive:

For this people's heart is waxed gross, and their ears are dull of hearing, and their eyes they have closed; lest at any time they should see with their eyes, and hear with their ears, and should understand with their heart, and should be converted, and I should heal them. (Matthew 13:13-15.)

Also, the author of Acts quotes Paul as having said the following concerning Isaiah's words:

Well spake the Holy Ghost by Esaias the prophet unto our fathers, Saying, Go unto this people, and say, Hearing ye shall hear, and shall not understand; and seeing ye shall see, and not perceive:

For the heart of this people is waxed gross, and their ears are dull of hearing, and their eyes have they closed; lest they should see with their eyes, and hear with their ears, and understand with their heart, and should be converted, and I should heal them. (Acts 28:25-27.)

2 NEPHI 21 *The importance of Isaiah chapter 11*

The eleventh chapter of Isaiah (which is quoted in 2 Nephi 21) is evidently one of the most important chapters in all scripture. Not only does Jacob quote it here from the brass plates of Laban, but on September 21, 1823, the resurrected angel Moroni quoted this chapter to Joseph Smith and said it was about to be fulfilled. Also, a section of the Doctrine and Covenants (section 113) is devoted primarily to an explanation of this chapter.

2 NEPHI 21:1-10   *The meanings of some of the terms*
used by Isaiah

The following questions and answers that relate to Isaiah
11:1-10 (and thus to 2 Nephi 21:1-10) are included in section
113 of the Doctrine and Covenants:

Who is the Stem of Jesse spoken of in the 1st, 2nd, 3rd, 4th and
5th verses of the 11th chapter of Isaiah?

Verily thus saith the Lord: It is Christ.

What is the rod spoken of in the first verse of the 11th chapter
of Isaiah, that should come of the Stem of Jesse?

Behold, thus saith the Lord: It is a servant in the hands of
Christ, who is partly a descendant of Jesse as well as of Ephraim, or
of the house of Joseph, on whom there is laid much power.

What is the root of Jesse spoken of in the 10th verse of the 11th
chapter?

Behold, thus saith the Lord, it is a descendant of Jesse, as well
as of Joseph, unto whom rightly belongs the priesthood, and the
keys of the kingdom, for an ensign, and for the gathering of my
people in the last days.

2 NEPHI 21:10-12   *A "second" gathering of Israel*

A careful reading of these verses would seem to indicate
they pertain to a time in the distant future from the days of
Isaiah when the remnants of Israel are to be gathered
together again. Concerning a possible intrepretation of these
verses, Elder LeGrand Richards has written:

From this scripture we learn that the events described were to
be in the future: "The Lord shall set his hand again the second time
to recover the remnant of his people." There could not be a
"second time" unless there had been a first. The first time was when
the Lord led Israel out of Egyptian bondage and captivity. When
did the Lord set his hand the "second time" to recover the remnant
of his people? This we will now consider. From the above scripture
we learn that three important events were to transpire: (1) He shall
set up an ensign for the nations; (2) he shall assemble the outcasts
of Israel; (3) he shall gather together the dispersed of Judah from
the four corners of the earth.

It is clear there are to be two gathering places—one for Israel
and one for Judah. . . .

When speaking of Israel, most people have the Jews in mind;
and when referring to the gathering of Israel, they have in mind the
return of the Jews to the land of Jerusalem. It should be remembered that the Jews, the descendants of Judah, represent but
one of the twelve branches, or tribes, of the house of Israel—the

family of Jacob.   145

The twelve tribes of Israel were divided under two great heads—Judah, comprising the smaller group, and Israel, the larger group. (*A Marvelous Work and a Wonder,* 1976 ed., revised and enlarged, pp. 202-3.)

2 NEPHI 24:8   *Meaning of the word "feller" in Isaiah*

The word *feller* as it is used in Isaiah 14:8 (and in 2 Nephi 24:8) refers to a person who fells or cuts down trees. Thus, literally, a feller is "one who fells" or "one who cuts off."

2 NEPHI 24:12-13   *Who is Lucifer?*

The term *Lucifer* is apparently the title or name of the personage in the pre-earthly existence who is now referred to as Satan or the devil. The fact that Isaiah refers to Lucifer and his role in the pre-earthly existence would seem to indicate that the Old Testament prophets were acquainted with the doctrine of a pre-earthly existence. It may be that Isaiah and others of the ancient prophets had access to the writings of Moses that are not in our present Old Testament but which were revealed anew to the Prophet Joseph Smith in December 1830. These writings of Moses include the following statement concerning Lucifer and his role in the pre-earthly councils:

Wherefore, because that Satan rebelled against me, and sought to destroy the agency of man, which I, the Lord God, had given him, and also, that I should give unto him mine own power; by the power of mine Only Begotten, I caused that he should be cast down;

And he became Satan, yea, even the devil, the father of all lies, to deceive and to blind men, and to lead them captive at his will, even as many as would not hearken unto my voice. (Moses 4:3-4.)

2 NEPHI 25:20-30   *The relationship between the law of Moses and the atonement of Jesus Christ*

The Book of Mormon prophets clearly understood that the law of Moses did not contain the fulness of the saving principles of the gospel of Jesus Christ. They realized the law of Moses was given to prepare the people for the greater truths which were to be revealed. In 2 Nephi 25:24, Nephi writes: "And, notwithstanding we believe in Christ, we keep the law of Moses, and look forward with steadfastness unto Christ, until the law shall be fulfilled." Unfortunately, some of the people subsequently misunderstood this prophecy of Nephi and assumed that the law of Moses was fulfilled when the Savior was born upon the earth. However, it was made clear to them that the law of Moses was not to be fulfilled until after the resurrection of the Savior. (See 3 Nephi 1:24-25.)

2 NEPHI 25, 29   *For a discussion of the major points in these chapters, see the material listed after 1 Nephi 19-22.*

2 NEPHI 26:16   *The voice "out of the dust" which "shall be as one that hath a familiar spirit"*

Nephi is evidently quoting from a statement found in Isaiah 29:4 when he refers to a destroyed people whose record shall come "out of the ground, and their speech shall be low out of the dust, and their voice shall be as one that hath a familiar spirit." (2 Nephi 26:16.) Some biblical scholars have maintained that witchcraft is being referred to in that portion of Isaiah 29:4 which says that the voice shall be "as one that hath a familiar spirit." These scholars evidently arrived at this interpretation because of similar wording in other parts of the Bible. For example, in Leviticus we read: "Regard not them that have familiar spirits, neither seek after wizards, to be defiled by them" (Leviticus 19:31), and "A man also or woman that hath a familiar spirit, or that is a wizard, shall surely be put to death" (Leviticus 20:27). (For further biblical references indicating that the term "familiar spirits" might sometimes refer to witches, see 1 Samuel 28:7; 2 Kings 21:6; 1 Chronicles 10:13; Isaiah 8:19 and 19:3.)

However, a careful reading of this scripture, particularly when read together with Nephi's explanation, would indicate that the term it "hath a familiar spirit" means that this record (the Book of Mormon) would speak with a "familiar voice" to those who already have the Bible. In other words, Nephi is evidently saying here that the doctrinal teachings of the Book of Mormon would seem familiar to people who had already read and accepted the Bible.

2 NEPHI 26:29   *Definition of "priestcraft"*

The word *priestcraft* is used in the Book of Mormon to refer to the teachings of those people who would make a craft (or business) out of being a priest (or religious leader) to the people. Nephi indicates one danger of priestcraft is that such professional religious leaders would be more concerned with teaching those things which were popular and acceptable unto the people than they would in preaching the word of God. Thus they seek to "get gain and praise of the world; but they seek not the welfare of Zion." (2 Nephi 26:29.)

Priestcraft should not be confused with priesthood. There is a great deal of difference between the two, as is indicated in the following statement by George Q. Cannon: "There is a difference between priestcraft and Priesthood. Priestcraft builds up itself, it is not authorized of God. Priestcraft oppresses the people; but the Priesthood of God emancipates men and women and makes them free." (*Journal of Discourses,* 13:55.)

In defining priestcraft and explaining why it must eventually be destroyed, Elder Bruce R. McConkie has written:

. . . false priests, professing ministers, those claiming but not possessing priesthood, are engaged, to a greater or lesser degree, in the iniquitous practice of priestcraft. Priesthood and priestcraft are two opposites; one is of God, the other of the devil.

Apostasy is born of priestcrafts (2 Ne. 10:5; 3 Ne. 16:10; D.& C. 33:4), for those who engage in them follow vain things, teach false doctrines, love riches, and aspire to personal honors. (Alma 1:12, 16.) Men are commanded to repent of their priestcrafts (3 Ne. 30:2), and eventually, in the millennial day, these great evils will be done away. (3 Ne. 21:19.) (*Mormon Doctrine* [Bookcraft, 1958], p. 534.)

2 NEPHI 27:9, 15-18   *The words of the book to be taken to one who is learned*

Nephi's prophecy concerning the words of the book which the translator shall "deliver . . . to another, that he may show them unto the learned" (2 Nephi 27:15) apparently refers (1) to Joseph Smith's giving a copy of some of the characters to Martin Harris and (2) to the subsequent visit of Martin Harris with Professor Charles Anthon. Sometime between December 1827 and February 1828, Joseph Smith copied a number of the characters from the plates in his possession and translated some of them by means of the Urim and Thummim. In February 1828, Martin Harris visited the Prophet in Pennsylvania, obtained a transcript of

148 the characters, and took it to Professor Charles Anthon of New York City. For an account of what occurred, we have the following statement made by Martin Harris to Joseph Smith:

I went to the city of New York, and presented the characters which had been translated, with the translation thereof, to Professor Charles Anthon, a gentlemen celebrated for his literary attainments. Professor Anthon stated that the translation was correct, more so than any he had before seen translated from the Egyptian. I then showed him those which were not yet translated, and he said that they were Egyptian, Chaldaic, Assyriac, and Arabic; and he said they were true characters. He gave me a certificate, certifying to the people of Palmyra that they were true characters, and that the translation of such of them as had been translated was also correct. I took the certificate and put it into my pocket, and was just leaving the house, when Mr. Anthon called me back, and asked me how the young man found out that there were gold plates in the place where he found them. I answered that an angel of God had revealed it unto him.

He then said to me, "Let me see that certificate." I accordingly took it out of my pocket and gave it to him, when he took it and tore it to pieces, saying that there was no such thing now as ministering of angels, and that if I would bring the plates to him he would translate them. I informed him that part of the plates were sealed, and that I was forbidden to bring them. He replied, "I cannot read a sealed book." I left him and went to Dr. Mitchell, who sanctioned what Professor Anthon had said respecting both the characters and the translation. (Joseph Smith 2:64-65.)

This experience apparently convinced Martin Harris that Joseph Smith was a prophet and that he had the gold plates. Thus he later served as a scribe for Joseph Smith during the translation of part of the Plates of Mormon, was privileged to be one of the three special witnesses, and was willing to mortgage his farm to raise money for the first edition of the Book of Mormon.

2 NEPHI 27:12-13   *The special witnesses of the Book of Mormon*

The Lord allowed Joseph Smith to have two sets of special witnesses to the Book of Mormon: (1) the three witnesses—Oliver Cowdery, David Whitmer, and Martin Harris, and (2) the eight witnesses—Christian Whitmer, Jacob Whitmer, Peter Whitmer, Jr., John Whitmer, Hiram Page, Joseph Smith, Sen., Hyrum Smith, Samuel H. Smith.

In 2 Nephi 27:12 the three persons who should behold   149
the record "by the power of God" evidently are the three
special witnesses. In their testimony they declared they had
seen an angel, had heard the voice of the Lord, and had been
shown the plates "by the power of God, and not of man."

In 2 Nephi 27:13, the few other witnesses who should
view the record "according to the will of God, to bear testimony of his word unto the children of men" evidently include the eight special witnesses.

(For further information on this topic, see the section on
the witnesses in the first chapter, "The Story of the Coming
Forth of the Book of Mormon.")

2 NEPHI 28:3-4   *Contention among the so-called Christian churches*

Nephi's prophecy concerning the contention that would
exist among Christian churches at the time the Book of
Mormon was to be translated is amply demonstrated by the
words of the Prophet Joseph Smith regarding the situation in
New York when he was approximately fourteen years of age.

Some time in the second year after our removal to Manchester,
there was in the place where we lived an unusual excitement on the
subject of religion. It commenced with the Methodists, but soon became general among all the sects in that region of country. Indeed,
the whole district of country seemed affected by it, and great multitudes united themselves to the different religious parties, which
created no small stir and division amongst the people, some crying,
"Lo, here!" and others, "Lo, there!" Some were contending for the
Methodist faith, some for the Presbyterian, and some for the
Baptist.

For, notwithstanding the great love which the converts to these
different faiths expressed at the time of their conversion, and the
great zeal manifested by the respective clergy, who were active in
getting up and promoting this extraordinary scene of religious feeling, in order to have everybody converted, as they were pleased to
call it, let them join what sect they pleased; yet when the converts
began to file off, some to one party and some to another, it was seen
that the seemingly good feelings of both the priests and the
converts were more pretended than real; for a scene of great confusion and bad feeling ensued—priest contending against priest, and
convert against convert; so that all their good feelings one for
another, if they ever had any, were entirely lost in a strife of words
and a contest about opinions. (Joseph Smith 2:5-6.)

150   2 NEPHI 28:7-8   *The teachings of modern theology concerning sin*

Any person who has carefully studied the teachings of modern theologians recognizes that many of them now teach there is no such thing as "sin against God"; they claim sin is simply doing wrong against oneself. In such a philosophy, the person can rationalize whether or not he is committing sin. Nephi's prophecy concerning the false teachings of the last days seems to be literally fulfilled in this modern theology, which even questions the existence of God and of life after death. The philosophy that "God is dead" comprises a significant part of modern theology. Concerning the inherent weakness of a philosophy of "Eat, drink, and be merry, for tomorrow we die" (2 Nephi 28:7), President John Taylor has written:

> If I am a being that came into the world yesterday, and leaves it again tomorrow, I might as well have one religion as another, or none at all; "let us eat and drink; for to-morrow we die." If I am an eternal being, I want to know something about that eternity with which I am associated. I want to know something about God, the devil, heaven, and hell. If hell is a place of misery, and heaven a place of happiness, I want to know how to escape the one, and obtain the other. If I cannot know something about these things which are to come in the eternal world, I have no religion. . . . If there is a God, I want a religion that supplies some means of certain and tangible communication with Him. If there is a heaven, I want to know what sort of a place it is. If there are angels, I want to know their nature, and their occupation, and of what they are composed. If I am an eternal being, I want to know what I am to do when I get through with time. . . . (*Journal of Discourses*, 1:151.)

2 NEPHI 28:21   *Is everything well in Zion?*

Nephi's warning against teaching that "all is well in Zion" evidently refers to a situation in which people say everything is well when actually it is not. Concerning such a condition, President Wilford Woodruff has warned:

> Can we fold our arms in peace and cry "all is peace in Zion," when, so far as we have the power of the priesthood resting upon us, we can see the condition of the world? Can we imagine that our garments will be clean without lifting our voice before our fellowmen and warning them of the things that are at their doors? No, we cannot. There never was a set of men since God made the world under a stronger responsibility to warn this generation, to lift up our

voices long and loud, day and night so far as we have the opportunity and declare the words of God unto this generation. We are required to do this. This is our calling. It is our duty. It is our business. (*Journal of Discourses*, 21:122.)

2 NEPHI 28:22   *Is there a devil?*

Students of comparative Christianity are well aware that many Christian churches today do not teach the actual existence of a devil. This condition was prophesied by Nephi wherein he stated that in the last days the devil would say to the people, "I am no devil, for there is none." (2 Nephi 28:22.) The Book of Mormon and other latter-day scriptures clearly and definitely teach the existence of the devil as a personage of spirit. Concerning some of these teachings of the Church, James E. Talmage has written:

Now, I know that it is not quite in accord with the advanced thought of the day, according to certain cults, to believe that there is a devil, a personage, a reality. Many who pose as super-thinkers seek to dismiss, with the old ideas, the old stories, fables they call them, that form the bulk of the very word of God recorded as sacred writ, the fact of Satan's existence.

But there is a personage known as Satan. Before he was cast out from heaven he was called Lucifer. He is just as truly a personage as are you or am I, though he is not embodied. He is in that unembodied state in which we existed prior to our birth into the flesh. And we read, as the Revelator tells us [Rev. 12:7-9], as Jude attests [Jude 6], that he was cast out from heaven because of his rebellion and all his angels or followers were cast out with him; numbering a third of the spirit-hosts of that particular class in heaven. [Rev. 12:4; D&C 29:36.] So they were many, and they are many . . .

Satan foresaw what would come to pass, and the prophet Nephi realized fully the claims that would be set up in the last days, these days. Read what goes before that which I shall read to you, and you will see that the prophet is referring to the time in which we live. He tells us that it will be necessary in this day that the kingdom of the devil shall shake, and he foretells that the devil will "rage in the hearts of the children of men, and stir them up to anger against that which is good."

"And others will he pacify, and lull them away into carnal security, that they will say: All is well in Zion; yea, Zion prospereth, all is well—and thus the devil cheateth their souls, and leadeth them away carefully down to hell.

"And behold, others he flattereth away, and telleth them there

152   is no hell; and he saith unto them: I am no devil, for there is none—and thus he whispereth in their ears, until he grasps them with his awful chains, from whence there is no deliverance." (2 Nephi 28:21-22.) (*Vitality of Mormonism* [Boston: Richard G. Badger, 1919], pp. 123-24.)

2 NEPHI 28:30   *Those who reject the additional word of God will have taken away even that which they have*

One of the principles upon which God operates is to give his children only as much of the law as they are able to live. Otherwise, if he gives laws to his children that they are not able to keep, then they would come under condemnation. God has said, "I will give unto the children of men line upon line, precept upon precept, here a little and there a little; and blessed are those who hearken unto my precepts, and lend an ear unto my counsel, for they shall learn wisdom; for unto him that receiveth I will give more; *and from them that shall say, We have enough, from them shall be taken away even that which they have.*" (2 Nephi 28:30. Italics added.)

In relationship to the coming forth of the Book of Mormon, this principle of the Lord works somewhat as follows:

1. "For unto him that receiveth, I will give more"—in other words, unto those who accept the Book of Mormon will be given additional scriptures (such as the Doctrine and Covenants and the Pearl of Great Price).

2. "And from them that shall say, We have enough, from them shall be taken away even that which they have"— those who believe the Bible is enough and who say they do not need the Book of Mormon, from them shall be taken away "even that which they have" (the Bible). Thus, readers of this prophecy should not be surprised to note that since 1830 the Bible has largely been "taken away" from the Christian world. When the Book of Mormon was published, most Christians and nearly all Christian ministers believed the Bible to be the true word of God. However, after these same people rejected the Book of Mormon, they largely lost their testimonies of the Bible until now only a comparatively few Christians (and very few Christian ministers) actually believe the Bible is the true word of God.

2 NEPHI 29:11-14   *The three scriptural witnesses*

"In the mouth of two or three witnesses shall every word be established." (2 Corinthians 13:1.) The Bible, which contains the preceding statement, is one of the scriptural witnesses in which the word of God is established. But where are the second or the third witnesses? Latter-day Saints believe that the Book of Mormon is a second witness for the gospel of Jesus Christ; and in 2 Nephi 29:11-14 the Lord mentions a third scriptural witness that is yet to come forth: the record of the lost tribes of Israel. Thus the great "triple combination" of the last days will evidently consist of three great scriptural witnesses that testify of each other and will also witness of the divinity of Jesus Christ and his gospel.

2 NEPHI 30:4-7   *The blessings of the Lamanites*

When read in context, these verses concerning the eventual blessings of the Lamanites quite clearly refer to the last days. Concerning the future destiny of the Lamanites as they come into the Church, President Spencer W. Kimball has written:

The Lamanites must rise in majesty and power. We must look forward to the day when they will be "white and delightsome," [2 Nephi 30:6], sharing the freedoms and blessings which we enjoy; when they shall have economic security, culture, refinement, and education; when they shall be operating farms and businesses and industries and shall be occupied in the professions and in teaching; when they shall be organized into wards and stakes of Zion, furnishing much of their own leadership; when they shall build and occupy and fill the temples, and serve in them as the natives are now serving in the Hawaiian Temple where I found last year the entire service conducted by them and done perfectly. And in the day when their prophet shall come, one shall rise . . . mighty among them . . . being an instrument in the hands of God, with exceeding faith, to work mighty wonders. . . . (2 Nephi 3:24.)

Brothers and sisters, the fluorescence of the Lamanites is in our hands. (*Conference Report,* October 1947, p. 22.)

2 NEPHI 31:5-21   *The baptism of Jesus Christ*

The New Testament mentions the baptism of Jesus Christ, but the exact reasons why the Savior submitted to baptism are not made clear in the Bible except in his statement that he was being baptized in order "to fulfil all righteousness." (Matthew 3:15.)

154   The Book of Mormon lists several reasons for the baptism of the Christ, including the one given by the Savior himself on the eastern continent: (1) "to fulfil all righteousness" (2 Nephi 31:5); in other words, the Savior was baptized in order to keep the commandments of the Lord. (2) "He humbleth himself before the Father." (2 Nephi 31:7.) (3) He "witnesseth unto the Father that he would be obedient unto him in keeping his commandments." (2 Nephi 31:7.) (4) "It showeth unto the children of men the straightness of the path, and the narrowness of the gate, by which they should enter, he having set the example before them." (2 Nephi 31:9.)

When we partake of the sacrament we renew the covenants we made at the time of baptism. In this regard, it is interesting to compare the major promises enumerated in the sacramental prayers with the reasons listed above as to why the Savior was baptized. The wording of the sacramental prayers also indicates that we should humble ourselves and witness unto the Father that we are willing to take upon us the name of his Son, and always remember him and keep his commandments. (Moroni 4 and 5.)

Although Nephi lived over five hundred years before the birth of the Savior, he knew by the power of revelation that the Savior was going to be baptized. Furthermore, he counseled his people to "do the things which I have told you I have seen that your Lord and your Redeemer should do; for, for this cause have they been shown unto me, that ye might know the gate by which ye should enter." (2 Nephi 31:17.) This scripture indicates clearly that baptism was practiced, at least among the Nephites, hundreds of years before the Savior was born.

Other evidence exists, in the scriptures and elsewhere, that baptism was also performed by other groups before the birth of Christ. The *Jewish Encyclopedia* indicates that baptism was a common practice in ancient Israel: "Baptism was practiced in ancient Judaism (Hasidic or Essene), first as a means of penitence . . . to receive the spirit of God, or to be permitted to stand in the presence of God, man must undergo baptism." (Vol. 2, p. 499.) Concerning the mode of baptism, the *Encyclopedia* says ". . . this [baptism] is only valid when performed by immersion in a natural fountain or stream or in a properly constructed [vessel]. This rule was, of 155 course, also preserved in the temple at Jerusalem." (Vol. 1, pp. 68-69.)

The fact that baptism was practiced in ancient Israel might help explain why the Savior was not criticized by the orthodox Jewish people when he was baptized. The Pharisees were quick to criticize the Savior whenever he did anything contrary to their law. However, not a single word of criticism concerning the baptism of Jesus Christ is found in the entire New Testament!

(If you desire additional information on the topic of baptism among the Nephites, see the discussion following 2 Nephi 9:23-24.)

2 NEPHI 33:10-11 *If you believe in the words of Christ, you will believe in the Book of Mormon*

In his farewell address, Nephi warns us as future readers of his record that we have the responsibility to decide whether or not we believe the things he has written. He also informs us that if we truly believe in Christ we will believe in his words, "for they are the words of Christ." (2 Nephi 33:10.) In conclusion, he warns: "And if they are not the words of Christ, judge ye—for Christ will show unto you, with power and great glory, that they are his words, at the last day." (2 Nephi 33:11.)

JACOB 1:11   *The new king called "Second Nephi"*

It is not clear who succeeded Nephi as king over the Nephites. Some Book of Mormon scholars have surmised that Nephi's successor was probably Jacob; they say Jacob failed to mention this here because of his modesty. However, other scholars feel that Nephi was probably succeeded as king by one of his sons.

JACOB 1:14   *Meaning of the terms "Nephites" and "Lamanites"*

In general, the terms "Nephites" and "Lamanites" are used with the same meaning for the first 500 years of Nephite history. The term *Nephites* refers to all those who followed after Nephi and to their descendants. The term *Lamanites* refers to those who followed after Laman and to their descendants. However, it is mentioned later in the Book of Mormon that there were no "ites" of any kind during the 200-year Golden Age immediately after the appearance of the resurrected Jesus Christ. (See 4 Nephi 17.)

After this 200-year period of righteousness, the terms "Lamanites" and "Nephites" are used again, but with somewhat different meanings than those used earlier in the Book of Mormon.

(For further information on the later use of these terms, see the material listed after 4 Nephi 20, 36-39.)

JACOB 1:19   *The responsibility of leadership*

The righteous leaders of the Nephites on the American continent apparently had the same keen sense of responsibility as was held by the righteous Hebrew leaders on the eastern continent. Jacob mentions that he and his brother Joseph, in becoming the religious leaders of the people, had taken upon themselves "the responsibility, answering the sins of the people upon our own heads if we did not teach them the word of God with all diligence." (Jacob 1:19.)

Ezekiel was one of the leaders of Israel on the eastern continent at about this same period. Concerning the responsibility of the leader to the people, Ezekiel recorded the following instructions from the Lord:

Again the word of the Lord came unto me, saying,

Son of man, speak to the children of thy people, and say unto them, When I bring the sword upon a land, if the people of the land take a man of their coasts, and set him for their watchman:

If when he seeth the sword come upon the land, he blow the trumpet, and warn the people;

Then whosoever heareth the sound of the trumpet, and taketh not warning; if the sword come, and take him away, his blood shall be upon his own head.

He heard the sound of the trumpet, and took not warning; his blood shall be upon him. But he that taketh warning shall deliver his soul.

But if the watchman see the sword come, and blow not the trumpet, and the people be not warned; if the sword come, and take any person from among them, he is taken away in his iniquity; but his blood will I require at the watchman's hand.

So thou, O son of man, I have set thee a watchman unto the house of Israel; therefore thou shalt hear the word at my mouth, and warn them from me. (Ezekiel 33:1-7.)

JACOB 2:18-19   *Legitimate use of riches*

The Book of Mormon does not teach that riches *per se* are evil. It does, however, indicate that the love of riches is evil, because then the craving for wealth is motivated by the wrong reasons.

However, Jacob promises here that if a person truly seeks the kingdom of God first and then desires riches, he will seek wealth for the right reasons: to clothe the naked, to feed the hungry, etc.

JACOB 2:23   *Jacob's teachings on whoredoms*

Jacob clearly taught that whoredoms are an abomination before the Lord. (Jacob 2:23, 28.) The word *whoredom* as used here by Jacob could refer either to the sin of fornication or to the sin of adultery.

The leaders of the Church in this dispensation have been strong in condemning these types of sins. Following is an official statement published over the signatures of the First Presidency of the Church concerning this matter:

To us of this Church, the Lord has declared that adulterers should not be admitted to membership (D&C 42:76); that adulterers in the Church, if unrepentant, should be cast out (D&C 42:75), but if repentant should be permitted to remain (D&C

42:74, 42:25) and, He said, "By this ye may know if a man repenteth of his sins—behold, he will confess them and forsake them." (D&C 58:43)

In the great revelation on the three heavenly glories, the Lord said, speaking of those who will inherit the lowest of these, or the telestial glory: "These are they who are liars, and sorcerers, and adulterers, and whoremongers, and whosoever loves and makes a lie." (D&C 76:103)

The doctrine of this Church is that sexual sin—the illicit sexual relations of men and women—stands, in its enormity, next to murder.

The Lord has drawn no essential distinctions between fornication, adultery, and harlotry or prostitution. Each has fallen under His solemn and awful condemnation.

You youths of Zion, you cannot associate in non-marital, illicit sex relationships, which is fornication, and escape the punishments and the judgments which the Lord has declared against this sin. The day of reckoning will come just as certainly as night follows day. They who would palliate this crime and say that such indulgence is but a sinless gratification of a normal desire, like appeasing hunger and thirst, speak filthiness with their lips. Their counsel leads to destruction; their wisdom comes from the Father of Lies.

You husbands and wives who have taken on solemn obligations of chastity in the holy temples of the Lord and who violate those sacred vows by illicit sexual relations with others, you not only commit the vile and loathsome sin of adultery, but you break the oath you yourselves made with the Lord Himself before you went to the altar for your sealing. You become subject to the penalties which the Lord has prescribed for those who breach their covenants with Him. . . .

But they who sin may repent, and, they repenting, God will forgive them, for the Lord has said, "Behold, he who has repented of his sins, the same is forgiven, and I, the Lord, remember them no more." (D&C 58:52)

By virtue of the authority in us vested as the First Presidency of the Church, we warn our people who are offending, of the degradation, the wickedness, the punishment that attend upon unchastity; we urge you to remember the blessings which flow from the living of the clean life; we call upon you to keep, day in and day out, the way of strictest chastity, through which only can God's choice gifts come to you and His Spirit abide with you.

How glorious is he who lives the chaste life. He walks unfearful in the full glare of the noon-day sun, for he is without moral infirmity. He can be reached by no shafts of base calumny, for his armor is without flaw. His virtue cannot be challenged by any just accuser, for he lives above reproach. His cheek is never blotched with shame, for he is without hidden sin. He is honored and respected by all mankind, for he is beyond their censure. He is loved by the Lord, for he stands without blemish. The exaltations of eternities await his coming. (Heber J. Grant, J. Reuben Clark, Jr., David O. McKay, *Conference Report,* October 1942, pp. 11-12.)

Also, Hyrum M. Smith reminds us that the law against adultery was one of the Ten Commandments and it is still binding upon the world:

"Thou shalt not commit adultery." Another soul destroying crime which is very rare among the Latter-day Saints. There is no other sin, save murder only, that will so soon destroy the spiritual and moral life of men—why, it is spiritual suicide to participate in any such deadly crime. We do not sustain it; we do not suffer it; we do not tolerate it; and we do not commit it, as a people. (Hyrum M. Smith, *Conference Report,* October 1906, pp. 44-45.)

JACOB 2:24-30   *Jacob's teachings on polygamy*

Jacob indicates that if the Lord commands people to practice polygamy in order to "raise up seed" unto himself, then the people should practice polygamy. (Jacob 2:30.) However, if the Lord does not command the people to practice polygamy, then a man should not have more than one wife. (Verse 27.) Jacob makes it clear that the Nephites were not to practice polygamy. (Jacob 2:25-27.)

JACOB 3:10   *The responsibility of parents*

The doctrine that parents are at least partially responsible for the acts of their children is clearly taught in latter-day scriptures. In fact, as is indicated in the following scripture, parents are responsible for the sins of their children if the parents do not teach them the gospel:

And again, inasmuch as parents have children in Zion, or in any of her stakes which are organized, that teach them not to understand the doctrine of repentance, faith in Christ the Son of the living God, and of baptism and the gift of the Holy Ghost by the laying on of the hands, when eight years old, the sin be upon the heads of the parents. . . .

And they shall also teach their children to pray, and to walk uprightly before the Lord. (D&C 68:25, 28.)

JACOB 3:14   *The "plates of Jacob"*

Apparently the "plates of Jacob" referred to here are the same set of plates referred to elsewhere as the small plates of

160   Nephi. Jacob admits these plates were "made by the hand of Nephi." (Jacob 3:14.) Evidently they are now called the plates of Jacob because the historian who is writing on the plates is now Jacob.

JACOB 4:14-17   *The blindness of the Jews*

In trying to explain why the Jewish people did not accept the Savior when he came, Jacob said it was because of the blindness of the Jews "which blindness came by looking beyond the mark." (Jacob 4:14.) Although the meaning of this idiomatic expression is not absolutely clear, some Book of Mormon scholars have suggested that the Jewish people were "looking beyond the mark" insofar as they expected the Savior to do at his first coming those things which it was prophesied he should do at his second coming. Thus, when the Savior did not lead the Jewish people to victory over their enemies during his earthly existence, he was largely rejected by the Jews. Jacob, however, prophesies that in the last days the Jews will once again build upon the sure foundation of Jesus Christ.

JACOB Chapter 5   *The allegory of Zenos concerning the tame and wild olive tree*

The remarkable allegory or parable of Zenos contained in the fifth chapter of Jacob makes up the longest single chapter in the Book of Mormon. One of the difficulties of the allegory—and of all allegories—is to know how literally it should be interpreted. The dictionary defines an allegory as "the veiled presentation, in a figurative story, of a meaning metaphorically implied but not expressly stated." In other words, an allegory is the description of one thing under the image of another. The images (or symbols) used by Zenos in his allegory together with their possible meanings are as follows:

1. A tame olive tree: this represents the house of Israel.

2. A wild olive tree: this refers to the gentiles—those who are not of the house of Israel by birth.

3. Natural branches of the tame olive tree that are grafted (planted) in the vineyard: these refer to various scatterings of portions of the house of Israel throughout the world.

4. The vineyard: this represents the world.

5. The grafting in of the branches of the wild olive tree into the tame olive tree: this refers to the conversion of the gentiles or the adoption by the gentiles of the covenants of the house of Israel.

6. The master or Lord of the vineyard: this evidently refers to the Lord of the earth—Jesus Christ.

7. The servant: this apparently refers to the prophet of the Lord; perhaps there was a different servant during each of these scatterings and gatherings.

These identical symbols were used by Paul in his letter to the Romans (see Romans 11:17-24), which might indicate Paul was acquainted with the allegory by Zenos. The ten "lost" tribes of Israel and the Lehite and Mulekite colonies could all be included among the various graftings (plantings) of the natural branches of the tame olive tree into the "nethermost part" of the vineyard. The last planting referred to (in Jacob 5:25, 40, 43-44) evidently refers to the Nephite-Lamanite groups that descended from the Lehite colony.

Concerning the importance of this parable by Zenos, Joseph Fielding Smith has written:

The parable of Zenos, recorded by Jacob in chapter five of his book, is one of the greatest parables ever recorded. This parable in and of itself stamps the Book of Mormon with convincing truth. No mortal man, without the inspiration of the Lord, could have written such a parable. . . . It is simple and very clear to the minds of those who earnestly seek to know the truth. . . .

In brief, it records the history of Israel down through the ages, the scattering of the tribes to all parts of the earth; their mingling with, or being grafted in, the wild olive trees, or in other words the mixing of the blood of Israel among the Gentiles. . . .

This remarkable parable portrays how, . . . branches of the olive tree (Israelites) were carried to all parts of the earth (the Lord's vineyard) and grafted into the wild olive trees (the Gentile nations). . . .

Today Latter-day Saints are going to all parts of the world as servants in the vineyard to gather this fruit and lay it in store for the time of the coming of the Master. This parable is one of the most enlightening and interesting in the Book of Mormon. How can any person read it without feeling the inspiration of this ancient prophet? (*Answers to Gospel Questions,* 4:141-42.)

JACOB 7:1-20 *The teachings of Sherem, the anti-Christ*

Sherem is one of the first avowed anti-Christs in the

162   Book of Mormon. It might be profitable, therefore, to review his teachings, because later anti-Christs (Nehor, Korihor, etc.) teach essentially these same things. Sherem (1) preached those things which were flattering unto the people (Jacob 7:2); (2) claimed that no man can tell of things to come (Jacob 7:7); (3) claimed to believe in the scriptures, but clearly did not understand them (Jacob 7:10-11); (4) denied the existence of Christ (Jacob 7:9); (5) would not accept evidence unless it could be perceived through the physical senses, and thus asked for a sign he could feel (Jacob 7:13).

JACOB 7:19   *The unpardonable sin*

When Sherem admitted he had been deceived by the devil, he feared lest he had committed "the unpardonable sin," for he had lied unto God and had denied the Christ. Although it is not clear in the Book of Mormon whether or not Sherem was guilty of committing the unpardonable sin, the Lord has explained in other scriptures the characteristics of those who do commit this sin. In the Doctrine and Covenants, the Lord has said:

Thus saith the Lord concerning all those who know my power, and have been made partakers thereof, and suffered themselves through the power of the devil to be overcome, and to deny the truth and defy my power—

They are they who are the sons of perdition, of whom I say that it had been better for them never to have been born;

For they are vessels of wrath, doomed to suffer the wrath of God, with the devil and his angels in eternity;

Concerning whom I have said there is no forgiveness in this world nor in the world to come—

Having denied the Holy Spirit after having received it, and having denied the Only Begotten Son of the Father, having crucified him unto themselves and put him to an open shame.

These are they who shall go away into the lake of fire and brimstone, with the devil and his angels—

And the only ones on whom the second death shall have any power. (D&C 76:31-37.)

Orson Pratt has explained the meaning of the term "second death," which is used in this scripture and which comes upon the sons of perdition:

Second death, What is that? After you have been redeemed from the grave, and come into the presence of God, you will have to

stand there to be judged; and if you have done evil, you will be   163
banished everlastingly from His presence—body and spirit united
together; this is what is called the second death. Why is it called the
second death? Because the first is the dissolution of body and spirit,
and the second is . . . a banishment—a becoming dead to the things
of righteousness. . . . (*Journal of Discourses*, 1:288.)

JACOB 7:27   *The use of the word "adieu"*

Some anti-LDS critics of the Book of Mormon have
raised the question as to how Jacob could possibly have used
such a word as *adieu* when this word clearly comes from the
French language, which was not developed until hundreds of
years after the time of Jacob. Such critics evidently overlook
the fact that the Book of Mormon is translation literature,
and Joseph Smith felt free in his translation to use any words
familiar to himself and his readers that would best convey
the meaning of the original author. It is interesting to note
that there is a Hebrew word *Lehitra 'ot,* which has essentially
the same meaning in Hebrew as the word *adieu* has in
French. Both of these words are much more than a simple
farewell; they include the idea of a blessing. Would it be un-
reasonable to remind these critics that *none of the words*
contained in the English translation of the book of Jacob
were used by Jacob himself? These words all come from the
English language, which did not come into existence until
long after Jacob's time!

ENOS

ENOS 1-10 *One means of receiving revelation*

Although small in number of verses, the book of Enos teaches some important concepts. For example, Enos tells us something concerning one way in which revelation can be received when he says "there came a voice unto me, saying" (verse 5) and "the voice of the Lord came into my mind again, saying" (verse 10). Concerning this type of revelation, President Harold B. Lee said:

Another way by which we receive revelation is the way that the Prophet Enos spoke of. After he'd gone up and received the great commission to carry on the work and to write the record, he pens this very significant statement in his record in the Book of Mormon. "And while I was thus struggling in the spirit, the voice of the Lord came into my mind saying—." In other words, sometimes we hear the voice of the Lord coming into our minds and when it comes the impressions are just as strong as though he were talking as with a trumpet into our ear. Jeremiah says something like that in the first chapter of the Book of Jeremiah: "Then the words of the Lord came unto me saying—." He was having the voice of the Lord into his mind, as Enos said. In the story of the Book of Mormon we have Nephi upbraiding his brothers, calling them to repentance and in his statement to them he gives voice to the same thought when he says, "And he hath spoken unto you in a still, small voice, but ye were past feeling, so that ye could not feel his words." Thus the Lord, by revelation, brings into our mind as though a voice were speaking. May I bear humble testimony, if I may be pardoned, to that fact? I was once in a situation where I needed help. The Lord knew I needed help and I was on an important mission. I was awakened in the hours of the morning as though someone had wakened me to straighten me out on something that I had planned to do in a contrary course, and there was clearly mapped out before me as I lay there that morning, just as surely as though someone had sat on the edge of my bed and told me what to do. Yes, the voice of the Lord comes into our minds and we are directed thereby. (*Brigham Young University Speeches of the Year,* October 15, 1952.)

ENOS 11-18 *The eternal nature of a covenant with the Lord*

Another important principle taught in the book of Enos

is that the Lord will keep all the covenants he has made with 165
his people. In verse 16, Enos tells us that the Lord
covenanted with him that the records of the Nephites would
come forth unto the Lamanites in the Lord's own due time.
That this covenant of the Lord was literally fulfilled is made
clear in the Doctrine and Covenants wherein the Lord said
to Joseph Smith:

Nevertheless, my work shall go forth, for inasmuch as the
knowledge of a Savior has come unto the world, through the testimony of the Jews, even so shall the knowledge of a Savior come
unto my people—

And to the Nephites, and the Jacobites, and the Josephites, and
the Zoramites, through the testimony of their fathers—

And this testimony shall come to the knowledge of the
Lamanites, and the Lemuelites, and the Ishmaelites, who dwindled
in unbelief because of the iniquity of their fathers, whom the Lord
has suffered to destroy their brethren the Nephites, because of their
iniquities and their abominations.

And for this very purpose are these plates preserved, which
contain these records—that the promises of the Lord might be
fulfilled, which he made to his people. (D&C 3:16-19.)

Another principle taught in this account is that our
prayers are not necessarily answered immediately. That the
Lord will answer our prayers if we keep our covenants and
are worthy is made clear by George Q. Cannon in the
following statement:

And, if they (the saints) will exercise their faith aright, there is no
good thing, which they can desire, that will be withheld from them.
Because you do not get all your prayers answered and your desires
granted immediately, you must not therefore be disheartened. Remember the instruction upon this point imparted by Jesus through
the parable of the importunate widow, and remember, also, that
though your prayers may not be answered immediately, if they are
offered in the name of Jesus and in faith, nothing being left undone
by you that is required, they will live on the records of heaven and
in the remembrance of the Lord, and yet bear fruit. The ancient
fathers asked for blessings in their prayers, which are even now
being granted—thousands of years after the death of their mortal
bodies. And many centuries ago the servants of the Lord among
the Nephites made known to the Lord the desires of their hearts
respecting their brethren in their prayers, and they yet await their
fulfilment; but they know the promise of the Lord is sure and cannot fail. . . . Though heaven and earth pass away, not one word that

166   the Lord has spoken, not one promise that he has made, can pass away or remain unfulfilled. If they have waited thus patiently for the fulfilment of their prayers, cannot we, if necessary, do so also? (*Millennial Star*, 25:74-75.)

JAROM 2   *The Book of Mormon is for the "benefit of the Lamanites"*

The writers of the Book of Mormon clearly understood that their writings were going to benefit the Lamanites and their descendants more than their own descendants. (Enos 11-17; Jarom 2.) Yet many of the writers continued with their recording efforts even during periods when the Lamanites were their bitter enemies. (Enos 20; Jarom 6-7; Mormon 2:2-3, 17-18.)

JAROM 8   *The high state of civilization among the Nephites*

Jarom's statement that in his days the Nephites had become skilled in "fine workmanship of wood, in buildings, and in machinery, and also in iron and copper, and brass and steel, making all manner of tools of every kind to till the ground, and weapons of war" would seem to indicate a very high state of civilization among these people of the fourth century B.C. Interestingly enough, archaeologists are now uncovering evidence from this time period that tends to verify this high state of civilization. Indeed, some archaeologists have now admitted that these people had some skills that we do not possess today.

OMNI

OMNI 1-3, 4-8, 9, 10-11, 12-30 *Why five writers in the Book of Omni?*

The first five books in our present Book of Mormon (1 Nephi, 2 Nephi, Jacob, Enos, and Jarom) comprise 129 pages, cover a period of approximately 239 years, and are written by four men. The brief book of Omni comprises less than three pages, covers a possible time period of 231 years, and is written by five different writers.

Although some of the five writers in the book of Omni attempt to explain why their writings are not more extensive, perhaps we should examine again the purpose of the small plates of Nephi and then relate this purpose to the reasons given by these men. The small plates of Nephi were to contain the religious history of the Nephite people. Thus the record on these plates primarily consisted of the prophecies and religious teachings of the Nephite leaders. The fact that the writings of five men occupy such a small segment as the book of Omni would indicate this was a period of great apostasy—thus there were no new prophecies or religious teachings to be added to the record.

The first three verses in this book were written by Omni, and he admits he was a wicked man. Verses 4-8 were written by Amaron, who states that the "more wicked part of the Nephites were destroyed" because of the judgments of God; this statement also indicates a period of apostasy and wickedness. The next writer, Chemish, wrote only one verse. Abinadom, the son of Chemish, wrote twice as much as his father—two verses! In these verses Abinadom states that he knows of no revelation nor prophecy except those that were written (verse 11); again this would indicate a period of great apostasy and wickedness. The final 19 verses (verses 12-30) were written by Amaleki, the son of Abinadom. His writings also indicate that he lived in a time of apostasy; in fact, it was during his lifetime that the Lord warned Mosiah to lead a small righteous group of people away from the wicked Nephites.

OMNI 12-19   *The people of Zarahemla*

Most Latter-day Saints refer to the people of Zarahemla as the "Mulekites," although the word *Mulekite* does not appear a single time in the Book of Mormon. The people of Zarahemla were descendants of a colony of people who left Jerusalem about 589 B.C. at the time of the Babylonian captivity. (Omni 15.) Included in this colony was Mulek (the ancestor of Zarahemla and one of the sons of Zedekiah, the king of Judah—Mosiah 25:2 and Helaman 8:21). Inasmuch as only descendants of Judah could serve as the rulers of the kingdom of Judah, Mulek and his descendants were of the tribe of Judah. Of course, representatives of some of the other tribes of Israel might have been included among the people of Zarahemla.

It is interesting to note that although the progenitors of Mosiah's group and of the people of Zarahemla left Jerusalem within about twelve years of each other, and evidently spoke the same language then, yet about four hundred years later their descendants could not even understand each other. The reason for this is that the language of the people of Zarahemla "had become corrupted" because they "had brought no records with them; and they denied the being of their Creator." (Omni 17.) Thus the earlier counsel to Nephi seems to be substantiated that "it is better that one man should perish" in order to obtain records and scriptures than "that a nation should dwindle and perish in unbelief." (1 Nephi 4:13.)

OMNI 13   *The land of Zarahemla is "down" from the land of Nephi*

The concept of going "up" when you go north and of going "down" when you go south is of relatively recent origin, and thus was not used by the Nephites. When the Nephites stated they went from Nephi down to Zarahemla, they were referring to elevation and not to direction. Zarahemla was definitely lower in elevation than Nephi because the river Sidon had its head in the land of Nephi but flowed down through the center of the land of Zarahemla. (Alma 16:6-7; 22:27-29.)

OMNI 20-22   *Coriantumr, the last of the Jaredites*

The Coriantumr who lived with the people of Zarahemla

170   for a short period was the last military leader of the Jaredite nation. (Ether 12:1; 13:20-22.) The Book of Mormon does not specifically state when Coriantumr lived with the people of Zarahemla, but it would have to be sometime after 589 B.C. (when the colony of Mulek first left Jerusalem) and before about 200 B.C. (when Mosiah and his group first came into the land of Zarahemla). The twentieth verse of Omni tells of a large stone that was brought to Mosiah and which contained an account of Coriantumr. However, this does not necessarily indicate that Coriantumr was still alive in the days of Mosiah; his stay of "nine moons" among the people of Zarahemla could have occurred decades or even centuries before the time of Mosiah.

OMNI 25, 30   *The end of the small plates of Nephi*

The first 132 pages in the current edition of the Book of Mormon came from the first-person account of the nine writers on the small plates of Nephi. These writers were Nephi, Jacob, Enos, Jarom, Omni, Amaron, Chemish, Abinadom, and Amaleki. Inasmuch as Amaleki did not have any children to whom he could give the plates, he delivered them to King Benjamin (Omni 25). Thus the same man, King Benjamin, came into control of both the small plates of Nephi and the large plates of Nephi, and apparently he decided to discontinue the small plates. Mormon did not abridge the writings on the small plates of Nephi; in fact, he had virtually nothing to do with these plates except that he put them "with the remainder" of his records. (Words of Mormon 5-6.)

THE WORDS OF MORMON

THE WORDS OF MORMON *The significance of the section entitled "The Words of Mormon"*

The two pages comprising The Words of Mormon are approximately five hundred years out of context. Note that the approximate date of the end of the book of Omni is 130 B.C. whereas the Words of Mormon are dated about 385 A.D. (See 4 Nephi 48 and Mormon 1:2; 6:5 for the major dates in the life of Mormon.) However, the approximate date of the beginning of the book of Mosiah is once again 130 B.C.

The Words of Mormon were apparently written near the end of Mormon's life for the purpose of connecting two major records. It was made known to Mormon "by the workings of the Spirit of the Lord" that the small plates of Nephi (which ended when Benjamin was a relatively young man) might be used to replace his abridgment of the book of Lehi (which ended when Benjamin was an old man about ready to die). So that a gap would not occur in the history of the Nephites, Mormon included the major events of the lifetime of King Benjamin in The Words of Mormon, thus connecting the account on the small plates of Nephi with Mormon's abridgment of the book of Mosiah.

THE WORDS OF MORMON 5-6, 9-18 *Possible interpretations of the Words of Mormon*

In verse 5, Mormon mentions that he is going to finish his record upon "these things" and that he will take the remainder of his record "from the plates of Nephi." Several questions have been raised concerning this brief verse by Mormon: (1) First of all, to what is he referring when he states he is going to finish *his record?* (2) To what plates is he referring when he says he will finish his record upon *these things?* (3) To what section of his writings is he referring when he talks of the *remainder* of his record?

Most Book of Mormon scholars have assumed that when Mormon refers to finishing "his record" he had in mind the rest of his writings in the small section entitled The Words of Mormon. Most scholars also assume that "these things" refer to the small plates of Nephi. If this interpretation is

172   correct, then the section entitled The Words of Mormon was written at the end of the small plates of Nephi. According to these scholars, the fact that Amaleki says the small plates of Nephi are already full (Omni 30) does not necessarily rule out the possibility of adding the brief notes that make up The Words of Mormon.

Mormon's reference to the "remainder" of his record is a little more confusing. Some scholars believe that here Mormon is referring to the rest of his writings in The Words of Mormon, the ideas of which he obtained from the large plates of Nephi. Other scholars, however, believe that Mormon is referring to that portion of his abridgment from the large plates of Nephi which he has not yet written on his plates of Mormon. Unfortunately, the pronoun reference in verse 5 does not make it possible to determine Mormon's meaning exactly.

MOSIAH

MOSIAH 1:1-2 *The beginning of Mormon's abridged record*

Note that the main story in the book of Mosiah is told in the third person rather than in the first person as was the custom in the earlier books of the Book of Mormon. The reason for this is that someone else is now telling the story, and that "someone else" is Mormon. With the beginning of the book of Mosiah we start our study of Mormon's abridgment of various books that had been written on the large plates of Nephi. (3 Nephi 5:8-12.) The book of Mosiah and the five books that follow—Alma, Helaman, 3 Nephi, 4 Nephi, and Mormon—were all abridged or condensed by Mormon from the large plates of Nephi, and these abridged versions were written by Mormon on the plates that bear his name, the plates of Mormon. These are the same plates that were given to Joseph Smith by the angel Moroni on September 22, 1827.

MOSIAH 1:1-5 *Were the brass plates written in Egyptian?*

The statement that "Lehi . . . having been taught in the language of the Egyptians therefore he could read" the engravings on the brass plates of Laban quite clearly indicates these plates were written in the Egyptian language. Thus they were almost certainly not started until after the flood and the tower of Babel, as there was no Egyptian language before those events. The brass plates were probably not started until after the Israelites went down into Egypt in the days of Joseph, although the writers on these plates may have had access to records that had been written earlier.

Two other evidences supporting this thesis are: (1) Laban "was a descendant of Joseph, wherefore he and his fathers had kept the records" (1 Nephi 5:16), and (2) the great prophecies "of Joseph, who was carried into Egypt . . . are written upon the plates of brass" (2 Nephi 4:1-2), as these records contained "the five books of Moses" (1 Nephi 5:11). Other writers continued recording on these plates "even down to the commencement of the reign of Zedekiah, king

174   of Judah" (1 Nephi 5:12)—the very year Lehi left Jerusalem (1 Nephi 1:4).

MOSIAH 1:18   *The temple in the land of Zarahemla*

This is the first reference to a temple in the land of Zarahemla. The building of a temple mentioned earlier in the Book of Mormon (2 Nephi 5:16) refers to the temple in the land of Nephi. Our present Book of Mormon does not provide any additional information concerning when or by whom this temple in Zarahemla was constructed.

MOSIAH 2:17   *Benjamin's statement on service*

One of the most widely quoted scriptures in the entire Book of Mormon is the statement of King Benjamin: "when ye are in the service of your fellow beings ye are only in the service of your God." (Mosiah 2:17.) In this statement Benjamin includes the essence of the two great commandments that were later enunciated by the Savior: (1) that we should love God with all our heart, soul, and mind, and (2) that we should love our neighbors as ourselves. (Matthew 22:37-40.)

If we truly love God and keep his commandments, we will serve our brothers because he has commanded us to love them. Therefore, as King Benjamin indicates, when we are in the service of our fellow beings we are only in the service of our God.

MOSIAH 2:38 and 3:27   *Hell is "like" an unquenchable fire*

The major Christian churches that believe in a place called hell refer to it as a place of endless burnings and punishment. The leaders of these churches evidently get this belief partially from their interpretation of such scriptures as Luke 16:28 (where hell is referred to as a "place of torment") and from Matthew 13:42 (where hell is referred to as a "furnace of fire," where there will be "wailing and gnashing of teeth"). However, the exact wording that hell is a place "where people are continually burning but are never consumed" is not found in the scriptures; largely this concept comes from false interpretations by men. In the Doctrine and Covenants the Lord has explained what is meant by the terms "endless torment" and "eternal damnation":

Nevertheless, it is not written that there shall be no end to this torment, but it is written *endless torment.*

Again, it is written *eternal damnation;* wherefore it is more express than other scriptures, that it might work upon the hearts of the children of men, altogether for my name's glory.

Wherefore, I will explain unto you this mystery, for it is meet unto you to know even as mine apostles.

I speak unto you that are chosen in this thing, even as one, that you may enter into my rest.

For, behold, the mystery of godliness, how great is it! For, behold, I am endless, and the punishment which is given from my hand is endless punishment, for Endless is my name. Wherefore—

Eternal punishment is God's punishment.

Endless punishment is God's punishment. (D&C 19:6-12. Italics added.)

The Book of Mormon indicates that hell as a place is not a place of eternal fire. However, the feeling of guilt, pain, and anguish that the sinner feels is "like an unquenchable fire" (Mosiah 2:38), and his torment is "as a lake of fire and brimstone" (Mosiah 3:27).

MOSIAH 3:11, 16-18   *Jesus Christ atones for the sins of children and those who have died without law*

Most of the so-called Christian churches today teach the doctrine of original sin. Essentially, this doctrine is that all of us are born sinful onto this earth because of the original transgression of Adam and Eve. One church has explained the doctrine of original sin as follows:

On account of their sin Adam and Eve lost sanctifying grace, the right to heaven, and their special gifts; they became subject to death, to suffering, and to a strong inclination to evil. . . .

On account of the sin of Adam, we, his descendants, come into the world deprived of sanctifying grace and inherit his punishment, . . .

This sin in us is called original sin. It is the state in which every descendant of Adam comes into the world, totally deprived of grace, through inheriting the punishment, not of Adam's personal sin, but of his sin as head of the human race. . . .

Because of original sin, heaven was closed to all men until the death of Our Lord Jesus Christ. Our Lord instituted the sacrament of Baptism in order to restore to us the right to heaven that Adam had lost.

. . . only Baptism can remit original sin; no one with any taint can enter heaven. (Louis LaVoire Morrow, *My Catholic Faith* [Kenosha, Wisc.: My Mission House, 1963], pp. 48-49, 269.)

As indicated in the last sentence of the above statement, the many churches that believe in the doctrine of original sin also usually teach that original sin can be removed only through baptism. Such teachings deny the right of unbaptized people, including unbaptized infants, to gain the presence of God (heaven). However, the Book of Mormon prophets clearly and definitely teach that the atonement of Jesus Christ fully atones: (1) for the original transgression of Adam and Eve, (2) for the sins of unbaptized infants who die before they are accountable, and (3) for the sins of all people who die without having an opportunity to receive the "will of God concerning them." In his famous discourse on the atonement, King Benjamin says concerning the Savior: ". . . his blood atoneth for the sins of those who have fallen by the transgression of Adam, who have died not knowing the will of God concerning them, or who have ignorantly sinned." (Mosiah 3:11.)

MOSIAH 3:15-27 *The relationship of the laws of justice and mercy to the atonement of Jesus Christ*

The law of justice works in relationship to the other laws of God in the moral realm. In essence, the law of justice might be explained as follows: (1) every law has both a punishment and a blessing attached to it; (2) whenever the law is transgressed (broken), a punishment (or suffering) must be inflicted; (3) whenever a law is kept (obeyed), a blessing (or reward) must be given.

The law of justice requires that God must be a God of order and that he must be just and impartial. Because of the law of justice, God can make such statements as these: "I, the Lord, am bound when ye do what I say; but when ye do not what I say, ye have no promise" (Doctrine and Covenants 82:10); "There is a law, irrevocably decreed in heaven before the foundations of this world, upon which all blessings are predicated—And when we obtain any blessing from God, it is by obedience to that law upon which it is predicated" (Doctrine and Covenants 130:20-21).

The law of mercy agrees entirely with the law of justice. However, the law of mercy introduces the possibility of vicarious payment of the laws that have been transgressed. In essence, the law of mercy might be paraphrased as follows: Whenever a law is transgressed (or broken), a payment (or suffering or atonement) must be made; however, the person who transgressed the law does not need to make payment *if* he will repent and *if* he can find someone else who is both able and willing to make payment. Note that the law of mercy insists that the demands of the law of justice be met fully. As Alma stated, ". . . justice exerciseth all his demands, and also mercy claimeth all which is her own; and thus, none but the truly penitent are saved. What, do ye suppose that mercy can rob justice? I say unto you, Nay; not one whit. If so, God would cease to be God." (Alma 42:24-25.)

The law of justice made the atonement of Jesus Christ necessary. When Adam fell, he transgressed a law that had physical and spiritual death as its punishment. Thus the law of justice demanded payment (or atonement) for the broken (or transgressed) law.

The law of mercy made the atonement of Jesus Christ possible. In order for Jesus Christ to pay fully for the law Adam had transgressed, it was necessary that the Savior be both able and willing to make atonement. He was willing to make payment because of his great love for mankind, and he was able to make payment because he lived a sinless life and because he was actually, literally, biologically the Son of God in the flesh. Thus he had the power to atone for the spiritual and physical deaths introduced by the fall of Adam and Eve. Because of this atonement (or payment), he is rightfully referred to as the Savior and Redeemer of all mankind.

Every person benefits unconditionally from two major aspects of the atonement: (1) the resurrection, and (2) the full payment for the original transgression of Adam and Eve. However, as Mosiah indicates, there are also some conditional aspects of the atonement, and in order to benefit from these a person must repent of his sins. Otherwise, "mercy . . . could have claim" upon the person "no more forever," for the law of mercy is made active in the life of a person only upon the conditions of repentance. (Mosiah 3:25-27.)

MOSIAH 3:19 and 4:2 *Why is the natural man "an enemy to God"?*

One of the most disputed issues among so-called Christian theologians has been the question of the basic nature of man. Some of these theologians have argued that man is

178   born evil into this world as an infant; thus the only way this evil can be removed is by receiving the sacrament of baptism. Still other theologians have argued that man is born innocent and remains basically good; some of them thus conclude that inasmuch as man is basically good he has no need for a redeemer to atone for his sins.

It should be clear to students of the Book of Mormon that the prophets definitely reject both the doctrine of the natural depravity of man and the doctrine that man is so good by nature he has no need for a redeemer. Benjamin, the prophet and king of the Nephites, said that "an angel from God" taught him that although infants are born in a state of innocence, after they become accountable they can become enemies to God if they do not accept the saving principles and ordinances of the gospel.

In explaining how man can be born innocent but yet can become an enemy to God, David H. Yarn has written:

In a modern revelation the Lord said:

"Every spirit of man was innocent in the beginning; and God having redeemed man from the fall, men became again, in their infant state, innocent before God. And that wicked one cometh and taketh away light and truth, through disobedience, from the children of men, and because of the tradition of their fathers." (Doctrine and Covenants 93:38, 39.)

Thus, from the beginning of man's mortal existence the wicked one, the devil, has engaged in taking away "light and truth." He has done this through men, individually and collectively—individually through disobedience and collectively through the tradition of their fathers.

Fundamentally the revelation teaches us that infants are innocent, but that they are born in a mortal world where men are agents unto themselves; where various factors influence decisions; and where, through the exercise of agency, men individually and in varying degrees have chosen to acknowledge or to deny God, to accept and practice His principles or to reject them. Consequently, although babies are innocent, by the time they reach the age of accountability they have become acquainted, through their own weaknesses and those of others, with a fallen world. Although not comprehending these words, they no doubt quite adequately understand that man has his failings. Perhaps this is in part what King Benjamin had in mind when he said:

"For the natural man is an enemy to God, and has been from the fall of Adam, and will be, forever and ever, unless he yields to the enticings of the Holy Spirit, and putteth off the natural man and becometh a saint through the atonement of Christ the Lord, and becometh as a child, submissive, meek, humble, patient, full of love, willing to submit to all things which the Lord seeth fit to inflict upon him, even as a child doth submit to his father." (Mosiah 3:19.)

Other scriptural passages speak of the natural man as carnal, sensual, and devilish. (See Alma 42:10; Moses 5:13.) These words may seem harsh, but it is probably impossible for us even to guess what the corrupt state of man would be had there not been periodic restorations of the Gospel in man's history and some glimmer of spiritual knowledge trickling down through the centuries.

It is important that the teaching of King Benjamin be distinguished from the apostate doctrine of depravity. Man is not born evil, but innocent. He is innocent until he reaches the age of accountability, but he grows up in a world of sin and as an agent makes choices from among a vast complex of enticements; and when he becomes accountable and refuses to make his will submissive to God by accepting Him and making covenants with Him, he is "carnal, sensual, and devilish."

An explanation of the matter suggests, however, that the words *carnal, sensual,* and *devilish,* must not be limited to their more narrow and specific connotations, but that they are accurately, though more broadly, interpreted by the scriptural phrase "enemy to God." That is to say, not all men who have not made the covenants with the Christ are given to indulging in degrading practices which are appropriately designated carnal, sensual, and devilish in a dictionary sense. Yet all men, regardless of how moral and how pure they may be with reference to such practices, are enemies to God until they yield to the enticings of the Holy Spirit, accept the Atonement of the Lord, and are submissive to His will. A significant point here is that what we conventionally call basic personal and social morality are not enough. In addition to these things one must do other things which are binding upon him by virtue of his covenantal relationship with the Father and the Son. Or, putting it in another way, for one not to be an enemy to God he must endeavor to do all things whatsoever the Lord his God shall command him. (See Abraham 3:25.)

Summarily put, the natural man (he who is carnal, sensual, and devilish, he who is an enemy to God) is the man who has not humbled himself before God and made covenants with God by receiving the revealed ordinances at the hands of God's authorized servants; or the man who, having done these things, has failed to live according to the covenants made in baptism and to the injunction given when he was confirmed a member of the Church—"Re-

180   ceive the Holy Ghost." (*Gospel Living in the Home* [Deseret Sunday School Union], pp. 50-51.)

MOSIAH 4:6-11   *The teachings of Benjamin on salvation*

When the people heard Benjamin's discourse and asked him how they could "apply the atoning blood of Christ that we may receive forgiveness of our sins, and our hearts may be purified" (Mosiah 4:2), Benjamin told them they (1) must believe in the goodness of God and in the atonement of Jesus Christ, (2) must repent of their sins and forsake them, and (3) must humble themselves before God and ask in sincerity of heart for forgiveness. (Mosiah 4:6-10.)

Although Benjamin did not specifically mention baptism by water and by the Holy Ghost, it seems reasonable to assume that the people whom Benjamin was addressing had already received these ordinances for the following reasons: (1) the Nephites had authority to baptize (2 Nephi 6:2); (2) they plainly understood that baptism was essential to salvation (2 Nephi 9:23-24); (3) apparently the righteous Nephites had practiced baptism from the beginning of the Book of Mormon (2 Nephi 31:17).

MOSIAH 7:17   *The temple in the land of Lehi-Nephi*

This is the first reference to a temple in the land of Lehi-Nephi. The two earlier temples mentioned in the Book of Mormon were located in the land of Nephi (2 Nephi 5:16) and in the land of Zarahemla (Mosiah 1:18). No further information is provided in our present Book of Mormon concerning when or by whom this temple in the land of Lehi-Nephi was first constructed.

MOSIAH 7:26   *The prophet of the land who was killed*

The prophet who is mentioned in this verse as having been killed because of the wickedness and abominations of the people is the prophet Abinadi. The teachings of Abinadi are found in Mosiah, chapters 11-17.

MOSIAH 8:7-12   *The land of destruction discovered by the scouts of Limhi*

The evidences of destruction that were discovered by the forty-three scouts sent out by King Limhi are the remains of the great Jaredite civilization of which we will read in the book of Ether.

MOSIAH 8:13-17   *Definition of a "seer"*

The word *seer* literally means one who sees: a see-er. Ammon says a seer is a person who has the right to use the "interpreters" or the Urim and Thummim. (Mosiah 8:13-17; see also Mosiah 28:10-16.) He states further: "a seer is a revelator and a prophet also; and a gift which is greater can no man have." (Mosiah 8:16.) Members of The Church of Jesus Christ of Latter-day Saints regularly sustain the members of the First Presidency, the Council of the Twelve Apostles, and the Patriarch to the Church as "Prophets, Seers, and Revelators."

MOSIAH 9:1   *The record of Zeniff*

Chapters 9 and 10 of Mosiah are evidently taken verbatim from a record originally prepared by Zeniff. Note that these two chapters are written in the first person: "I, Zeniff," etc. Beginning with chapter 11, the account is written in the third person, although these materials also evidently come from the record of Zeniff.

MOSIAH 9:9   *The crops of the Nephites*

Although the equivalent of the word *corn* is used in some Semitic languages to refer to various types of cereals, including wheat, Joseph Smith would probably translate it here so it would be clear to the understanding of his readers in the United States. Thus, the "corn" here is probably maize, which is frequently called corn in the Americas. It is not clear what crops are referred to by the titles of "neas" and "sheum."

MOSIAH 10:6   *The king of the Lamanites*

Evidently the Lamanites have used the same procedure as the Nephites did in their early history of naming their kings after their earliest leader. Jacob 1:11 mentions that the kings who succeeded Nephi were known as "second Nephi, third Nephi, and so forth, according to the reigns of the kings." Thus it should not be too surprising to discover that the king of the Lamanites in approximately 178 B.C. was still known as "King Laman" (Mosiah 10:6), although the original leader after whom the king was named had lived some four hundred years before. Also, later in the Book of Mormon we discover that the son who succeeded this king is also known as Laman. (See Mosiah 24:3.)

182

MOSIAH 10:12-17   *False traditions of the Lamanites*

False traditions had been handed down by the Lamanites from generation to generation, and, with the passage of time, some of these false teachings were apparently accepted by many of the Lamanites as being true. Some of these false teachings were:

1. That Laman and Lemuel were driven out of the land of Jerusalem "because of the iniquities of their father." (Actually Lehi and his group were led away from Jerusalem and impending destruction because of the righteousness of Lehi.)

2. That Laman and Lemuel were "wronged" by their brethren "in the wilderness" . . . "while crossing the sea" . . . "while in the land of their first inheritance." (The Lord was directing the righteous leaders, Lehi and Nephi, as to what should be done.)

3. That Nephi had wrongfully "taken the ruling of the people" out of the hands of Laman and Lemuel. (The Lord designated Nephi as the new leader because of his faithfulness in keeping the commandments.)

4. That Nephi robbed Laman and Lemuel by taking "the records which were engraven on the plates of brass." (Nephi was rightfully entitled to these records because he was God's chosen religious leader of the group.)

Because of these false traditions the Lamanites had taught their children that they should hate, rob, and murder the Nephites; therefore, the Lamanites had "an eternal hatred towards the children of Nephi." (Mosiah 10:17.)

MOSIAH 11:1   *The wicked King Noah*

Mormon evidently now begins abridging the original record of Zeniff. Note that chapter 11 is primarily written in the third person, whereas chapters 9 and 10 were written in the first person. Note also how Mormon tells us in one brief statement of the wicked character of King Noah: "he did not walk in the ways of his father."

MOSIAH 13:5   *A clarification of a biblical text*

Notice the following interesting reference concerning Abinadi as he made his defense before Noah and the wicked priests: "the Spirit of the Lord was upon him; and his face shone with exceeding luster, *even as Moses' did while in the mount of Sinai,* while speaking with the Lord." (Italics added.) This statement is of particular interest because of the controversy among biblical scholars and translators concerning the facial appearance of Moses after he had talked with the Lord on the mount of Sinai. The King James Version renders Exodus 34:30 as follows: "And when Aaron and all the children of Israel saw Moses, behold, the skin of his face shone; and they were afraid to come nigh him." However, the Catholic translators of the Douay Version followed the pattern of the Septuagint Bible by translating the same verse as follows: "And he knew not that his face was horned from the conversation with the Lord. And Aaron and the children of Israel seeing the face of Moses horned, were afraid to come near." Because of this faulty interpretation, the great sculptor Michelangelo put horns on his famous statue of Moses! The Book of Mormon again comes to the support of its companion scripture, the Bible, and clarifies an area of controversy; the face of Moses "shone" when he came off the mount.

MOSIAH 14:1-12   *Isaiah's prophecy of the Savior*

Biblical scholars have long disputed whether or not chapter 53 of Isaiah really pertained to the life and mission of Jesus Christ. The fact that Abinadi quotes this chapter (Mosiah 14) in an attempt to convince the people of the coming of the Messiah would indicate that these particular writings of Isaiah definitely do pertain to Jesus Christ.

MOSIAH 15:1-4   *Jesus Christ as the "Father" and the "Son"*

Jesus Christ is referred to several times in the Book of Mormon as both the Father and the Son. (Mosiah 15:1-4; Ether 3:14.) The question might well be asked: In what way (or in what sense) is Jesus Christ both the "Father" and the "Son"? The words *Father* and *Son* are titles rather than names; thus they may be used to refer to more than one person. The term *Father* may rightfully be used to refer to Jesus Christ in the following areas:

(1) Jesus Christ is the Father of those who accept the gospel because it is through his atonement that the gospel is made active on this earth. (Mosiah 5:7; 15:10-13; see also D&C 25:1; 39:1-4; and Ether 3.)

184   (2) Jesus Christ is the Father of this earth in the sense that he created this earth under the direction of his Father. (Mosiah 15:4; 16:15; see also Alma 11:38-39; 3 Nephi 9:15; Ether 4:7; D&C 45:1.)

(3) Jesus Christ is the Father because of divine investiture of power—that is, Jesus Christ has been given the power to act for and represent his Father on this earth. (Read particularly D&C 93:2-4, 17.)

(4) Other dictionary definitions of *Father* that might be used to refer to Jesus Christ are as follows: "one to whom respect is due"; "one who cares as a father might"; "an originator, source, or prototype"; "one who claims or accepts responsibility."

The term *Son* also has varied meanings. Jesus Christ is rightfully referred to as the Son in the following senses: (1) Jesus Christ is the firstborn of God in the spirit (Colossians 1:15-19; D&C 93:21); (2) Jesus Christ is the Only Begotten Son of God in the flesh (Jacob 4:5, 11; Alma 12:33-34; 13:5; John 1:18, 3:16); (3) Jesus Christ submitted his will to the will of his Father (Mosiah 15:2-7).

President Joseph Fielding Smith made the following observations concerning these verses:

The statement of Abinadi [indicates] . . . that Jesus Christ is both Father and Son to us [Mosiah 15:1-4]. . . .

What's wrong with that scripture? What is a father? *One who begets or gives life.* What did our Savior do? He begot us, or gave us life from death, as clearly set forth by Jacob, the brother of Nephi. If it had not been for the death of our Savior, Jesus Christ, the spirit and body would never have been united again. As Jacob states:

And our spirits must have become like unto him, and we become devils, angels to a devil, to be shut out from the presence of our God, and to remain with the father of lies, in misery, like unto himself; yea, to that being who beguiled our first parents, who transformeth himself nigh unto an angel of light, and stirreth up the children of men unto secret combinations of murder and all manner of secret works of darkness.

O how great the goodness of our God, who prepareth a way for our escape from the grasp of this awful monster; yea, that monster, death and hell, which I call the death of the body, and also the death of the spirit.

And because of the way of deliverance of our God, the Holy One of Israel, this death, of which I have spoken, which is the temporal, shall deliver up its dead; which death is the grave.

And this death of which I have spoken, which is the spiritual death, shall deliver up its dead which spiritual death is hell; wherefore, death and hell must deliver up their dead, and hell must deliver up its captive spirits, and the grave must deliver up its captive bodies, and the bodies and the spirits of men will be restored one to the other; and it is by the power of the resurrection of the Holy One of Israel.

O how great the plan of our God! For on the other hand, the paradise of God must deliver up the spirits of the righteous and the grave deliver up the body of the righteous; and the spirit and the body is restored to itself again, and all men become incorruptible, and immortal, and they are living souls, having a perfect knowledge like unto us in the flesh, save it be that our knowledge shall be perfect. [2 Nephi 9:9-13.]

If there had been no redemption from death our spirits would have been taken captive by Satan and we would have become subject to Satan's will forever.

What did our Savior do? He begot us in that sense. He became a father to us because he gave us immortality or eternal life through his death and sacrifice upon the cross. I think we have a perfect right to speak of him as Father.

King Mosiah put his people under covenant to take upon them the name of Christ. And this was 124 years before the birth of Christ. I want to read a verse or two from this pledge.

And now, because of the covenant which ye have made ye shall be called the children of Christ, his sons, and his daughters; for behold, this day he hath spiritually begotten you; for ye say that your hearts are changed through faith on his name; therefore, ye are born of him and have become his sons and his daughters. [Mosiah 5:7.]

Is there anything wrong in our calling Jesus Christ our spiritual Father?

And under this head [this wonderful king said] ye are made free and there is no other head whereby ye can be made free. There is no other name given whereby salvation cometh; therefore I would that ye should take upon you the name of Christ, all you that have entered into the covenant with God that ye should be obedient unto the end of your lives.

And it shall come to pass whosoever does this shall be found at the right hand of God, for he shall know the name by which he is called; for he shall be called by the name of Christ.

And now it shall come to pass, that whosoever shall not take upon him the name of Christ must be called by some other name; therefore, he findeth himself on the left hand of God. [Mosiah 5:8-10.]

The Son of God has a perfect right to call us his children, spiritually begotten, and we have a perfect right to look on him as our Father who spiritually begot us.

Now if these critics would read carefully the Book of Mormon they would find that when the Savior came and visited the Nephites he told them that he had been sent by his Father. He knelt before them and he prayed to his Father. He taught them to pray to his Father, but that did not lessen in the least our duty and responsibility of looking upon the Son of God as a Father to us because he spiritually begot us. (*Answers to Gospel Questions* [Deseret Book Co., 1957-66] 4:177-80.)

MOSIAH 15:11-19   *Who are "they who have published peace"?*

When the wicked priests of King Noah started to question Abinadi, they asked him to interpret the following words of Isaiah: "How beautiful upon the mountains are the feet of him that bringeth good tidings; that publisheth peace; that bringeth good tidings of good; that publisheth salvation; that saith unto Zion, Thy God reigneth." (Mosiah 12:21; Isaiah 52:7.) The possible interpretation of this scripture has been debated by many biblical scholars, because this verse of Isaiah is frequently quoted. Who are they who bring "good tidings," who publish peace, who publish salvation? Abinadi gives the answer in Mosiah 15:11-19: those who are heirs of the kingdom of God including "all the holy prophets ever since the world began." (Mosiah 15:12-13.) Abinadi mentions specifically "the founder of peace, yea, even the Lord." (Mosiah 15:18.)

MOSIAH 16:1-5   *The wicked remain as though there had been no redemption made*

Abinadi's teaching that the wicked remain "as though there was no redemption made" (Mosiah 16:5) should not be interpreted to mean that the wicked are not resurrected. It is made abundantly clear elsewhere in the Book of Mormon that everyone who has lived on this earth will be resurrected from the dead, regardless of whether or not they keep the commandments of God. (See 2 Nephi 9:22; Alma 11:41; 33:22.)

However, Abinadi realizes that in order to be fully redeemed, a person must be worthy to return to the presence of our Heavenly Father. Thus, if a person "persists in his own carnal nature, and goes on in the ways of sin and rebellion against God" (Mosiah 16:5), then he cannot be worthy to return to God's presence. He remains "as though there was no redemption made" so far as regaining the presence of God is concerned.

MOSIAH 16:6-7 *Abinadi's testimony of the Savior's mission*

Although he lived nearly 150 years before the birth of Christ, Abinadi was so certain Jesus Christ was going to be born on the earth that he sometimes referred to the life of the Savior in the past tense. He was aware, of course, that he was doing this. In Mosiah 16:6 he states: ". . . and now if Christ *had not* come into the world, *speaking of things to come as though they had already come,* there could have been no redemption." (Italics added.)

MOSIAH 17:2-4 *The introduction of Alma*

One of the wicked priests of King Noah is a man named Alma, who is a descendant of Nephi. When first introduced in the Book of Mormon, Alma is a young man in the process of being converted by Abinadi. (Mosiah 17:2.) Much of the religious history of the Nephite nation for the next three hundred years is concerned with this man and his descendants. Alma not only begins a religious revival among his own people, but later he is given power by King Mosiah to establish churches throughout all the land of Zarahemla. (See Mosiah 25:19.)

Still later we read that Alma's son (also called Alma) succeeds his father as the religious leader of the people and also becomes the first chief judge over the Nephite nation. Other descendants of Alma the elder who become great religious leaders of the Nephites include his grandson (Helaman); great-grandson (Helaman, the son of Helaman); great-great-grandson (Nephi, the son of Helaman who is the son of Helaman); and great-great-great-grandson (Nephi the second, who is also the chief disciple of the resurrected Jesus Christ). Abinadi may have felt that he had failed as a missionary; so far as the record indicates, his only convert was Alma. However, as mentioned above, the missionary efforts of Abinadi affected the religious life of the Nephites for hundreds of years.

MOSIAH 18:4 *The land called Mormon*

The word *Mormon* is used chronologically for the first

188   time in Mosiah 18:4. Although the word appears earlier than this in the Book of Mormon it has always referred to the name of the great prophet, historian, and military leader who lived several hundred years after the time of Christ. The place called "Mormon" referred to in Mosiah 18:4 received its name "from the king." No further information is given concerning this king.

MOSIAH 18:12-18   *The baptism of Alma and his authority to baptize*

The Book of Mormon does not specifically state whether or not Alma had been baptized before or how he got his authority to baptize. The record merely says that Alma immersed himself in the water when he baptized Helam (Mosiah 18:14-15) and that "Alma, having authority from God, ordained priests." (Mosiah 18:18.) Alma may have been ordained by Abinadi, but the record is not clear on this point. Joseph Fielding Smith feels that Alma held the priesthood before he became involved with King Noah. (*Answers to Gospel Questions,* 3:203-4.)

MOSIAH 19:20   *The death of King Noah*

When the followers of King Noah "caused that he should suffer, even unto death by fire" (Mosiah 19:20), they were fulfilling the prophecy of Abinadi made to King Noah that "ye shall suffer, as I suffer, the pains of death by fire" (Mosiah 17:18).

MOSIAH 22:14   *The records possessed by the Nephites*

The early history contained in the Book of Mormon is obtained from three sets of plates: the brass plates of Laban, the small plates of Nephi, and the large plates of Nephi. However, when Limhi's people join with the people of King Mosiah in the land of Zarahemla they bring with them two additional sets of plates: (1) their own records, which are known as the record of Zeniff, and (2) the "records which had been found by the people of Limhi," which are later identified as the records of Ether. (See Ether 1:1-2.) When Alma and his people come into the land of Zarahemla, they also evidently bring their own records with them. (See Mosiah 25:6 and also the superscription before Alma, chapter 23.)

MOSIAH 23:3; 24:25 *The distance from the land of Nephi to the land of Zarahemla*

The story of the flight of Alma and his people gives us the best clue in the Book of Mormon to the distance between the lands of Nephi and Zarahemla. It takes Alma and his group eight days to go from the waters of Mormon (in the borders of the land of Nephi—Mosiah 18:4) to the land of Helam (Mosiah 23:3). Then when they finally leave Helam, it takes them an additional twelve days of travel to go to the land of Zarahemla. (Mosiah 24:25.) Thus approximately twenty days are spent *in travel* by Alma and his group in going from the borders of the land of Nephi to the land of Zarahemla.

MOSIAH 23:8 *The value of a monarchy*

The Book of Mormon gives several valuable principles concerning different types of government. Mosiah 23:8 indicates that a monarchy would be a good system of government "if it were possible that ye could always have just men to be your kings." Thus, apparently nothing is inherently wrong with a monarchal system of government. In fact, the scriptures indicate that when Jesus Christ comes on the earth during the Millennium he will rule as King of kings; this evidently means we will then have a monarchal system of government.

MOSIAH 23:16-17 *Was Alma the elder the "founder" of the church among the Nephites?*

In the part of the Book of Mormon where we first read that Alma was the "founder of their church," the pronoun *their* refers only to the people who were with Alma in the wilderness; it does not refer to the entire Nephite nation. Thus when the statement is read in context, the true meaning is clear; this meaning is also clarified later in the record when it states that King Mosiah gave authority to Alma over the churches in Zarahemla. (Mosiah 26:8.) A brief historical setting of this period is provided by Joseph Fielding Smith in his answer to the question "Did the Nephites Have a Church Organization before the Days of Alma?"

It should be remembered that Alma had been one of the priests of King Noah in the land of Lehi-Nephi. It should also be taken into consideration that the colony in that land separated themselves from the main body of the Church in Zarahemla. In the days of Amaleki, who kept the Nephite record, a company of Nephites under Zeniff desired to occupy the land which was *first* settled by the Nephites, and entered into an agreement with the Lamanites to possess that land. There they established an independent kingdom which they possessed for many years, however in constant war and bondage to the Lamanites. In course of time, under King Noah, they became very wicked. It was at this time that the prophet Abinadi was murdered, and Alma, having accepted the teachings of Abinadi, gathered around him all who were willing to keep the commandments of the Lord, and doing so he brought upon himself and his followers the wrath of the wicked king, and they had to flee from their homes into the wilderness, with the intention of making their way back to the land of Zarahemla. The story of their flight, suffering, and blessings from the hand of the Lord were recorded in the Book of Mosiah. While in the wilderness Alma organized his group of believers into a branch of the Church and is spoken of as their founder.

The main body of the Nephites, under the second King Mosiah, was still intact in the land of Zarahemla. The reference stating that Alma was the founder of their church has reference only to the refugees who were fleeing from the land of the Nephites' first inheritance. In course of time they found their way back to the main body of the Church and Alma was consecrated as the high priest over the Church in all of the lands occupied by the Nephites. (*Answers to Gospel Questions,* 3:39-40.)

MOSIAH 24:3-4 *The language of the Nephites is taught to the Lamanites*

During the hundreds of years when the Nephites and Lamanites had lived apart, their languages had changed to such an extent that it was difficult for them to communicate with each other. During the period of history between 145 and 123 B.C., however, the king of the Lamanites "appointed teachers of the brethren of Amulon" (the wicked priests of King Noah who were Nephites by birth) to teach the Nephite language "among all the people of the Lamanites." (Mosiah 24:4.) Thus the two groups evidently start speaking the same language again. This fact takes on added significance later in the Book of Mormon when we read about the missionary efforts between these two groups.

MOSIAH 25:13 *The manner of naming the people*

The Book of Mormon peoples evidently had the custom

of taking upon themselves the name of their leader. Thus the two early groups were known as the Nephites and Lamanites because the names of their first leaders were Nephi and Laman. Later, when a small group of Nephites headed by Mosiah came down into the land of Zarahemla, they discovered that the people there were called "the people of Zarahemla" after the name of their leader. (Omni 14.) Now when the two peoples of Zarahemla and Nephi combined together, they become known as Nephites "because the kingdom had been conferred upon none but those who were descendants of Nephi." (Mosiah 25:13.)

MOSIAH 27:11-17   *The appearance of an angel*

Although angels from God have appeared to righteous people, President Wilford Woodruff indicated that God always has a purpose in sending such messages:

One of the Apostles said to me years ago, "Brother Woodruff, I have prayed for a long time for the Lord to send me the administration of an angel. I have had a great desire for this, but I have never had my prayers answered." I said to him that if he were to pray a thousand years to the God of Israel for that gift, it would not be granted, unless the Lord had a motive in sending an angel to him. I told him that the Lord never did nor never will send an angel to anybody merely to gratify the desire of the individual to see an angel. If the Lord sends an angel to anyone, He sends him to perform a work that cannot be performed only by the administration of an angel. I said to him that those were my views. The Lord had sent angels to men from the creation of the world, at different times, but always with a message or with something to perform that could not be performed without. I rehearsed to him different times when angels appeared to men. Of course, I referred to the angel visiting Joseph Smith. The Revelator John said that in the last days an angel would fly in the midst of heaven, having the everlasting Gospel to preach to them that dwelt on the earth. The reason it required an angel to do this work was, the Gospel was not on the earth. The Gospel and the Priesthood had been taken from among men. Hence God had to restore it again.

Now, I have always said, and I want to say it to you, that the Holy Ghost is what every Saint of God needs. It is far more important that a man should have that gift than he should have the ministration of an angel, unless it is necessary for an angel to teach him something that he has not been taught. (Address given at Weber Stake Conference, Ogden, Utah, October 19, 1896, and published in *Deseret Weekly,* 53:641.)

MOSIAH 27:14-16   *Power of the prayers of the righteous*

The Lord has promised that if we ask in faith for that which is right, we shall receive. (3 Nephi 18:20.) However, he has not promised the manner or the time in which the prayer will be answered. When the angel appeared to Alma the younger and the four sons of Mosiah, the angel made it clear that he had not appeared to them because of their own worthiness. Rather, he said, "for this purpose have I come to convince thee of the power and authority of God, *that the prayers of his servants might be answered according to their faith."* (Mosiah 27:14. Italics added.) Also the angel pled with them to repent of their sins and "seek to destroy the church no more" *that the prayers of the righteous members of the church might be answered.* (Mosiah 27:16. Italics added.) Evidently it was primarily because of the faithful prayers of Alma the elder and the other members of the church that the angel appeared to Alma the younger and the four sons of Mosiah.

MOSIAH 27:34   *The sons of King Mosiah*

The order of the birth of the four sons of Mosiah is never made clear in the Book of Mormon. The listing in Mosiah 27:34 would indicate that Ammon was the first born followed by Aaron, then Omner, and Himni. Also, the fact that Ammon was the leader on their missionary journey to the Lamanites would seem to indicate that Ammon was the eldest. (See Alma, chapters 17-26.) However, when King Mosiah asked his people to select his successor, they first desired that Aaron should be their king and their ruler. (Mosiah 29:1-2.) In this single instance it appears as though Aaron may have been the eldest son.

MOSIAH 28:11-13   *The holy interpreters*

The "two stones" that were used by Mosiah in translating the records written on the gold plates found by the people of Limhi were evidently the Urim and Thummim. (Mosiah 28:11-13.)

MOSIAH 28:11-19   *The records of Ether*

Mosiah's translation of the gold plates discovered by the people of Limhi was evidently made available to the people of Mosiah (Mosiah 28:11, 18), and Mormon promises that an account of this record "shall be written hereafter; for behold, it is expedient that all people should know the things which are written in this account" (Mosiah 28:19). Mormon's son Moroni later abridges the account contained in these records, and his abridgment appears in our present Book of Mormon as the book of Ether.

MOSIAH 29:25-27 *The strength—and weakness—of a democracy*

Among the principles of government contained in the Book of Mormon is that a monarchy is a good system of government *if* the people can be assured they will always have good and righteous kings. (Mosiah 23:8.) However, the weakness of a monarchy is that "ye cannot dethrone an iniquitous king save it be through much contention, and the shedding of much blood." (Mosiah 29:21.)

Thus, because his people could not be assured of always having righteous kings, Mosiah proposes to them a system of judges who would be chosen "by the voice of this people." (Mosiah 29:25.) He indicates that the value of this system of democratic government is that "it is not common that the voice of the people desireth anything contrary to that which is right." (Mosiah 29:26.) However, he also warns that this type of democracy has a weakness: "if the time comes that the voice of the people doth choose iniquity, then is the time that the judgments of God will come upon you." (Mosiah 29:27.)

ALMA 1:2-16   *Nehor, the advocator of priestcraft*

Nephi, the son of Lehi, had warned his people against the evils of priestcraft, which he defined as "men preach and set themselves up for a light unto the world, that they may get gain and praise of the world; but they seek not the welfare of Zion." (2 Nephi 26:29.) The warning of Nephi concerning the evils of priestcraft is amply demonstrated by Nehor, who taught that "every priest and teacher ought to become popular; and they ought not to labor with their hands, but . . . they ought to be supported by the people." (Alma 1:3.)

Alma the younger, the chief judge of the people, accuses Nehor not only of being guilty of preaching priestcraft but also of endeavoring to enforce it by the sword. Furthermore, he warns the Nephites that if priestcraft were to be enforced among them "it would prove their entire destruction." (Alma 1:12.) Alma was very concerned about this matter because the Lord had warned the Nephites they were to keep the commandments of the Lord or they would be destroyed.

ALMA 2:1-31   *Amlici, who desired to be king*

Soon after the establishment of a system of elected judges among the Nephites, several revolts take place against this type of government. The first of these revolts is headed by Amlici, who, in addition to being an avowed kingman, is also a follower of the order of Nehor and thus advocates priestcraft. (Alma 2:1.) Although Amlici is not successful in his desire to obtain the kingship, he precipitates a civil war that results in the deaths of over 19,000 people. (Alma 2:19.)

ALMA 3:4-9   *The Amlicites mark themselves "with red in their foreheads"*

The Amlicites who escaped from Alma and his armies joined with the attacking Lamanite armies. Evidently they soon felt the need of marking themselves so their new allies, the dark-skinned Lamanites, could identify them as these two groups battled against the Nephites. Thus the Amlicites "marked themselves with red in their foreheads after the manner of the Lamanites." (Alma 3:4.)

This statement has two possible interpretations: (1) the Lamanites had red skin so the Amlicites marked themselves with red, or (2) the Lamanites marked themselves with red, and the Amlicites imitated them by marking themselves with red. Regardless of which interpretation is correct, this statement may provide a clue concerning the origin of painted war faces among this people, which continued to the coming of the white man some 1600 years later.

ALMA 5:14, 21 *Have all members of the church been spiritually reborn?*

The baptism of water which qualifies one for membership in the church does not assure one of the spiritual rebirth necessary to regain the presence of God. The "right" to receive the Holy Ghost is bestowed upon a person when he is confirmed a member of the Church and after he has been baptized by water. But unless a person fully repents of his sins and *actually receives* the Holy Ghost, he cannot be sanctified and be born again spiritually. (See Alma 7:14, 21; 3 Nephi 27:19-20; and John 3:5.) Thus Alma correctly asked his brethren of the Church, "have ye spiritually been born of God?" (Alma 5:14.) (See also material listed after Alma 7:14.)

ALMA 6:1 *The ordaining of "priests" and "elders"*

Alma ordained "priests" and "elders" to "preside and watch over the church." (Alma 6:1.) However, it is not clear whether this quotation means he was ordaining them to specific offices in the priesthood; the words *priests* and *elders* are sometimes used in a general way to denote religious leaders. Concerning whether or not these terms referred to specific offices in the priesthood, Elder Bruce R. McConkie has written:

In general terms a *priest* is a minister. One so designated (if he is a true priest) must in fact hold the priesthood; yet the designation *priest,* when so used, has no reference to any particular office in the priesthood. Thus among the Nephites it was the practice to consecrate priests and teachers, give them administrative responsibility, and send them out to preach, teach, and baptize. (Mosiah 23:17; 25:19; 26:7; Alma 4:7; 15:13; 23:4.) These priests and teachers held the Melchizedek Priesthood. (*Doctrines of Salvation,* vol. 3, p. 87.) . . .

Book of Mormon prophets gave the title *priest* to officers known in this dispensation as *high priests.* That is, they were priests of the Melchizedek Priesthood, or as Alma expressed it, *"the Lord God ordained priests, after his holy order, which was after the order of his Son."* (Alma 13:1-20.) Since there was no Aaronic Priesthood among the Nephites in Alma's day (there being none of the lineage empowered in pre-meridian times to hold that priesthood), there was no need to distinguish between priests of the lesser and greater priesthoods. (*Mormon Doctrine*, 2nd ed., pp. 598-99.)

The reference referred to by Elder McConkie in *Doctrines of Salvation* includes the following statement:

The Nephites did not officiate under the authority of the Aaronic Priesthood. They were not descendants of Aaron, and there were no Levites among them. There is no evidence in the *Book of Mormon* that they held the Aaronic Priesthood until after the ministry of the resurrected Lord among them, but the *Book of Mormon* tells us definitely, in many places, that the priesthood which they held and under which they officiated was the Priesthood after the *holy order*, the order of the Son of God. This higher priesthood can officiate in every ordinance of the gospel, and Jacob and Joseph, for instance, were consecrated priests and teachers after this order. (Joseph Fielding Smith, *Doctrines of Salvation*, 3:87.)

ALMA 7:10 *Was the Savior born "at Jerusalem"?*

Alma said that the Savior should be "born of Mary, at Jerusalem which is the land of our forefathers." (Alma 7:10.) Inasmuch as the Savior was evidently born at Bethlehem, not in Jerusalem, how should we interpret Alma's statement? At first glance the statement appears to be in error. However, archaeological evidences that have come forth since the Book of Mormon was published indicate that in 600 B.C. Bethlehem was probably a part of the "greater" land of Jerusalem. In this connection, it is of interest to note that the Book of Mormon refers to the *land* of Jerusalem, not the city; also, Bethlehem is only about six miles from the city of Jerusalem. (If you desire additional information on this subject, read *An Approach to the Book of Mormon*, pp. 81-82, by Hugh Nibley.)

ALMA 7:14 *"Be born again"*

Alma indicated that a person must be "born again" in order to inherit the kingdom of heaven. (Alma 7:14.) Concerning the importance of this rebirth, Elder Bruce R. McConkie has written:

...To gain salvation in the celestial kingdom men must be *born again* (Alma 7:14); born of water and of the Spirit (John 3:1-13); born of God, so that they are changed from their "carnal and fallen state, to a state of righteousness," becoming new creatures of the Holy Ghost. (Mosiah 27:24-29.) They must become newborn babes in Christ (1 Pet. 2:2); they must be "spiritually begotten" of God, be born of Christ, thus becoming his sons and daughters. (Mosiah 5:7.)

The first birth takes place when spirits pass from their pre-existent first estate into mortality; the second birth or birth "into the kingdom of heaven" takes place when mortal men are born again and become alive to the things of the Spirit and of righteousness. The elements of water, blood, and Spirit are present in both births. (Moses 6:59-60.) The second birth begins when men are baptized in water by a legal administrator; it is completed when they actually receive the companionship of the Holy Ghost, becoming new creatures by the cleansing power of that member of the Godhead.

Mere compliance with the formality of the ordinance of baptism does not mean that a person has been born again. No one can be born again without baptism, but the immersion in water and the laying on of hands to confer the Holy Ghost do not of themselves guarantee that a person has been or will be born again. The new birth takes place only for those who actually enjoy the gift or companionship of the Holy Ghost, only for those who are fully converted, who have given themselves without restraint to the Lord. Thus Alma addressed himself to his "brethren of the church," and pointedly asked them if they had "spiritually been born of God," received the Lord's image in their countenances, and had the "mighty change" in their hearts which always attends the birth of the Spirit. (Alma 5:14-31.)

Those members of the Church who have actually been born again are in a blessed and favored state. They have attained their position, not merely by joining the Church, but through faith (1 John 5:1), righteousness (1 John 2:29), love (1 John 4:7), and overcoming the world. (1 John 5:4.) *"Whosoever is born of God doth not continue in sin; for the Spirit of God remaineth in him; and he cannot sin, because he is born of God, having received that holy Spirit of promise."* (*Inspired Version,* 1 John 3:9.) (*Mormon Doctrine,* 2d ed., pp. 100-1.)

Elder Mark E. Petersen has also emphasized the importance of this rebirth:

Unless a man is born again, he cannot see the Kingdom of God. I do not believe that a person will ever see the Kingdom of

198   God unless he is born again. . . . That birth of the spirit means something more than most of us normally realize. Through proper teaching, a conviction is born in our soul. Faith develops. Through it we see how important it is to become like Christ. We see ourselves as we are in contrast to a Christlike soul. A desire for a change-over is born within us. The change-over begins. We call it repentance. Through our faith and as part of our conversion or change from one state to another, we begin to see sin in its true light. . . . We strive with all our souls to become like the Savior. (Address to seminary and institute of religion personnel, BYU, July 11, 1956.)

President David O. McKay has indicated that a real rebirth also involves a change in feeling:

. . . No man can sincerely resolve to apply to his daily life the teachings of Jesus of Nazareth without sensing a change in his own nature. The phrase, "born again," has a deeper significance than many people attach to it. This *changed feeling* may be indescribable, *but it is real.* Happy the person who has truly sensed the uplifting, transforming power that comes from this nearness to the Savior, this kinship to the Living Christ. (*Conference Report,* April 1962, p. 7.)

ALMA 10:2   *The writing upon the wall of the temple*

In his introduction, Amulek mentions he is "the son of Giddonah, who was the son of Ishmael, who was a descendant of Aminadi . . . who interpreted the writing which was upon the wall of the temple, which was written by the finger of God." (Alma 10:2.) This is the only time Aminadi is mentioned, and our present Book of Mormon gives no further details concerning the writing written by the finger of God upon the wall of the temple. Evidently an account of this incident was recorded on the large plates of Nephi, but Mormon did not include it in his abridgment.

ALMA 10:3   *Lehi is a descendant of Manasseh*

In further identifying himself, Amulek mentioned that his forefather Aminadi "was a descendant of Nephi, who was the son of Lehi . . . who was a descendant of Manasseh, who was the son of Joseph who was sold into Egypt. . . ." (Alma 10:3.) Earlier in the Book of Mormon it was mentioned that Lehi was a descendant of Joseph. (1 Nephi 5:14.) However, Joseph had two sons, Manasseh and Ephraim, and this is the first time the Book of Mormon indicates that Lehi was a descendant of Joseph's eldest son, Manasseh.

Some students of the Book of Mormon have wondered how descendants of Joseph were still living in Jerusalem in 600 B.C. when most members of the tribes of Ephraim and Manasseh were taken into captivity by the Assyrians about 721 B.C. A scripture in 2 Chronicles may provide a clue to this problem. This account mentions that in about 941 B.C. Asa, the king of the land, gathered together at Jerusalem all of Judah and Benjamin "and the strangers with them out of Ephraim and Manasseh." (2 Chronicles 15:9.) These "strangers. . . out of Ephraim and Manasseh" who were gathered to Jerusalem in approximately 941 B.C. may have included the forefathers of Lehi and Ishmael.

Concerning the fact that Ishmael was also a descendant of Joseph, Elder Erastus Snow said:

Whoever has read the Book of Mormon carefully will have learned that the remnants of the house of Joseph dwelt upon the American continent; and that Lehi learned by searching the records of his fathers that were written upon the plates of brass, that he was of the lineage of Manasseh. The Prophet Joseph informed us that the record of Lehi was contained on the 116 pages that were first translated and subsequently stolen, and of which an abridgement is given us in the first Book of Nephi, which is the record of Nephi individually, he himself being of the lineage of Manasseh; but that Ishmael was of the lineage of Ephraim, and that his sons married into Lehi's family, and Lehi's sons married Ishmael's daughters, thus fulfilling the words of Jacob upon Ephraim and Manasseh in the 48th chapter of Genesis, which says: "And let my name be named on them, and the name of my fathers Abraham and Isaac; and let them grow into a multitude in the midst of the land." Thus these descendants of Manasseh and Ephraim grew together upon this American continent, with a sprinkling from the house of Judah, from Mulek descended, who left Jerusalem eleven years after Lehi, and founded the colony afterwards known as Zarahemla and found by Mosiah—thus making a combination, an intermixture of Ephraim and Manasseh with the remnants of Judah, and for aught we know, the remnants of some other tribes that might have accompanied Mulek. And such have grown up on the American continent. (*Journal of Discourses*, 23:184-85.)

ALMA 11:3-19   *The Nephite monetary system*

The monetary system used by the Nephites is briefly explained by Mormon as he recounts the story of Alma and Amulek in the city of Ammonihah. The basic unit is a senine of gold (or a senum of silver, which has the same value). If a

200   value of "1" is attributed to this unit, the monetary system of the Nephites might be summarized as follows: Leah equals $\frac{1}{8}$; shiblum = $\frac{1}{4}$; shiblon = $\frac{1}{2}$; antion of gold = $1\frac{1}{2}$; senum of silver or senine of gold = 1; amnor of silver or seon of gold = 2; ezrom of silver or shum of gold = 4; onti of silver or limnah of gold = 7. One senine of gold (or senum of silver) = wages of a judge for one day. The Nephite monetary system was based on a barley standard, with a senine of gold or a senum of silver equal to a measure of barley. (Alma 11:7.)

ALMA 11:32-37   *Can God save (or redeem) people "in their sins"?*

Amulek taught that God cannot save people "*in* their sins." The Lord can save (or redeem) them *from* their sins after they have repented, but he cannot save them *in* their sins because they have not repented of their wickedness. (Read also Helaman 5:10-11.)

ALMA 11:41   *The status of the wicked*

Amulek said to Zeezrom, ". . . the wicked remain as though there had been no redemption made, except it be the loosing of the bands of death." (Alma 11:41.) In essence, Amulek is saying that the wicked are all resurrected, but they are not redeemed into the presence of God unless they repent of their sins and become spotless before him. (See also Mosiah 16:5; 3 Nephi 27:19-20.)

ALMA 11:41-45   *The temporal death and permanent resurrection of the body*

The Book of Mormon uses the adjective *temporal* when referring to the death of the body, and the adjective *spiritual* when referring to a separation from God because of sin. Concerning the temporal or physical death that will come upon every person who has lived on this earth, President Joseph F. Smith has written:

Every man that is born into the world will die. It matters not who he is, nor where he is, whether his birth be among the rich and the noble, or among the lowly and poor in the world, his days are numbered with the Lord, and in due time he will reach the end. We should think of this. Not that we should go about with heavy hearts or with downcast countenances; not at all. I rejoice that I am born to live, to die, and to live again. . . . I am speaking now of the temporal death, the death of the body. All fear of this death has been removed from the Latter-day Saints. They have no dread of the temporal death, because they know that as death came upon them by the transgression of Adam, so by the righteousness of Jesus Christ shall life come unto them, and though they die they shall live again. Possessing this knowledge, they have joy even in death, for they know that they shall rise again and shall meet again beyond the grave. They know that the spirit dies not at all; that it passes through no change, except the change from imprisonment in this mortal clay to freedom and to the sphere in which it acted before it came to this earth. (Joseph F. Smith, *Conference Report,* October 1899, p. 70.)

However, every person will be resurrected from this physical death, or, as Amulek phrased it, "all shall be raised from this temporal death. The spirit and the body shall be reunited again in its perfect form . . . they can die no more; their spirits uniting with their bodies, never to be divided." (Alma 11:42-43, 45.) President Charles W. Penrose has explained the immortal qualities of the resurrected body as follows:

. . . we are told in the Book of Mormon, as well as in the Doctrine and Covenants, that in the resurrection from the dead, when all shall be raised, "every man in his order," the spirit and the body will be joined together, and they will "not die after;" we are there told that the resurrection will come to *all* mankind, the great and the small, the good and the bad, all races and tribes and beings who are of the seed of Adam will be raised from the dead, and their bodies will not die after. (*Conference Report,* October 1911, p. 50.)

The exact type of body that resurrected beings will have after the resurrection has not been made clear in the scriptures except that it will be an immortal, glorified body animated by spirit. For example, the Book of Mormon prophets clearly teach that the actual physical body will be resurrected; "both limb and joint shall be restored to its proper frame, even as we now are at this time." (Alma 11:43). Unfortunately, the teachings in the New Testament concerning a resurrected body have been misinterpreted by many Christian theologians; thus many churches teach that the actual physical body is not resurrected. Concerning the false teachings of many of the Christian churches, President Joseph Fielding Smith has said:

These modern blind teachers of the blind have a very false understanding of what is meant by a spiritual body. They have

202   based their conclusion on the statement that Paul makes that the body is raised a spiritual body, and that flesh and blood cannot inherit the kingdom of God. They cannot conceive in their minds a body raised from the dead, being composed of flesh and bones, quickened by spirit and not by blood. When Paul spoke of the *spiritual* body he had no reference at all to the *spirit* body and there they have made their mistake. They have confused the spiritual body, or, in other words, the body quickened by the spirit, with the body of the spirit alone. They think that those who believe in the resurrection of the literal body believe that it shall be raised again, quickened by blood, which is not the case. I want to read another verse from the Doctrine and Covenants: (Sec. 88:15-20, 25-30, quoted.)

After the resurrection from the dead our bodies will be spiritual bodies, but they will be bodies that are tangible, bodies that have been purified, but they will nevertheless be bodies of flesh and bones, but they will not be blood bodies, they will no longer be quickened by blood but quickened by the spirit which is eternal and they shall become immortal and shall never die. (*Conference Report,* April 1917, pp. 62-63.)

ALMA 12:3   *God knows all our thoughts*

Amulek said to Zeezrom: "[God] knows all thy thoughts, and thou seest that thy thoughts are made known unto us by his Spirit." (Alma 12:3.) This gift of discernment is one of the gifts of the Holy Spirit, and it is through the proper use of this gift that the evils and designs of wicked men are made known to the prophets of God. In further explanation of this principle, Ammon, one of the sons of Mosiah, said: "[God] knows all the thoughts and intents of the heart; for by his hand were they all created from the beginning." (Alma 18:32.)

ALMA 12:14   *Of what will we be judged at the final judgment?*

Alma and Benjamin both state we shall be judged of our words, our works, and our thoughts. (Alma 12:14; Mosiah 4:30.) Elsewhere in the Book of Mormon it is made clear that we shall also be judged of our responsibilities concerning the welfare of others. (Jacob 1:18-19; Mosiah 2:20-28, 36-41; Mosiah 4:19-30.) Perhaps the most difficult area of judgment for people to understand is that which deals with our thoughts. Yet the Savior very clearly taught that we shall be responsible for what we think (Matthew 5:27-28), and this truth has also been taught by other prophets (1 Chronicles 28:9; Job 42:2; Psalm 94:11; Romans 2:16). The following statements by two of the Presidents of the Church in this dispensation are interesting in this regard:

In reality a man cannot forget anything. He may have a lapse of memory; he may not be able to recall at the moment a thing that he knows or words that he has spoken; he may not have the power at his will to call up these events and words; but let God Almighty touch the mainspring of the memory and awaken recollection, and you will find then that you have not even forgotten a single idle word that you have spoken! I believe the word of God to be true, and, therefore, I warn the youth of Zion, as well as those who are advanced in years, to beware of saying wicked things, of speaking evil, and taking in vain the name of sacred things and sacred beings. Guard your words, that you may not offend even man, much less offend God. (Joseph F. Smith, quoted in *Latter-day Prophets Speak* [Bookcraft, 1948], pp. 56-57.)

We read something like this, "But I say unto you, that every idle word that men shall speak, they shall give account thereof in the day of judgment." Now, this is a remarkable declaration. . . . God has made each man a register within himself, and each man can read his own register, so far as he enjoys his perfect faculties. This can be easily comprehended.

Let your memories run back, and you can remember the time when you did a good action, you can remember the time when you did a bad action; the thing is printed there, and you can bring it out and gaze upon it whenever you please. . . . Where do you read all this? In your own book. You do not go to somebody else's book or library, it is written in your own record, and you there read it. Your eyes and ears have taken it in, and your hands have touched it; and then your judgment, as it is called, has acted upon it—your reflective powers. Now, if you are in possession of a spirit or intellectuality of that kind, whereby you are enabled to read your acts, do you not think that that being who has placed that spirit and that intelligence within you holds the keys of that intelligence, and can read it whenever he pleases? Is not that philosophical, reasonable, and scriptural? I think it is. . . . Well, then, upon this principle we can readily perceive how the Lord will bring into judgment the actions of men when he shall call them forth at the last day. (John Taylor, *Journal of Discourses*, 11:77-78.)

If I had time to enter into this subject alone, I could show you upon scientific principles that man himself is a self-registering machine, his eyes, his ears, his nose, the touch, the taste, and all the various senses of the body are so many media whereby man lays up for himself a record which perhaps nobody else is acquainted with

204   but himself; and when the time comes for that record to be unfolded all men that have eyes to see, and ears to hear will be able to
read all things as God Himself reads them and comprehends them,
and all things, we are told, are naked and open before Him with
whom we have to do. (John Taylor, quoted in *Latter-day Prophets
Speak*, p. 57.)

The Book of Mormon clearly teaches that God knows
our thoughts (Alma 18:32) and that we shall be held
responsible for them.

ALMA 12:16-22   *For information on the topic of spiritual
death, read the material listed after 2 Nephi 9:6-12.*

ALMA 13:9, 14-19   *Who or what is "without beginning
of days or end of years"?*

Melchizedek is one of the most misinterpreted persons in
the Bible. He lived approximately 2000 B.C., was a contemporary of Abraham, and was one of the most righteous men
who ever lived on the earth. Yet little is known about him,
and the little that is said about him in the Bible has been
misunderstood by most biblical scholars. For example, in the
book of Hebrews we read the following concerning this great
prophet:

For this Melchisedec, king of Salem, priest of the most high
God . . .

To whom also Abraham gave a tenth part of all; first being by
interpretation King of righteousness, and after that also King of
Salem, which is, King of peace;

Without father, without mother, without descent, having
neither beginning of days, nor end of life; but made like unto the
Son of God; abideth a priest continually. (Hebrews 7:1-3.)

Some biblical scholars have interpreted these verses to
mean that Melchizedek was born without a mother or a
father! In other words, they believe that the words "without
father, without mother, without descent, having neither beginning of days nor end of life" refer to Melchizedek. That
these words do not refer to Melchizedek, but instead refer to
the priesthood he held, is made clear in both the Doctrine
and Covenants and the Book of Mormon. Section 84 of the
Doctrine and Covenants contains the following statement
concerning the priesthood of God: " . . . Abraham received
the priesthood from Melchizedek, who received it through
the lineage of his fathers. . . . Which priesthood continueth in

the church of God in all generations, and is without beginning of days or end of years." (D&C 84:14, 17.) Concerning this high priesthood the Book of Mormon states, " . . . which calling, and ordinance, and high priesthood, is without beginning or end—Thus they become high priests forever, after the order of the Son, the Only Begotten of the Father, who is without beginning of days or end of years." (Alma 13:8-9.)

ALMA 13:18 *Melchizedek reigned "under his father"*

The statement that Melchizedek reigned "under his father" should not necessarily be interpreted to mean that he reigned at the same time his father was king or even while his father was living. The term "under his father" evidently is a Hebrew idiom meaning that he "takes the place of his father" or "reigns in his father's stead." (For several examples of similar terminology in the Bible, see Genesis 36:33-39.)

ALMA 14:11 *The destruction of the righteous*

It is difficult for mortals—who see events only through eyes that are restricted by time—to see things in their proper relationship so far as the eternities are concerned. Thus, because we as mortals have only limited vision it is understandable why we sometimes desire or wish for things in this life that would not be for our best welfare in the eternities to come. For example, if we had unlimited power and followed our mortal feelings, we would probably never suffer pain, or disease, or even death. But would this be the best thing for us in eternity?

It appears only natural that Amulek should plead with Alma to exercise the power of the priesthood and save the righteous people from being burned to death. However, Alma, through the impressions of the Spirit, was able to see things through the eyes of eternity and thus said: "The Spirit constraineth me that I must not stretch forth mine hand; for behold the Lord receiveth them up unto himself, in glory; and he doth suffer . . . that the people may do this thing unto them, according to the hardness of their hearts, that the judgments which he shall exercise upon them in his wrath may be just." (Alma 14:11.)

Essentially this same idea is expressed by a later Book of Mormon prophet, who says: "For the Lord suffereth the

206 righteous to be slain that his justice and judgment may come upon the wicked; therefore ye need not suppose that the righteous are lost because they are slain; but behold, they do enter into the rest of the Lord their God." (Alma 60:13.)

Concerning the fact that we should live righteous lives and then leave the final judgment to God as to what should be done with our lives, President Spencer W. Kimball has said:

Now, we find many people critical when a righteous person is killed, a young father or mother is taken from a family, or when violent deaths occur. Some become bitter when oft-repeated prayers seem unanswered. Some lose faith and turn sour when solemn administrations by holy men seem to be ignored and no restoration seems to come from repeated prayer circles. But if all the sick were healed, if all the righteous were protected and the wicked destroyed, the whole program of the Father would be annulled and the basic principle of the Gospel, free agency, would be ended.

If pain and sorrow and total punishment immediately followed the doing of evil, no soul would repeat a misdeed. If joy and peace and rewards were instantaneously given the doer of good, there could be no evil—all would do good and not because of the rightness of doing good. There would be no test of strength, no development of character, no growth of powers, no free agency, no Satanic controls.

Should all prayers be immediately answered according to our selfish desires and our limited understanding, then there would be little or no suffering, sorrow, disappointment, or even death; and if these were not, there would also be an absence of joy, success, resurrection, eternal life, and godhood. ("Tragedy or Destiny," *Improvement Era,* March 1966, pp. 180, 210.)

ALMA 18:9 *Horses and chariots*

Two major questions have been raised by anti-LDS critics of the Book of Mormon concerning the statement that there were horses and chariots on the American continents before the time of Christ (Alma 18:9). These critics have maintained: (1) no horses existed on the American continents before the time of Columbus, and (2) the people who lived on the American continents did not know the principle of the wheel before the coming of Columbus. However, since the publication of the Book of Mormon, considerable archaeological evidence has come forth to reinforce its claims that there were horses on the American continents before the time of Columbus and that these early peoples did know the principle of the wheel.

ALMA 18:13 *Meaning of the word "Rabbanah"*

The Lamanite word "Rabbanah," meaning "powerful or great king," is strikingly similar to other Semitic words having essentially the same meaning. For example, the New Testament word *rabboni* clearly refers to one who is a leader (John 20:16). Also the word *rabbi,* which is used frequently by Jewish people, designates "one who teaches or leads." That the spoken language of both the Nephites and the Lamanites is derived from the Hebrew is made quite clear in several places in the Book of Mormon. In fact, even as late as the fourth century A.D. one Book of Mormon prophet said, ". . . if our plates had been sufficiently large we should have written in Hebrew." (Mormon 9:33.)

ALMA 18:23 *Possible meaning of the word "guile"*

Although the word *guile* is frequently used to mean "deceitful cunning" or "treachery," it can also denote the use of strategy. It is evidently used in the latter sense in Alma 18:23; in other words, Ammon *planned* or *used strategy* in arranging the questions he asked King Lamoni.

ALMA 19 *Abish, the Lamanitish woman*

If for no other reason, Abish, the Lamanitish woman, is distinguished because her actual name appears in the Book of Mormon. She is one of only three women in the entire Nephite-Lamanite-Mulekite-Jaredite records to have her name in the Book of Mormon. The other two are Sariah, the wife of Lehi (1 Nephi 2:5), and Isabel, the harlot (Alma 39:3).

The brief account of the conversion of Abish is not clear. The statement that Abish had been converted "unto the Lord for many years, on account of a remarkable vision of her father" (Alma 19:16) may have two possible interpretations. One interpretation is that Abish herself had this vision and in her vision she saw her father. Another possible interpretation is that the vision was actually had by the father of Abish. Regardless of which interpretation is correct, this conversion of Abish plays an important role in converting large numbers of Lamanites.

208

ALMA 20:2-3 *The four sons of Mosiah and their missionary companions*

The Book of Mormon does not specifically state how many missionary companions accompanied the four sons of Mosiah on their long-term mission (about fourteen years!—see Mosiah 28:1, 8-9; Alma 17:6; Alma 16:21); yet the record clearly indicates there were additional missionaries (Mosiah 28:1; Alma 22:35), and at least two of them, Muloki and Ammah, are mentioned by name (Alma 20:2-3).

ALMA 21:2 *The wicked Amalekites and Amulonites*

The Amalekites are mentioned for the first time in Alma 21:2; the exact source of their name is never made clear in the Book of Mormon. The Amulonites mentioned here are the descendants and the followers of Amulon, the wicked priest of King Noah. (Mosiah 23:31-35; Mosiah 24:3-4.) Both of these groups of people believed in the "order of the Nehors" (Alma 21:4; read also Alma 1:2-6, 15-16), and they were so hardened in wickedness that only one Amalekite and no Amulonites were converted by the four sons of Mosiah and their companions (Alma 23:14).

ALMA 22:18 *What does it mean "to give away" all one's sins?*

The king of the Lamanites promised the Lord, "I will give away all my sins to know thee." (Alma 22:18.) As is evident in his subsequent life, the king was promising the Lord that he would repent of all of his sins, forsake them, and start keeping the commandments of God. Some students of the Book of Mormon have wondered concerning the miraculous and almost instantaneous conversions of King Lamoni (Alma 18:40-43 and 19:1-36) and the king of the Lamanites (Alma 22:15-23). However, it is possible for people to be immediately converted to the gospel if they are sincere in wanting to repent of their sins and in learning the truth. Concerning how long it takes a person to repent, Heber C. Kimball said:

On the day of Pentecost, when Peter proclaimed the Gospel, about 3,000 souls were added to the Church that day. How long did it take them to repent? No longer than they were willing to believe, and put away their sins, with a determination to forsake them, and not sin again. (*Journal of Discourses*, 1:36.)

ALMA 22:32 *The narrow neck of land*

One of the most widely quoted verses concerning the geography of Book of Mormon lands is Alma 22:32, wherein the historian states that "the land of Nephi and the land of Zarahemla were nearly surrounded by water, there being a small neck of land between the land northward and the land southward." Earlier in this verse the historian mentions that "it was only the distance of a day and a half's journey for a Nephite, on the line Bountiful and the land Desolation, from the east to the west sea."

Some students of the Book of Mormon interpret this verse to mean that the entire narrow neck of land separating the land northward from the land southward could be traversed by a Nephite in a day and a half. However, a careful reading of this verse does not necessarily justify this conclusion. The historian's statement concerning a line "from the east to the west sea" does not necessarily mean the same as though he had said that the line existed from the east *sea* to the west sea. The statement may mean that it was a day and a half's journey for a Nephite from the east *of the line* to the west sea.

In Helaman 4:7 the author mentions this same area again: "And there they did fortify against the Lamanites, from the west sea, even unto the east; it being a day's journey for a Nephite, on the line which they had fortified." Again, note that the word *sea* does not follow the word *east*. Also, a Nephite can now travel this distance in only one day's journey, and it is quite clear the distance being covered is "the line which they had fortified" and not necessarily the distance between two seas.

ALMA 23:17 *Possible meanings of the term "Anti-Nephi-Lehi"*

The Lamanites converted by the four sons of Mosiah and their missionary companions took upon themselves the name of "Anti-Nephi-Lehies." (Alma 23:17; Alma 24:1-5.) The "Nephi-Lehi" part of the title probably had reference to the lands of Nephi and Lehi (or the people then living in those lands) rather than to the descendants of Nephi or Lehi.

However, Dr. Hugh Nibley has found "a Semitic and common Indo-European root corresponding to anti that means 'in the face of' or 'facing,' as of one facing a mirror,

210 and by extension either 'one who opposes' or 'one who imitates.' " (Quoted in Eldin Ricks, *Book of Mormon Study Guide*, p. 63.) Thus the term "Anti-Nephi-Lehies" might refer to those who imitate the teachings of the descendants of Nephi and Lehi.

ALMA 24:16-17 *A possible source for a tradition of the American Indians*

The converted Lamanites (Anti-Nephi-Lehies) refused to take up their arms against their brethren because, as they stated, "it has been all that we could do, (as we were the most lost of all mankind) to repent of all our sins." (Alma 24:6, 11.) As part of a covenant with God that they would give up their own lives rather than shed the blood of anyone else in time of war, they "took their swords, and all the weapons which were used for the shedding of man's blood, and they did bury them up deep in the earth." (Alma 24:17.) It is entirely possible that this interesting incident could have served as the source of the "bury-the-hatchet" tradition of showing peace, which was a common practice among some of the tribes of American Indians when Columbus and other white men came to their lands.

ALMA 24:19 *Problems of writing on plates of ore*

Mormon wrote his abridgment of the large plates of Nephi on "plates of ore" that he had made with his own hands. He does not mention the technique used in writing the language characters on the metal plates (etching, embossing, etc.), but students have sometimes wondered how Mormon could correct something he had already written. Alma 24:19 might give us some clue to this matter. Concerning the converted Lamanites, Mormon had written that "they buried their weapons of peace." Then, evidently realizing that he had not intended exactly what he had written, he added "or they buried the weapons of war, for peace." Other examples of similar changes in the Book of Mormon are found in Mosiah 7:8, Alma 50:32, Helaman 3:33, and 3 Nephi 16:4.

ALMA 29:8 *The Lord giveth to all nations that which "he seeth fit that they should have"*

Sometimes it is difficult to understand why some groups of people are given so much more knowledge than other groups, especially when one remembers we are all children of our Heavenly Father and thus are spiritual brothers and sisters to each other. However, we should remember that we will be judged according to that knowledge and those opportunities which we have. Thus, simply because one group of people has less knowledge or understanding than another does not mean they are less worthy or righteous. Alma says: " . . . the Lord doth grant unto all nations, of their own nation and tongue . . . all that he seeth fit that they should have." (Alma 29:8.) We should not presume to judge why God deals with nations the way that he does, but should acknowledge that this is all done in the wisdom and justice of God.

ALMA 30:6-59   *Some of the teachings of Korihor, the anti-Christ*

The teachings of the anti-Christs in the Book of Mormon are essentially the same, although Korihor adds a few teachings to those proposed by Nehor. Some of the major teachings of Korihor are: (1) No man can know of anything which is to come—Alma 30:13. (2) Prophecies are simply foolish traditions—Alma 30:14. (3) "Ye cannot know of things which ye do not see"—Alma 30:15. (4) There is no such thing as sin and, therefore, there is no need for an atonement and you do not receive a remission of your sins—Alma 30:16-17. (5) There is no existence after death—Alma 30:18. (6) God is "a being who never has been seen or known, who never was nor ever will be"—Alma 30:28.

In essence, Korihor denies the existence of God, the need for a Savior, the power of the priesthood, and the power of prophecy. He apparently accepts only those things which he can perceive through the five physical senses.

ALMA 30:6, 12, 30-59   *Was Korihor an agnostic or an atheist?*

The position of the agnostic is "I don't know whether or not there is a God, but I don't believe there is; furthermore, I don't believe anyone can *know* that there is a God." The atheistic position is "I *know* there is not a God." This position cannot be defended by reason or logic, for how can a person *know* there is no God unless he has the power of God to see everything and everywhere in the entire universe at one time? Perhaps Alma had this fallacy in mind when he

212   told Korihor, "I know that thou believest, but *thou art possessed with a lying spirit.*" (Alma 30:42. Italics added.) Korihor's position in Alma 30:48 is essentially that of the agnostic: "I do not deny the existence of a God, but I do not believe that there is a God."

Inasmuch as it is impossible to prove there is *not* a God, some people have also tried to argue that it is impossible to prove there is a God. However, this argument does not necessarily follow. God can be, and has been, proven to many people. James E. Talmage suggests that "the evidence upon which mankind rest their conviction regarding the existence of a Supreme Being, may be classified for convenience of consideration under the three following heads: (1) the evidence of history and tradition, (2) the evidence furnished by the exercise of human reason, (3) the conclusive evidence of direct revelation from God. (*Articles of Faith,* p. 30.) The Book of Mormon is primarily concerned with the highest or most conclusive evidence—direct revelation from God.

ALMA 30:29-30   *The trial of Korihor*

When the people resisted Korihor and his teachings, they "caused that he should be bound; and they delivered him up into the hands of the officers." (Alma 30:29.) The officers before whom Korihor was taken included Alma (who was the religious leader) and Nephihah ("the chief judge who was governor over all the land"—Alma 30:29). The fact that Korihor was brought before Alma would seem to indicate that Korihor was or had been a member of the church.

ALMA 31:13-18, 26-35   *How should we pray?*

Several places in the scriptures the prophets have warned us to avoid "vain repetition" in our prayers and have encouraged us to pray according to our needs and sincere feelings. This chapter contains classic examples both of what we should not do and what we should do when praying. The example of a wrong prayer is the memorized, rote prayer of the apostate Zoramites. (Alma 31:15-18.) The example of an effective prayer is the humble and sincere petition of Alma. (Alma 31:26-35.)

ALMA 31:15-18   *The unvarying prayer of the apostate Zoramites*

Notice how many elements of apostasy are indicated in the set prayer of the apostate Zoramites: (1) They believe God is a spirit only (verse 15). (2) They do not believe in the divinity of Jesus Christ (verse 16). (3) They do not accept the teachings of the prophets because the "tradition" of their brethren "was handed down to them by the childishness of their fathers"; nevertheless, they readily accepted some of the false teachings or "traditions" which had been passed down by other people (verse 16). (4) They believe in "double predestination"—i.e., God has "elected" them to be saved, but he has elected everyone else to be cast down to hell (verses 17 and 18). Also, note other common practices of religious groups in a state of apostasy: the repetition of memorized prayers in worship, and the relegation of religion to a "Sunday" activity (verses 22 and 23).

ALMA 31:21   *The Rameumptom or holy stand*

The name of the holy stand of the apostate Zoramites, upon which they stood when they offered their weekly prayer, was the "Rameumptom." Although this name may look strange in English, it has appropriate Semitic roots recognizable to students of Semitic languages. The preface "ram" is frequently used to indicate a high place. For example, later in the Book of Mormon we read of the hill Ramah. Also, in modern Israel are the town of Ramallah (located in the tops of the Judean hills just north of Jerusalem) and Rameem (which literally means "the heights" and is located on the top of the hills near the Lebanese border).

ALMA 32:10-11   *Which day of the week is the "right" day to worship God?*

Each day of the week is used by one or more religious groups as the "official" day of worship. In the United States, Saturday and Sunday are the major days of worship: Saturday for the Jewish groups and the Seventh-day Adventists, Sunday for the Catholic and most of the Protestant churches. The prophet Alma indicates that we should worship God at all times and should not restrict our worship of him to just one day a week. He also clearly indicates we do not have to be in a synagogue or church in order to worship God.

214 ALMA 32:12-14   *What does it mean to be "compelled to be humble"?*

Whenever people do not humble themselves before God or even think of God except in times of dire need or danger, they are being "compelled to be humble" through the seriousness of the circumstance. Such people are more blessed than those who never think of God, but how much better it would be for them if they were humble and prayerful before God at all times—in prosperity as well as in poverty, in health as well as sickness.

ALMA 32:17-43   *Alma's teachings on the subject of faith*

Perhaps the definition of faith most widely quoted by Latter-day Saints is the one given by Alma: "Faith is not to have a perfect knowledge of things; therefore if ye have faith ye hope for things which are not seen, which are true." (Alma 32:21.) This definition is even more complete and meaningful than the definition given by Paul as recorded in our present New Testament: "Now faith is the substance of things hoped for, the evidence of things not seen." (Hebrews 11:1.)

It is interesting to note that both of these prophets include hope as an element of faith; yet, as Alma points out, faith is more than mere hope or the "desire to believe." (Alma 32:26-27.) On the other hand, faith is *not* knowledge, "for if a man knoweth a thing" he has no need to exercise faith or even to believe, for "he knoweth it." (Alma 32:18.) Alma's comparison of faith to the planting of a seed beautifully and clearly illustrates this principle. (Alma 32:28-43.) One of the best expositions of the distinctions between belief, faith, and knowledge is that given by Elder James E. Talmage:

The terms faith and belief are sometimes regarded as synonyms; nevertheless each of them has a specific meaning in our language, although in earlier usage there was little distinction between them, and therefore the words are used interchangeably in many scriptural passages. Belief, in one of its accepted senses, may consist in a merely intellectual assent, while faith implies such confidence and conviction as will impel to action. Dictionary authority justifies us in drawing a distinction between the two, according to present usage in English; and this authority defines belief as a mental assent to the truth or actuality of anything, excluding, however, the moral element of responsibility through such assent, which responsibility is included by faith. Belief is in a sense passive, an agreement or acceptance only; faith is active and positive, embracing such reliance and confidence as will lead to works. Faith in Christ comprises belief in Him, combined with trust in Him. One cannot have faith without belief; yet he may believe and still lack faith. Faith is vivified, vitalized, living belief.

. . . Neither belief nor its superior, actual knowledge, is efficient to save; for neither of these is faith. If belief be a product of the mind, faith is of the heart; belief is founded on reason, faith largely on intuition. . . .

The mere possession of knowledge gives no assurance of benefit therefrom. It is said that during an epidemic of cholera in a great city, a scientific man proved to his own satisfaction, by chemical and microscopical tests, that the water supply was infected, and that through it contagion was being spread. He proclaimed the fact throughout the city, and warned all against the use of unboiled water. Many of the people, although incapable of comprehending his methods of investigation, far less of repeating such for themselves, had faith in his warning words, followed his instructions, and escaped the death to which their careless and unbelieving fellows succumbed. Their faith was a saving one. To the man himself, the truth by which so many lives had been spared was a matter of knowledge. He had actually perceived, under the microscope, proof of the existence of death-dealing germs in the water; he had demonstrated their virulence; he knew of what he spoke. Nevertheless, in a moment of forgetfulness he drank of the unsterilized water, and soon thereafter died, a victim to the plague. His knowledge did not save him, convincing though it was; yet others, whose reliance was only that of confidence or faith in the truth that he declared, escaped the threatening destruction. He had knowledge; but, was he wise? Knowledge is to wisdom what belief is to faith, one an abstract principle, the other a living application. Not possession merely, but the proper use of knowledge constitutes wisdom. (*Articles of Faith*, pp. 96-100.)

ALMA 33:3-17 *The strong testimonies of Zenos and Zenock*

The prophets Zenos and Zenock are mentioned several times in the Book of Mormon, and each time they are mentioned we learn something new about these remarkable prophets. In 1 Nephi 19:10-17 we read of the strong and clear witness of these prophets concerning the divine mission of Jesus Christ, and here in Alma 33:17 we learn that at least one of these prophets, Zenock, sealed his testimony with his

216   life, for the people of his day "stoned him to death."

ALMA 33:19   *A "type" of the coming of Jesus Christ*

In his discourse on the coming life and mission of Jesus Christ, Alma mentions the testimonies of several earlier prophets concerning this event, including this statement about Moses: ". . . he was spoken of by Moses; yea, and behold a type was raised up in the wilderness, that whosoever would look upon it might live. And many did look and live." (Alma 33:19.)

The "type" mentioned by Alma evidently refers to the brass serpent that was lifted up on a pole by Moses when he was leading the people of Israel out of Egypt. This symbol is discussed later in the Book of Mormon; see the material listed after Helaman 8:13-15.

ALMA 34:9-16   *For a discussion of the major points covered in these verses, see the material listed after Mosiah 3:15-27.*

ALMA 34:32-35   *Is it possible to repent after death?*

We should not conclude from these statements by Amulek that it is impossible for a person to repent once he has left this earth life. Other scriptures indicate that repentance may be obtained under certain conditions beyond the veil of mortality. For example, Peter mentions that after the crucifixion of Jesus Christ, the Savior "preached unto the spirits" of those who had died during the days of Noah (1 Peter 3:18-20) so that they "might be judged according to men in the flesh, but live according to God in the spirit" (1 Peter 4:6). However, we do not know the full conditions of repentance in the post-earthly spirit world, and, as Brother Talmage has stated, ". . . to suppose that the soul who has wilfully rejected the opportunity of repentance in this life will find it easy to repent there is contrary to reason. To procrastinate the day of repentance is to deliberately place ourselves in the power of the adversary." (*Articles of Faith,* p. 115.)

ALMA 34:33   *What is the "night of darkness" wherein no labor can be performed?*

Amulek warns us not to procrastinate the day of our repentance, because if we do not improve our time while in this life, "then cometh the night of darkness wherein there can be no labor performed." (Alma 34:33.) The "night of darkness" referred to by Amulek is that period of a person's existence when he loses the *will* to repent. Thus when a person loses the desire to repent or decides he is not going to repent, then his "night of darkness" has come whether it is in this life or in the life to come.

ALMA 34:34-35   *Danger of deathbed repentance*

Several weaknesses and dangers are inherent in the doctrine of deathbed repentance. One of these is that we never know when we are going to die; therefore, there may not be time to repent. Furthermore, as Amulek warns us, "Ye cannot say, when ye are brought to that awful crisis [death], that I will repent, that I will return to my God. Nay, ye cannot say this; for that same spirit which doth possess your bodies at the time that ye go out of this life, that same spirit will have power to possess your body in that eternal world." (Alma 34:34.) Then Amulek counsels us to repent of our sins so that we will be prepared for death whenever it should come. Essentially this same advice is given by President Lorenzo Snow:

All men and women who are worthy to be called Latter-day Saints should live hour by hour in such a way that if they should be called suddenly from this life into the next they would be prepared. The preparation should be such that we should not fear to be called away suddenly into the spirit life. It is our privilege to so live as to have the spirit of light and intelligence to that extent that we shall feel satisfied that all will be well if we should be called away at any hour. (*Conference Report,* October 1899, p. 2.)

ALMA 36:6-10   *Is there a discrepancy between Alma 36:10 and Mosiah 27:23?*

Some readers of the Book of Mormon have claimed there is a discrepancy in the accounts of the conversion of Alma as recorded in Mosiah 27:23 and Alma 36:10. It is true that one account mentions "two days and two nights" and the other says "three days and three nights," but there is no apparent discrepancy because they are not referring to exactly the same thing. In the account in the book of Mosiah the time element clearly refers to the period of fasting by the priests; no exact length of time is indicated for Alma's unconscious state. Note the major details of the account: After Alma was confronted by an angel and realized the enormity of his sins, he fell to the earth almost as if dead. Then he was carried to his father in this helpless condition. The father of Alma then called in the priests of the church and *"after they had fasted and prayed for the space of two days and two nights,* the limbs of Alma received their strength, and he stood up." (Mosiah 27:22-23. Italics added.) In the account in the book of Alma, however, the term "three days and three nights" clearly refers to the *total time* Alma could not open his mouth nor use his limbs. (Alma 36:10.)

ALMA 36:14   *The "murder" of spiritual life*

In recounting his sinful past to his son Helaman, Alma said that he had "murdered" many people, and then he adds, "or rather led them away unto destruction." (Alma 36:14.) As Alma mentions later to his son Corianton, the murder of a human physical body is a grave sin. However, an even more serious sin is to murder the spiritual life of a person or, in other words, to purposely lead one away from the saving principles of the gospel. Concerning such people Alma says: ". . . whosoever murdereth against the light and knowledge of God, it is not easy for him to obtain forgiveness." (Alma 39:6.)

ALMA 37:23, 38   *Use of the words "Gazelem" and "Liahona"*

Two interesting words that appear for the first time in the book of Alma are *Gazelem* (Alma 37:23) and *Liahona* (Alma 37:38). Possible meanings of these two words are given by Reynolds and Sjodahl as follows:

Gazelem is a name given to a servant of God. The word appears to have its roots in Gaz—a stone, and Aleim, a name of God as a revelator, or the interposer in the affairs of men. If this suggestion is correct, its roots admirably agree with its apparent meaning—a seer.

Liahona. This interesting word is Hebrew with an Egyptian ending. It is the name which Lehi gave to the ball or director he found outside his tent the very day he began his long journey through the "wilderness" after his little company had rested for some time in the Valley of Lemuel. (1 Nephi 16:10; Alma 37:88)

L is a Hebrew preposition meaning "to," and sometimes used to express the possessive case. *Iah* is a Hebrew abbreviated form of "Jehovah," common in Hebrew names. *On* is the Hebrew name of the Egyptian "City of the Sun." . . . *L-iah-on* means, therefore, literally, "To God is Light"; or, "of God is Light." That is to say, God gives light, as does the Sun. The final *a* reminds us that the Egyptian form of the Hebrew name *On* is *Annu,* and that seems to be the form Lehi used. (*Commentary on the Book of Mormon,* 4:162, 178.)

ALMA 37:35-37 *Learn wisdom—learn to keep the commandments of God*

The word *wisdom* in the Book of Mormon is used to denote the wise or effective use of knowledge; it not only concerns the acquisition of knowledge, but also the right use of knowledge. To Alma some of the best advice he could leave his son Helaman was to "learn wisdom in thy youth; yea, learn in thy youth to keep the commandments of God." (Alma 37:35.) Wise indeed is the person who will learn the commandments of God and then obey them so he can receive the promised blessings.

ALMA 37:38-46 *"It is . . . easy to give heed to the word of Christ"*

The Liahona was given to Lehi and his colony to direct them in their journey to the promised land. All they needed to do was exercise faith in God, and the Liahona would show the direction they were to go. Alma compares living the laws of the gospel with following the guidance of the Liahona: ". . . it is as easy to give heed to the word of Christ, which will point to you a straight course to eternal bliss, as it was for our fathers to give heed to this compass, which would point unto them a straight course to the promised land." (Alma 37:44.) Thus Alma indicates it is relatively easy to heed the word of Christ—just keep the commandments. However, he warns Helaman and also us not to "be slothful because of the easiness of the way." (Alma 37:46.)

ALMA 38:9-14 *The counsel of Alma to his son Shiblon*

Although Alma's counsel to his son Shiblon occupies only one brief chapter in the Book of Mormon, yet it is filled with good advice for young people of all times and places. Among other things, Alma counsels Shiblon (and, indirectly, all of us): (1) to "learn wisdom . . . that there is no other way or means whereby man can be saved, only in and through Christ"; (2) to teach the word of God; (3) to "be diligent and temperate in all things"; (4) to be humble—not to boast of wisdom or strength; (5) to "use boldness, but not overbearance"; (6) to bridle the passions; (7) to refrain from idleness; (8) to pray with sincerity of heart and not "to be heard of men"; (9) to acknowledge unworthiness before God and to ask him for forgiveness of sin.

ALMA 39:3 *Isabel, the harlot*

The harlot Isabel is one of only three women mentioned by name in our present Book of Mormon from the entire Nephite-Lamanite-Mulekite-Jaredite records. The other two women mentioned are Sariah, the wife of Lehi (1 Nephi 2:5), and Abish, the Lamanite woman (Alma 19:16).

ALMA 39:1-6 *The sins of murder and adultery*

Although the Lord has not provided an extensive list of sins in the order of their severity, he has indicated the following as the three most grievous or serious sins a person can commit on this earth: (1) the unpardonable sin of denying the Holy Ghost once it has had place in you, (2) murder, or the shedding of innocent blood, and (3) unchastity. The unpardonable sin will be discussed in greater detail in the next note. Concerning murder, the authorities of the Church have published the following brief statement:

> One of the most serious of all sins and crimes against the Lord's plan of salvation is the sin of murder or the destruction of human life. It seems clear that to be guilty of destroying life is the act of "rebellion" against the plan of the Almighty by denying an individual thus destroyed in mortality, the privilege of a full experience in this earth-school of opportunity. It is in the same category as the rebellion of Satan and his hosts and therefore it would not be surprising if the penalties to be imposed upon a murderer were to be of similar character as the penalties meted out to those spirits which were cast out of heaven with Satan. (Quoted in Doxey, *The Doctrine and Covenants Speaks,* 1:240.)

The teaching of the Church is equally strong on the sin of unchastity or adultery, as is indicated by the following statement by Joseph Fielding Smith:

> I call your attention to this statement by the Prophet Joseph Smith: "If a man commit adultery, he cannot receive the celestial kingdom of God. Even if he is saved in any kingdom, it cannot be the celestial kingdom."

> Of course, a man may, according to the Doctrine and Covenants, 132:26, receive forgiveness, if he is willing to pay the penalty for such a crime: that is he "shall be destroyed in the flesh,

and shall be delivered unto the buffetings of Satan unto the day of redemption," which is the time of the resurrection. We cannot destroy in the flesh, so what the Lord will require in lieu thereof, I do not know. . . .

We have been taught that adultery is a crime second only to the shedding of innocent blood. We cannot treat it lightly. For a man to destroy another man's home is too serious an offense to be readily forgiven. Such a man should not be permitted to come back in the Church, under any circumstances, at least until years have elapsed. He should be placed on probation for that length of time to see if he can, or will, remain clean. Even then I confess I do not know what disposition the Lord will make of him. To permit him to come back within a short time has a very evil effect upon other members of the Church who begin to think that this enormous crime is not so serious after all. . . .

If a man thinks the Lord has placed upon him a seal by which he is exempt from his transgressions and is bound to inherit eternal life, no matter what he does, as long as he does not commit murder, or shed innocent blood, or deny the Holy Ghost, he is in the gall of bitterness, as a Nephite prophet would have said.

No man is promised salvation who is not cleansed from all his sins, and if a man sins deliberately, thinking he is exempt, he will be damned! (*Doctrines of Salvation,* 2:93-94, 99.)

ALMA 39:4-7　*What is the difference between an "unpardonable" and an "unforgivable" sin?*

In the counsel to his son Corianton, Alma indicates that the three most serious sins a person can commit on this earth are (1) the sin against the Holy Ghost, (2) murder—the shedding of innocent blood, and (3) unchastity. The Lord indicates the seriousness of all these sins in his revelations to Joseph Smith as recorded in the Doctrine and Covenants. The most serious of these sins is to deny the Holy Ghost and become a son of perdition. The Lord has defined this sin in these words:

Thus saith the Lord concerning all those who know my power, and have been made partakers thereof, and suffered themselves through the power of the devil to be overcome, and to deny the truth and defy my power—

They are they who are the sons of perdition, of whom I say that it had been better for them never to have been born;

For they are vessels of wrath, doomed to suffer the wrath of God, with the devil and his angels in eternity;

Concerning whom I have said there is no forgiveness in this

222   world nor in the world to come—

Having denied the Holy Spirit after having received it, and having denied the Only Begotten Son of the Father, having crucified him unto themselves and put him to an open shame.

These are they who shall go away into the lake of fire and brimstone, with the devil and his angels—

And the only ones on whom the second death shall have any power. (D&C 76:31-37.)

This is an *unpardonable* sin because it cannot be paid for (or pardoned) either by the sinner himself or through the atonement of Jesus Christ.

The second most serious sin is to commit murder—that is, to willfully shed innocent blood. Concerning this sin, the Lord has said: "Thou shalt not kill; and he that kills shall not have forgiveness in this world, nor in the world to come." (D&C 42:18.) Thus this is an *unforgivable* sin, which means that Jesus Christ cannot pay for (or "atone for" or "foregive") the penalty demanded by the broken law. This sin is a pardonable sin, however; that is, the sinner can eventually make full payment himself, and be received into a state of pardon. Apparently one reason this sin is unforgivable is that forgiveness is based upon repentance, and a murderer cannot fully repent of his sin for he cannot make restitution of the life he has taken.

The third most serious sin is unchastity. The Lord has said, "Thou shalt not commit adultery; and he that committeth adultery, and repenteth not, shall be cast out. But he that has committed adultery and repents with all his heart, and forsaketh it, and doeth it no more, thou shalt forgive; But if he doeth it again, he shall not be forgiven, but shall be cast out." (D&C 42:24-26.) Thus adultery is both pardonable and forgivable, but if committed again after a person understands the law it is unforgivable.

The word *pardon* as used in the scriptures means to be sanctified, to be clean, to reach a point where a broken law has no further claim upon the sinner. Thus the most serious sin is *unpardonable* because the law will always have a claim upon the sinner, and the sinner will always remain unclean; he cannot ever regain the presence of God, for "no unclean thing can enter into his kingdom." (3 Nephi 27:19.) All unpardonable sins are of necessity also unforgivable.

The word *forgiveness* as used in the scriptures indicates

one is "given something before." Thus when a person repents of a sin, Jesus Christ, through his atonement, pays for (or atones for) part of the broken law *before* the person makes *full* payment. Thus he is "fore-given" that part of the penalty paid for by Jesus Christ. Forgiveness is possible only upon repentance; thus those who refuse to repent "remain as though there had been no redemption made, except it be the loosing of the bands of death." (Alma 11:41; read also D&C 19:15-20.)

ALMA 39:9   *What does it mean to "cross yourself"?*

In his patriarchal blessing to his son Corianton, Alma says: "I would that ye should repent and forsake your sins, and go no more after the lusts of your eyes, but cross yourself in all these things; for except ye do this ye can in nowise inherit the kingdom of God. Oh, remember, and take it upon you, and cross yourself in these things." (Alma 39:9.) The question is sometimes asked concerning the meaning of the expression "cross yourself in all these things." Some people evidently read into this statement something that is not intended; they think it pertains to the practice of physically drawing a cross as it is done by members of some Christian churches.

The meaning of the expression "cross yourself" is clarified in other scriptures. For example, 3 Nephi 12:30 says: "For it is better that ye should deny yourselves of these things, wherein ye will take up your cross, than that ye should be cast into hell." In Matthew 16:24 the Savior says, "If any man will come after me, let him deny himself, and take up his cross, and follow me." Both of these scriptures indicate that to "cross yourself" means to deny yourself. In the Inspired Version of the New Testament the Savior makes it absolutely clear that this is the meaning of the term: "And now for a man to take up his cross, is to deny himself all ungodliness, and every worldly lust, and keep my commandments." (Matthew 16:26.)

ALMA 40:11-14   *Where is the post-earthly spirit world?*

Alma's statement that "the spirits of all men" upon death "are taken home to that God who gave them life" apparently does not mean that the post-earthly spirit world is in the actual, physical presence of God the Father. Concerning this statement by Alma, Brigham Young has said:

It reads that the spirit goes to God who gave it. Let me render this Scripture a little plainer; when the spirits leave their bodies they are in the presence of our Father and God; they are prepared then to see, hear and understand spiritual things. But where is the spirit world? It is incorporated within this celestial system. Can you see it with your natural eyes? No. Can you see spirits in this room? No. Suppose the Lord should touch your eyes that you might see, could you then see the spirits? Yes, as plainly as you now see bodies. . . . (Ludlow, *Latter-day Prophets Speak,* p. 26.)

Concerning the location of the post-earthly spirit world, President Young has said further:

When you lay down this tabernacle, where are you going? Into the spiritual world. . . . Where is the spirit world? It is right here. Do the good and evil spirits go together? Yes, they do. Do they both inhabit one kingdom? Yes, they do. Do they go to the sun? No. Do they go beyond the boundaries of the organized earth? No, they do not. They are brought forth upon this earth, for the express purpose of inhabiting it to all eternity. Where else are you going? No where else, only as you may be permitted. (Ibid., p. 26.)

The above two statements by Brigham Young would indicate that the post-earthly spirit world is not the same place as the world of resurrected beings. This is also the teaching of Parley P. Pratt:

The world of resurrected beings, and the world of spirits, are two distinct spheres, as much so as our own sphere is distinct from that of the spirit world.

Where then does the spirit go, on its departure from its earthly tabernacle? It passes to the next sphere of human existence, called the world of spirits, a vail being drawn between us in the flesh, and that world of spirits. Well, says one, is there no more than one place in the spirit world? Yes, there are many places and degrees in that world, as in this. Jesus Christ, when absent from his flesh, did not ascend to the Father, to be crowned, and enthroned in power. Why? Because he had not yet a resurrected body, and had therefore a mission to perform in another sphere. Where then did he go? To the world of spirits. . . . (*Journal of Discourses,* 1:9.)

Heber C. Kimball, a member of the First Presidency for many years, suggested that we will never go back to the actual presence of God the Father until we are fully worthy of this honor.

When we escape from this earth, we suppose we are going to heaven? Do you suppose you are going to the earth that Adam came from? that Eloheim came from? where Jehovah the Lord came from? No. When you have learned to become obedient to the Father that dwells upon this earth, to the Father and God of this earth, and obedient to the messengers He sends—when you have done all that, remember you are not going to leave this earth. You will never leave it until you become qualified, and capable, and capacitated to become a father of an earth yourselves. (Ibid., p. 356.)

ALMA 40:12 *The status of people in the post-earthly spirit world*

Alma is told by an angel of God that there are two major divisions in the post-earthly spirit world: (1) paradise, which is "a state of rest, a state of peace" (Alma 40:12), and (2) outer darkness, where the "spirits of the wicked, yea, who are evil" go and there shall be "weeping, and wailing, and gnashing of teeth, and this because of their own iniquity" (Alma 40:13).

Even those who go into paradise will not know perfect happiness, however. Perfect joy or happiness is possible only in a resurrected state, as is indicated in this statement from the Doctrine and Covenants: "For man is spirit. The elements are eternal, and spirit and element, inseparably connected, receive a fulness of joy; And when separated, man cannot receive a fulness of joy." (D&C 93:33-34.)

Essentially this same idea is taught by Orson Pratt:

When our spirits leave these bodies, will they be happy? Not perfectly so. Why? Because the spirit is absent from the body; it cannot be perfectly happy while a part of the man is lying in the earth. How can the happiness be complete when only a part of the redemption is accomplished? You cannot be perfectly happy until you get a new house. You will be happy, you will be at ease in paradise; but still you will be looking for a house where your spirit can enter, and act as you did in former times, only more perfectly, having superior powers. Consequently, all the holy men that have lived in days of old, have looked forward to the resurrection of their bodies; for then their glory will be complete. (*Journal of Discourses,* 1:289-90.)

ALMA 40:14-26 *A clarification of the teachings of Alma on the resurrection*

Alma admits he is not sure whether or not all of the people who died before the resurrection of Jesus Christ will be resurrected before any of the people who died after the time of Christ. (Alma 40:18-21.) However, he says, "I give it

226   as my opinion, that the souls and the bodies are reunited, of the righteous, at the resurrection of Christ." (Alma 40:20.) Alma is correct, of course, in this assumption. Other prophets in the Book of Mormon make it clear that the righteous who have died will be resurrected at the time of the resurrection of the Savior. For example, Abinadi prophesied as follows:

> And now, the resurrection of all the prophets, and all those that have believed in their words, or all those that have kept the commandments of God, shall come forth in the first resurrection; therefore, they are the first resurrection.
>
> They are raised to dwell with God who has redeemed them; thus they have eternal life through Christ, who has broken the bands of death.
>
> And these are those who have part in the first resurrection; and these are they that have died before Christ came, in their ignorance, not having salvation declared unto them. And thus the Lord bringeth about the restoration of these; and they have a part in the first resurrection, or have eternal life, being redeemed by the Lord.
>
> And little children also have eternal life.
>
> But behold, and fear, and tremble before God, for ye ought to tremble; for the Lord redeemeth none such that rebel against him and die in their sins; yea, even all those that have perished in their sins ever since the world began, that have wilfully rebelled against God, that have known the commandments of God, and would not keep them; these are they that have no part in the first resurrection. (Mosiah 15:22-26.)

Thus Abinadi makes it very clear that the wicked will have no part in the first resurrection; the wicked, no matter when they lived, will have to wait until the final resurrection. The term "first resurrection" is used in the scriptures as a synonym for "the resurrection of the just." Thus, if one comes forth the first opportunity he has to be resurrected after he dies, he comes forth in the morning of *his* first resurrection.

ALMA 40:23   *The resurrection of the body*

The prophets of the Book of Mormon definitely teach that all mankind will be resurrected from the dead. One of the best descriptions of this resurrected body is provided by Alma wherein he states: "the soul shall be restored to the body, and the body to the soul; yea, and every limb and joint shall be restored to its body; yea, even a hair of the head shall not be lost; but all things shall be restored to their proper and perfect frame." (Alma 40:23.)

The prophets of this dispensation have also taught that the actual, physical body will be resurrected and, through the law of restoration, will essentially become perfect. The Prophet Joseph Smith taught the following concerning the resurrected body:

As concerning the resurrection, I will merely say that all men will come from the grave as they lie down, whether old or young; there will not be "added unto their stature one cubit," neither taken from it; all will be raised by the power of God, having spirit in their bodies, and not blood. Children will be enthroned in the presence of God and the Lamb with bodies of the same stature that they had on earth, having been redeemed by the blood of the Lamb; they will there enjoy the fulness of that light, glory and intelligence, which is prepared in the celestial kingdom. "Blessed are the dead who die in the Lord, for they rest from their labors and their works do follow them." [Revelation 14:13.] (*History of the Church,* 4:555-56.)

Concerning the process of restoring a body to a state of perfection in the resurrection, President Joseph F. Smith has written:

The death that came by the fall of our first parents is eradicated by the resurrection of the Son of God, and you and I cannot help it. You will come forth from your graves, these same mortal bodies as they are now, bearing the marks just as much as Christ's body bore the marks that were upon him. They will come forth from their graves, but they will be immediately immortalized, restored to their perfect frame, limb and joint. And the poor, unfortunate creature who has lost a leg or an arm or a finger will have it restored to its proper frame, every joint to its place, and every part to its part, and it will be made perfect (Alma 40:23), for that is the law of restoration that God has instituted by which His own purpose cannot fail, by which his own designs concerning His children must be consummated. Now this is the restoration I believe in. . . . What is more desirable than that we should meet with our fathers and our mothers, with our brethren and our sisters, with our wives and our children, with our beloved associates and kindred in the spirit world, knowing each other, identifying each other by the marks we knew in the flesh and by the associations that familiarize each to the other in mortal life? What do you want better than that? What is there for any religion superior to that? I know of nothing. . . . (Doxey, *The Latter-day Prophets and the Doctrine and Covenants* [Deseret Book Co., 1963], 3:168.)

Melvin J. Ballard has also provided a description of the resurrected body:

The fact of the resurrection does not depend upon a man's belief or unbelief. It is a fact, whether he believes it or not. But man's state in the resurrection is established by himself; hence the part we can play in planning a glorious resurrection. He has laid down terms by which he will return this house to us not as it was, old and decrepit, but strong, and vigorous and beautiful, for I believe with the prophets, that in the resurrection from the dead, whether it shall take place immediately at the resurrection or thereafter when the restitution of all things comes, there will be no maimed or crippled bodies. (Alma 40:23.)

When you see men and women in the resurrection, we shall see them in the very bloom of their glorious manhood and womanhood, and he has promised all who would keep his commandments and obey the gospel of the Lord Jesus Christ, the restoration of their houses, glorified, immortalized, celestialized, fitted to dwell in the presence of God.

To those who cannot subscribe to those terms, and yet obey others, the lesser law, Jesus has promised a terrestrial body, not so glorious, and yet immortal and eternal, and still to those who cannot do so much, but only obey in part, a telestial body suited to the kingdom in which they dwell. Thus we fix our status in that resurrection, though the resurrection is a fact without our action. Our action makes it either glorious—the resurrection of the just; or the resurrection of the unjust. (*Sermons and Missionary Services of Melvin J. Ballard* [Deseret Book Co., 1949], p. 186.)

President Joseph Fielding Smith also indicated that in the resurrection all things will be restored to their proper and perfect frame:

A little sound thinking will reveal to us that it would be inconsistent for our bodies to be raised with all kinds of imperfections. Some men have been burned at the stake for the sake of truth. Some have been beheaded, and others have had their bodies torn asunder; for example, John the Baptist was beheaded and received his resurrection at the time of the resurrection of our Redeemer. It is impossible for us to think of him coming forth from the dead holding his head in his hands; our reason says he was physically complete in the resurrection. He appeared to the Prophet Joseph Smith and Oliver Cowdery with a perfect resurrected body.

When we come forth from the dead, our spirits and bodies will be reunited inseparably, never again to be divided, and they will then be assigned to the kingdom to which they belong. *All de-*

*formities and imperfections will be removed, and the body will con-
form to the likeness of the spirit,* for the Lord revealed, "that which
is spiritual being in the likeness of that which is temporal; and that
which is temporal in the likeness of that which is spiritual; the spirit
of man in the likeness of his person, as also the spirit of the beast,
and every other creature which God has created." (D&C 77:2.)
(*Doctrines of Salvation,* 2:289.)

ALMA 41:10 *What is the basis of Alma's statement
"wickedness never was happiness"?*

Every law has both a blessing and a punishment affixed
to it. Whenever the law is obeyed, a blessing is given that
results in happiness (joy). Whenever the law is disobeyed, a
punishment is given which results in unhappiness (misery).
Thus "wickedness never was happiness" and it never will be.
(See 2 Nephi 2:13.) Samuel the Lamanite included the same
thought in these words to the wicked Nephites: " . . . ye have
sought all the days of your lives for that which ye could not
obtain; and *ye have sought for happiness in doing iniquity,
which thing is contrary to the nature of* that *righteousness*
which is in our great and Eternal Head." (Helaman 13:38.
Italics added.)

ALMA 42:12-25 *For a discussion of "The Relationship
of the Laws of Justice and Mercy to the Atonement of
Jesus Christ," see the material listed under Mosiah 3:15-
27.*

ALMA 42:22 *Who or what "inflicteth the punishment"
demanded by a broken law?*

Inasmuch as every law has both a punishment and a
blessing affixed to it, punishments (or miseries) are the
natural result of disobedience to the law, whereas blessings
are the natural results of obedience. Thus, when a person
transgresses a law (or sins) and suffering or punishment
results, he brings upon himself the suffering and the "law
inflicteth the punishment." (Read Helaman 14:30-31.) It is
foolish to blame God for our suffering, for if all men were
100 percent righteous there would be no suffering. The
following analogy might help to illustrate this point: If you
counsel a person not to touch a hot stove or he will be
burned, and he then disregards your counsel, touches the hot
stove, and is burned, what caused him to be burned—you or
the stove? Likewise, if the Lord commands you not to do a

230 certain thing or you will suffer, and you then disregard the counsel of the Lord, commit the sin, and then suffer, who caused your suffering—the Lord, or your willful disobedience of divine law?

ALMA chapters 43-62 *The Nephite-Lamanite wars of 74-61* B.C.

One of the most difficult aspects of the reading of this part of the book of Alma is to keep in mind the battlefronts, cities, and leaders involved in each war. The first skirmish in the long struggle took place between Zerahemnah (the Lamanite leader) and Moroni and Lehi (two of the chief Nephite leaders). The account of this struggle is recorded in Alma 43-44. The second phase of the battle occurred when the new Lamanite king, Amalickiah, sent his armies down to attack the Nephite cities of Noah and Ammonihah; however, the Lamanites were quickly and decisively defeated.

The main war started when "Amalickiah did himself come down, at the head of the Lamanites." (Alma 51:12.) There are two major fronts in this war. The battle on the *eastern front* (chapters 51-52, 53:1-7, 54-55, 59-62) concerns the cities of Lehi, Morianton, Omner, Gid, Mulek, Nephihah, and Bountiful. The Nephite leaders are Teancum, Lehi, and Moroni (after he helps fortify the land in the south and the west); the Lamanite leaders are Amalickiah, Jacob, and Ammoron (who soon leaves for the west front for several years and then returns). The battle on the *west sea coast* (chapters 53:8-23; 56-58) involves the cities of Zeezrom, Cumeni, Antiparah, Judea, Manti, and the "city by the sea." The Nephite leaders here are Helaman, Antipus, Gid, and Teomner; the only Lamanite leader named is Ammoron.

It is well to keep in mind that you are not reading about the battles in chronological order. Many of the battles on the eastern front that you read about first actually occurred after some of the major battles on the western front. For example, the "decoy method" of capturing cities was employed by Helaman and Antipus in their attempt to recapture the city of Antiparah on the western front (Alma 56:20, 27-57) before it was used successfully by Moroni and Teancum in recapturing the city of Mulek on the eastern front (Alma 52:19-26).

Mormon inserted a series of letters that help to keep us informed of the proceedings on the two fronts. Note particularly (1) Moroni's letter to Ammoron and Ammoron's angry reply—chapter 54; (2) Helaman's lengthy letter to Moroni—chapters 56-58; (3) Moroni's two letters to Pahoran—chapters 59:3 and 60; and (4) Pahoran's answer to Moroni—chapter 61.

ALMA 43:13   *The "Lamanites" of about 74 B.C.*

For hundreds of years the descendants of Lehi had been divided into two major groups, the Nephites and the Lamanites. These terms were originally used to denote those who followed after the first two major leaders, Nephi and Laman. However, by the period of 74 B.C., several dissident and apostate Nephite groups had joined with the Lamanites and had become known as Lamanites. Thus the historian says the Lamanites "were a compound of Laman and Lemuel, and the sons of Ishmael, and all those who had dissented from the Nephites, who were Amalekites and Zoramites, and the descendants of the priests of Noah." (Alma 43:13.)

The "descendants of the priests of Noah" in this verse refer to Amulon and his brethren, and their descendants. (See Mosiah 23:31-32.) The Zoramites refer to the apostate Nephites who had previously lived in the land of Antionum. The Book of Mormon does not provide any further information concerning the apostate group known as the "Amalekites." The "Amlicites" were another apostate Nephite group that previously had joined with the Lamanites. (See Alma 2 and 3.) However, the Amlicites are not mentioned in this new listing, and whether or not they have any connection with the Amalekites is not made clear.

ALMA 43:17-19   *Military strategy and techniques used by Moroni*

Notice the new and surprising military strategy and techniques used by Moroni in these military campaigns. Moroni prepared his people with breastplates, arm-shields, thick clothing, and shields to protect their heads. (Alma 43:19.) He also fortified the Nephite cities by having the people cast up "heaps of earth round about all the cities. . . . And upon the top of these ridges of earth he caused that there should be

232   timbers . . . built up to the height of a man. . . . And he caused that upon these works of timbers there should be a frame of pickets built . . . and they were strong and high. And he caused towers to be erected that overlooked those works of pickets, and he caused places of security to be built upon those towers." (Alma 50:1-4.) In actual battle, Moroni often used decoy and encircling tactics to confuse and defeat the enemy. (Alma 43:27-35.)

Moroni may have obtained some of his new ideas on warfare from Mosiah's translation of the twenty-four gold plates of Ether, which contained an account of the wars and contentions of the people of Jared. (See Alma 37:23-29.) If so, this may have given him an advantage over the Lamanites, because they did not have access to this record.

ALMA 43:45-47   *Justification for defensive warfare*

Although the Nephites were commanded by the Lord not to begin a war, they were also counseled by him: "Inasmuch as ye are not guilty of the first offense, neither the second, ye shall not suffer yourselves to be slain by the hands of your enemies." (Alma 43:46.) The Lord further instructed the Nephites: "Ye shall defend your families even unto bloodshed." (Alma 43:47.) Thus the Nephites felt justified in resisting the invasion of the Lamanites, so long as the Nephites were fighting for their lives, their homes, and their liberty.

ALMA 44:12-14   *A brief note concerning the "scalping" of Zerahemnah*

The question might be raised as to whether or not the "scalping" of the Lamanite leader, Zerahemnah, might have led to the scalping tradition of the American Indian. (Alma 44:12-14.) However, recent evidence would seem to indicate the American Indian did not have a scalping tradition until *after* the coming of the white man—that is, until the seventeenth century A.D. Apparently it was the white man who started the scalping custom, when some of the early colonists offered money for the scalps or hair of dead Indians. In order to get even with the evil white men who killed Indians just for their scalps (in much the same way as they would kill a buffalo for its hide), the Indians started to kill and scalp the whites in return.

ALMA 45:19   *Was Moses translated?*

Joseph Fielding Smith answers this question "Yes" in these words: "Moses, like Elijah, was taken up without tasting death, because he had a mission to perform. . . . and it had to be performed *before* the crucifixion of the Son of God, and it could not have been done in the spirit." (*Doctrines of Salvation,* 2:107, 110.) President Smith is referring here to the mission Moses performed on the mount of transfiguration when he appeared to the Savior and to Peter, James, and John. (See Matthew 17:1-13.)

Alma 45:19 would also seem to indicate that Moses was translated, wherein it states that Moses "was taken up by the Spirit, or buried by the hand of the Lord." These words also help to explain the real meaning of Deuteronomy 34:5-6, which states that the Lord "buried" Moses.

ALMA 46:12-24   *Moroni's Title of Liberty*

One of the most fascinating stories in the entire Book of Mormon is the account of Moroni and the Title of Liberty, which he used to rally the Nephites in defense of their lands and liberty. This story is filled with types, shadows, and idiomatic expressions foreign to most of us in the modern world, but they were not strange to the ancient eastern mind, as is indicated in the following quotation from Dr. Hugh Nibley:

To the modern and the western mind all this over-obvious dwelling on types and shadows seems a bit overdone, but not to the ancient or Oriental mind. The whole Arabic language is one long commentary on the deepseated feeling, so foreign to us but so characteristic of people who speak synthetic languages, that if things are *alike* they are the *same.* . . .

One of the most remarkable aspects of the story is the manner in which Moroni sought to stir up patriotic fervor by appealing to ancient and traditional devices. He connected the whole business of the rent garment with the story of the tribal ancestors Jacob and Joseph, and suggested that ". . . those who have dissented from us . . ." were the very ". . . remnant of the seed of Joseph . . ." to which the dying Jacob prophetically referred. [Alma 46:27.] It was not merely a resemblance or a type, but the very event foreseen by the patriarch of old. . . .

In the tenth century of our era the greatest antiquarian of the Moslem world, Muhammad ibn-Ibrahim ath-Tha'labi, collected in Persia a great many old tales and legends about the prophets of Israel. . . . Among other things, Tha'labi tells a number of stories,

234   which we have not found anywhere else, about Jacob and the garment of Joseph. In one, Joseph's brethren bring his torn garment to their father as proof that he is dead, but Jacob after examining the garment, ("and there were in the garment of Joseph three marks of tokens when they brought it to his father") declares that the way the cloth is torn shows him that their story is not true. . . .

    . . . aside from the great symbolic force of the tale, there can be no doubt that the story told by Moroni as one familiar to all the people actually was one that circulated among the Jews in ancient times. . . . It was totally unknown to the world in which Joseph Smith lived.

    These interesting little details are typical apocryphal variations on a single theme, and the theme is the one Moroni mentions; the rent garment of Joseph is the symbol both of his suffering and his deliverance, misfortune and preservation. Such things in the Book of Mormon illustrate the widespread ramifications of the Book of Mormon culture, and the recent declaration of Albright and other scholars that the ancient Hebrews had cultural roots in every civilization of the Near East. This is an acid test that no forgery could pass; it not only opens a window on a world we dreamed not of, but it brings to our unsuspecting and uninitiated minds a first glimmering suspicion of the true scope and vastness of a book nobody knows. (*An Approach to the Book of Mormon*, pp. 171-80.)

ALMA 46:23-27   *Joseph's coat of many colors*

    The Book of Mormon provides the biblical scholar with additional information on the famed "coat of many colors" which was given to Joseph by his father, Jacob. The Bible does not mention what happened to Joseph's coat after it was smeared with blood by Joseph's brothers and taken to Jacob, but according to the Book of Mormon, the coat was preserved, and, miraculously, part of the coat never decayed. The Book of Mormon account is partially substantiated by the following story by the great Moslem historian, Muhammad ibn-Ibrahim ath-Tha'labi, concerning what took place when Joseph finally met his brothers in Egypt:

    And when Joseph had made himself known unto them (his brethren) he asked them about his father, saying, "What did my father after (I left)?" They answered, "He lost his eyesight (from weeping)." Then he gave them his garment (*qamis,* long outer shirt). According to ad-Dahak that garment was of the weave (pattern, design) of Paradise, and the breath (spirit, odor) of Paradise was in it, *so that it never decayed* or in any way deteriorated (and that was) a sign (omen). And Joseph gave them that garment, and it was the very one that had belonged to Abraham, having already had a long history. And he said to them, "Go, take this garment of mine and place it upon the face of my father so he may have sight again, and return (to me) with all your families." And when they had put Egypt behind them and come to Canaan their father Jacob said, "Behold, I perceive the spirit (breath, odor) of Joseph, if you will not think me wandering in my mind and weakheaded from age . . ." (for, he knew that upon all the earth there was no spirit [breath, odor]) of Paradise save in that garment alone. . . . And as-Sadi says that Judah said to Joseph, "It was I who took the garment bedaubed with blood to Jacob, and reported to him that the bear had eaten Joseph; so give me this day thy garment that I might tell him that thou art living, that I might cause him to rejoice now as greatly as I caused him to sorrow then." And Ibn-Abbas says that Judah took the garment and went forth in great haste, panting with exertion and anxiety . . . and when he brought the garment he laid it upon his face, so that his sight returned to him. And ad-Dahak says that his sight returned after blindness, and his strength after weakness, and youth after age, and joy after sorrow. (Quoted in Nibley, *An Approach to the Book of Mormon,* pp. 178-79.)

ALMA 46:40   *The fevers at "some seasons of the year"*

Very little information is provided in the Book of Mormon concerning the climate where the Nephites and Lamanites lived. However, some scholars have assumed that the reference to fevers that occurred at certain seasons of the year in the land of Zarahemla might indicate this particular land was in a tropical or semitropical area. However, as noted by the historian, the effects of these fevers were not too serious "because of the excellent qualities of the many plants and roots which God had prepared to remove the cause of diseases." (Alma 46:40.)

ALMA 48:14   *Nephites not to wage offensive war*

Although the Nephites were permitted by the Lord to fight for their rights and liberties when attacked by the Lamanites (see Alma 43:46-47), nevertheless they had been warned by the Lord "never to give an offense, yea, and never to raise the sword except it were against an enemy, except it were to preserve their lives." (Alma 48:14.) (For further information concerning the teachings of the Lord and the prophets on war, see the materials listed after 3 Nephi 3:20-21.)

ALMA 51:26   *The capture of the city of Nephihah*

Although the historian of this part of the record mentions in Alma 51:25 that the Lamanites decided not "to go against the city of Nephihah to battle," in the next verse the historian records that the Lamanites went on "taking possession of many cities, the city of Nephihah, and the city of Lehi . . . ," etc. Although it is not clear whether or not the historian intended to include the city of Nephihah in this list, it is evident that the city is captured later by the Lamanites. (See Alma 59:7-9.)

ALMA 53:6   *A puzzling reference to the "land of Nephi"*

Concerning one of Moroni's exploits against the Lamanites, the historian writes: "And it came to pass that Moroni had thus gained a victory over one of the greatest of the armies of the Lamanites, and had obtained possession of the city of Mulek, which was one of the strongest holds of the Lamanites *in the land of Nephi. . . .*" (Alma 53:6. Italics added.) The reference to the city of Mulek as "one of the strongest holds of the Lamanites in the land of Nephi" is puzzling because the city of Mulek is evidently located in the greater land of Zarahemla. (See Alma 51:26.)

Here are three possible explanations of this puzzle: (1) Perhaps this land is being called "the land of Nephi" by the Lamanites because they now possess it as they also possess the land of Nephi in the south. (2) The Nephites could have a "land of Nephi" in the north, although such a land has not been mentioned before and is not mentioned later. (3) The phrase "in the land of Nephi" might be used to identify those particular Lamanites mentioned in the verse and to differentiate them from Lamanites living in other parts of the country.

ALMA 53:8   *The west sea is now to the south*

When the Nephites first landed in the promised land, they gave names to some of the seas and lands around them. At that time the sea to the west of their landing place was evidently called the "west sea." Later, Nephi left this land, took his followers, and went northward where they settled in the land of Nephi. The descendants of Nephi and his group lived there for several hundred years. Then Mosiah, under the inspiration of the Lord, led a group of Nephites even farther north to the land of Zarahemla. The major group of the Nephites is now located in the land of Zarahemla, far north of the original landing place. Thus, the original "west sea" is actually far to the south of where they are now living, and they refer to "the west sea, south." (Alma 53:8.)

ALMA 54:24 *The false claim of the Lamanites to the right of government*

One reason listed by Ammoron (the apostate Nephite who has now become the leader of the Lamanites) for waging his war against the Nephites is that he wants "to avenge" the wrongs of the Lamanites and "to maintain and to obtain their rights to the government." (Alma 54:24.) When Lehi died soon after arriving in the promised land, Laman and his followers felt they should succeed him as the rulers of the colony because Laman was the eldest son of Lehi and Sariah. However, the Lord designated the righteous Nephi as the new leader. Thus for hundreds of years the Lamanites had passed down the tradition that the Nephites had "robbed them" by taking away their right to the government. (For further information on the false traditions of the Lamanites, see the material listed after Mosiah 10:12-17.)

ALMA 56:46-48; 57:25-26 *The 2,000 stripling sons of Helaman*

One of the great war stories in the Book of Mormon is the account of the 2,000 young warriors who are descendants of Lamanite converts and who fight under the leadership of Helaman in the war between the Lamanites and the Nephites. The parents of these warriors had taken a covenant not to take up arms against their enemies, and Helaman would not allow them to break this covenant. However, the sons of these people had not entered into the covenant; therefore, they were willing to go to battle. Because of their great faith, valor, and courage, these young warriors were protected by the Lord through several battles, and not one lost his life.

This story is frequently told to illustrate the importance of correct teaching in the home and the blessings that come from honoring parents. These young men told Helaman that "they had been taught by their mothers, that if they did not doubt, God would deliver them." Then they added: "We do not doubt our mothers knew it." (Alma 56:47-48.)

238   In a letter to Moroni, Helaman attributes the success and preservation of his warrior sons to the power of God and to their faith: "And we do justly ascribe it [their preservation] to the miraculous power of God, because of their exceeding faith in that which they had been taught to believe—that there was a just God, and whosoever did not doubt, that they should be preserved by his marvelous power." (Alma 57:26.)

ALMA 60:13   *For information on why the Lord might suffer the righteous to be slain, read the material listed after Alma 14:11.*

ALMA 63:5-8   *Hagoth, the shipbuilder*

Several migrations from the land southward into the land northward took place in the decade between 60 and 50 B.C. Some of these immigrants and many of their supplies were shipped into the land northward on ships built by Hagoth. However, in about 55 B.C. Hagoth and "many more people" entered into a ship, started for the land northward, and were never heard of again. (Alma 63:7.)

HELAMAN

HELAMAN 1:2-34; 2:1-2 *The new chief judges*

The reign of judges began in the year 92 B.C. of the Christian calendar, and from then until 52 B.C. only three chief judges had served: Alma the younger, Nephihah, and Pahoran. However, in the year 52 B.C. Pahoran died and within the next two years three additional chief judges were selected: (1) Pahoran the second was selected to succeed his father, but he was murdered by Kishkumen (Helaman 1:9); (2) Pacumeni succeeded Pahoran the second, but he was killed by Coriantumr in war (Helaman 1:21); (3) Helaman the second (the son of Helaman who was the son of Alma the younger) then became the new chief judge (Helaman 2:1-2).

HELAMAN 2:2-14 *The band of Gadianton*

The introduction to the band of Gadianton (also known as the "Gadianton Robbers") would indicate that this group was organized by Kishkumen. However, upon the death of Kishkumen, "Gadianton, who was exceeding expert in many words, and also in his craft, to carry on the secret work of murder and of robbery . . . became the leader of the band of Kishkumen." (Helaman 2:4.)

Gadianton then led his followers into the wilderness, and they are not mentioned again in the record for several years. But, as Mormon promised, "more of this Gadianton shall be spoken hereafter." (Helaman 2:12.)

HELAMAN 3:16 *The meaning of the term "Lamanite"* about 45 B.C.

In the days of Helaman, the word *Lamanite* was being used to refer to the wicked people who had joined with the blood descendants of Laman and his early followers. Thus the wicked who joined with the Lamanites were "no more called the Nephites, becoming wicked, and wild, and ferocious, yea, even becoming Lamanites." (Helaman 3:16.)

It is quite evident that some of the Lamanites converted by Nephi and Lehi in the prison were really apostate Nephites, for Aminadab said that they had had the gospel preached unto them by "Alma, and Amulek, and Zeezrom."

240   (Helaman 5:41.) So far as the Book of Mormon relates, the only missionary venture engaged in by these three men together was to the apostate Zoramites who were then living in the land of Antionum. (Alma 31:3-6.)

HELAMAN 4:7   *For information on the narrow neck of land and the line of fortification, see the material listed after Alma 22:32.*

HELAMAN 4:11-13   *Pride—one cause of war*

Although the Book of Mormon lists several causes of war (wickedness, greed, personal ambition, selfishness, etc.), one of the most frequently listed causes is pride. Perhaps it should be obvious how pride could lead to war, because pride causes a person to feel he is better than others. Therefore, when a person or a nation is lifted up in "the pride of their hearts" they feel others should not have the same rights and privileges they have; thus they are willing to fight either to prevent other people from getting these rights or to gain other privileges for themselves.

HELAMAN 5:10-11   *Jesus Christ can redeem people from their sins*

When Alma and Amulek were doing missionary work in the city of Ammonihah, the investigator Zeezrom asked Amulek if God could save people *in* their sins. "And Amulek answered and said unto him: I say unto you he shall not, for it is impossible for him to deny his word. . . . And I say unto you again that he cannot save them in their sins; for I cannot deny his word, and he hath said that no unclean thing can inherit the kingdom of heaven; therefore, how can ye be saved, except ye inherit the kingdom of heaven? Therefore, ye cannot be saved in your sins." (Alma 11:34, 37.)

Many years after the above experience Helaman explained these teachings of Amulek to his sons Nephi and Lehi, as follows:

And remember also the words which Amulek spake unto Zeezrom, in the city of Ammonihah; for he said unto him that the Lord surely should come to redeem his people, but that he should not come to redeem them in their sins, but to redeem them from their sins.

And he hath power given unto him from the Father to redeem them from their sins because of repentance; therefore he hath sent his angels to declare the tidings of the conditions of repentance, which bringeth unto the power of the Redeemer, unto the salvation of their souls. (Helaman 5:10-11.)

Thus Jesus Christ cannot redeem people *in* their sins (because they are still wicked), but he can redeem them *from* their sins (because they have repented from them).

HELAMAN 5:21   *The prison in the land of Lehi-Nephi*

During their missionary journey to the Lamanites, Nephi and Lehi are thrown into the same prison "in which Ammon and his brethren were cast by the servants of Limhi." (Helaman 5:21.) Thus we find that Nephi and Lehi are doing missionary work in the land of Lehi-Nephi, because this is where Ammon and his brethren were thrown into prison by King Limhi. (See Mosiah 7:2-7.)

HELAMAN 5:41   *The identification of the apostate Zoramites*

The Book of Mormon does not expressly give the identity of the people who are in the prison at the time of the miraculous manifestation mentioned in Helaman 5. However, a clue as to who these people were is given by Aminadab when he said unto them, "You must repent, and cry unto the voice, even until ye shall have faith in Christ, who was taught unto you by Alma, and Amulek, and Zeezrom." (Helaman 5:41.) The only time Alma and Amulek and Zeezrom were on a missionary trip together was to the apostate Zoramites who were then living in the land of Antionum. (See Alma 31:1-8.) The Zoramites later fled from this area and joined with the Lamanites in the greater land of Nephi, and from this statement by Aminadab we learn they have now occupied the land of Lehi-Nephi, which had just been deserted by Limhi and his people.

Again, the Book of Mormon proves to be a very complex book but also a wonderfully consistent one.

HELAMAN 6:10; 8:21   *Were all the sons of King Zedekiah killed?*

Zedekiah was the king of Judah at the time Lehi and his colony fled from Jerusalem. (1 Nephi 1:4.) A few years later when the Babylonians besieged Jerusalem, they "slew the sons of Zedekiah before his eyes." (2 Kings 25:7.) Most people have assumed all of the sons of Zedekiah were killed

242   at that time; however, the Book of Mormon records that the
sons of Zedekiah were slain "all except it were Mulek."
(Helaman 8:21.)

HELAMAN 6:13   *Fine-twined linen*

The term "fine-twined linen" was evidently used quite
extensively by the Hebrews; it appears nine times in the
Book of Mormon and is used thirty-two times in the biblical
book of Exodus. It is not clear what material was used to
make the linen mentioned in the Book of Mormon. Hunter
and Ferguson discuss this problem as follows:

The Book of Mormon makes reference to "linen," without qualify-
ing it. It may be that the early Nephites had flax-linen. On the
other hand, flax . . . was not found in America at the time of the
Conquest. . . . The present scientific view is that linen from flax did
not exist in ancient America. Cotton, of course, was commonly used
in ancient Middle America. However, the word for *linen* would
have been in the vocabulary of settlers coming from Jerusalem in
600 B.C. It occurs many times in the Old Testament. However, Bible scholars have suggested that the various Hebrew words that
have been translated "linen" in the Old Testament are, for the most
part, of uncertain meaning, and in some cases varieties of cotton
are meant. In the United States today we sometimes refer to cotton
products as "linen." Thus, perhaps the Nephites did not have flax,
but rather used their word for "linen" in a broader sense.

The Hebrew background of the Nephites is reflected by its use.
(Milton R. Hunter and Thomas Stuart Ferguson, *Ancient America
and the Book of Mormon* [Oakland: Kolob Book Co., 1950], pp.
316-17.)

HELAMAN 6:25-30   *The origin of the secret oaths*

In his farewell instructions to his son Helaman, Alma
warns him to withhold from the Nephites those references
from Jaredite history pertaining to "all their oaths, and their
covenants, and their agreements in their secret abominations; yea . . . ye shall keep these secret plans of their oaths
and their covenants from this people." (Alma 37:27, 29.) But
in Helaman 6, which covers a period about fifty years later
than Alma's instructions to his son, it is obvious that the
Nephites (especially the Gadianton Robbers) are in
possession of these secret oaths and covenants. The historian
hastens to inform us, however, that these "secret oaths and
covenants did not come forth unto Gadianton from the
records which were delivered unto Helaman; but behold,

they were put into the heart of Gadianton by that same be-ing who did entice our first parents to partake of the forbid-den fruit." (Helaman 6:26.) In subsequent verses the his-torian makes it clear that these secret oaths and covenants came from the devil, "he who is the author of all sin." (He-laman 6:30.)

HELAMAN 7:7   *The good old days*

The prophet Nephi (the son of Helaman) apparently believes in the sayings that "the grass is always greener on the other side of the fence" and "the good old days are best." After he and his teachings are rejected by the people, Nephi laments:

Oh, that I could have had my days in the days when my father Nephi first came out of the land of Jerusalem, that I could have joyed with him in the promised land; then were his people easy to be entreated, firm to keep the commandments of God, and slow to be led to do iniquity; and they were quick to hearken unto the words of the Lord—

Yea, if my days could have been in those days, then would my soul have had joy in the righteousness of my brethren. (Helaman 7:7-8.)

However, students of the Book of Mormon probably re-member that all things were not perfect during this early time period. This was the time of bitter hatred between the Lamanites and Nephites when they finally broke away from each other. In fact, Jacob (the brother of Nephi, who had grown up during this period) expressed his feelings concern-ing this same period as follows: ". . . we being a lonesome and a solemn people, wanderers, cast out from Jerusalem, born in tribulation, in a wilderness, and hated of our brethren, which caused wars and contentions; wherefore, we did mourn out our days." (Jacob 7:26.)

HELAMAN 8:13-15   *The "brazen serpent" lifted up by Moses*

According to the Bible, when the people of Israel were being bitten by serpents and some of the people were dying, the Lord commanded Moses to make a serpent "and set it upon a pole: and it shall come to pass, that every one that is bitten, when he looketh upon it, shall live. And Moses made a serpent of brass, and put it upon a pole, and it came to pass, that if a serpent had bitten any man, when he beheld

244   the serpent of brass, he lived." (Numbers 21:8-9.) That is the end of the account in the Bible. However, the account in the Book of Mormon indicates that when Moses lifted up the brazen serpent he did "bear record that the Son of God should come. And as he lifted up the brazen serpent in the wilderness, even so shall he be lifted up who should come. And as many as should look upon that serpent should live, even so as many as should look upon the Son of God with faith, having a contrite spirit, might live, even unto that life which is eternal." (Helaman 8:14-15).

The Savior also indicated that the "brazen serpent lifted up by Moses" was a type (shadow, or example) of his own crucifixion when he said: "And as Moses lifted up the serpent in the wilderness, even so must the Son of man be lifted up: That whosoever believeth in him should not perish, but have eternal life." (John 3:14-15.)

Some scholars of the Book of Mormon have wondered if this story of the serpent as given in the book of Helaman did not account for the "serpent motif" in the art and architecture of some of the American Indian cultures. Also, it is of interest to note that one of the names given by some of the American Indians to the great white God who appeared out of the eastern sky was the name of *Quetzalcoatl,* which literally means the bird-serpent, or the serpent of precious plumage.

HELAMAN 8:19-20   *References to ancient prophets not mentioned in the Bible*

Four ancient prophets whose writings do not appear in our present Bible are mentioned in the Book of Mormon. These four prophets and the Book of Mormon references to them are as follows: (1) Zenos, who is mentioned 12 times in the Book of Mormon, in 1 Nephi 19:10, 12, 16; Jacob 5:1; 6:1; Alma 33:3, 13, 15; 34:7; Helaman 8:19; 15:11; and 3 Nephi 10:16; (2) Zenock, who is mentioned five times in the Book of Mormon, in 1 Nephi 19:10; Alma 33:15; 34:7; Helaman 8:20; and 3 Nephi 10:16; (3) Neum, who is mentioned once in the Book of Mormon, in 1 Nephi 19:10; (4) Ezias, who is mentioned once in the Book of Mormon, in Helaman 8:20. The reference in Helaman 8:19-20 to three of these prophets seems to indicate they lived sometime between the "days of Abraham" and the time of Isaiah.

HELAMAN 8:21   *Mulek and the tribe of Judah*

Mulek was the son of Zedekiah, the king of Judah, who was spared at the time of the Babylonian captivity and who later came to the Americas. The descendants of Mulek were included among the people of Zarahemla, and later they were numbered among the Nephites. Thus, among the combined Nephite-Lamanite-Mulekite peoples are represented at least three of the twelve tribes of ancient Israel: (1) the tribe of Manasseh, represented by the descendants of Lehi; (2) the tribe of Ephraim, represented by the descendants of Ishmael; (3) the tribe of Judah, represented by the descendants of Mulek. (For further information concerning the lineage of Lehi, Ishmael, and Mulek, see the material listed after Helaman 6:10 and after Alma 10:3.)

HELAMAN 10:6-9   *The sealing power of the priesthood*

Because of the righteousness and great faith of Nephi, the Lord promised him: "Behold, I give unto you power, that whatsoever ye shall seal on earth shall be sealed in heaven; and whatsoever ye shall loose on earth shall be loosed in heaven; and thus shall ye have power among this people." (Helaman 10:7.) This is the same sealing power of the priesthood that was later promised by the Savior to Peter on the eastern continent: "And I will give unto thee the keys of the kingdom of heaven: and whatsoever thou shalt bind on earth shall be bound in heaven: and whatsoever thou shalt loose on earth shall be loosed in heaven." (Matthew 16:19.) This sealing power can be used not only to seal things on earth so they will be sealed in heaven (such as priesthood ordinances, marriages, etc.), but also actually to "seal the heavens" so it cannot rain. This power was used by Nephi during the drought mentioned in Helaman 11:4-17.

HELAMAN 10:16-17   *Nephi went forth "in the Spirit"*

The term "in the Spirit," which is used to indicate how Nephi taught the people, evidently means that Nephi went forth "by the power of the Spirit." It does *not* mean Nephi's body was separated from his spirit; rather it probably means he was protected in his missionary work by the power of the Spirit.

 HELAMAN 12:2-8   *Mormon's lament on human frailties*

When Mormon reviews the wickedness of the people who were living shortly before the birth of Christ, he points out that "at the very time" the Lord prospers the people with riches and other blessings, "then is the time that they do harden their hearts, and do forget the Lord their God." (Helaman 12:2.) Thus, after observing that the people do not keep the commandments of the Lord, Mormon laments: "O how great is the nothingness of the children of men; yea, even they are less than the dust of the earth. For behold, the dust of the earth moveth hither and thither, to the dividing asunder, at the command of our great and everlasting God." (Helaman 12:7-8.)

This statement should not be interpreted that Mormon believes men are worth even less than the dust of the earth. Rather Mormon is saying that men sometimes appear to be less wise than the dust of the earth. When the Lord tells the dust of the earth to move, it obeys, whereas when the Lord tells men to do something, they frequently do not obey.

 HELAMAN 13-16   *The prophecies of Samuel the Lamanite*

Inasmuch as there are no quotation marks in the entire Book of Mormon, it is sometimes a little difficult to tell exactly where a direct quotation begins and ends. In verses 8 through 20 of chapter 13 of Helaman, Samuel is apparently quoting directly from the words of an angel. The remainder of Samuel's sermon was "put into his heart" by the Lord. (Helaman 13:5.) Thus his entire sermon was given under the influence of the Lord, and it contains the following remarkable prophecies in rather detailed form:

1. The eventual destruction of the Nephites: ". . . four hundred years pass not away save the sword of justice falleth upon this people. Yea, heavy destruction awaiteth this people, and it surely cometh unto this people, and nothing can save this people save it be repentance and faith on the Lord Jesus Christ." (Helaman 13:5-6.)

2. The destruction of the city of Zarahemla. In fact, Samuel said that the Lord had not destroyed the city of Zarahemla because of the few righteous people who lived

there, but, he warned, "when ye shall cast out the righteous from among you, then shall ye be ripe for destruction." (Helaman 13:12-14.)

3. The birth of the Savior: ". . . five years more cometh . . . then cometh the Son of God to redeem all those who shall believe on his name." (Helaman 14:1-2.) At the time of his birth, there should be no darkness for a "day and a night and a day," "great lights in heaven," including a new star "such an one as ye never have beheld," and many signs and wonders in heaven which shall cause the people to fall to the earth in amazement. (Helaman 14:3-7.)

4. The death of the Savior: ". . . in that day that he shall suffer death the sun shall be darkened and refuse to give his light unto you; and also the moon and the stars; and there shall be no light upon the face of this land, even from the time that he shall suffer death, for the space of three days, to the time that he shall rise again from the dead." (Helaman 14:20.) There shall also be "thunderings and lightnings for the space of many hours, and the earth shall shake and tremble"; many mountains shall be "laid low, like unto a valley, and there shall be many places which are now called valleys which shall become mountains . . . and many cities shall become desolate. And many graves shall be opened, and shall yield up many of their dead; and many saints shall appear unto many." (Helaman 14:21-25.)

5. The treasures of the people shall become slippery: ". . . whoso shall hide up treasures in the earth shall find them again no more, because of the great curse of the land. . . . And the day shall come that they shall hide up their treasures, because they have set their hearts upon riches; and because they have set their hearts upon their riches, I will hide up their treasures when they shall flee before their enemies." (Helaman 13:18, 20.) "And behold, the time cometh that he curseth your riches, that they become slippery, that ye cannot hold them; and in the days of your poverty ye cannot retain them." (Helaman 13:31.)

Samuel's final warning to the Nephites was that the Lord would "utterly destroy them" unless they repented of their sins. (Helaman 15:17.) Some of the people heeded this warning by Samuel, and they sought out Nephi, confessed their sins, and desired to be baptized. (Helaman 16:1.) Others, however, did not believe the words of Samuel; they became angry at him and tried to kill him. (Helaman 16:2, 6-8.)

HELAMAN 13:38 *Happiness is not obtained through doing iniquity*

Samuel the Lamanite reminds the wicked people of his day: ". . . ye have sought all the days of your lives for that which ye could not obtain; and ye have sought for happiness in doing iniquity, which thing is contrary to the nature of that righteousness which is in our great and Eternal Head." (Helaman 13:38.) Samuel's teachings are very similar to those of Alma the younger ("wickedness never was happiness"—Alma 41:10), and to those of Lehi (2 Nephi 2:11-27).

(For further information on this subject, including a diagram showing the relationship between wickedness and unhappiness, see the material listed after 2 Nephi 2:11-27.)

HELAMAN 14:12 *Who was the "Creator of all things from the beginning"?*

Jesus Christ is referred to as the "Creator of all things from the beginning." (Helaman 14:12.) In fact, Jesus Christ once introduced himself to the Nephites as follows: "Behold, I am Jesus Christ the Son of God. I created the heavens and the earth, and all things that in them are." (3 Nephi 9:15. See also Moses 1:33 and 2:1; and D&C 45:1-3.) (For further information on Jesus Christ as the Creator see the material listed after 3 Nephi 9:15.)

HELAMAN 14:15-17 *The spiritual deaths*

The Book of Mormon mentions two major types of spiritual death. The term "first spiritual death" refers to the original transgression of Adam and Eve when they were cast out of the Garden of Eden and to the condition which comes upon a person when he commits his first sin. Jesus Christ atoned for the first spiritual death of Adam and Eve, and each individual person can be redeemed from his "first spiritual death" upon the conditions of repentance. However, the "second spiritual death" is much more serious. This term is used in the Book of Mormon to refer to a death which takes place after physical death wherein the person is "cut off again as to things pertaining to righteousness." (Helaman 14:18.) This second spiritual death refers essentially to the state or condition of those who become sons of perdition. (For further information on the use of the term spiritual death in the Book of Mormon, see the material listed after 2 Nephi 9:6-12.)

HELAMAN 14:25 *"Many graves shall be opened . . . and many saints shall appear"*

Samuel the Lamanite prophesied that on the American continents at the time of the resurrection of Jesus Christ "many graves shall be opened, and shall yield up many of their dead; and many saints shall appear unto many." (Helaman 14:25.) This prophecy is not only literally fulfilled later in the Book of Mormon, but also, during his appearance to the righteous Nephites, the resurrected Jesus Christ instructed that an account of the fulfillment of this prophecy should be written in their records. In fact, the Savior says he commanded Samuel the Lamanite to prophesy concerning this event. (See 3 Nephi 23:9-13.)

A similar event of graves being opened also occurred on the eastern continent at the time of the resurrection of the Savior: "And the graves were opened; and many bodies of the saints which slept arose, and came out of the graves after his resurrection, and went into the holy city, and appeared unto many." (Matthew 27:52-53.)

HELAMAN 14:30-31 *The importance of free agency*

Samuel the Lamanite warns us that when we disobey God we cannot use the excuse that we were forced to commit sin. He says:

. . . remember, my brethren, that whosoever perisheth, perisheth unto himself; and whosoever doeth iniquity, doeth it unto himself; for behold, ye are free; ye are permitted to act for yourselves; for behold, God hath given unto you a knowledge and he hath made you free.

He hath given unto you that ye might know good from evil, and he hath given unto you that ye might choose life or death; and ye can do good and be restored unto that which is good, or have that which is good restored unto you; or ye can do evil, and have that which is evil restored unto you. (Helaman 14:30-31.)

This gift of free agency is one of the greatest gifts ever given to man by God. It is true that without free agency man could not be condemned in the justice of God, but it is also true that without it man could not be blessed for keeping the laws. President David O. McKay has explained the value and importance of free agency as follows:

A fundamental principle of the gospel is free agency, and references in the scriptures show that this principle is (1) essential to man's salvation; and (2) may become a measuring rod by which the actions of men, of organizations, of nations may be judged.

"Therefore," we are told in the scripture, "cheer up your hearts, and remember that ye are free to act for yourselves—to choose the way of everlasting death or the way of eternal life." (2 Nephi 10:23.) . . .

"My independence is sacred to me," said Brigham Young, "it is a portion of that same Deity that rules in the heavens. There is not a being upon the face of the earth who is made in the image of God, who stands erect and is organized as God is, that would be deprived of the free exercise of his agency so far as he does not infringe upon other's rights, save by good advice and a good example." (*Discourses of Brigham Young,* 1943 ed., p. 62.)

The history of the world with all its contention and strife is largely an account of man's effort to free himself from bondage and usurpation.

Man's free agency is an eternal principle of progress, and any form of government that curtails or inhibits its free exercise is wrong. Satan's plan in the beginning was one of coercion, and it was rejected because he sought to destroy the agency of man which God had given him.

When man uses this God-given right to encroach upon the rights of another, he commits a wrong. Liberty becomes license, and the man, a transgressor. It is the function of the state to curtail the violator and to protect the individual.

Next to the bestowal of life itself, the right to direct our lives is God's greatest gift to man. Freedom of choice is more to be treasured than any possession earth can give. It is inherent in the spirit of man. It is a divine gift to every normal being. Whether born in abject poverty or shackled at birth by inherited riches, everyone has the most precious of all life's endowments—the gift of free agency, man's inherited and inalienable right. It is the impelling source of the soul's progress. It is the purpose of the Lord that man becomes like him. In order for man to achieve this, it was necessary for the Creator first to make him free. To man is given a special endowment, not bestowed upon any other living thing. God gave to him the power of choice. Only to the human being did the Creator say: ". . . thou mayest choose for thyself, for it is given unto thee; . . ." (Moses 3:17.) Without this divine power to choose, humanity cannot progress.

With free agency, however, there comes responsibility. If man is to be rewarded for righteousness and punished for evil, then common justice demands that he be given the power of independent action. A knowledge of good and evil is essential to man's progress on earth. If he were coerced to do right at all times or helplessly enticed to commit sin, he would merit neither a blessing for the first nor punishment for the second. Man's responsibility is correspondingly operative with his free agency. Actions in harmony with divine law and the laws of nature will bring happiness, and those in opposition to divine truth, misery. Man is responsible not only for every deed, but also for every idle word and thought.

Freedom of the will and the responsibility associated with it are fundamental aspects of Jesus' teachings. Throughout his ministry he emphasized the worth of the individual and exemplified what is now expressed in modern revelation as "his work and his glory." (Moses 1:39.) Only through the divine gift of soul freedom is such progress possible. (*Conference Report,* October 1965, pp. 7-8.)

THIRD NEPHI

Origin of the title "Third Nephi"

In the first edition of the Book of Mormon, the book that is now known by the title of "Third Nephi" was known only as "The Book of Nephi the son of Nephi, who was the son of Helaman." This original title was used until the edition of 1879 when, at the recommendation of Orson Pratt, the heading "Third Nephi" was added before the title of this book and the words "Fourth Nephi" were added before the title of the book that follows.

3 NEPHI 1:1   *Meaning of the term "*A.D.*1"*

The chronological material listed on the bottom of each page in the Book of Mormon did not appear in the first edition. These chronological notes were first added in the edition of 1920 at the recommendation of a committee headed by Elder James E. Talmage. The abbreviation B.C. is used to designate the number of years before the time of Christ. The abbreviation A.D. (from the Latin *Anno Domini,* meaning "in the year of our Lord") is used to indicate the number of years since the birth of Christ. Note that this calendar system does not go through a zero number. Thus the year before the birth of Christ is 1 B.C. and the year in which the Savior is born is A.D. 1. According to the calendar systems previously used by the Nephites, the year A.D. 1 occurs in the ninety-second year of the reign of judges (the record says the "ninety and first year *had passed away*") and in the six hundredth year from the time Lehi left Jerusalem. (3 Nephi 1:1.)

3 NEPHI 1:2-3   *The disappearance of Nephi the son of Helaman*

The great leader Nephi about whom we read so much in the book of Helaman turned the record over to his son Nephi at the beginning of this new book and then "departed out of the land, and whither he went, no man knoweth." (3 Nephi 1:3.) The disappearance of Nephi the son of Helaman is somewhat similar to the disappearance seventy-three years earlier of his great-great-grandfather, Alma the younger. The

Book of Mormon provides no further information concerning what became of these two great prophets.

3 NEPHI 1:12-14   *The statement of the Savior the day before his birth*

The day before the Savior was born on the eastern continent, he spoke to the prophet Nephi on this continent and said:

Lift up your head and be of good cheer; for behold, the time is at hand, and on this night shall the sign be given, and on the morrow come I into the world...

... to do the will, both of the Father and of the Son—of the Father because of me, and of the Son because of my flesh. And behold, the time is at hand, and this night shall the sign be given. (3 Nephi 1:13-14.)

This pre-birth statement of the Savior again indicates something concerning the nature and power of pre-earthly beings. Also, the Savior's statement that he was to do the will "of the Father *because of me*" evidently refers to his status as the first born spiritual child of our Heavenly Father. His statement that he is coming into the world to "fulfill all things" and to do the will "of the Son *because of my flesh*" evidently refers to his coming mission on earth as the Savior and Redeemer of the world.

3 NEPHI 1:24-25   *The law of Moses not fulfilled at the birth of the Savior*

About five hundred years before the birth of the Savior, Nephi the son of Lehi had prophesied that at the coming of the Christ the law of Moses "shall be fulfilled." (2 Nephi 25:24.) Thus at the sign of the birth of Christ, some of the descendants of Nephi claimed "it was no more expedient to observe the law of Moses" because according to their interpretation of the scriptures the law of Moses had been fulfilled. (3 Nephi 1:24.) However, it was made known unto them "that the law was not yet fulfilled, and that it must be fulfilled in every whit." (3 Nephi 1:25.)

Later, during the three days between his crucifixion and resurrection, the Savior spoke to the righteous Nephites living on the American continent and said "in me is the law of Moses fulfilled." (3 Nephi 9:17.) Still later the resurrected Savior appeared to the Nephites and taught, ". . . verily I say unto you, one jot nor one tittle hath not passed away from

254 the law, but in me it hath all been fulfilled." (3 Nephi 12:18.) Evidently the law of Moses was fulfilled by the Savior at the time of his crucifixion and resurrection.

(For further information on the topic "The Relationship Between the Law of Moses and the Atonement of Jesus Christ" see the material listed after 2 Nephi 25:20-30.)

3 NEPHI 2:5-8   *The Nephite calendar systems*

The Nephites used three systems of reckoning time:

(1) The first method was to determine the number of years since father Lehi left Jerusalem; this system was used from 600 B.C. to 92 B.C. (Mosiah 29:44-47; Alma 1:1.)

(2) The second method was to calculate the number of years from the beginning of the reign of the judges; this system was used for about 100 years, from 91 B.C. to A.D. 9. (3 Nephi 2:5-7.)

(3) The last method was to "reckon their time from this period when the sign was given, or from the coming of Christ" (3 Nephi 2:7-8); this system was used for the remainder of their record.

3 NEPHI 3:20-21   *Is war ever justified?*

Although the Gadianton Robbers had threatened to come to battle against the Nephites "on the morrow month," when the Nephites asked their military leader Gidgiddoni to attack the robbers first, Gidgiddoni said: "The Lord forbid; for if we should go up against them the Lord would deliver us into their hands." (3 Nephi 3:21.) This counsel of the Lord not to wage offensive war has apparently been given to people of all dispensations, as is indicated in this statement in the Doctrine and Covenants:

Behold, this is the law I gave unto my servant Nephi, and thy fathers, Joseph, and Jacob, and Isaac, and Abraham, and all mine ancient prophets and apostles.

And again, this is the law that I gave unto mine ancients, that they should not go out unto battle against any nation, kindred, tongue, or people, save I, the Lord, commanded them.

And if any nation, tongue, or people should proclaim war against them, they should first lift a standard of peace unto that people, nation, or tongue;

And if that people did not accept the offering of peace, neither the second nor the third time, they should bring these testimonies before the Lord;

Then I, the Lord, would give unto them a commandment, and justify them in going out to battle against that nation, tongue, or people.

And I, the Lord, would fight their battles, and their children's battles, and their children's children's, until they had avenged themselves on all their enemies, to the third and fourth generation.

Behold, this is an ensample unto all people, saith the Lord your God, for justification before me. (D&C 98:32-38.)

This principle is also the teaching of the Church at this time, as is indicated in the following statement by President George Q. Cannon:

We must proclaim peace; do all in our power to appease the wrath of our enemies; make any sacrifice that honorable people can to avert war, with all its horrors, entailing as it does dreadful consequences so numerous that they cannot be mentioned. It is our duty, I say, as a nation. The influence of the Latter-day Saints should be used in this direction. We should seek to quell these feelings of anxiety to fight and to shed blood. Our influence should go forth like oil poured upon the troubled waters, quieting the waves of discontent and wrath that are aroused by this fearful spirit. . . .

Not only ought we to extend the offering of peace the first time to a nation that proclaims war against us, but again the second time; and if that should be rejected, again the third time; and if it be rejected the third time, then:

"They should bring these testimonies before the Lord."

Go to the Lord and say, "Here are our testimonies. We have offered peace the first time; we have offered it twice; we have offered it three times; but our offerings are rejected, and this nation is determined to have war with us. Now we bring these testimonies before thee, Lord." . . .

I do not look for our nation to do this. It is scarcely to be expected, in the nature of things, that they would do it. But it is the true principle, and we as a people should use our influence for this purpose. Our prayers should ascend to God; our petitions should ascend to the government of our nation to do everything that honorable people can to avert war. We have no fear of the effect of the combinations against us. . . . But the promise of God is that if we will do right as a nation, if we will serve Him, they shall not have power over us, or be able to bring us into bondage; and in the end we shall prevail. This is a glorious promise which is made to the inhabitants of the land. . . .

To us as Latter-day Saints these principles are of the utmost importance. I do not want to see our young men get filled with the spirit of war and be eager for the conflict. God forbid that such a

256 spirit should prevail in our land, or that we should contribute in any manner to the propagation of a spirit of that kind! But one may say, "Is it not our duty to defend our country and our flag? Is it not our duty to maintain the institutions which the Lord has given to us?" Certainly it is. And it is no part of cowardice to take the plan that the Lord has pointed out. No man need be afraid that the Lord or any just man will look upon him as a coward. (*Conference Report,* April 1898, pp. 86-87.)

The principle behind this counsel apparently is related to the principle of repentance, as is indicated in this statement by President Joseph Fielding Smith:

> The law of forgiveness and retribution . . . applies to individuals and to families, as well as to the Church at large. We are under commandment to forgive our enemies and suffer their abuses and smiting the first time and second time, also the third time. This is to be done in patience, and in humility and prayer, hoping that the enemy might repent. If the enemy come upon us for the fourth time we are justified in meting out retribution, but even then there is to come a reward if we patiently endure, and the Lord will reward us abundantly. For all these abuses we will be rewarded if we endure them in patience. Perchance the enemy may repent, and that we should most sincerely desire. This may to the most ordinary human being be a hard law to follow; but nevertheless it is the word of the Lord. One of the best illustrations of this spirit of enduring wrong rather than retaliating is found in the story of the people of Ammon in the Book of Mormon. Because they refused to take up arms to defend themselves, but would rather lay down their lives than shed blood even in their own defense, they brought many of their enemies to repentance and to the kingdom of God. [Alma 24:17-25; 27:3.] This is the doctrine of Jesus Christ as taught in the Sermon on the Mount. [Matt. 5:21-22, 43-44.] If all peoples would accept this doctrine there could be no war, and all difficulties could be adjusted in righteousness. This doctrine was taught, so the Lord declared, to his people anciently. There are many things in the Old Testament in relation to the wars and battles of the Israelites in the meagre record which has come down to us, which are made to appear to us that these people were cruel and vengeful, but the Lord says they went out to battle when they were guided by prophets and the spirit of revelation when the Lord commanded them. (Joseph Fielding Smith, *Church History and Modern Revelation* [Salt Lake City: The Council of the Twelve Apostles, 1953], 1:434-35.)

3 NEPHI 5:8-12   *The writings of Mormon are only a small abridgment*

When Mormon abridged the material from the large plates of Nephi over to his own plates, he said he did not write "even a hundredth part" of that which was written in their records, including the large plates. Thus, apparently our present Book of Mormon consists of only about one percent of the original Nephite record.

3 NEPHI 5:20   *Lehi's disappearance from Jerusalem was secret*

When Lehi and his colony left Jerusalem in about 600 B.C., their leaving was evidently kept secret from the other people in Jerusalem. Mormon tells us concerning Lehi's departure, "no one knew it save it were himself and those whom he brought out of that land." (3 Nephi 5:20.)

3 NEPHI 6-7   *The "reign of judges" replaced by other forms of government*

Between A.D. 26 and 30 the people became very wicked, and "the church was broken up in all the land save it were among a few of the Lamanites who were converted unto the true faith." (3 Nephi 6:10-14.) The "chief judges, and they who had been high priests and lawyers" entered into a covenant to destroy "the people of the Lord" and to "destroy the governor, and to establish a king over the land, that the land should no more be at liberty but should be subject unto kings." (3 Nephi 6:21-30.) This secret society did not succeed in establishing a king over the land; but "they did destroy upon the judgment seat, yea, did murder the chief judge of the land." (3 Nephi 7:1.) The people were so divided they could not agree on a form of centralized government, so "they did separate one from another into tribes, every man according to his family and his kindred and his friends; and thus they did destroy the government of the land." (3 Nephi 7:2.)

3 NEPHI 6:10-15   *The apostasy from the church in about A.D. 30*

Despite the miraculous signs given at the birth of Christ, within thirty years many members of the church had apostatized. Apparently the beginning cause of this apostasy was the pride of the people. Because of this pride "the people began to be distinguished by ranks, according to their riches and their chances for learning. . . . And thus there became a great inequality in all the land, insomuch that the church began to be broken up." (3 Nephi 6:12, 14.) Apparently pride is the first slope down on the "roller coaster" so far as both apostasy and war are concerned. When people start to believe they are better than others, then they start ridiculing and persecuting other people, and apostasy and war are the inevitable results.

3 NEPHI 7:2-3　*The people were divided into tribes*

It is of interest to note that when the central government was destroyed, the people divided "into tribes, every man according to his family and his kindred and friends." (3 Nephi 7:2.) The strong family ties indicated here are reminiscent of the emphasis of the early Hebrews on the family. After the appearance of the resurrected Jesus Christ to these people, they again have a strong central government for over three hundred years. However, after that time, the government begins to disintegrate and by the close of the Book of Mormon almost complete anarchy exists. Apparently after A.D. 400 the people divide into tribes again, for this is the system of government they had when the white man came almost 1,000 years later.

3 NEPHI 7:18-20　*The great faith and power of Nephi the son of Nephi*

The prophet Nephi of approximately A.D. 32 was so righteous and had such great faith that "angels did minister unto him daily." (3 Nephi 7:18.) Although Nephi used this power to try to bless his people (he even raised his own brother from the dead), the wicked people "were angry with him because of his power." (3 Nephi 7:20.) Thus, despite the great signs and miracles that had been performed for the people, they still disbelieved. Once again this indicates that signs do not convert unless the conversion of faith follows.

3 NEPHI 8:5　*An exact date for the crucifixion of Jesus Christ*

The New Testament account of the crucifixion of Christ would seem to indicate that the Savior was crucified the very week he became thirty-three years of age. The Book of Mormon not only substantiates this account, but also provides us with an exact date of the crucifixion. According to the Nephite calendar system, the Savior was crucified "in the thirty and fourth year, in the first month, on the fourth day of the month." (3 Nephi 8:5.) Although we are not certain when the first month of the Nephite calendar would occur, if the Nephites were using the same calendar system as the Hebrews, the first month would be in the spring of the year sometime between about the middle of March and the middle of April.

3 Nephi 9:15 *Jesus Christ is the Creator of the heavens and the earth*

While the body of the Savior lay in the tomb on the eastern continent, he spoke to the righteous Nephite survivors on the western continent and introduced himself with these words: "Behold, I am Jesus Christ the Son of God. I created the heavens and the earth, and all things that in them are." (3 Nephi 9:15.) The concept that Jesus Christ created the heavens and the earth was taught earlier in the Book of Mormon by Samuel the Lamanite when he identified the Savior as "Jesus Christ, the Son of God, the Father of heaven and of earth, the Creator of all things from the beginning." (Helaman 14:12.)

Other scriptures also teach that Jesus Christ created both the heavens and the earth. In Moses 1:33 God the Father (Eloheim) states: "And worlds without number have I created; and I also created them for mine own purpose; and by the Son I created them, which is mine Only Begotten."

Also, in the Doctrine and Covenants the Savior introduces himself to the members of the Church in this dispensation as follows: "Hearken, O ye people of my church, to whom the kingdom has been given; hearken ye and give ear to him who laid the foundation of the earth, who made the heavens and all the hosts thereof, and by whom all things were made which live, and move, and have a being." (D&C 45:1.)

3 NEPHI 9:17 *How to become sons and daughters unto Christ*

After introducing himself as the Creator of the heavens and earth, the Savior informs the people "as many as have received me, to them have I given to become the sons of

260 God; ánd even so will I to as many as shall believe on my name." (3 Nephi 9:17.) The Savior's statement in this scripture is quite similar to a statement he made to the Brother of Jared over 2,000 years earlier as a pre-earthly spirit: "In me shall all mankind have light, and that eternally, even they who shall believe on my name; and they shall become my sons and my daughters." (Ether 3:14).

King Benjamin also taught his people how they could become the sons and daughters of Christ. After telling his people about the life and mission of the Savior, he encouraged his people to enter into a covenant to accept Christ and to serve him (this covenant evidently included the ordinance of baptism). Then he said: ". . . because of the covenant which ye have made ye shall be called the children of Christ, his sons, and his daughters; for behold, this day he hath spiritually begotten you." (Mosiah 5:7.)

3 NEPHI 10:16-17 *The Nephites are descendants of the Prophets Zenos and Zenock*

The prophets Zenos and Zenock are quoted several times by the prophets of the Book of Mormon. A possible reason for this propensity in quoting them becomes evident in this reading assignment: the Nephites are descendants of the prophets Zenos and Zenock! The historian records: ". . . the prophet Zenos did testify of these things, and also Zenock spake concerning these things, because *they testified particularly concerning us, who are the remnant of their seed."* (3 Nephi 10:16. Italics added.) (For additional information on the prophets Zenos and Zenock, see the material listed after Helaman 8:19-20.)

3 NEPHI 11 *The time of the appearance of the resur- rected Jesus Christ to the Nephites*

Some readers of the Book of Mormon disagree as to the exact time of the appearance of the resurrected Jesus Christ to the Nephites in the land Bountiful. One view is that he came to the American continent immediately after his resurrection; a second opinion is that he came about forty days after his resurrection at the time of his "ascension into heaven" on the eastern continent; a third view is that he came almost a year after his resurrection. The statements that refer to this problem are as follows:

And it came to pass in the thirty and fourth year, in the first month, on the fourth day of the month, there arose a great storm, such an one as never had been known in all the land. (3 Nephi 8:5.)

And it came to pass that in the ending of the thirty and fourth year, behold, I will show unto you that the people of Nephi who were spared, and also those who had been called Lamanites, who had been spared, did have great favors shown unto them, and great blessings poured out upon their heads, insomuch that soon after the ascension of Christ into heaven he did truly manifest himself unto them—

Showing his body unto them, and ministering unto them; and an account of his ministry shall be given hereafter. Therefore for this time I make an end of my sayings. (3 Nephi 10:18-19.)

Other verses that might indirectly throw light on this question are 3 Nephi 11:1-3 and 3 Nephi 19:1-5.

3 NEPHI 11   *The Indian title or name of Quetzalcoatl*

Many American tribes have a tradition of the appearance of a great white God to their ancestors of many years ago. The name or title frequently given to this personage, especially among the Quiché tribes of Central America, is Quetzalcoatl, which literally means "bird-serpent" or "serpent of precious plumage." It is interesting to speculate that perhaps this title was given to the resurrected Jesus Christ because he had been lifted up on a cross as the serpent had been lifted up on a stick by Moses. (Helaman 8:13-16. See also Numbers 21:6-9 and John 3:14.) Also, he appeared to them by descending out of the sky like a bird. (3 Nephi 11:8.) This theory might also explain why the very first thing the Savior did after his appearance to the Nephites was to invite the people to feel the prints of the nails in his hands and feet that they might know that "it was he, of whom it was written by the prophets, that should come." (3 Nephi 11:14-15.)

3 NEPHI 11:16-21   *The meaning of the word "Hosanna"*

At the time of the appearance of the resurrected Jesus Christ to the Nephites, the multitude went forth, felt the resurrected body of the Savior, and testified that "it was he, of whom it was written by the prophets, that should come" and then cried out "with one accord, saying: Hosanna!" (3 Nephi 11:15-16.) The word *Hosanna* is a transliteration of a Hebrew word of supplication which means in essence "Oh,

262   grant salvation." Evidently the people were asking the Savior to teach them the way to salvation; thus it is not surprising that he immediately teaches them the basic principles and ordinances of the gospel.

3 NEPHI 11:21-34   *The teachings of the Savior on baptism*

Baptism is perhaps the most basic and fundamental of all the ordinances in the gospel of Jesus Christ. Yet, the teachings on baptism in the New Testament must not be too clear, for wide diversities exist among Christian churches concerning such fundamentals as: (1) the necessity and purpose of baptism, (2) the age of baptism, (3) whether or not priesthood power is necessary to baptize, (4) the mode or method of baptism, and (5) the words to be used in the baptismal prayer.

However, the Savior clarifies many of the essential concepts on baptism in a few brief verses in the Book of Mormon. In chapter 11 of 3 Nephi, he indicates: (1) baptism is for the remission of sins (verse 23), (2) thus a person who is baptized should be old enough to repent of his sins (verse 23), (3) priesthood authority or power is needed in order for a person to baptize (verses 21-22), (4) baptism should be performed by immersion (verses 23-27), and (5) the person baptizing should say the words: "Having authority given me of Jesus Christ, I baptize you in the name of the Father, and of the Son, and of the Holy Ghost. Amen" (verse 25).

Some students have raised the question as to why the words of the baptismal prayer in the Book of Mormon differ slightly from the prayer listed in the Doctrine and Covenants. In this dispensation the Lord has counseled us to use these words in baptizing a person, after calling the candidate by name: "Having been commissioned of Jesus Christ, I baptize you in the name of the Father, and of the Son, and of the Holy Ghost. Amen." (D&C 20:73.) The only difference in the two prayers is the introductory statement. In the Book of Mormon the disciples were counseled to say "having authority given me of Jesus Christ," whereas in this dispensation we are told to say "having been commissioned of Jesus Christ."

One possible explanation for this difference may be associated with the problem of translation. For example, it is not always possible to translate exact words into other languages; thus, the baptismal prayer is not exactly the same in all languages. Another possibility for explaining this difference is that the disciples in the Book of Mormon received their authority *directly* from Jesus Christ; therefore, they rightfully could say "having authority given me of Jesus Christ." However, in this dispensation priesthood bearers have been given the power to baptize from John the Baptist, who was commissioned by Jesus Christ to come to earth and restore this authority. Therefore, in this dispensation we use the words "having been commissioned of Jesus Christ."

3 NEPHI 12-14 *Contributions of the Book of Mormon to a correct understanding of the Sermon on the Mount*

It is perhaps safe to say that the Sermon on the Mount is the most quoted and the least understood of all the teachings of Jesus. The translation of Matthew's account of this sermon in our present New Testament (Matthew 5-7) has caused many people to raise questions concerning the authenticity of the sermon. They ask such questions as the following: Why did the Savior teach that people were better off being poor in spirit than not poor in spirit, or that they were more blessed mourning than not mourning? When he said "Blessed are they which do hunger and thirst after righteousness: for they shall be filled," with what are they to be filled: hunger, thirst, or righteousness? Also, why did he counsel the people to "take no thought for your life, what ye shall eat, or what ye shall drink; nor yet for your body, what ye shall put on"? What if all people literally followed this admonition? Who would plant and harvest the crops, feed the children, manufacture the clothes, etc. It is evident there is something wrong with the translation of the Sermon on the Mount in our present New Testament.

When the resurrected Jesus Christ appeared to the Nephites, he gave them the same sermon. In fact, he specifically told the Nephites, "Behold, ye have heard the things which I taught before I ascended to my Father." (3 Nephi 15:1.) However, the account of this sermon in the Book of Mormon is much more complete and makes much more sense than the New Testament account. For example, in the Book of Mormon the Savior prefaced his sermon by indicating the teachings that were to follow applied only to

264 those who would "come down into the depths of humility
and be baptized . . . [and] be visited with fire and with the
Holy Ghost, and . . . receive a remission of their sins." (3
Nephi 12:2.) Then he related these prerequisite conditions to
each of the Beatitudes that followed: "Yea, blessed are the
poor in spirit *who come unto me,* for theirs is the kingdom of
heaven. *And again,* blessed are all they that mourn, for they
shall be comforted." (3 Nephi 12:3-4. Italics added.) This
more complete version of the sermon changes the entire emphasis of the Beatitudes. Here the Savior is not saying "you
are more blessed if you mourn than if you do not mourn,"
but he is saying "If you are called upon to mourn, then you
are blessed if you come unto me, are baptized, receive the
Holy Ghost, etc." Thus, if you do truly hunger and thirst
after righteousness, you shall be filled "with the Holy
Ghost." (3 Nephi 12:6.)

It is also of interest to note that each of the Beatitudes in
the Book of Mormon begins with the coordinating conjunction "and," which helps to relate them back to the introductory statement.

3 NEPHI 12:1-2   *The introductory verses to the Sermon on the Mount*

Before delivering the Sermon on the Mount on the
eastern continent and his similar sermon to the Nephites, the
Savior stated that what he was about to say pertained to
those who were willing to believe in his words, "come down
into the depths of humility and be baptized" so that they
could "be visited with fire and with the Holy Ghost," and
could "receive a remission of their sins." (3 Nephi 12:2. See
also Matthew 5:3-4 of the Inspired Version.)

Unfortunately, this introductory statement does not appear in either the King James or the Catholic version of the
Bible. Thus most Christians have a misconception as to the
meaning of the Sermon on the Mount. They assume that this
sermon was meant either for the whole world or for only the
chosen disciples. However, the Book of Mormon and the Inspired Version of the Bible indicate that the major parts of
this sermon were intended for all those who were willing to
accept Christ and keep his commandments.

The Beatitudes in the Book of Mormon are listed in the same order as those in the New Testament. However, some significant differences of wording should be noted:

·1. Each Beatitude in the Book of Mormon begins with a conjunction that relates it to the previous Beatitude and helps to relate all of the Beatitudes to the introductory statement of the Savior.

2. The Beatitude that reads in the New Testament "Blessed are the poor in spirit: for theirs is the kingdom of heaven" is clarified in the Book of Mormon: "*Yea,* blessed are the poor in spirit *who come unto me,* for theirs is the kingdom of heaven." (3 Nephi 12:3. Italics added.) The word *yea* and the clause "who come unto me" relate this Beatitude to the conditional introductory statement of the Savior.

3. The Beatitude that reads in the New Testament "Blessed are they which do hunger and thirst after righteousness: for they shall be filled" is clarified in the Book of Mormon as follows: "*And* blessed are *all* they who do hunger and thirst after righteousness, for they shall be filled *with the Holy Ghost.*" (3 Nephi 12:6. Italics added.)

4. The Beatitude in the New Testament that reads "Blessed are they which are persecuted for righteousness' sake: for theirs is the kingdom of heaven" has been clarified in the Book of Mormon: "*And* blessed are *all* they who are persecuted for *my name's sake,* for theirs is the kingdom of heaven." (3 Nephi 12:10. Italics added.)

3 NEPHI 12:22   *Meaning of the word "raca"*

In the New Testament the Savior counseled his followers: ". . . whosoever is angry with his brother without a cause shall be in danger of the judgment: and whosoever shall say to his brother, Raca, shall be in danger of the council." (Matthew 5:22.) The Savior's teachings on this subject in the Book of Mormon are the same except the phrase "without a cause" is deleted. The word *raca* is used in both accounts, however, and students often wonder what this word means. In the original Semite tongue *raca* means *vain* or *empty.* Thus, the Savior is telling us not to call other people by such derogatory titles.

266   3 NEPHI 12:31-32   *The teachings of the Savior on divorce*

Divorce was definitely discouraged by Jesus Christ. In the New Testament when the Pharisees asked "Is it lawful for a man to put away his wife for every cause?" the Savior replied: "Have ye not read, that he which made them at the beginning made them male and female, And said, For this cause shall a man leave father and mother, and shall cleave to his wife: and they twain shall be one flesh? Wherefore they are no more twain, but one flesh. What therefore God hath joined together, let not man put asunder." (Matthew 19:4-6.) Then the Pharisees asked, "Why did Moses then command to give a writing of divorcement, and to put her away?" (Note: Moses did not "command" divorce, but in Deuteronomy 24:1-4 he required a man to give his wife a bill of divorcement if he should separate from her or should "send her out of his house.") And Jesus answered: "Moses because of the hardness of your hearts suffered you to put away your wives; but from the beginning it was not so. And I say unto you, Whosoever shall put away his wife, except it be for fornication, and shall marry another, committeth adultery: and whoso marrieth her which is put away doth commit adultery." (Matthew 19:8-9.)

It should be remembered that the "putting away of a wife" referred to by Jesus was not equal to a legal divorce. As James E. Talmage has indicated, "Jesus announced no specific or binding rule as to legal divorces; the putting away of a wife, as contemplated under the Mosaic custom, involved no judicial investigation or action by an established court." (*Jesus the Christ,* p. 474.)

These same ideas on marriage and divorce are included in the Savior's statement in the Book of Mormon. Divorce (or permanent separation) is not good; but if a couple decides to separate permanently, they should follow the legal procedures. This requirement is equally applicable to the man or the woman, for if a man "puts away his wife" but does not give her a legal divorce, he causes both her and any subsequent husband she might marry to commit adultery. (3 Nephi 12:31-32; compare Matthew 5:31-32; 19:3-9; Luke 16:18.) In this regard, it is well to remember that the word *divorce* as used by the Savior in 3 Nephi 12:32 is not a legal term; it simply implies a separation or "putting away." The legal term used by the Savior is "writing of divorcement." (3 Nephi 12:31.)

3 NEPHI 12:48 *The Savior said, ". . . ye should be perfect even as I"*

In closing a major part of the Sermon on the Mount on the eastern continent, the Savior said: "Be ye therefore perfect, even as your Father which is in heaven is perfect." (Matthew 5:48.) To the Nephites, the Savior makes a significant addition: "Therefore I would that ye should be perfect even as I, or your Father who is in heaven is perfect." (3 Nephi 12:48.) When the Savior delivered this sermon on the eastern continent, he was just beginning his ministry; he had not yet brought about the atonement in the Garden of Gethsemane nor had he been resurrected from the dead. Thus, at that time he was not perfect in every sense. However, when he appeared to the Nephites as a glorified, resurrected God of glory, then he could rightfully counsel them to be perfect "even as I."

3 NEPHI 13:9-13 *The Book of Mormon account of "the Lord's Prayer"*

A comparison of the Lord's Prayer in the Book of Mormon (3 Nephi 13:9-13) and the New Testament (Matthew 6:9-13) indicates these changes: (1) the personal pronoun *who* is used in the Book of Mormon to refer to God rather than the impersonal pronoun *which;* (2) the term "Thy kingdom come" is omitted from the Book of Mormon account, perhaps because the church (or "kingdom") had already been established among the Nephites; (3) the Book of Mormon says "on" earth rather than "in" earth; (4) the sentence "Give us this day our daily bread" is omitted from the Book of Mormon account. The remainder of the two prayers is the same.

Some Latter-day Saints have raised the question as to why the clause "Lead us not into temptation" appears in the Book of Mormon account whereas the Prophet Joseph Smith apparently later changed this in his inspired revision of the Bible to read "And suffer us not to be led into temptation." The following statement is a possible answer to this question:

268   Few of the present generation can comprehend the attitude of the Protestant Christian world to the Bible at the time the Book of Mormon was published. Every word in it was regarded as sacred and the word of God. The people worshipped the book rather than the Author. Such was the condition of the minds of those to whom the latter-day gospel was carried. Therefore, not to put fresh obstacles in the way of the honest, or further hurt their susceptibilities, the Lord, in his divine wisdom and loving kindness, permitted those portions of the Bible that were incorporated in the Book of Mormon to appear in the identical language to which the people were accustomed. It was only when a change was absolutely necessary that he permitted it. If this supposition be correct, then in no case would this precaution have to be observed more strictly than in the utterances of the Redeemer himself, as, for instance, in the Lord's prayer.

To show how clearly the text of the Old Testament has been followed, we draw attention to some peculiarities in the extracts from the prophecies of Isaiah that appear in the Book of Mormon. In the second verse of the twenty-second chapter of the second book of Nephi, the word Jehovah appears with every letter capitalized. It is so printed in the Bible where this same verse occurs. (Isa. 12:2.) Elsewhere in the Book of Mormon the word appears with only the first letter a capital. In the same chapter (verse 6.) Zion is spelled Sion; in all other places it is spelled with a Z. But in this place it is copied letter for letter from the corresponding verse in Isaiah (12:6.) In Isaiah (6:2, 6.) the double plural—both Hebrew and English—appears in the word seraphions. It so appears when quoted in the Book of Mormon. The word silverlings appears (II Nephi 17:23.) in the reproduction of Isaiah 7:23. Now silverlings were as unknown to English speaking people at the time the Book of Mormon was translated as they were to the Nephites. These are small things, but they have weight when considered in this connection.

Another thing that must be remembered: it was not until considerably later in the history of the Prophet Joseph Smith, that it was shown to him that the more correct translation of this portion of the prayer would be, "Suffer us not to be led into temptation." (*Improvement Era*, 4:306-7.)

3 NEPHI 13:14-15   *Forgive others*

At the end of the Lord's Prayer, the Savior reminds the Nephites that if they are to pray sincerely "forgive us our debts, as we forgive our debtors" (3 Nephi 13:11), they must be willing to forgive others: "For, if ye forgive men their trespasses your heavenly Father will also forgive you; But if ye forgive not men their trespasses neither will your Father forgive your trespasses." (3 Nephi 13:14-15.)

President Spencer W. Kimball has explained what it means to forgive others:

Remember that we must forgive even if our offender did not repent and ask forgiveness. . . .

It frequently happens that offenses are committed when the offender is not aware of it. Something he has said or done is misconstrued or misunderstood. The offended one treasures in his heart the offense, adding to it such other things as might give fuel to the fire and justify his conclusions. Perhaps this is one of the reasons why the Lord requires that the offended one should make the overtures toward peace. . . .

To the Nephites the Lord said:

". . . if . . . thy brother hath aught against thee—Go thy way unto thy brother, and first be reconciled to thy brother, and then come unto me with full purpose of heart, and I will receive you." (3 Nephi 12:23-24.)

And to the disciples in Judea he said:

"Therefore if thou bring thy gift to the altar, and there rememberest that thy brother hath ought against thee;

"Leave there thy gift before the altar and go thy way; first be reconciled to thy brother, and then come and offer thy gift." (Matt. 6:23-24.)

Do we follow that commandment or do we sulk in our bitterness, waiting for our offender to learn of it and to kneel to us in remorse?

And this reconciliation suggests also forgetting. Unless you forget, have you forgiven? . . .

The Lord forgets when he has forgiven, and certainly must we. He inspired Isaiah to say:

"I, even I, am he that blotted out thy transgressions for mine own sake, and will not remember thy sins." (Isaiah 43:25.)

And again in our dispensation, he said:

"Behold, he who has repented of his sins, the same is forgiven; and I, the Lord, remember them no more." (D&C 58:42.)

And we are instructed by him that:

". . . thou shalt forgive him with all thine heart. . . ." (D&C 98:45.)

No bitterness of past frictions can be held in memory if we forgive with all our hearts. (*Conference Report,* October 1949, pp. 132-33.)

3 NEPHI 13:25-26   *Some specific teachings of the Savior to his disciples*

The way the Sermon on the Mount appears in the present King James Version would indicate that the entire sermon was given either to the whole world or to the Savior's chosen disciples only, depending on the interpretation placed upon Matthew 5:1-2. However, the Book of Mormon indicates that although most of the sermon was intended for the multitude, at least a portion of it was intended only for the chosen leaders. In the New Testament there is no break between the teachings "Ye cannot serve God and mammon" and "Therefore I say unto you, Take no thought for your life," etc. (Matthew 6:24-25.) However, in the Book of Mormon the Savior pauses between these two statements, turns from the multitude, and speaks only to "the twelve whom he had chosen." (3 Nephi 13:25.) The next ten verses are directed only to these chosen leaders.

3 NEPHI 15:4-8   *The Savior gave the law to Moses . . . and later fulfilled it*

Jesus identifies himself as the God who gave the law to Moses on the Mount of Sinai: "Behold, I am he that gave the law." (3 Nephi 15:5.) Furthermore, he indicates that through his atonement in the Garden of Gethsemane and at the time of his resurrection he fulfilled the law that he had given unto Moses. (3 Nephi 15:4-8.)

3 NEPHI 15:11-24   *"Other sheep I have which are not of this fold"*

During his earthly ministry, the Savior taught the people on the eastern continent as follows: "And other sheep I have, which are not of this fold: them also I must bring, and they shall hear my voice; and there shall be one fold, and one shepherd." (John 10:16.) In teaching the Nephite disciples, the resurrected Jesus Christ relates this teaching on the eastern continent; then he said concerning the Nephites, ". . . ye are they of whom I said: Other sheep I have which are not of this fold." (3 Nephi 15:21.) Thus the appearance of the resurrected Christ to the Nephites at least partially fulfilled his promise that his "other sheep" should hear his voice.

3 NEPHI 16:1-3; 17:4   *The promised appearance of the*
Savior to the lost tribes of Israel

After teaching the Nephites concerning his prophecy that he had "other sheep" that were not of the fold at Jerusalem, he then said to the Nephites: "And verily, verily, I say unto you that I have other sheep which are not of this land, neither of the land of Jerusalem . . . they of whom I speak are they who have not as yet heard my voice; neither have I at any time manifested myself unto them. But I have received a commandment of the Father that I shall go unto them . . . therefore I go to show myself unto them." (3 Nephi 16:1-3.)

In the next chapter he makes it clear that these "other sheep" not of the land of Jerusalem nor of the Americas are the lost tribes of Israel. Therefore, he says, ". . . now I go unto the Father, and also to show myself unto the lost tribes of Israel, for they are not lost unto the Father, for he knoweth whither he hath taken them." (3 Nephi 17:4.)

Earlier in the Book of Mormon (2 Nephi 29:11-14), the Lord promises that in the mouths of three great scriptural witnesses the divinity of Christ would be established. It is of interest to note that evidently the resurrected Jesus Christ appeared to all of the peoples who were to write these great scriptural witnesses. He appeared as a resurrected being to the Jews, from whom we get the Bible; he appeared as a resurrected being to the Nephites, from whom we get the Book of Mormon; and he promises here that he is going to appear as a resurrected being to the lost tribes of Israel, from whom shall come the third great scriptural witness.

3 NEPHI 17:14-15   *A prayer by the Savior*

Although the Savior undoubtedly frequently prayed while he was on the earth, only a few of his prayers are listed in the scriptures. One account of his praying is in 3 Nephi 17:14-25, and the witnesses of this prayer testified: "The eye hath never seen, neither hath the ear heard, before, so great and marvelous things as we saw and heard Jesus speak unto the Father; And no tongue can speak, neither can there be written by any man, neither can the hearts of men conceive so great and marvelous things as we both saw and heard Jesus speak; and no one can conceive of the joy which filled

272   our souls at the time we heard him pray for us unto the Father." (3 Nephi 17:16-17.) Perhaps this description helps explain why we do not have more accounts in the scriptures of the prayers of the Savior; even for the righteous Nephites the experience was so overpowering that "they were overcome." (3 Nephi 17:18.)

3 NEPHI 18:1-2   *The sacrament of the Lord's Supper*

The Book of Mormon account of the sacrament of the Lord's Supper greatly clarifies the four accounts given in the New Testament. (See Matthew 26:26-29; Mark 14:22-25; Luke 22:19-20; and 1 Corinthians 11:24-27.) Also, the account in the Book of Mormon (3 Nephi 18:1-12) would indicate that the Catholic doctrine of real presence (or transubstantiation) is not true. The Catholics define their doctrine as follows:

The Catholic Church has always interpreted the words: "This is My Body; This is My Blood," which occur in the four accounts of the Last Supper, in a strictly literal sense. No explanation of these simple words can make their meaning clearer. . . .

The doctrine of the Real Presence is undoubtedly a great mystery like the Creation, the Blessed Trinity and the Incarnation, but it is not impossible, because it does not imply any self-contradiction. If God can create the universe out of nothing, why cannot He change the substance of bread and wine into His Body and Blood? . . .

Non-Catholics declare the doctrine of the Real Presence impossible, because they think it involves a self-contradiction. They suppose that it requires the same thing to be both bread and not bread at the same time. This is not the Catholic teaching. After Consecration the species of bread is not really bread, but the Body of Christ, for the substance of the bread has been changed into the substance of Christ's Body. What is not changed is the "accidents or the sensible qualities of the bread; viz., its color, taste," etc. But the reality of a thing lies in its substance, the invisible part of it, not in the accidents, or visible part. . . .

This is certainly a mysterious doctrine, hard to understand, because there is nothing like it in all our experience. But the mysteries of Christianity are all unique, because they pertain to divine things. (*The Question Box* [Houston: The Question Box, 1950], pp. 251, 254-55.)

The Book of Mormon, however, indicates that when we partake of the emblems of the sacrament we should do so *in remembrance* of the body and the blood of Jesus Christ; we are not partaking of the actual flesh and blood of the Savior. Also, the Lord has said:

Listen to the voice of Jesus Christ, your Lord, your God, and your Redeemer, whose word is quick and powerful. For, behold, I say unto you, that it mattereth not what ye shall eat or what ye shall drink when ye partake of the sacrament, if it so be that ye do it with an eye single to my glory—remembering unto the Father my body which was laid down for you, and my blood which was shed for the remission of your sins. (D&C 27:1-2.)

The Book of Mormon also clarifies the following points concerning the sacrament:

1. It should be administered to only by those who have the proper authority ("there shall one be ordained among you, and to him will I give power that he shall break bread and bless it"—3 Nephi 18:5).

2. It should be given to those people who are members of the Church ("unto all those who shall believe and be baptized in my name"—3 Nephi 18:5).

3. It is a remembrance ordinance of the atonement of Jesus Christ ("this shall ye do in remembrance of my body, which I have shown unto you . . . and . . . in remembrance of my blood, which I have shed for you"—3 Nephi 18:7, 11).

4. It is a covenant ordinance, and those who partake of it promise that they will keep all the commandments of God ("this doth witness unto the Father that ye are willing to do that which I have commanded you"—3 Nephi 18:10); ("And if ye do always remember me ye shall have my Spirit to be with you"—3 Nephi 18:11).

5. It should be partaken of often by members of the Church ("And I give unto you a commandment that ye shall do these things. And if ye shall always do these things blessed are ye. . . . And behold, ye shall meet together oft"— 3 Nephi 18:12, 22).

6. It should not be partaken of by one who is unworthy ("ye shall not suffer any one knowingly to partake of my flesh and blood unworthily"—3 Nephi 18:28-29).

3 NEPHI 18:15-25 *Some teachings of the Savior on prayer*

The best recorded sermon on prayer given by the Savior is found in the Book of Mormon, 3 Nephi 18. In eleven brief verses the Savior gives the following counsel and reasons for

274 praying: We should pray because he has set the example (verse 16); we should pray lest we should enter into temptation (verse 18); we should pray so that we will not be led away captive by the devil (verse 15); we should pray "unto the Father" in the name of Jesus Christ (verse 19); we should pray for things which are right for us (verse 20); we should pray in faith (verse 20); we should pray with our families so that our wives and children may be blessed (verse 21); we should meet together and pray often (verse 22); we should pray for others to meet with us (verse 23); we should pray as an example for others (verse 24).

3 NEPHI 18:28-29 *Do not partake of the sacrament unworthily*

The Savior counseled his disciples to see that no unworthy person partook of the sacrament, "For whoso eateth and drinketh my flesh and blood unworthily eateth and drinketh damnation to his soul." (3 Nephi 18:29.) This same admonition that we are not to partake of the sacrament unless we are worthy and are willing to keep the commandments of the Lord has been given to us in this dispensation. (See D&C 46:4.)

Concerning the evil of partaking of the sacrament unworthily, President David O. McKay has said: "To partake of the sacrament unworthily is to take a step toward spiritual death. No man can be dishonest within himself without deadening the susceptibility of his spirit. Sin can stun the conscience as a blow on the head can stun the physical senses. He who promises one thing and deliberately fails to keep his word, adds sin to sin. On natural principles such a man 'eats and drinks condemnation to his soul.'" (*Conference Report,* October 1929, pp. 14-15.)

3 NEPHI 18:36-39 *The disciples receive the power to give the Holy Ghost*

When the Savior left his disciples after his first appearance to them, "he touched with his hand the disciples whom he had chosen, one by one, even until he had touched them all, and spake unto them as he touched them. . . . the disciples bare record that he gave them power to give the Holy Ghost. And I will show unto you hereafter that this record is true." (3 Nephi 18:36-37.)

Evidently the pronoun *I* in this quotation refers to the historian Mormon when he promises "I will show unto you hereafter that this record is true"; that is, Mormon is going to show later in his record that the Savior did give the disciples the power to bestow the Holy Ghost. Some persons might question whether or not Mormon does indicate this later in his record. However, it is of interest to note that as soon as Moroni starts writing, he gives us the exact wording of the prayer of the Savior on this occasion. (See Moroni 2.)

3 NEPHI 19:4, 11-13 *The baptism of the twelve Nephite disciples*

The question has sometimes been raised by readers of the Book of Mormon as to why the Nephite disciples had to be rebaptized when it was quite evident that they had already received the ordinance of baptism. The record indicates that the twelve disciples desired *most* that "the Holy Ghost should be given unto them." (3 Nephi 19:9.) They prayed to the Father for this blessing; then Nephi "went down into the water and was baptized. And he came up out of the water and began to baptize. And he baptized all those whom Jesus had chosen. And . . . when they were all baptized and had come up out of the water, the Holy Ghost did fall upon them, and they were filled with the Holy Ghost and with fire." (3 Nephi 19:11-13.)

Concerning the baptism of the Nephites at this particular time, President Joseph Fielding Smith has written: "When Christ appeared to the Nephites on this continent, he commanded them to be baptized, although they had been baptized previously for the remission of their sins. . . . The Savior commanded Nephi and the people to be baptized again, *because he had organized anew the Church under the gospel. Before that it had been organized under the law.* For the same reason Joseph Smith and those who had been baptized prior to April 6, 1830, were again baptized on the day of the organization of the Church." (*Doctrines of Salvation,* 2:336.)

3 NEPHI 19:20-23 *A prayer given by the Savior*

With the exception of the Lord's Prayer, which he gave to us as an example, the scriptures contain very few personal prayers of the Savior. However, a notable exception to this is

3 Nephi 19:20-23, which contains the exact words of a personal prayer given by the Savior. This prayer is a classic example for several reasons. First, the prayer is very personal. This brief prayer of only four verses contains forty personal pronouns used by the Savior. Also, the prayer contains the thanks of the Savior to our Heavenly Father (verse 20) and a petition to the Father for a future blessing (verse 21). Another interesting feature of this prayer is that the Savior explains to the Father why the Nephites are praying directly to him rather than to the Father: ". . . they pray unto me because I am with them." (3 Nephi 19:22.) Elsewhere the Savior clearly taught that we should pray unto the Father in the name of the Savior. (See 3 Nephi 18:20.)

3 NEPHI 19:28-29 *How we may become one with the Father and the Son*

One of the most disputed doctrines of Christianity involves the characteristics of God and the other members of the Godhead. Because of certain statements in the New Testament indicating that members of the Godhead are one, some theologians have taught that the members of the Godhead are one in substance. However, a careful reading of the New Testament indicates this is not the meaning. For example, in his great prayer of supplication, the Savior prays to the Father for his chosen disciples and then adds: "Neither pray I for these alone, but for them also which shall believe on me through their word; That they all may be one; as thou, Father, art in me, and I in thee, that they also may be one in us: that the world may believe that thou hast sent me. And the glory which thou gavest me I have given them; *that they may be one, even as we are one.*" (John 17:20-22. Italics added.)

It is clear from this scripture that the Savior is not praying for the people to become one in substance with him and the Father. This statement is further clarified by the Savior in the Book of Mormon where he indicates again that he is praying for all those who will believe on him. Then he adds: "Father, I pray not for the world, but for those whom thou hast given me out of the world, because of their faith, that they may be purified in me, . . . that I may be glorified in them." (3 Nephi 19:29.)

Thus the way we may become one with the Father and

the Son is to keep the commandments of the Lord so that we might be sanctified or purified and be worthy to have their presence with us.

3 NEPHI 20:6-7   *The miracle of providing the bread and wine for the sacrament*

A miracle has been defined as the use of natural law in a way that is not fully understood. In this sense the term *miracle* could be used to describe electricity, for no scientist professes to understand all the laws upon which electricity is based. Certainly the Savior's providing bread and wine for the sacrament could be termed a miracle. The Savior did not circumvent natural law; rather, he used the law in a way we do not fully understand. Many people can make bread by taking wheat and adding other ingredients such as yeast and sugar; this process also requires the presence of the ingredients plus heat and time. However, Jesus Christ, the Creator of the heavens and the earth, was able to apply these natural laws almost instantaneously. That is, although there was no bread present, he was able to reach out his hands, gather the elements, and break bread that could be used in the sacrament.

3 NEPHI 20:14-16   *A remnant of Jacob to be given great power in the last days*

The Savior taught the righteous Nephites that several generations after his appearance to them their descendants would become wicked again; finally the Gentiles would be brought to occupy the lands that had been given for the inheritance of the Nephites. However, the Savior also tells the Nephites that "if the Gentiles do not repent after the blessing which they shall receive, . . . Then shall ye, who are a remnant of the house of Jacob, go forth among them; and ye shall be in the midst of them who shall be many; and ye shall be among them as a lion among the beasts of the forest, and as a young lion among the flocks of sheep, who, if he goeth through both treadeth down and teareth in pieces, and none can deliver." (3 Nephi 20:15-16.) Later in his sermon the Savior repeats this prophecy (3 Nephi 21:12); then he says: "wo be unto the Gentiles except they repent." (3 Nephi 21:14.)

A possible interpretation of this prophecy has been given by Daniel H. Wells as follows:

278   To add to the sufferings and great calamities of the American nation, they will be greatly distressed by the aborigines, who will "marshall themselves, and become exceeding angry," and vex them "with a sore vexation." This event, we believe, may not take place in its fulness until the nation has been greatly weakened by the death of millions in their own revolutionary battles. To what extent the Indians will have power over the nation, is not stated in this revelation; but from what Jesus informed their forefathers at the time of his personal ministry among them, as recorded in the Book of Mormon, they will have power in a great measure over the whole nation. In speaking upon this subject, Jesus prophesies as follows:

"Therefore, it shall come to pass, that whosoever will not believe in my words, who am Jesus Christ, which the Father shall cause him" (Joseph Smith) "to bring forth unto the Gentiles, and shall give unto him power that he shall bring them forth unto the Gentiles, (it shall be done even as Moses said) they shall be cut off from among my people who are of the covenant; and my people, who are a remnant of Jacob, shall be among the Gentiles, yea, in the midst of them, as a lion among the beasts of the forest, as a young lion among the flocks of sheep, who, if he go through, both treadeth down and teareth in pieces, and none can deliver." [3 Nephi 21:11-12.]

. . . It appears more improbable, now, to the people of the United States, that the Indians should ever become so powerful an enemy and so dreadful a scourge to them, . . . that they would ever engage in so dreadful a civil war as that now raging. Yet this will as surely be fulfilled as have the other portions of this prophecy. (*Millennial Star*, 27:187.)

3 NEPHI 20:29-31, 46   *Prophecies of the Savior now in the process of fulfillment*

Many prophecies of the Savior concerning the house of Israel have already been fulfilled. Some of these were fulfilled before the coming forth of the Book of Mormon, but many of them have been fulfilled since the publication of this holy scripture. However, others of these prophecies of the Savior are now in the process of fulfillment and still others are in the future.

For example, in verse 29 the Savior promises that in the last days the house of Israel should be gathered together to "the land of their fathers for their inheritance, which is the land of Jerusalem, which is the promised land unto them forever, saith the Father." (3 Nephi 20:29.) This prophecy was made by the Savior in A.D. 34 and it was published in the Book of Mormon in 1830. Yet it was not until 1948, 118 years after the publication of the Book of Mormon, that the modern state of Israel was established and these people could gather home to the land of their inheritance.

Also, in verse 30 the Savior prophesies: "And it shall come to pass that the time cometh, when the fulness of my gospel shall be preached unto them." Again, the great missionary program of the Church was not organized in 1830 when the Book of Mormon was published. However, since that time the gospel has been taken to many peoples upon the earth, including many of the Jewish people. In verse 31 the Savior continues: "And they shall believe in me, that I am Jesus Christ, the Son of God, and shall pray unto the Father in my name." So far this prophecy has been only partially fulfilled; the acceptance of Jesus Christ by the Jewish people as a whole is still in the future.

3 NEPHI 21:1-7, 9, 12, 22-29   *Teachings of the Savior on the gathering of Israel*

This statement by the Savior is one of the most significant statements in all scripture concerning the gathering of Israel in the last days. It is of particular significance because (1) it is given by the resurrected Jesus Christ himself, (2) he clearly indicates that these aspects of the gathering are to take place in the last days, and (3) the gathering of Israel includes much more than the gathering of the Jewish people to the land of Israel.

Elder LeGrand Richards has pointed out the major concepts that are included in these brief verses:

In considering the above declaration, it should be remembered that the Book of Mormon was published and given to the world in 1830, the year the Church was organized, when Joseph Smith was only twenty-four years old. And yet this statement covers all the essential points with respect to the gathering of latter-day Israel, to wit:

1. That the New Jerusalem would be established in the land of America.

2. That the church of Jesus Christ would be established in the land of America.

3. That the church would be established among the gentiles. . . .

4. That at the time that his church would be established among the gentiles in America, it would be a sign that the time had arrived, "That I shall gather in, from their long dispersion, my people, O house of Israel, and shall establish again among them my Zion." (3 Nephi 21:1.)

5. That the accomplishment of these things shall precede the second coming of the Christ: "And I also will be in the midst." (3 Nephi 21:25.)

6. That at that time, the Lord would set his hand to gather his people from among all nations: "Yea, and then shall the work commence, with the Father, among all nations, in preparing the way whereby his people may be gathered home to the land of their inheritance." (3 Nephi 21:28.)

7. These declarations of the Savior confirm the statements of the prophets already referred to, to the effect that Israel would be sifted among all nations. (*A Marvelous Work and a Wonder,* p. 207.)

3 NEPHI 21:4   *The destiny of America*

Elder Mark E. Petersen has explained the significance of this verse as follows:

I take you back now to the time when the Savior was ministering in America. I hope that each one of you will read 3 Nephi 21. It is extremely significant. It is meaningful to us as Americans and as Latter-day Saints who live right now. You will recall that the Savior was talking to the Nephites about the Gentiles who would occupy this country in the latter days. He talked about the destiny of America, and explained why there would be a United States. Among other things, he said this:

"... it is wisdom in the Father that they [the Gentiles in this country] should be established in this land, and be set up as a free people by the power of the Father...."

Then he gives the reason. He had been talking about the gospel; he had been talking about the predictions; he had been talking about ... the records which eventually became the Book of Mormon. He said that this great modern nation of the Gentiles should be established on this land as a free people. And now I quote directly:

"... that these things might come forth from them unto a remnant of your seed, that the covenant of the Father may be fulfilled which he hath covenanted with his people, O house of Israel." (3 Nephi 21:4.)

That is the reason there is an America. That is the destiny of America. The Almighty kept this land free from other people until such time as he was ready to establish our nation....

So, . . . this is God's land. He raised it up specially as he has raised up no other nation. He has given us our flag. So far as I am concerned the flag of the United States is the flag of Almighty God. Old Glory to me stands for everything that the gospel of Christ stands for, because Old Glory was raised up because there was to be a restoration of the gospel. I cannot separate my flag and my religion. I would fight for my flag as I would fight for my religion. (*BYU Speeches of the Year,* 1968.)

3 NEPHI 21:22-26 *Who shall build the "New Jerusalem" of the last days?*

The "New Jerusalem" of the last days will be built on the American continent by (1) "the remnant of Jacob," (2) the Gentiles who "shall come into the covenant and be numbered among . . . the remnant of Jacob," and (3) "as many of the house of Israel as shall come." (3 Nephi 21:22-25. Read also 3 Nephi 20:22; Ether 13:1-12.) After quoting extensively from chapters 20 and 21 of 3 Nephi, President Marion G. Romney explained the role of the "remnant of Jacob" in building the New Jerusalem:

From these declarations by Jesus, it is certain that the believing, repentant, righteous, faithful Indians shall be among "the remnant of Jacob" who are to build the New Jerusalem to which the Savior will come.

As early as 1831 the Lord assured the Prophet Joseph that "before the great day of" his coming should arrive "Jacob shall flourish in the wilderness, and the Lamanites shall blossom as the rose." (D&C 49:24.)

Some fifty-seven years ago, Hyrum M. Smith and Janne M. Sjodahl, commenting on this prophecy, wrote:

"The American Indians are, indeed, flourishing today. On Government reservations they enjoy a measure of prosperity beyond the dreams of their fathers. In Indian Territory they have attained a high degree of both civilization and prosperity. Indians now occupy Government offices and seats in legislative assemblies, in schools and pulpits, and in every walk of life. They are flourishing. This is all the more remarkable because at one time the general belief was that they were a vanishing race. When the United States became an independent nation, the number of Indians in North America was estimated at three millions, and in the year 1876 at only one million three hundred thousand. In 1907 the decrease had been checked, and an increase to one million four hundred and seventy-four thousand was reported. Only a prophet inspired by God could have foreseen such a decided turn in the tide of Indian affairs." (*D&C Commentary,* p. 287.)

In 1849, Orson Pratt wrote:

". . . the fulness of the gospel, with its heavenly powers and blessings is now in the midst of many powerful tribes or nations of Israel or Indians; and thus has the prophecy of Jesus been in part fulfilled. The remainder of this great prophecy will soon come to pass, and then many of the Indian nations will become a civilized and Christian people, after which the Indians, who are the remnant of Joseph, will build [Had I been writing this I should have said, "Will assist in building"] the city called the New Jerusalem or Zion, being assisted by the Gentile Saints.

"If the Gentile Saints had built up the city of Zion in Jackson county, Missouri, before the gospel had been taken from among that nation, and before many of the Indian nations became converted, it would have falsified the prediction of Jesus in the Book of Mormon.

"The converted remnants of Joseph are to be the principal actors in the great work of the building up of the city of Zion [I believe this is true. I also believe that the said "remnants of Joseph" include the descendants of Ephraim]; after which the Indian nations will be gathered in one to the city of Zion and the surrounding country; then the powers of heaven will be revealed, and Jesus will descend in his glory and dwell in the midst of Zion." (*Millennial Star,* October 1, 1849, p. 293.)

That the Lord will continue to bless and prosper the Indians and all the rest of us in preparing Zion for the coming of the Savior, I humbly pray, in the name of Jesus Christ. Amen. (*BYU Speeches of the Year,* 1972.

3 NEPHI 22:1-3 *The desolate cities of the Gentiles to be inhabited*

In describing some of the events of the last days including the destructions to come upon the Gentiles if they do not repent, the Savior quotes from chapter 54 of Isaiah. Among the prophecies contained in this chapter is the promise to the house of Israel that in the last days "thy seed shall inherit the Gentiles and make the desolate cities to be inhabited." (3 Nephi 22:3. See also Isaiah 54:3.)

3 NEPHI 22:15-17 *Prophecies concerning the house of Israel in the last days*

An additional prophecy by Isaiah (and repeated here by the Savior) concerns the gathering of the house of Israel in the last days. Isaiah warns the house of Israel that after they are gathered together, the nations of the earth "shall surely gather together against thee, not by me; whosoever shall gather together against thee shall fall for thy sake. . . . No weapon that is formed against thee shall prosper." (3 Nephi 22:15, 17.) Some biblical scholars have assumed that the prophecies in Isaiah were fulfilled before the coming of Jesus Christ. However, the fact that the Savior quotes these prophecies from Isaiah 54 and relates them to the events of the last days would indicate they pertain to the dispensation of the fulness of times.

3 NEPHI 23:7-14   *The value of the scriptures*

It is of interest to note how important, the scriptures are in the eyes of the Lord. The resurrected Jesus Christ not only read the records of the Nephites and asked the people to do the same, but he also commanded that an important element that had been omitted should be added to the records to make them complete. (3 Nephi 23:7-14.) Thus he was not only supporting the testimony of his servant, Samuel the Lamanite, but he was also helping to make the scriptures complete in and of themselves so far as testimony is concerned.

3 NEPHI 24-25   *The prophecies of Malachi*

Malachi, the last writer in our present Old Testament, lived approximately 400 B.C. Since his writings were not included on the brass plates of Laban, the Savior gave the words of Malachi to the Nephites. The angel Moroni also referred to these prophecies during his first visit with Joseph Smith, but he changed them as follows:

For behold, the day cometh that shall burn as an oven, and all the proud, yea, and all that do wickedly shall burn as stubble; for they that come shall burn them, saith the Lord of Hosts, that it shall leave them neither root nor branch.

And again, he quoted the fifth verse thus: *Behold, I will reveal unto you the Priesthood, by the hand of Elijah the prophet, before the coming of the great and dreadful day of the Lord.*

He also quoted the next verse differently: *And he shall plant in the hearts of the children the promises made to the fathers, and the hearts of the children shall turn to their fathers. If it were not so, the whole earth would be utterly wasted at his coming.* (Joseph Smith 2:37-39.)

It should be noted that Moroni's alterations of the Bible and Book of Mormon texts were probably for emphasis and clarification rather than correction.

284   3 NEPHI 24:8-10   *A reference to tithing*

Although the Nephites evidently lived the law of tithing, the only definite reference to this subject in the Book of Mormon appears in the Savior's quotation from Malachi:

Will a man rob God? Yet ye have robbed me. But ye say: Wherein have we robbed thee? In tithes and offerings. . . .

Bring ye all the tithes into the storehouse, that there may be meat in my house; and prove me now herewith, saith the Lord of Hosts, if I will not open you the windows of heaven, and pour you out a blessing that there shall not be room enough to receive it. (3 Nephi 24:8, 10. See also Malachi 3:8, 10.)

3 NEPHI 25:5-6   *The coming of Elijah*

Malachi closes his book with the statement by the Savior that "before the coming of the great and dreadful day of the Lord" Elijah should come to "turn the heart of the fathers to the children, and the heart of the children to their fathers, lest I come and smite the earth with a curse." (3 Nephi 25:5-6. See also Malachi 4:5-6; Joseph Smith 2:37-39.)

Many biblical scholars have assumed that the prophesied "second coming of Elijah" took place during the lifetime of the Savior when Elijah appeared on the Mount of Transfiguration. (See Mark 9:4.) However, the fact that the Savior quoted this prophecy to the Nephites after his resurrection would indicate the fulfillment was still in the future. Also, a careful wording of this scripture indicates that the prophesied coming of Elijah pertained not to the first coming of the Savior, but to his second coming; Malachi said that Elijah the prophet should be sent before the coming of "the *great and dreadful* day of the Lord." The first coming of the Savior was a great day, but it was not dreadful; however, the second coming of the Savior will be both a great day (for the righteous) and a dreadful day (for the wicked).

Final proof that this prophecy pertains to the last days is found in the statement by Joseph Smith that on September 21, 1823, the angel Moroni quoted this prophecy and said it was about to be fulfilled. (See Joseph Smith 2:36-40.) Most Latter-day Saints believe this prophecy was fulfilled on April 3, 1836, when Elijah appeared in the Kirtland Temple and restored the sealing powers of the priesthood. The Doctrine and Covenants records the following concerning this visitation:

. . . another great and glórious vision burst upon us; for Elijah the prophet, who was taken to heaven without tasting death, stood before us, and said:

Behold, the time has fully come, which was spoken of by the mouth of Malachi—testifying that he [Elijah] should be sent, before the great and dreadful day of the Lord come—

To turn the hearts of the fathers to the children, and the children to the fathers, lest the whole earth be smitten with a curse—

Therefore, the keys of this dispensation are committed into your hands; and by this ye may know that the great and dreadful day of the Lord is near, even at the doors. (D&C 110:13-16.)

3 NEPHI 26:2-11   *Only a few of the teachings of the Savior are found in the Book of Mormon*

In teaching the gospel to the righteous Nephites, the Savior explains why the fulness of the gospel has not been revealed to all the people upon the earth. Mormon then explains why he did not write all of the statements of the Savior into his own record: "And now there cannot be written in this book even a hundredth part of the things which Jesus did truly teach unto the people; . . . these things . . . are a lesser part of the things which he taught the people; . . . I was about to write them, all which were engraven upon the plates of Nephi, but the Lord forbade it, saying: I will try the faith of my people." (3 Nephi 26:6, 8, 11.)

In explanation as to why he did not allow his greater truths to be revealed, the Savior said that it was "expedient" to give his lesser teachings first to try the faith of the people. Then he warns: "And if it so be that they will not believe these things, then shall the greater things be withheld from them, unto their condemnation." (3 Nephi 26:10.)

3 NEPHI 26:21 and 27:1-8   *The name of the true church of Jesus Christ*

In answer to a question among the disciples as to what the name of the church should be, the Savior said that the church should be called after his name if it is established by him, and if it is built upon his gospel. (3 Nephi 27:8.) The Savior also reminds his disciples of the scripture that says, ". . . ye must take upon you the name of Christ." (3 Nephi 27:5.) Thus the name of the true church is The Church of Jesus Christ. However, to differentiate the true church of

286   Christ on the earth now from the church established during the meridian of time, the Savior has directed that in this dispensation the name of his church should be The Church of Jesus Christ of Latter-day Saints. (D&C 115:4.)

3 NEPHI 27:13-18   *The atonement of Jesus Christ*

In explaining his gospel to the Nephites of about A.D. 34, the resurrected Jesus Christ also explained why it was necessary for him to come here upon this earth and atone for sin and provide for the resurrection. Concerning this dual contribution of the Savior and Redeemer of mankind, B. H. Roberts has written:

The effect of Adam's transgression was to destroy the harmony of things in this world. As a consequence of his fall man is banished from the presence of God—a spiritual death takes place and man becomes sensual, devilish, unholy, is cursed, we say, with a strong inclination to sinfulness. Man is also made subject to a temporal death, a separation of the spirit and body. Much might have been gained by this union of his spirit with his body of flesh and bone could it have been immortal, but that is now lost, by this temporal death, this separation of spirit and body. These conditions would have remained eternally fixed as the result of the operation of law—inexorable law, called "the justice of God," admitting of nothing else; for the law was given to eternal beings and by them violated, and man is left in the grasp of eternal justice, with all its consequences upon his head and the head of his progeny. And the justice of the law admitted the conditions, admitted that the penalties affixed should be effective, but this is justice—stern, unrelenting justice; justice untempered by mercy. But mercy must in some way be made to reach man, yet in a way also that will not destroy justice; for justice must be maintained, else all is confusion—ruin. If justice be destroyed—if justice be not maintained— "God will cease to be God." Hence mercy may not be introduced into the divine economy of this world without a vindication of the broken law by some means or other, for divine laws as well as human ones are mere nullities if their penalties be not in force.

The penalty of the law then, transgressed by Adam, must be executed, or else an adequate atonement must be made for man's transgression. This the work of the Christ. He makes the atonement. He comes to earth and assumes responsibility for this transgression of law, and gathers up into his own soul all the suffering due to the transgression of the law by Adam. All the suffering due to individual transgression of law—the direct consequences of the original transgression—from Adam to the end of the world.

The burden of us all is laid upon him. He will bear our griefs and carry our sorrows. He will be wounded for our transgressions, and be bruised for our iniquities. The chastisement of our peace will be upon him; on him is laid the iniquity of us all; by his stripes shall we be healed. That is to say, having gathered into himself all the suffering and sorrows due to all the sinning that shall be in the world, he is able to dictate the terms upon which man may lay hold of mercy—by which mercy may heal his wounds—and these terms he names in the conditions of the gospel, the acceptance of which brings complete redemption. The Christ brings to pass the resurrection of the dead. The spirit and the body are eternally reunited; the temporal death—one of the effects of Adam's transgression—is overcome. There is no more physical death; the "soul"—the eternally united spirit and body are now to be immortal as spirit alone before was immortal. The man so immortal is brought back into the presence of God, and if he has accepted the terms of the gospel by which he is redeemed from the effects of his own, as well as from Adam's transgression, his spiritual death is ended, and henceforth he may be spiritually immortal as well as physically immortal—eternally with God in an atmosphere of righteousness—the spiritual death is overcome.

Such I make out to be the Book of Mormon doctrine of the atonement, and the redemption of man through the gospel. (*New Witnesses for God,* 3:216-18.)

For additional review on the important subject of the atonement, re-read the materials following 2 Nephi 9:6-9 and Mosiah 3:15-27.

3 NEPHI 27:13-21   *A review of the gospel of Jesus Christ*

One of the conditions to be met by the true church is that it should be based upon the gospel of Christ. After explaining this point to his disciples, the Savior then reviews the gospel of Jesus Christ. One of the high points of all scripture is found in 3 Nephi 27:13-21 wherein the Savior outlines the essential doctrines of the gospel and explains their importance. He then summarizes the gospel in one brief statement: "Now this is the commandment: Repent, all ye ends of the earth, and come unto me and be baptized in my name, that ye may be sanctified by the reception of the Holy Ghost, that ye may stand spotless before me at the last day. Verily, verily, I say unto you, this is my gospel. . . ." (3 Nephi 27:20-21.)

Thus a major purpose of the gospel is to provide those

288   principles and ordinances which enable us to become sanctified and worthy to live again in the presence of our Heavenly Father. Concerning the importance of the atonement of Jesus Christ and the gospel plan of salvation, President Marion G. Romney has said:

The atonement of the Master is the central point of world history. Without it, the whole purpose for the creation of earth and our living upon it would fail. . . .

From the days of Adam to the days of Jesus Christ, every people who understood the gospel offered blood sacrifices, using animals or birds without blemish. This they did in contemplation of the great event which was to take place in the Meridian of Time.

When Jesus was about to go through that terrible suffering incident to the atonement, he took his disciples with him to the Passover. . . .

Jesus then went into the Garden of Gethsemane. There he suffered most. He suffered greatly on the cross, of course, but other men had died by crucifixion; in fact, a man hung on either side of him as he died on the cross. But no man, nor set of men, nor all men put together, ever suffered what the Redeemer suffered in the Garden. He went there to pray and suffer. One of the New Testament writers says that it ". . . was as it were great drops of blood falling down to the ground." (Luke 22:44.)

In this dispensation the Lord, calling upon the people to repent, tells them that unless they repent they must suffer even as he suffered. He describes that suffering in these words:

"Which suffering caused myself, even God, the greatest of all, to tremble because of pain, and to bleed at every pore, and to suffer both body and spirit—and would that I might not drink the bitter cup, and shrink—

"Nevertheless, glory be to the Father, and I partook and finished my preparations unto the children of men." (D&C 19:18-19.)

. . . I cannot here discuss with you in detail what the atonement of the Savior means to us. But without it, no man or woman would ever be resurrected. . . . And so all the world, believers and nonbelievers, are indebted to the Redeemer for their certain resurrection, because the resurrection will be as wide as was the fall, which brought death to every man.

There is another phase of the atonement which makes me love the Savior even more, and fills my soul with gratitude beyond expression. It is that in addition to atoning for Adam's transgression, thereby bringing about the resurrection, the Savior by his suffering paid the debt for my personal sins. He paid the debt for your personal sins and for the personal sins of every living soul that ever dwelt upon the earth or that ever will dwell in mortality upon the earth. But this he did conditionally. The benefits of this suffering for our individual transgressions will not come to us unconditionally in the same sense that the resurrection will come regardless of what we do. If we partake of the blessings of the atonement as far as our individual transgressions are concerned, we must obey the law.

And it is perfectly just that we are required to obey it because through the fall of Adam, man's free agency was preserved. We had nothing to do with death's coming into the world; death came as a consequence of Adam's fall. But we have everything to do with our own acts. When we commit sin, we are estranged from God and rendered unfit to enter into his presence. No unclean thing can enter into his presence. We cannot of ourselves, no matter how we may try, rid ourselves of the stain which is upon us as a result of our own transgressions. That stain must be washed away by the blood of the Redeemer, and he has set up the way by which that stain may be removed. That way is the gospel of Jesus Christ. The gospel requires us to believe in the Redeemer, accept his atonement, repent of our sins, be baptized by immersion for the remission of our sins, receive the gift of the Holy Ghost by the laying on of hands, and continue faithfully to observe, or do the best we can to observe, the principles of the gospel all the days of our lives. (*Conference Report,* October 1953, pp. 34-36.)

3 NEPHI 27:19-20 *The fulness of the gospel*

In the Doctrine and Covenants, section 20, verses 8-10, the Lord has said that the Book of Mormon contains "the fulness of the gospel of Jesus Christ to the Gentiles and to the Jews also." Many people have raised the question as to how the Book of Mormon could actually contain the fulness of the gospel when it doesn't even refer to such important ordinances as the temple endowment and marriage for eternity. Concerning this question, Joseph Fielding Smith has written:

First of all, let us consider what the Lord means by "a fulness of the gospel." He did not mean to convey the impression that every truth belonging to exaltation in the kingdom of God had been delivered to the Nephites and was recorded in the Book of Mormon, to be delivered to Gentiles and Jews in this dispensation. Neither would this statement imply that every truth belonging to the celestial kingdom and exaltation therein was to be found within the covers of the Book of Mormon. There are many truths belonging to the exaltation that have not been revealed, nor will they be revealed to man while he is in mortality. We must concede it to be a fact that there are many things related to the exaltation which cannot be received now and do not concern mortal men. These truths were not given to the Nephites; neither can they be given to us in this present day, for they do not in any way apply to the needs of the mortal condition, nor could we comprehend them while we are in mortality. These things belong to the kingdom of God and will be revealed to those who attain to the celestial exaltation.

. . . . The fulness of the gospel then, as expressed in the Doctrine and Covenants, has reference to the principles of salvation by which we attain unto this glory. Therefore the Lord has revealed in the Book of Mormon all that is needful to direct people who are willing to hearken to its precepts, to a fulness of the blessings of the kingdom of God. The Book of Mormon then, does contain all the truths which are essential for Gentiles and Jews or any other people, to prepare them for this glorious exaltation in the celestial kingdom of God.

It is beyond dispute, or should be, that the Book of Mormon teaches that the first principles of the gospel are, faith in God; repentance from sin; baptism for the remission of sins; the gift of the Holy Ghost, obedience to divine law and that man cannot be saved in ignorance of these divine truths. It teaches that "wickedness never was happiness," and that no man can be saved without repentance of sin. (*Answers to Gospel Questions,* 3:95-97.)

President Charles W. Penrose has also written on this subject:

Now, some of our brethren have taken up quite a discussion as to the fulness of the everlasting gospel. We are told that the Book of Mormon contains the fulness of the gospel, that those who like to get up a dispute, say that the Book of Mormon does not contain any reference to the work of salvation for the dead, and there are many other things pertaining to the gospel that are not developed in that book, and yet we are told that book contains "the fulness of the everlasting gospel." Well, what is the fulness of the gospel? You read carefully the revelation in regard to the three glories, section 76, in the Doctrine and Covenants, and you find there defined what the gospel is. There God, the Eternal Father, and Jesus Christ, His Son, and the Holy Ghost, are held up as the three persons in the Trinity—the one God, the Father, the Word, and the Holy Ghost, all three being united and being one God. When people believe in that doctrine and obey the ordinances which are spoken of in the same list of principles, you get the fulness of the gospel for this reason: If you really believe so as to have faith in our Eternal Father and in his Son, Jesus Christ, the Redeemer, and will hear Him, you will learn all about what is needed to be done for the salvation of the living and the redemption of the dead.

When people believe and repent and are baptized by Divine authority, and the Holy Ghost is conferred upon them as a gift, they receive the everlasting gospel. We used to call it, and it is now called in the revelations, the "Gift of the Holy Ghost," the Holy Ghost, the spirit that proceeds from the presence of the Father throughout the immensity of space, which guides, directs, enlightens, which is light in and of itself, which is the spirit of intelligence, the "light of truth." . . . (*Conference Report,* April 1922, pp. 27-28.)

3 NEPHI 28 *Were the twelve Nephite disciples really apostles?*

Although the words *disciple* (one who follows) and *apostle* (one who is sent) have distinct and separate meanings, the two terms are used somewhat interchangeably in the New Testament. The Book of Mormon tends to use the word *disciple* except when referring to the apostles who were called by Jesus when he lived on the earth on the eastern continent. In fact, *apostle* is used in only sixteen verses in the entire Book of Mormon. In some of the verses the word *apostle* refers to John the Beloved (1 Nephi 14:20, 24, 25, 27); in others it refers to the twelve selected by Jesus on the eastern continent (1 Nephi 11:34-36; 12:9; 13:24, 26, 39, 40, 41); and in the other verses it is used in a more general sense (Mormon 9:18; Ether 12:41; Moroni 2:2). It is doubtful that the word *apostle* is ever used in the Book of Mormon to refer to the chosen twelve of the Nephites. However, Joseph Fielding Smith indicates that they were apostles in the sense that they were special witnesses of the Savior. His statement follows:

The twelve men chosen by our Savior among the Nephites are called disciples in the Book of Mormon. . . .

While in every instance the Nephite twelve are spoken of as disciples, the fact remains that they had been endowed with divine authority to be special witnesses for Christ among their own people. Therefore, they were virtually apostles to the Nephite race, although their jurisdiction was . . . eventually to be subject to the authority and jurisdiction of Peter and the twelve chosen in Palestine. According to the definition prevailing in the world an apostle is a witness for Christ, or one who evangelizes a certain nation or people. "A zealous advocate of a doctrine or cause." Therefore the Nephite twelve became apostles, as special witnesses, just as did Joseph Smith and Oliver Cowdery in the Dispensation of the Fulness of Times.

When the Savior taught the Nephites he informed them that he had "other sheep" which were not of the Nephites, neither of the land of Jerusalem, and these also were to hear his voice and be ministered to by him. It is reasonable for us to conclude that among these others who were hidden from the rest of the world, he likewise chose disciples—perhaps twelve—to perform like functions and minister unto their people with the same fulness of divine authority. (*Answers to Gospel Questions,* 1:121-22.)

Also, the Prophet Joseph Smith, in a letter written dated March 1, 1842, refers to some of the teachings of the Book of Mormon: "This book also tells us that our Savior made His appearance upon this continent after His resurrection; that He planted the Gospel here in all its fulness, and richness, and power, and blessing; that they had Apostles, Prophets. . . ." (*History of the Church,* 4:538.)

This statement by the Prophet would also indicate that the term *apostle* could rightfully be used in referring to the chosen twelve Nephite leaders.

3 NEPHI 28:1-8, 13-17, 37-40   *The nature of translated beings*

One of the beliefs of the Latter-day Saints that help to make them a "peculiar people" in the eyes of others is that concerning translated beings; that is, Latter-day Saints believe there are people now living on the earth whose physical bodies have been changed or "translated" into another order or state of existence. Although this doctrine is almost unique with Latter-day Saints, it should not be so, for it is clearly taught in the New Testament. After his resurrection, Jesus Christ appeared to some of his disciples at the sea of Tiberias. He counseled his disciples and commanded Peter to "feed my sheep." Then Peter asked the Master concerning the future mission of John the Beloved. The account of the conversation is written in the book of John as follows:

Peter . . . saith to Jesus, Lord, and what shall this man do?

Jesus saith unto him, If I will that he tarry till I come, what is that to thee? follow thou me.

Then went this saying abroad among the brethren, that that disciple should not die: yet Jesus said not unto him, He shall not die; but, If I will that he tarry till I come, what is that to thee? (John 21:21-23.)

A more complete account of this experience is given in the Doctrine and Covenants (section 7), but the New Testament account is sufficiently clear to indicate that John the Beloved was to live on the earth until the Savior should come in his glory.

The Savior gave the three Nephite disciples in the Book of Mormon the same promise he had given earlier to John: ". . . ye shall never taste of death; but ye shall live to behold all the doings of the Father unto the children of men, even until all things shall be fulfilled according to the will of the Father, when I shall come in my glory with the powers of heaven. And . . . ye shall be changed in the twinkling of an eye from mortality to immortality; and then shall ye be blessed in the kingdom of my Father." (3 Nephi 28:7-8.)

This statement has raised the question in the minds of some readers as to whether or not John and the three Nephite disciples are still mortal—that is, must these men still suffer a physical death? The answer to this question is "Yes; they are still mortal, for they still must die." The Savior clearly indicated this when he told the three Nephite disciples, *"when I shall come in my glory ye shall be changed* in the twinkling of an eye *from mortality to immortality."* (3 Nephi 28:8. Italics added.) Thus their spirits will be separated from their bodies (which is physical death) but will come back into their bodies (which is their resurrection) in the "twinkling of an eye"—that is, almost immediately.

Some people are confused on this subject by the following two statements by the Savior: ". . . ye shall never taste of death . . . ye shall never endure the pains of death." (3 Nephi 28:7-8.) These statements *do not* mean the same as though the Savior had said "Ye shall never die." This is made clear in a revelation by the resurrected Jesus Christ to the Prophet Joseph Smith: "And it shall come to pass that *those that die in me shall not taste of death,* for it shall be sweet unto them; And they that die not in me, wo unto them, for their death is bitter." (D&C 42:46-47. Italics added.) In other words, death will be either a sweet or a bitter experience for people: if they are righteous, death will be a sweet experience—they will not taste of death nor feel the pains of death; if they are wicked, death will be a bitter experience. But both groups of people *must die.* As Paul stated, "For as in Adam all die,

294 even so in Christ shall all be made alive." (1 Corinthians 15:22.)

Joseph Fielding Smith has written the following concerning the present mortal condition of John the Beloved and the three Nephite disciples: ". . . translated beings are still mortal and will have to pass through the experience of death . . . although this will be instantaneous. . . . Translated beings have not passed through death; that is, they have not had the separation of the spirit and the body." (*Answers to Gospel Questions*, 1:165; 2:46.)

And finally, the Prophet Joseph Smith has indicated that translated beings have future missions to perform: "Translated bodies cannot enter into rest until they have undergone a change equivalent to death. Translated bodies are designed for future missions." (*History of the Church*, 4:425.)

3 NEPHI 29:8   *Latter-day Saints are not to ridicule the people of the house of Israel*

The gospel of Jesus Christ invokes us to love our neighbor as ourselves, and if all mankind lived this commandment there would be no persecution or hatred of other peoples. The Savior knew that some groups of people would be persecuted, including the Jewish people. However, he told the Nephites that in the last days he would remember the covenants made with the house of Israel. Therefore, he tells the Nephites and us: "Yea, and ye need not any longer hiss, nor spurn, nor make game of the Jews, nor any of the remnant of the house of Israel." (3 Nephi 29:8.)

FOURTH NEPHI

TITLE OF "FOURTH NEPHI"   *For information concerning the origin of the title of "Fourth Nephi," see the material listed after Title of Third Nephi.*

4 NEPHI 14   *New disciples ordained*

As the original twelve Nephite disciples chosen by the Savior passed away, new disciples were chosen to take their place. This practice evidently continued as long as the Nephites were righteous enough to have a church organization amongst them. The three Nephite disciples who were promised by the Savior that they should live on the earth until his second coming (3 Nephi 28:4-8) apparently continued to work with the people for several hundred years; both Mormon and Moroni were ministered to by them (Mormon 8:11).

4 NEPHI 19-21, 47   *Evidences of long life among the Nephites*

Several instances could be cited to indicate that many of the Nephites lived to a rather old age. For example, Jacob, the son of Lehi, was born during the eight-year trek from Jerusalem to Bountiful—that is, between 600 B.C. and 592 B.C. Jacob's son Enos died sometime after 420 B.C. (Enos 25.) Thus the lives of Jacob and his son Enos covered at least 172 years. Other examples can be taken from the book of Fourth Nephi. The four historians who wrote during the period covered by the book of Fourth Nephi and the approximate number of years each of them had the record are as follows: (1) Nephi (the son of the Nephi who was a disciple of Jesus Christ)—from about A.D. 34 to A.D. 111 (see the subtitle of the book of Fourth Nephi and 4 Nephi 18-19); (2) Amos (the son of the historian Nephi mentioned above)—from A.D. 111 to A.D. 194 (4 Nephi 19-21); (3) Amos (the son of Amos listed above)—from A.D. 194 to A.D. 306 (4 Nephi 21, 47); (4) Ammaron (the brother of Amos mentioned in 3, above)—from A.D. 306 until A.D. 321, when he hid up the records in the hill Shim (4 Nephi 47-49; Mormon 1:3).

The life expectancy of the people was quite long during this period; the first historian kept the record for 77 years, the second for 84 years, and the third for 112 years! Of course, their age when they obtained the record would have to be added to the figures listed above to determine their age at the time of death.

4 NEPHI 20, 36-39   *New meaning of the terms "Nephites" and "Lamanites"*

During the golden age of the people of Lehi after the appearance of the resurrected Jesus Christ there were no people known as ". . . Lamanites, nor any manner of -ites." (4 Nephi 17.) However, approximately A.D. 194 there was "a small part of the people who had revolted from the church and taken upon them the name of Lamanites; therefore there began to be Lamanites again in the land." (Verse 20.)

In A.D. 231 "there arose a people who were called the Nephites, and they were true believers in Christ . . . therefore the true believers in Christ, and the true worshipers of Christ . . . were called Nephites. . . . And it came to pass that they who rejected the gospel were called Lamanites." (Verses 36-38.)

The terms *Nephites* and *Lamanites* for the remainder of the Book of Mormon are determined by this division, which had taken place by A.D. 231. In other words, the Lamanites of the last two hundred years of Book of Mormon history are descendants of those who revolted against the true church of Christ between about A.D. 194 and 231.

4 NEPHI verses 24-27   *The steps of apostasy*

The small book of Fourth Nephi provides a classic example of the steps that lead to apostasy. In the first part of this book the historian tells of an almost perfect society. In fact, he says concerning these people: ". . . surely there could not be a happier people among all the people who had been created by the hand of God." (Verse 16.) However, by the end of this brief book the historian has to record that "both the people of Nephi and the Lamanites had become exceeding wicked one like unto another. And it came to pass that the robbers of Gadianton did spread over all the face of the land; and there were none that were righteous save it were the disciples of Jesus." (Verses 45-46.)

Significantly the historian records step by step the things that led the people from the state of nearly perfect happiness to a state of exceeding wickedness:

(1) A small part of the people revolted from the church—verse 20.

(2) The people became "exceeding rich"—verse 23.

(3) Some of the people began to be "lifted up in pride, such as the wearing of costly apparel"—verse 24.

(4) After the people were built up in pride, "from that time forth they did have their goods and their substance no more common among them"—verse 25.

(5) The people began to be divided into classes—verse 26.

(6) The people began to "build up churches unto themselves to get gain, and began to deny the true church of Christ"—verse 26.

(7) Many churches were established "which professed to know the Christ, and yet they did deny the more parts of his gospel"—verse 27.

(8) These churches which professed to know Christ did administer "that which was sacred [the sacrament] unto him whom it had been forbidden because of unworthiness. And this church did multiply exceedingly because of iniquity, and because of the power of Satan who did get hold upon their hearts"—verses 27-28.

(9) Another church was established "which denied the Christ; and they did persecute the true church of Christ, . . . and they did despise them because of the many miracles which were wrought among them"—verse 29.

(10) ". . . the people did harden their hearts and seek to kill" the few remaining righteous people, including the three Nephite disciples—verse 31.

(11) The "wicked part of the people began again to build up the secret oaths and combinations of Gadianton"—verse 42.

(12) And finally, the people became "proud in their hearts" and "vain like unto their brethren," thus "both the people of Nephi and the Lamanites had become exceeding wicked one like unto another. . . . and there were none that were righteous save it were the disciples of Jesus"—verses 43-46.

MORMON 1:1-7   *The boyhood of Mormon*

Mormon does not provide us with very much information concerning his boyhood, but the scanty details he does provide indicate:

1. He was born probably in A.D. 310 or 311. (He was about ten years of age in A.D. 321—see 4 Nephi 48 and Mormon 1:2.)

2. He was a descendant of Nephi. (Mormon 1:5.)

3. His father's name was Mormon, and he was named after the land of Mormon. (Mormon 1:5 and 3 Nephi 5:12.)

4. He was evidently born in the land northward. (Mormon 1:2, 6.)

5. At the age of fifteen he was "visited of the Lord." (Mormon 1:15.)

6. Despite his testimony of the divinity of Christ, he was "forbidden" to preach repentance unto the wicked people. (Mormon 1:16.)

7. In his "sixteenth year" he was appointed leader of the Nephite armies, and he and his armies defended the Nephites from the Lamanites. (Mormon 2:2.)

Elder Sterling W. Sill has written concerning the boyhood and manhood of Mormon as follows:

Mormon has an interesting and remarkable history. At age 15, like Samuel at Shiloh, he received a personal visitation from the Lord. And at age 16 he was launched upon what so far as I can find was the greatest military career in history, stretching as it did over a period of 58 years. (Mormon 1:15, 2:16.)

It is interesting to imagine the kind of qualities that a young man would need to have to attract a personal visit from the Lord at such a young age, and then when only sixteen years old to win for himself the leadership of a great national army.

Mormon possessed in great abundance the qualities that make a leader believed in, loved and followed, only one of these will be mentioned here and that was that Mormon had to be restrained in his desire to preach the gospel. If you would like to develop a good fault, here is one of the best I know of. Most of us have to be coaxed and begged and reminded to do our duty. Mormon had to be held back. (Mormon 1:16-17.)

. . . No one had to push Mormon, neither were his abilities confined to one field. He was a prophet, general, author, historian, and almost the last survivor of a great civilization . . . If you think it an inspiration that a 16 year old boy could win the leadership of a great national army what would you think of a man between the ages of 65 and 74 who was still the best man among his entire people for this top position of leadership, and in those days the general marched at the head and not in the rear of his troops. (Mormon 6:11) It is one thing to shoot a guided missile at an enemy a thousand miles away, but it is quite another thing to meet the enemy face to face, and with a sword or a battle axe, take on all comers, old and young, on any basis they might choose to elect; and still be in there fighting at age 74. No weakling or coward survives a test like that. His leadership and great skill in battle must have been an inspiration to those fortunate companions in arms who were privileged to fight at his side . . .

Mormon impresses his greatness upon us in many ways. He was a greater general than Washington. Washington led a little Revolutionary army for just a few months, and the total American dead was 4,435. . .

Mormon was a greater statesman than Lincoln. Lincoln undoubtedly received inspiration from God during the years that he was trying to hold the Union together, but Mormon talked with God directly over this long period.

Mormon was a greater author than Shakespeare. Shakespeare wrote a great literature, much of which is good and much of which is bad. But Mormon wrote by direct command of God a literature which if followed would save the world. (*The Upward Reach* [Bookcraft, 1962], pp. 248-49, 252-54.)

MORMON 1:15-16   *Mormon "was visited of the Lord"*

Mormon writes in his record the following brief statement concerning one of the greatest events in his life: ". . . being fifteen years of age and being somewhat of a sober mind, therefore I was visited of the Lord, and tasted and knew of the goodness of Jesus." (Mormon 1:15.) This statement indicates that he was evidently the recipient of a personal visitation by the Savior.

MORMON 2:17-18   *Mormon abridges his own record from the large plates of Nephi*

When Ammaron turned the responsibility of the records over to Mormon, he indicated that Mormon should "engrave on the plates of Nephi all the things that [he] had observed concerning his people." (Mormon 1:4.) Thus Mormon's major record of the events of his day was written on the large plates of Nephi. However, later in his life he was com-

300   manded by the Lord to make a separate set of plates, the plates of Mormon. He then abridged onto his own plates all of the writings from the large plates of Nephi, including his own writings. Concerning his writings on these two sets of plates, Mormon said: "And upon the plates of Nephi I did make a full account of all the wickedness and abominations; but upon these plates [the plates of Mormon] I did forbear to make a full account of their wickedness and abominations. . . ." (Mormon 2:18.)

Earlier in his writings, Mormon indicated he did not write on the plates of Mormon even one hundredth part of the things that were written on the large plates of Nephi. (3 Nephi 26:6-8.)

MORMON 3:10 and 4:4   *Mormon's teachings on war*

After Mormon had led his armies to victory in at least three major encounters, the Nephites

began to boast in their own strength, and began to swear before the heavens that they would avenge themselves of the blood of their brethren who had been slain by their enemies.

And they did swear by the heavens, and also by the throne of God, that they would go up to battle against their enemies, and would cut them off from the face of the land. (Mormon 3:9-10.)

When the Nephite soldiers decided to attack the Lamanites first, Mormon refused to lead them in offensive war. This position was not only justified by earlier teachings of the prophets and the counsel of the Lord (see 3 Nephi 3:20-21; Alma 43:46; Alma 48:14), but was also vindicated by subsequent events: the Nephite armies began to be defeated from that time forth. (For further information on the teachings of the Book of Mormon concerning war, read the material listed after 3 Nephi 3:20-21.)

MORMON 3:17-22   *God's system of providing judges*

Although Jesus Christ is the eventual judge of all mankind, he has established a system of judges to help him in this responsibility. For example, Mormon indicates that the twelve apostles of the Savior on the eastern continent are to judge the twelve tribes of Israel. (Mormon 3:18.) Thus the twelve Nephite disciples on the American continent are to be judged by the twelve apostles on the eastern continent (see 1 Nephi 12:9-10; Mormon 3:19)), and in turn these twelve Nephite disciples will judge the "remnant of the people," which refers to the descendants of Lehi and Ishmael.

MORMON 4:10-12   *The thirst for blood and war*

Once the Nephite soldiers started to wage offensive war they soon became so bloodthirsty they were concerned only with the taking of human life. Thus both the Nephites and Lamanites became obsessed with the desire to kill. Concerning this situation Mormon writes:

And it is impossible for the tongue to describe, or for man to write a perfect description of the horrible scene of the blood and carnage which was among the people, both of the Nephites and of the Lamanites; and every heart was hardened, so that they delighted in the shedding of blood continually.

And there never had been so great wickedness among all the children of Lehi, nor even among all the house of Israel, according to the words of the Lord, as was among this people. (Mormon 4:11-12.)

The leaders of this dispensation have also warned against the dangers of starting an offensive war. President Charles W. Penrose has said:

Now if a nation essays to go forth against another nation for the purpose of conquest, to gain territory, to grasp something that does not belong to that nation, then the nation thus assailed has the right to resist even to the shedding of blood, as it was in this land in the war for independence. But we have to be careful as to what spirit we are guided by. If we want to go out to battle, to encroach upon other peoples' liberties and rights, to gain their lands, to destroy their property without any right or reason, that is one thing; but if somebody comes against us to destroy us and our property and our homes and our rights and our privileges, either on land or sea, then we have the right under the divine law to rise for our own protection and take such steps as are necessary. But, . . . we Latter-day Saints must watch ourselves and not give way to passion and desire to shed blood and to destroy, for that is the power of the evil one. We do not want to imitate any nation that is bent on a policy of destruction, to destroy where they cannot rule, to break down and trample under foot where they cannot dominate. If we have that desire, it is the spirit of the wicked one. . . .

There is a very great difference between arising to go forth for conquest, for blood, for plunder, to gain territory and power in the earth, and in fighting to defend our own possessions in the spirit of justice and righteousness and equity, and standing up like men for those things that we have a right to contend for. (*Conference*

Report, April 1917, pp. 21-22.)

(For further information concerning the teachings of modern prophets on this subject, read the material listed after 3 Nephi 3:20-21.)

MORMON 5:14   *One purpose of the Book of Mormon is to persuade the Jews to believe in Jesus Christ*

Several purposes for the coming forth of the Book of Mormon have been listed within the book itself. However, one purpose listed frequently is that the Book of Mormon is to help persuade "the unbelieving of the Jews . . . that Jesus is the Christ, the Son of the living God; that the Father may bring about, through his most Beloved, his great and eternal purpose, in restoring the Jews, or all the house of Israel, to the land of their inheritance, which the Lord their God hath given them, unto the fulfilling of his covenant." (Mormon 5:14.)

This purpose is also listed by Moroni in the section that now comprises the title page of the Book of Mormon: "Which is to show unto the remnant of the House of Israel what great things the Lord hath done for their fathers; and that they may know the covenants of the Lord, that they are not cast off forever—And also to the convincing of the Jew and Gentile that JESUS is the CHRIST, the ETERNAL GOD, manifesting himself unto all nations."

MORMON 6:11   *How long did the "battle of Cumorah" last?*

The Book of Mormon is not absolutely clear on this point. It states that the battle of Cumorah started when "three hundred and eighty and four years had passed away," that is, A.D. 385. (Mormon 6:5.) After the battle was completed and the Lamanites had killed most of the Nephites, Mormon took the Nephite survivors with him and they "did behold on the morrow, when the Lamanites had returned unto their camps," the terrible scene of destruction. (Mormon 6:11, 15.) This could mean "on the morrow" after the battle was completed, regardless of how long the battle lasted.

MORMON 6:11-15   *The number of Nephite fatalities*

In order to compare the number of fatalities among the Nephites at the battle of Cumorah with the fatalities among

the U.S. citizens in the major wars of this country, the
following information is provided:

UNITED STATES CASUALTIES IN MAJOR WARS
BATTLE DEATHS

	Numbers Engaged	Army	Navy	Marine	Air Force	Total
Revolutionary War (1775-1783)	---	4,004	342	49	--	4,435
War of 1812 (1812-1815)	286,730	1,950	265	45	--	2,260
Mexican War (1846-1848)	78,718	1,721	1	11	--	1,733
Civil War (1861-1865)	2,213,363	138,154	2,112	148	--	140,414
Spanish-American (1898)	306,760	369	10	6	--	385
World War I (1917-1918)	4,734,991	50,510	431	2,461	--	53,402
World War II (1941-1945)	16,112,566	234,874	39,379	19,733	--	293,986
Korean War (1950-1953)	5,720,000	27,704	458	4,267	1,200	33,629

BATTLE DEATHS OF THE MAJOR COUNTRIES INVOLVED IN WORLD WAR II

Austria	280,000
China	1,319,958
France	201,568
Germany	3,250,000 (from all causes)
Japan	1,270,000
Netherlands	280,000 (from all causes)
Poland	664,000
Rumania	350,000
United States	293,986
U.S.S.R.	6,115,000 (from all causes)
United Kingdom	357,116 (from all causes)
Yugoslavia	305,000

°Information Please Almanac (New York: McGraw-Hill, 1958 ed.), pp. 414-15.

Original source: U.S. Department of Defense.

304   MORMON 7:8-9   *The Book of Mormon and the Bible testify of each other*

Chapter 7 of the "book of Mormon" is the last chapter written by Mormon himself. In virtually the concluding verses of this chapter, Mormon bears his testimony concerning the importance of the record he has written. Unfortunately, many students of the Bible do not realize the significance and importance of Mormon's statement because he uses pronouns to refer to the Bible and the Book of Mormon. In the following quotation of Mormon's writings, the exact scripture referred to will be inserted in brackets:

Therefore repent, and be baptized in the name of Jesus, and lay hold upon the gospel of Christ, which shall be set before you, not only in this record [the Book of Mormon] but also in the record which shall come unto the Gentiles from the Jews, which record shall come from the Gentiles unto you [the Bible].

For behold, this [the Book of Mormon] is written for the intent that ye may believe that [the Bible]; and if ye believe that [the Bible] ye will believe this also [the Book of Mormon]; and if ye believe this [the Book of Mormon] ye will know concerning your fathers, and also the marvelous works which were wrought by the power of God among them. (Mormon 7:8-9.)

(For further information concerning the Bible and the Book of Mormon as scriptural witnesses, see Appendix A, "The Book of Mormon as Part of God's System of Witnesses.")

MORMON 8:2-5   *Were all of the Nephites destroyed except Moroni?*

The two key words to consider in this question are *Nephites* and *destroyed.*

It is well to remember that the word *Nephite* apparently had a different meaning near the close of the Book of Mormon than it did before A.D. 231. (See 4 Nephi 20, 36-39.) From approximately 544 B.C. to A.D. 34 (Jacob 1:13-14) the term *Nephite* referred either to the descendants of Nephi and those who went with him into the wilderness (2 Nephi 5:5-8) or to those who joined with this group. From about A.D. 34 to nearly A.D. 194, there were not "any manner of -ites" among the descendants of Lehi. (4 Nephi 17.) By A.D. 194, however, a group of people revolted from the church and took upon themselves the name of Lamanites (4 Nephi 20), and by A.D. 231 those who had remained true to the church became known as Nephites (4 Nephi 36). For the remainder of the

Book of Mormon, the term Nephite apparently refers to the
descendants of those who had been faithful in A.D. 231.

Concerning whether or not all of the Nephites were destroyed, Hugh Nibley has written the following:

Are there not many Latter-day Saints who will insist that every American of pre-Columbian descent must be a Lamanite because, forsooth, there were once Nephites and Lamanites, and the Nephites were destroyed? Yet the Book of Mormon itself makes such an interpretation impossible. The Nephites were destroyed, we are told, but . . . what does the Book of Mormon mean by "destroyed"? The word is to be taken, as are so many other key words in the book, in its primary and original sense: "to unbuild; to separate violently into its constituent parts; to break up the structure." To destroy is to wreck the structure, not to annihilate the parts. Thus in I Nephi 17:31 we read of Israel in Moses' day that, "According to his word he did destroy them; and according to his word he did lead them . . ." bringing them together *after* they had been "destroyed," i.e., scattered, and needed a leader. "As one generation hath been destroyed among the Jews," according to II Nephi 25:9, ". . . even so they have been destroyed from generation to generation according to their iniquities." A complete slaughter of any one generation would of course be the end of their history altogether, but that is not what "destroyed" means. Of the Jews at Jerusalem Nephi says (I Nephi 17:43), "I know that the day must shortly come that they must be destroyed, save only a few. . . ." Later, "after the Messiah hath arisen from the dead . . . behold Jerusalem shall be destroyed again . . ." (II Nephi 25:15). In these two cases what actually happened was that the Jews were all scattered "save a few only" that remained in the land. The Israelites upon entering the Promised Land, we are told, drove out "the children of the land, yea, unto the scattering them to destruction" (I Nephi 17:32). Here it is plainly stated that the destruction of the Canaanites was their scattering—as is known to have been the case. Likewise of the Nephites: ". . . and after thy seed shall be destroyed, and dwindle in unbelief, and also the seed of thy brethren, behold these things shall be hid up" (I Nephi 13:35), where both Nephites and Lamanites dwindle in unbelief *after* they have been destroyed.

Only once in the Book of Mormon do we read of a case of annihilation, when we are specifically told that "every living soul of the Ammonihahites was destroyed" (Alma 16:9), where not only the social structure but each individual is undone. In other instances the Lord promises that he will not utterly destroy the descendants of Lehi's youngest son, Joseph (II Nephi 3:3), or of

306 Lemuel (id., 4:9), and even Nephi is told that God "will not suffer that the Gentiles will utterly destroy the mixture of thy seed which are among thy brethren" (I Nephi 13:30), even though the promises and fulfillment were that the Nephites should be "destroyed" (Ether 8:21), and even though Moroni can say: "there is none, save it be Lamanites" (Ether 4:3). (*Lehi in the Desert and the World of the Jaredites,* pp. 240-42.)

Also, it is of interest to note that the Lord has referred to Nephites in this dispensation. (See D&C 3:16-19.)

MORMON 8:26-41 *Conditions of the last days*

After the death of Mormon, his son Moroni writes the last two chapters (chapters 8 and 9) in his father's book, the "book of Mormon." Moroni evidently intends at first that these chapters should conclude his father's record; therefore, he outlines why the record is to be published in the last days and also prophesies the conditions existing when the book is to come forth. According to Moroni's prophecy, the Book of Mormon was to come forth in a day when:

1. "It shall be said that miracles are done away." (Mormon 8:26.)

2. The power of God shall be denied. (Mormon 8:28.)

3. Churches will become defiled and "lifted up in the pride of their hearts." (Mormon 8:28.)

4. There shall "be heard of wars, rumors of wars, and earthquakes in divers places." (Mormon 8:30.)

5. "There shall be great pollutions upon the face of the earth . . . murders, and robbing, and lying, and deceivings, and whoredoms, and all manner of abominations." (Mormon 8:31.)

6. People will say there is no sin, "Do this, or do that, and it mattereth not." (Mormon 8:31.)

7. "There shall be churches built up that shall say: Come unto me, and for your money you shall be forgiven of your sins." (Mormon 8:32.)

8. People will love their money and substance more than they will love "the poor and the needy, the sick and the afflicted." (Mormon 8:37.)

9. People will be ashamed to take upon them the name of Christ. (Mormon 8:38.)

10. People will build up "secret abominations to get gain." (Mormon 8:40.)

Moroni truly saw our day and knew of the conditions of 307
which he prophesied, as is indicated in this statement:

Behold, the Lord hath shown unto me great and marvelous
things concerning that which must shortly come, at that day when
these things shall come forth among you.

Behold, I speak unto you as if ye were present, and yet ye are
not. But behold, Jesus Christ hath shown you unto me, and I know
your doing. (Mormon 8:34-35.)

MORMON 9:1 *Moroni's address to unbelievers*

As indicated in the preceding note, Moroni at first evidently intended this chapter to be the last one in the entire
Book of Mormon. Thus he addresses himself to "those who
do not believe in Christ." (Mormon 9:1.) Then in a powerful,
logical, and forceful manner he outlines the major teachings
of the gospel of Jesus Christ and indicates why all men must
understand and apply these principles if they are to find the
peace and happiness they desire. He says the gospel is not
restricted to a chosen few, but is available "unto all, even
unto the ends of the earth." (Mormon 9:21.) Finally he concludes a portion of his address with this stirring statement:

. . . I speak unto you as though I spake from the dead; for I
know that ye shall hear my words.

Condemn me not because of mine imperfection, neither my
father, because of his imperfection, neither them who have written
before him; but rather give thanks unto God that he hath made
manifest unto you our imperfections, that ye may learn to be more
wise than we have been. (Mormon 9:30-31.)

MORMON 9:32-34 *The script of the plates of Mormon*

Moroni's statement in Mormon 9:32-34 pertains to the
plates of Mormon and does not necessarily pertain to the
small plates of Nephi from which we get the first 132 pages
in our present Book of Mormon. Concerning the script of the
plates of Mormon, Moroni says: ". . . we have written this
record according to our knowledge, in the characters which
are called among us the reformed Egyptian, being handed
down and altered by us, according to our manner of speech."
(Mormon 9:32.) He seems to indicate in the following verse
that the Nephites are still speaking a version of Hebrew, for
he admits that "if our plates had been sufficiently large we
should have written in Hebrew; but the Hebrew hath been
altered by us also." (Mormon 9:33.)

ETHER   *The title and the superscription to the book of Ether*

The present title of the book of Ether and the superscription to the book were apparently not included by Moroni on the plates of Mormon. Both of these were first included in the Book of Mormon in the edition of 1879, as is indicated in the following statement by Sidney B. Sperry:

The title of the book is now "The Book of Ether"; in the early editions of the Book of Mormon the title was simply "Book of Ether." The article seems to have been first added by Elder Orson Pratt in the 1879 edition. Immediately beneath the title of the book there now occurs an explanatory note in italics which reads: *The record of the Jaredites, taken from the twenty-four plates found by the people of Limhi in the days of king Mosiah.* This is wanting in all but the current editions of the Book of Mormon and is not to be regarded as part of the original text. The note seems to have been inserted by the committee appointed to edit the text now in common use. (*The Book of Mormon Testifies* [Bookcraft, 1952], p. 347.)

ETHER 1:1-2   *Moroni's abridgment of the record of Ether*

It is not made absolutely clear in the Book of Mormon whether Moroni made his abridgment of the record of Ether from Mosiah's earlier translation (see Mosiah 28:1-20) or whether Moroni took his account directly from the plates of Ether—in which case he would have needed to translate the record as well as abridge it. Sidney B. Sperry has suggested the following concerning this question:

From Ether 1:2 one naturally assumes that Moroni made his abridgment directly from the plates themselves. If he did so, we are driven to the conclusion that it was necessary for him to find his way into the hill Cumorah, where his father had hidden them. Inasmuch as the language of the plates was that of the Jaredite people, it would have been incumbent upon Moroni to translate them by means of the holy "interpreters" or Urim and Thummim before he could abridge them. This would have been a tremendous task, because Moroni says (Ether 15:33) that he had not written the hundredth part of the record, and as it is we have fifteen chapters or about thirty-one and one-half printed pages in our current edition. It seems much more reasonable—for the writer at least—to believe that Moroni abridged the translation of the Book of Ether which had been made many hundreds of years before by king Mosiah. (Mosiah 28:1-20) This translation would also have been available to Moroni in the hill. (Ibid., pp. 346-47.)

ETHER 1:6-33   *The genealogies of the Jaredite leaders*

It is not clear from the record whether or not the genealogies listed in Ether 1:6-33 are complete. Thirty names are listed, but in three instances the word *descendant* is used in place of the word *son,* which might indicate a gap of several generations. It may be that the original word could be translated as both son and descendant; thus, the translator would have to know the exact sense in which the word was originally used.

Verse 6 states that Ether was a descendant of Coriantor. However, Ether 11:23 reads "Coriantor begat Ether." Therefore, Ether is Coriantor's son. Also, verse 16 states that Aaron was a "descendant of Heth," but Ether 10:31 says that Heth "begat" Aaron. However, verse 23 mentions that Morianton was a "descendant of Riplakish," and Ether 10:9 also uses the same word *descendant.* This is the one place where the list of genealogies may not be complete.

ETHER 1:33-37   *Did the Jaredites speak and write the "Adamic" language?*

The key word in the verses that pertain directly to the problem (Ether 1:34-37) is *confound.* What does it mean when the record states that the Lord "did not confound the language of Jared"? Does it mean the same as saying that the Lord did not *change* the language of Jared? If so, Jared and his people apparently spoke and wrote the language of Adam, because so far as we know there was only one language before the "great tower" of Babel. However, another possible interpretation is that the language of Jared and his brother (and their friends and families) was changed, but it was changed the same for all of them so that they continued to understand each other and thus they were not "confounded."

In his book *The Way to Perfection* Joseph Fielding Smith indicates he believes Jared and his people did speak and write the Adamic language even after they arrived in the promised land, which was "choice above all the earth."

(Ether 1:38.) (*The Way to Perfection* [Genealogical Society of Utah, 1931], p. 60.)

ETHER 1:34 *The name of the brother of Jared*

It is not clear why the name of the brother of Jared does not appear in the Book of Mormon. However, the following are possible reasons: (1) He may have omitted his name out of modesty (John the Beloved did essentially this same thing in the Gospel of John, which he wrote). (2) The book of Ether is clearly a family record of Jared, not of the brother of Jared; Ether—the final writer and perhaps the abridger of the record—was a descendant of Jared and might naturally have emphasized the achievements of his direct ancestor rather than the brother of his ancestor. (3) Moroni may have omitted the name in his abridgment because of difficulty in translating (or transliterating) the name into the Nephite language.

Although the actual name of the brother of Jared is not mentioned in the scriptures, many Latter-day Saints quote the following story related by George Reynolds to indicate that his name was revealed to the Prophet Joseph Smith after the translation of the Book of Mormon:

While residing in Kirtland Elder Reynolds Cahoon had a son born to him. One day when President Joseph Smith was passing his door he called the Prophet in and asked him to bless and name the baby. Joseph did so and gave the boy the name of Mahonri Moriancumer. When he had finished the blessing he laid the child on the bed, and turning to Elder Cahoon he said, the name I have given your son is the name of the brother of Jared; the Lord has just shown (or revealed) it to me. Elder William F. Cahoon, who was standing near, heard the Prophet make this statement to his father; and this was the first time the name of the brother of Jared was known in the Church in this dispensation. ("The Jaredites," *Juvenile Instructor,* 27:282. Also *Improvement Era,* 8:705.)

In connection with this name, it is interesting to note that the major encampment of the Jaredites on the shore of "that great sea which divideth the lands" was called "Moriancumer." (Ether 2:13.)

ETHER 2:3 *Meaning of the Jaredite term "deseret"*

The word *deseret* is evidently transliterated from the original record, but fortunately the interpretation is included in Moroni's abridgment: "a honey bee." (Ether 2:3.) This is one of the few Jaredite words transliterated in our present Book of Mormon; therefore it is of special significance to the scholars.

Dr. Hugh Nibley has written extensively on the background of this word, including the following ideas:

By all odds the most interesting and attractive passenger in Jared's company is *deseret,* the honeybee. We cannot pass this creature by without a glance at its name and possible significance, for our text betrays an interest in *deseret* that goes far beyond respect for the feat of transporting insects, remarkable though that is. The word *deseret* we are told (Ether 2:3), "by interpretation is a honeybee," the word plainly coming from the Jaredite language, since Ether (or Moroni) must interpret it. Now it is a remarkable coincidence that the word *deseret,* or something very close to it, enjoyed a position of ritual prominence among the founders of the classical Egyptian civilization, who associated it very closely with the symbol of the bee. The people, the authors of the so-called Second Civilization, seem to have entered Egypt from the northeast as part of the same great outward expansion of peoples that sent the makers of the classical Babylonian civilization into Mesopotamia. Thus we have the founders of the two main parent civilizations of antiquity entering their new homelands at approximately the same time from some common center—apparently the same center from which the Jaredites also took their departure, . . . the Egyptian pioneers carried with them a fully developed cult and symbolism from their Asiatic home. Chief among their cult objects would seem to be the bee, for the land they first settled in Egypt was forever after known as "the land of the bee," and was designated in hieroglyphic by the picture of a bee, while every king of Egypt "in his capacity of 'King of Upper and Lower Egypt'" bore the title, "he who belongs to the sedge and the bee."

From the first, students of hieroglyphic were puzzled as to what sound value should be given to the bee-picture. . . . We know that the bee sign was not always written down, but in its place the picture of the Red Crown, the majesty of Lower Egypt was sometimes "substituted for superstitious reasons." If we do not know the original name of the bee, we do know the name of this Red Crown—the name it bore when it was substituted for the bee. The name was *dsrt* (the vowels are not known, but we can be sure they were all short). . . . (*Lehi in the Desert and the World of the Jaredites,* pp. 184-85.)

ETHER 2:8-12   *The people on the promised land to serve Jesus Christ or be destroyed*

Before the Jaredites ever arrive in the promised land,

312   they are warned by the Lord "that whoso should possess this land of promise, from that time henceforth and forever, should serve him, the true and only God, or they should be swept off when the fulness of his wrath should come upon them." (Ether 2:8.) This promise is particularly significant because the Book of Mormon literally documents the fulfillment of the promise and warning in the case of both the Jaredites and the Nephites. Moroni inserts this promise and later records its tragic fulfillment for the benefit of this generation. He says:

And this cometh unto you, O ye Gentiles, that ye may know the decrees of God—that ye may repent, and not continue in your iniquities until the fulness come, that ye may not bring down the fulness of the wrath of God upon you as the inhabitants of the land have hitherto done.

Behold, this is a choice land, and whatsoever nation shall possess it shall be free from bondage, and from captivity, and from all other nations under heaven, if they will but serve the God of the land, who is Jesus Christ, who hath been manifested by the things which we have written. (Ether 2:11-12.)

ETHER 2:12   *The "choice land"*

Although America has been identified as a choice land, yet, as Elder Mark E. Petersen has indicated, the people in America must serve Jesus Christ if they are to receive the promised blessings.

Another ancient prophet spoke directly to modern America, foretelling the assistance God will give us if we serve him. Said he: ". . . this is a choice land, and whatsoever nation shall possess it shall be free from bondage, and from captivity, and from all other nations under heaven, if they will but serve the God of the land, who is Jesus Christ. . . . " (Ether 2:12.)

And that prophet also said, even as did Lincoln, that if we in America fail to serve Jesus Christ, we will face certain destruction. This is a divine warning, first from the prophet of old and then from the inspired President of Civil War days.

Oh, America, turn to God. But do not give him mere lip service. Obey him with all your hearts, might, mind, and strength.

Let us save ourselves from the present crisis in the only certain way, remembering that "man shall not live by bread alone, but by every word that proceedeth out of the mouth of God." (Matthew 4:4.) (*Conference Report,* April 1968, pp. 62-63.)

President Joseph Fielding Smith also indicated that the

people in America must keep the commandments if they are 313 to be protected:

These passages of scripture from the *Book of Mormon* are true; (Ether 2:7-12) this nation is not exempt, and the people, if they continue to pursue the course of evil and ungodliness that they are now treading, shall eventually be punished. If they continue to disregard the warning voice of the Lord, deny their Redeemer, turn from his gospel unto fables and false theories, and rebel against all that he has through his servants in this day declared for the salvation of man; and if they increase in the practice of iniquity, I want to say to you, that if they do these things, *the judgments of the Lord will come upon this land, and this nation will not be saved;* we will not be spared from war, from famine, from pestilence and finally from destruction, as a nation.

Therefore, I call upon the people not only Latter-day Saints, but to all throughout the whole land to repent of their sins and to accept the Lord Jesus Christ, who is our Redeemer and the God of this land. Turn from your evil ways, repent of your sins and receive the fulness of the gospel through the waters of baptism and obedience, that the judgments which shall be poured out upon the ungodly may pass you by. (*Doctrines of Salvation,* 3:321-22.)

ETHER 2:19-20 *The Jaredite barges*

The record of Ether provides only a brief description of the barges built by the Jaredites to cross the great sea. Evidently the directions for building the barges had been given by the Lord. (See Ether 2:16.) The only additional information provided is: (1) "they were exceeding tight, even that they would hold water like unto a dish" (Ether 2:17); (2) "the sides thereof were tight like unto a dish; and the ends thereof were peaked; and the top thereof was tight like unto a dish; and the length thereof was the length of a tree; and the door thereof, when it was shut, was tight like unto a dish" (Ether 2:17); and (3) because of the tightness of the barge, evidently it was difficult to obtain either light or air.

The difficulty of obtaining light was met by the sixteen molten stones that were made to shine when they were touched by the finger of the Lord. (See Ether 3:1-6 and 6:2-3.)

In providing a solution for the difficulty of obtaining air, the Lord informed Jared: "Behold, thou shall make a hole in the top *thereof,* and also in the bottom *thereof;* and when thou shalt suffer for air, thou shalt unstop the hole *thereof,*

314   and receive air. And if it so be that the water come in upon
thee, behold, ye shall stop the hole *thereof,* that ye may not
perish in the flood." (Page 542 of the first edition. Italics added.) This quotation is taken from the first edition of the Book
of Mormon because the four *thereofs* underlined above appear in the early editions, but for some unexplainable
reasons were deleted from the 1920 edition and all subsequent editions (perhaps the revising committee thought
they were superfluous). A careful reading of this verse in the
first edition seems to indicate that the terms "in the top" and
"in the bottom" do not refer to the barge itself. Rather, they
refer to the top and bottom of something else such as a
chamber or cylinder (designated here as "thereof") which
could be used to admit air.

Dr. Hugh Nibley has explained the possible significance
of the "thereofs" and the possibility of an air chamber as
follows:

An exacting editor by removing those very significant *"thereofs"*
has made it appear that when Jared wanted air he was to open the
top window of the boat and admit fresh air from the outside. But
that is *not* what the original edition of the Book of Mormon says.
For one thing, the ships had no windows communicating with the
outside—"ye cannot have windows . . . " (2:23); each ship had an
airtight door (2:17), and that was all. Air was received not by opening and closing doors and windows, but by unplugging air holes
("thou shalt *unstop* the *hole* thereof, and receive air . . . "), this being done *only* when the ship was not on the surface—"when thou
shalt *suffer* for air" i.e., when they were not able to open the
hatches, the ships being submerged. (2:20.)

This can refer only to a reserve supply of air, and indeed the
brother of Jared recognizes that the people cannot possibly survive
on the air contained within the ships at normal pressure: ". . . we
shall perish, for in them we cannot breathe, save it is the air which
is in them; therefore we shall perish." (2:19.) So the Lord recommended a device for trapping (compressing) air, with a "hole in the
top thereof and also in the bottom thereof," not referring to the
ship but to the air chamber itself. Note the peculiar language:
"unstop" does not mean to open a door or window but to unplug a
vent, here called a "hole" in contrast to the door mentioned in
verse 17; it is specifically an air hole—"when thou shalt suffer for
air, thou shalt unstop the hole *thereof,* and receive air." (1st Ed.)
When the crew find it impossible to remain on the surface—"and if
it so be that the water come in upon thee" (2:20), they are to plug

up the air chamber: "ye shall stop up the hole thereof, that ye may not perish in the flood." This, I believe, refers to replenishing the air supply on the surface, lest the party suffocate when submerged—"that ye may not perish in the flood." (*A Book of Mormon Treasury* [Bookcraft, 1959], pp. 136-37.)

It is entirely feasible that such an air chamber could have been constructed in each boat. Some of the advantages of such an air chamber have been suggested by A. L. Zobell, Sr., as follows:

A tube is built from the bottom to the top of the barge, housing in both holes completely. Now we have a funnel right through the boat. Water can come into the tube as high as the water line of the vessel.

The model of the barge we have built has a stop hole both in front and in back of the tube. . . . These stop holes can easily be opened or closed as needed.

The purpose of the bottom hole is at least two-fold: First, it acted as a stabilizer to keep the barge at an even keel; second, it could be used to get rid of refuse. ("Jaredite Barges," *Improvement Era,* April 1941, pp. 211, 252.)

ETHER 2:22-24; 3:3-6 *How the brother of Jared received a blessing*

President Harold B. Lee has discussed some of the principles utilized by the Lord in helping the brother of Jared build the barges:

The Lord gave to the brother of Jared, that great prophet, a blueprint of the ships that he was to construct, by which he was to take his people across large bodies of water to a promised land. As he surveyed these and began to build, he faced two problems: (1) no provision was made for ventilation and (2) there was no light. The ventilation problem was solved rather simply by having holes at proper places that could be opened and closed; but the matter of light was one that he could not quite solve. So the brother of Jared cried to the Lord, saying, ". . . behold, I have done even as thou hast commanded me; and I have prepared the vessels for my people, and behold there is no light in them. Behold, O Lord, wilt thou suffer that we shall cross this great water in darkness?" (Eth. 2:22.)

Notice how the Lord dealt with this question. He said to the brother of Jared, "What will ye that I should do that ye may have light in your vessels?" (Eth. 2:23.)—as much as to say, "Well, have you any good ideas? What would you suggest that we should do in order to have light?" And then the Lord said, "For behold, ye can-

316   not have windows, for they will be dashed to pieces; neither shall ye take fire with you, for ye shall not go by the light of fire.

"For behold, you shall be as a whale in the midst of the sea; for the mountain waves shall dash upon you. Nevertheless, I will bring you up again out of the depths of the sea; for the winds have gone forth out of my mouth, and also the rains and the floods have I sent forth." (Eth. 2:23-24.)

Then the Lord went away and left him alone. It was as though the Lord were saying to him, "Look, I gave you a mind to think with, and I gave you agency to use it. Now you do all you can to help yourself with this problem; and then, after you've done all you can, I'll step in to help you."

The brother of Jared did some thinking. Then he gathered up sixteen stones, molten out of rock, and carried them in his hands to the top of the mount called Shelem, where he cried unto the Lord, "O Lord, thou hast said that we must be encompassed about by the floods. Now behold, O Lord, and do not be angry with thy servant because of his weakness before thee; for we know that thou art holy and dwellest in the heavens, and that we are unworthy before thee; because of the fall our natures have been evil continually; nevertheless, O Lord, thou hast given us a commandment that we must call upon thee, that from thee we may receive according to our desires." (Eth. 3:2.)

Now, what is he doing? He is confessing his sins before he asks again. He has come to the conclusion that before he is worthy to seek a blessing he must keep the basic laws upon which the blessings he seeks are predicated.

Then he says, "Behold, O Lord, [I know that] thou hast smitten us because of our iniquity, and hast driven us forth, and for these many years we have been in the wilderness; nevertheless, thou hast been merciful to us. O Lord, look upon me in pity, and turn away thine anger from this thy people. . . . " (Eth. 3:3.) The brother of Jared is confessing the sins of the people, because the blessing he wants is not just for himself; it is for his whole people. Having done all that he knew how to do, he came again with a specific request and said:

"And I know, O Lord, thou hast all power, and can do whatsoever thou wilt for the benefit of man; therefore touch these stones, O Lord, with thy finger, and prepare them that they may shine forth in darkness; and they shall shine forth unto us in the vessels which we have prepared, that we may have light while we shall cross the sea.

"Behold, O Lord, thou canst do this. We know that thou art able to show forth great power, which looks small unto the understanding of men.

"And it came to pass that when the brother of Jared had said these words, behold, the Lord stretched forth his hand and touched the stones one by one with his finger. And the veil was taken from off the eyes of the brother of Jared, and he saw the finger of the Lord; and it was as the finger of a man, like unto flesh and blood; and the brother of Jared fell down before the Lord, for he was struck with fear." (Eth. 3:4-6.)

This is the principle in action. If you want the blessing, don't just kneel down and pray about it. Prepare yourselves in every conceivable way you can in order to make yourselves worthy to receive the blessing you seek. ("How to Receive a Blessing from God," *Improvement Era,* October 1966, pp. 862-63, 896.)

ETHER 3:5-16   *The appearance of the pre-earthly Jesus Christ to the brother of Jared*

One of the spiritual highlights of the entire Book of Mormon is the appearance of the pre-earthly Jesus Christ to the brother of Jared. The conversation of the Savior with the brother of Jared sheds tremendous light on the pre-earthly role of Jesus Christ as well as the later role he is to play as the Savior and Redeemer of the world. It is significant to note, for example, that even in the pre-earthly existence Jesus Christ referred to himself as both the Father and the Son. Even before his birth on the earth the Savior indicates how all members of the human race can become his sons and daughters. (For further information on these topics, see the materials following Mosiah 15:1-14 and following 3 Nephi 9:17.)

Another significant part of the Savior's statement is the reference to his pre-earthly spirit body. He says to the brother of Jared: "Seest thou that ye are created after mine own image? Yea, even all men are created in the beginning after mine own image." (Ether 3:15.) This statement seems to indicate that in the scripture that says "God created man in his own image" (Genesis 1:27), the word *God* refers not to Elohim but to Jesus Christ, and the word *image* refers not to the physical resurrected body of Elohim but to the pre-earthly spiritual body of Jesus Christ.

ETHER 3:15   *How is it possible to reconcile Ether 3:15 with Moses 7:4 and Doctrine and Covenants 107:54?*

In Ether 3:15 the pre-earthly Jesus Christ told the brother of Jared: "And never have I showed myself unto

318 man whom I have created, for never has man believed in me as thou hast." This statement introduces something of a problem inasmuch as we read in Moses 7:4 that the Lord talked with Enoch "even as a man talketh one with another, face to face"—and Enoch lived on the earth *before* the time of the brother of Jared! Also, in the Doctrine and Covenants 107:54 it states that the "Lord appeared" unto Adam and his descendants.

Some people explain this problem by stating that the Lord referred to in Moses and the Doctrine and Covenants is God the Father (Elohim) rather than Jesus Christ. However, another possible interpretation is that Jesus Christ is the Lord mentioned on each of these occasions, but that he is essentially saying in Ether 3:15 that he has never *had* to show himself unto man before. This interpretation gains additional weight when considered in connection with the following verses: Ether 3:9, 19-20, 26. In these verses the Lord makes it very clear that the brother of Jared came before him with greater faith than any other man (Ether 3:9), that the brother of Jared "could not be kept from within the veil" (Ether 3:20), and that the Lord "could not withhold anything from him, for he knew that the Lord could show him all things" (Ether 3:26).

Concerning the possible contradiction between Ether 3:15 and Moses 7:4, Joseph Fielding Smith has written:

There is no contradiction. When Adam was in the Garden of Eden and before the Fall, he was in the presence of God the Father. He walked with God, for he was free from sin and in possession of an eternal body that could have endured forever. When he and Eve partook of the forbidden fruit, they were cast out of the presence of the Father and became subject to death, or mortal. From that time forth Jesus Christ became the Advocate and Mediator between the Father and mankind. This fall brought the first, or spiritual death, as well as mortality on Adam. Now there are several references in the Old Testament which declare that the Lord appeared to Enoch and talked with him. Enoch wrote that the Lord commanded him to get on the mount Simeon, and there said Enoch:

"I saw the Lord; and he stood before my face, and he talked with me, even as a man talketh one with another, face to face." [Moses 7:4.]

In the Bible all that is written is the following:

"And Enoch walked with God after he begat Methuselah three hundred years, and begat sons and daughters:

"And all the days of Enoch were three hundred sixty and five years:

"And Enoch walked with God: and he was not; for God took him." [Genesis 5:22-24.]

It is true that the Savior appeared to the prophets before the flood, but it is evident that he did not reveal himself in the fulness as he did to the Brother of Jared. Talking "face to face," as stated in this revelation, does not mean that the Lord did not appear in a cloud; or, that his body was partially hidden from the view of the prophet. All of this could occur and yet the Lord still be partially, if not completely, hidden from the prophet's view. The great difference rests in this, which the conversation of the Lord with the Brother of Jared clearly indicates: The Savior was conversing with the Brother of Jared in person. . . .

So the Savior showed to the Brother of Jared his entire body just as it would appear when he dwelt among men in the flesh.

It is a reasonable conclusion for us to reach, and fully in accordance with the facts, that the Lord had never before revealed himself so completely and in such a manner. We may truly believe that very few of the ancient prophets at any time actually beheld the full person of the Lord. (*Answers to Gospel Questions,* 2:123-25.)

ETHER 3:23-24   *The two stones given by the Lord to the brother of Jared*

Reynolds and Sjodahl have written the following concerning the two stones given to the brother of Jared by the Lord:

These Two Stones, which are also known as the *Interpreters* (Ether 4:5; Mosiah 28:20) and *Urim and Thummim* (Pearl of Great Price, Joseph Smith 2:52; Doctrine and Covenants 17:1) were, as we read here, entrusted into the care of Moriancumer, before he descended from the ever memorable scene of his vision and revelations. They were delivered to him with the admonition that they were to be sealed up, together with the sacred records that were to be kept, and thus be hidden from the eyes of the world, until they, in the due time of the Lord, were to come forth. The purpose of the *Stones* is stated to be to *magnify,* that is to say, to make clear "the things which ye shall write."

According to the Doctrine and Covenants (17:1), the Sacred Instruments deposited in the Hill Cumorah and delivered to the Prophet Joseph, [were] the Urim and Thummim received by the Brother of Jared on the Mount. When the Prophet Joseph received the *Stones,* September 22, 1827, they were framed in silver bows

320 and fastened to a *breastplate* (Pearl of Great Price, Joseph Smith 2:35). From the Doctrine and Covenants, 130:8-9, where God is said to dwell on a globe which is a Urim and Thummim, and that the Earth is to be sanctified and made immortal—*made like unto a crystal and will be a Urim and Thummim to the inhabitants thereon*—we conclude that that was the nature of the Stones. They were crystals. The Prophet Joseph Smith further adds to our information that the *white stone* mentioned in the Revelation 2:17, will become a Urim and Thummim to each who receives one, and that a *white stone* will be given to everyone who is privileged to come into the Celestial Kingdom. On the stone a new name is written. By this means *things pertaining to a higher order of kingdoms, even all kingdoms, will be made known. (Commentary on the Book of Mormon, 6:87.)*

ETHER 4:4-5; 5:1 *The sealed portion of the plates of Mormon*

Moroni wrote his account of the vision of the brother of Jared on the plates of Mormon, but he was commanded by the Lord to "seal up" this account. (Ether 4:4-5.) Joseph Smith was commanded not to translate this sealed portion. It is not absolutely clear what portion of the plates of Mormon was sealed. Joseph Smith simply said: "The volume was something near six inches in thickness, a part of which was sealed." (*History of the Church,* 4:537.) George Q. Cannon said that "about one-third" was sealed (*Young Peoples' History of Joseph Smith,* p. 25), whereas Orson Pratt maintained that the sealed portion comprised "about two-thirds" of the plates. (*Journal of Discourses,* 3:347.) Neither of these two brethren indicate where they obtained their information.

ETHER 4:4-8 *The sealed portion yet to be revealed*

Moroni wrote on the plates of Mormon an account of "the very things which the brother of Jared saw" in his great vision of the pre-earthly Jesus Christ. (Ether 4:4.) Concerning the importance of this vision, Moroni adds "there never were greater things made manifest than those which were made manifest unto the brother of Jared." (Ether 4:4.)

The Lord has indicated that the contents of the vision of the brother of Jared should not be revealed in a day when the people are wicked. Thus Moroni was commanded to write the account of the vision, but he was also commanded to "seal up the interpretation thereof. . . . For the Lord said unto me: They shall not go forth unto the Gentiles until the day that they shall repent of their iniquity, and become clean before the Lord." (Ether 4:5, 6.)

It is not clear in the Book of Mormon exactly when the sealed record is to be revealed. However, some of the prior conditions that must exist are enumerated. For example, the Lord said that before the record is revealed the people must exercise faith in him "even as the brother of Jared did." (Ether 4:7.) Also, the Savior indicated that the people must "become sanctified" in him. (Ether 4:7.) Only then will the sealed portion of the records be revealed.

ETHER 4:16   *The revelation of John the Revelator to come forth*

An additional record that is yet to come forth is an account of the writings of John the Revelator. After the house of Israel returns to the Savior and keeps his commandments, the Savior has promised that the record of John will be revealed to them. In the Doctrine and Covenants we read the following concerning the record of John that is yet to come forth:

And I, John, bear record that he [the Son of God] received a fulness of the glory of the Father;

And he received all power, both in heaven and on earth, and the glory of the Father was with him, for he dwelt in him.

And it shall come to pass, that if you are faithful you shall receive the fulness of the record of John. (D&C 93:16-18.)

ETHER 5:2-4   *For information on the promised three special witnesses of the Book of Mormon, read the material following 2 Nephi 27:12-13 and the chapter in this book on the special witnesses.*

ETHER 7:6   *The Jaredite land of Moron*

Moroni, the abridger of the Jaredite record and the last historian of the Nephites, is in an ideal position to indicate some of the geographical relationships between the lands of the Jaredites and the lands of the Nephites. Unfortunately, Moroni does not give us very much information concerning this matter. However, he does indicate that the "land of Moron" of the Jaredites "was near the land which is called Desolation by the Nephites." (Ether 7:6.) Inasmuch as the land of Moron was the capital land of the Jaredites and the Nephite land of Desolation was north of the narrow neck of land, it is assumed that the major portion of the Jaredite civi-

322   lization lived north of the narrow neck of land.

ETHER 8:9-26   *The origin of the secret combinations among the Jaredites*

Ether 8:9 indicates that the Jaredites brought a record with them when they came to the promised land. Later in this same chapter Moroni suggests that this record contained the sacred oaths and covenants that had been handed down from the time of Cain. (Verse 15.)

ETHER 8:18-26   *Moroni's warning against secret combinations*

Moroni says that one of the major reasons he abridged the record of the Jaredites was to warn the gentiles that they should not allow "murderous combinations" to get power over them. (Ether 8:23.) Concerning the destructive influences of such secret oaths and combinations, Moroni states: ". . . they have caused the destruction of this people of whom I am now speaking, and also the destruction of the people of Nephi. And whatsoever nation shall uphold such secret combinations, to get power and gain, until they shall spread over the nation, behold, they shall be destroyed." (Ether 8:21-22.)

In commenting on these verses Elder Ezra Taft Benson has said:

One of the most urgent, heart-stirring appeals made by Moroni as he closed the Book of Mormon was addressed to the gentile nations of the last days. He foresaw the rise of a great world-wide secret combination among the gentiles which ". . . *seeketh to overthrow the freedom of all lands, nations, and countries; . . .*" (Ether 8:25, Italics added.) He warned each gentile nation of the last days to purge itself of this gigantic criminal conspiracy which would seek to rule the world. . . .

The Prophet Moroni described how the secret combination would take over a country and then fight the work of God, persecute the righteous, and murder those who resisted. Moroni therefore proceeded to describe the workings of the ancient "secret combinations" so that modern man could recognize this great political conspiracy in the last days: "Wherefore, O ye Gentiles, it is wisdom in God that these things should be shown unto you, that thereby ye may repent of your sins, and suffer not that these murderous combinations shall get above you, which are built up to get power and gain—and the work, yea, even the work of destruction come upon you, . . .

"Wherefore, the Lord commandeth you, when ye shall see these things come among you that ye shall awake to a sense of your awful situation, because of this secret combination which shall be among you; . . .

"For it cometh to pass that whoso buildeth it up seeketh to overthrow the freedom of *all* lands, nations and countries; and it bringeth to pass the destruction of *all* people, for it is built up by the devil, who is the father of all lies; . . . " (Ether 8:23-25. Italics added.)

The Prophet Moroni seemed greatly exercised lest in our day we might not be able to recognize the startling fact that the same secret societies which destroyed the Jaredites and decimated numerous kingdoms of both Nephites and Lamanites would be precisely the same form of criminal conspiracy which would rise up among the gentile nations in this day.

The strategems of the leaders of these societies are amazingly familiar to anyone who has studied the tactics of modern communist leaders.

The Lord has declared that before the second coming of Christ it will be necessary to ". . . destroy the secret works of darkness, . . ." in order to preserve the land of Zion—the Americas. (2 Nephi 10:11-16.)

The world-wide secret conspiracy which has risen up in our day to fulfill these prophecies is easily identified. President [David O.] McKay has left no room for doubt as to what attitude Latter-day Saints should take toward the modern "secret combinations" of conspiratorial communism. In a lengthy statement on communism, he said:

". . . *Latter-day Saints should have nothing to do with the secret combinations* and groups antagonistic to the constitutional law of the land, which the Lord 'suffered to be established,' and which 'should be maintained for the rights and protection of all flesh according to just and holy principles.' " (*Gospel Ideals,* by David O. McKay, p. 306. Italics added.) (*Conference Report,* October 1961, pp. 71-72.)

ETHER 10:23-26 *The high state of civilization among the Jaredites*

It is possible that approximately one-third of the time period of the Jaredite civilization is covered in the brief account in chapter 10. Although the record is scanty, the few details presented indicate these people had a high state of civilization. For example, the historian mentions that the people:

324

(1) "were exceedingly industrious, and they did buy and sell and traffic one with another, that they might get gain" (Ether 10:22);

(2) did work in "all manner of ore, and they did make gold, and silver, and iron, and brass, and all manner of metals; . . . And they did work all manner of fine work" (Ether 10:23);

(3) had "silks, and fine-twined linen; and they did work all manner of cloth" (Ether 10:24);

(4) "did make all manner of tools to till the earth, both to plow and to sow, to reap and to hoe, and also to thrash. And they did make all manner of tools with which they did work their beasts" (Ether 10:25-26);

(5) "did make all manner of weapons of war. And they did work all manner of work of exceedingly curious workmanship" (Ether 10:27).

Interestingly enough, recent archaeological discoveries also indicate that a populous people with a high state of civilization once lived on the American continents during the exact period indicated in the Book of Mormon.

ETHER 12:6 *Moroni's definition of faith*

The Book of Mormon contains at least two classic definitions of faith. Alma the younger defined faith as follows: ". . . faith is not to have a perfect knowledge of things; therefore if ye have faith ye hope for things which are not seen, which are true." (Alma 32:21.) Moroni's definition is ". . . faith is things which are hoped for and not seen." (Ether 12:6.) These definitions of faith are somewhat similar to the definition of Paul: ". . . faith is the substance of things hoped for, the evidence of things not seen." (Hebrews 11:1.)

ETHER 12:26-27 *Men have weaknesses that they might be humble*

As Moroni is about ready to complete his record, he fears lest the people will mock at his writings because of his own weaknesses and imperfections. Therefore, he prays to the Lord concerning this matter. The Lord answers his petition in these words:

Fools mock, but they shall mourn; and my grace is sufficient for the meek, that they shall take no advantage of your weakness;

And if men come unto me I will show unto them their weakness. I give unto men weakness that they may be humble; and my grace is sufficient for all men that humble themselves before me; for if they humble themselves before me, and have faith in me, then will I make weak things become strong unto them. (Ether 12:26-27.)

Even though we might have weaknesses, if we have faith in the Lord as he indicated, then our weaknesses may be turned into strengths.

ETHER 12:30 *The moving of a mountain through faith*

In the New Testament the Savior said that "if ye have faith as a grain of mustard seed, ye shall say unto this mountain, Remove hence to yonder place; and it shall remove." (Matthew 17:20.) Many people have assumed that the Savior was simply giving a dramatic illustration to portray the great power of faith. However, he may have been referring to an actual incident, for Ether 12:30 says that the brother of Jared "said unto the mountain Zerin, Remove—and it was removed."

ETHER 12:38-39 *Moroni's personal witness of the Savior*

One major purpose for the coming forth of the Book of Mormon is to witness of the divinity of Jesus Christ. It therefore seems fitting and proper that many of the writers in this book should be personal witnesses of the Savior. Most of our present Book of Mormon was written by four men: Nephi, Jacob, Mormon, and Moroni, and all four of these men personally saw the Savior and visited with him. We have read earlier concerning the appearance of the Lord to Nephi (2 Nephi 11:2), Jacob (2 Nephi 11:3), and Mormon (Mormon 1:15), and now Moroni says: "I have seen Jesus ... he hath talked with me face to face" (Ether 12:39).

ETHER 13:2-11 *The "new Jerusalem" on this continent*

In the book of Revelation in the New Testament, John also mentions a "new Jerusalem" of the last days: "And I saw a new heaven and a new earth: for the first heaven and the first earth were passed away; and there was no more sea. And I John saw the holy city, new Jerusalem, coming down from God out of heaven, prepared as a bride adorned for her husband." (Revelation 21:1-2.)

President Joseph Fielding Smith wrote the following

326 concerning this holy city referred to by John:

The prevailing notion in the world is that this is the city of Jerusalem, the ancient city of the Jews which in the day of regeneration will be renewed, but this is not the case. We read in the Book of Ether that the Lord revealed to him many of the same things which were seen by John. . . . In his vision, in many respects similar to that given to John, Enoch saw the old city of Jerusalem and also the new city which has not yet been built, and he wrote of them as follows . . . [see Ether 13:2-11].

In the day of regeneration, when all things are made new, there will be three great cities that will be holy. One will be the Jerusalem of old which shall be rebuilt according to the prophecy of Ezekiel. One will be the city of Zion, or of Enoch, which was taken from the earth when Enoch was translated and which will be restored; and the city Zion, or New Jerusalem, which is to be built by the seed of Joseph on this the American continent.

"And righteousness will I send down out of heaven; and truth will I send forth out of the earth, to bear testimony of mine Only Begotten; his resurrection from the dead; yea, and also the resurrection of all men; and righteousness and truth will I cause to sweep the earth as with a flood, to gather out mine elect from the four quarters of the earth, unto a place which I shall prepare, an Holy City, that my people may gird up their loins, and be looking forth for the time of my coming; for there shall be my tabernacle, and it shall be called Zion, a New Jerusalem.

"And the Lord said unto Enoch: Then shalt thou and all the city meet them there, and we will receive them into our bosom, and they shall see us; and we will fall upon their necks, and they shall fall upon our necks, and we will kiss each other;

"And there shall be mine abode, and it shall be Zion, which shall come forth out of all the creations which I have made; and for the space of a thousand years the earth shall rest." [Moses 7:62-64.]

After the close of the millennial reign we are informed that Satan, who was bound during the millennium, shall be loosed and go forth to deceive the nations. Then will come the end. The earth will die and be purified and receive its resurrection. During this cleansing period the City Zion, or New Jerusalem, will be taken from the earth; and when the earth is prepared for the celestial glory, the city will come down according to the prediction in the Book of Revelation. (*Answers to Gospel Questions* 2:103, 105, 106.)

ETHER 13:20-21 *The prophet Ether warns Coriantumr*

Before the final days of destruction came upon the Jaredites, the Lord commanded Ether "that he should go and prophesy unto Coriantumr that, if he would repent, and all his household, the Lord would give unto him his kingdom and spare the people—Otherwise they should be destroyed, and all his household save it were himself." (Ether 13:20-21.) Unfortunately, the subsequent record indicates that Coriantumr and his people did not repent, and the prophesied destruction came upon them.

ETHER 14:2   *Did the Jaredites practice polygamy?*

The early Nephite records indicate quite clearly that the Nephites were not to practice polygamy. The prophet Jacob was commanded by the Lord to say to his people: ". . . there shall not any man among you have save it be one wife." (Jacob 2:27.) However, Jacob later makes it clear that if the Lord wants his people to "raise up seed" unto him, then he might command them to practice polygamy. (Jacob 2:30.) It is not clear, however, whether or not the Jaredites were commanded by the Lord to practice polygamy. The following evidences have been cited which might indicate that they did practice polygamy: (1) Many of the men had large numbers of sons and daughters. For example, the brother of Jared had 22 sons and daughters (Ether 6:20) and Orihah had 31 sons and daughters (Ether 7:2).

(2) Riplakish had "many wives and concubines" (Ether 10:5). He was condemned by the Lord for his wickedness, but it is not clear whether or not this condemnation was because of his "many wives."

(3) Ether 14:2 states that "every *man* kept the hilt of his sword in his right hand, in the defence of his property and his own life and of his *wives* and children." This verse seems to indicate that the people practiced polygamy, but whether or not it was sanctioned by the Lord is not made clear in the record.

ETHER 15:2   *The war casualties among the Jaredites*

The great civil war among the Jaredites may have been the bloodiest war ever fought on the American continents. Even before the last great battle, the historian records that "two millions of mighty men, and also their wives and their children" had been killed. (Ether 15:2.) And these casualties were for only one of the armies involved! In order to compare the extent of these casualties with those suffered by the Nephites during the battle of Cumorah, re-read Mormon

328   6:10-15. Also, to compare the extent of these casualties with those suffered by the United States, see the table and materials listed following Mormon 6:11-15.

ETHER 15:11   *The Jaredite hill Ramah*

The hill Ramah was one of the major hills in the lands of the Jaredites. Later when the Nephites moved into this area, they evidently called this same hill by the name of Cumorah. Moroni says that the hill Ramah "was that same hill where my father Mormon did hide up the records unto the Lord, which were sacred." (Ether 15:11.) In Mormon 6:6 this hill is identified as the hill Cumorah.

ETHER 15:29-30   *The final battle between Coriantumr and Shiz*

Many people have raised questions concerning the plausibility of Coriantumr and Shiz being the last survivors of the great Jaredite armies numbering millions of men. Hugh Nibley has written the following concerning this problem:

The insane wars of the Jaredite chiefs ended in the complete annihilation of both sides, with the kings the last to go. The same thing had almost happened earlier in the days of Akish, when a civil war between him and his sons reduced the population to thirty. (Ether 9:12) This all seems improbable to us, but two circumstances peculiar to Asiatic warfare explain why the phenomenon is by no means without parallel: (1) Since every war is strictly a personal contest between kings, the battle *must* continue until one of the kings falls or is taken. (2) And yet things are so arranged that the king must be very *last* to fall, the whole army existing for the sole purpose of defending his person. This is clearly seen in the game of chess, in which all pieces are expendable except the king, who can never be taken. "The *shah* in chess," writes M. E. Moghadem, "is *not* killed and does *not* die. The game is terminated when the *shah* is *pressed into a position from which he cannot escape.* This is in line with all good traditions of chess playing, and back of it the tradition of capturing the king in war rather than slaying him whenever that could be accomplished." You will recall the many instances in the book of Ether in which kings were kept in prison for many years but not killed. In the code of medieval chivalry, taken over from central Asia, the person of the king is sacred, and all others must perish in his defense. After the battle the victor may do what he will with his rival—and infinitely ingenious tortures were sometimes devised for the final reckoning—but as long as the war went on, the king could not die, for whenever he did die, the war was over, no matter how strong his surviving forces. Even so, Shiz was willing to spare *all* of Coriantumr's subjects if he could only behead Coriantumr with his own sword. In that case, of course, the subjects would become his own. The circle of warriors, "large and mighty men as to the strength of men" (Ether 15:26) that fought around their kings to the last man, represent that same ancient institution, the sacred "shieldwall," which our own Norse ancestors took over from Asia and which meets us again and again in the wars of the tribes, in which on more than one occasion the king actually *was* the last to perish. So let no one think the final chapter of Ether is at all fanciful or overdrawn. Wars of extermination are a standard institution in the history of Asia. (*The World of the Jaredites,* pp. 235-36.)

MORONI

MORONI chapters 1-10   *The writings of Moroni*

The contributions of Moroni in our present Book of Mormon consist of the following writings: Mormon 8 and 9; Ether 1-15; Moroni 1-10. However, not all of these were written completely by Moroni, as is indicated in the following statement by J. N. Washbùrn:

> There is no more convincing evidence of the variety of material and structure in the *Book of Mormon* than the difference between the records of Ether and Moroni. Just turn the page, and the change hits the eye forcefully. And yet both come to us from the same writer, Moroni, son of Mormon.
>
> The Book of Ether is narrative almost throughout. That is, it is narrative with rich commentary in pertinent places. The Book of Moroni contains no narrative at all. The nearest thing to it is in Chapter 9.
>
> This book which bears the name of Moroni is not without its variable aspects, its unexpected elements, though by now the reader of the *Book of Mormon* has come to expect the unexpected. Chapters 1-6 are clearly the work of Moroni. Chapter 7 is from Mormon by way of Moroni; in it the son presents the teachings of the father on various topics.
>
> Chapters 8-9 were actually written by Mormon and attached by Moroni to his book. It is a fair exchange for the two chapters which Moroni added to the book begun by his father. . . .
>
> Chapter 10, the last addition of Moroni to the writings, is in some ways unsurpassed. It is very choice, containing in its short compass a number of elements that are brought together only by virtue of the fact that they are timely and good. They appear like oddments, like "fillers," but extremely valuable ones. They lack something in connection or continuity. They are obviously end-materials. (*The Contents, Structure and Authorship of the Book of Mormon* [Bookcraft, 1954], pp. 70-71.)

Another interesting difference between the actual writings of Moroni and his abridgments was pointed out by E. Cecil McGavin in a series of radio talks over KSL radio in 1941. According to Brother McGavin, the term "and it came to pass" is ùsed by Moroni 117 times in forty pages of his abridgment of the records of the Jaredites. Yet in thirteen pages of his own writing, consisting of over 7,000 words, he does not use the expression a single time. (Quoted in ibid., pp. 160-61.)

MORONI 1:1-4 *Some "Nephites" survived the battle of Cumorah*

Moroni's book that bears his own name was evidently written sometime between A.D. 400 and 421. Thus it was written at least fifteen years after the beginning of the battle of Cumorah. Yet Moroni indicates that some Nephites are still alive, for he says the Lamanites are putting to death every Nephite "that will not deny the Christ." (Moroni 1:2.) (For further information concerning this question see the material listed after Mormon 8:2-5.)

MORONI 2:1-3 *The ordination prayer by the Savior*

In 3 Nephi 18:39, Mormon tells of the departure of the resurrected Jesus Christ from his chosen twelve disciples at the end of his first visit to them. Before departing, the Savior "touched with his hand the disciples whom he had chosen, . . . even until he had touched them all, and spake unto them as he touched them. . . . the disciples bear record that he gave them power to give the Holy Ghost. And I will show unto you hereafter that this record is true." (3 Nephi 18:36-37.) Here in chapter 2 of his own book, consisting primarily of a series of small "appendices," Moroni includes the exact words of the Savior in this prayer. In speaking to his disciples, the Savior said: ". . . in my name shall ye give it [the Holy Ghost], for thus do mine apostles." (Moroni 2:2.) This is the only time the word *apostles* is used in the Book of Mormon in such a way that it might refer to the twelve Nephite disciples. (For further information as to the use of the words *apostle* and *disciple,* see the material following 3 Nephi 28.)

MORONI 3:1-4 *The ordaining of priests and teachers*

Moroni includes in this short appendix a prayer used in ordaining priests and teachers. Note that in this prayer they (1) prayed unto the father, (2) prayed in the name of Christ, (3) stated the office to which the person was to be ordained, (4) included a brief blessing and admonition, and (5) closed with the word *amen.*

MORONI 4:1-3 *The sacramental prayer on the bread*

The third brief appendix listed by Moroni is the prayer

332   used on the sacramental bread. This prayer is identical to the prayer in the Doctrine and Covenants 20:77. In the prayer the partakers of the sacrament covenant to do three things: (1) remember the body of Jesus Christ; (2) witness unto the Father that they are willing to take upon them the name of Christ; (3) witness unto the Father that they will always remember Christ and will keep his commandments. The Lord's promise in the covenant is that if we do these things, he will bless us that we might always have his spirit to be with us.

Some readers of the Book of Mormon have wondered about Moroni's statement that the elder or priest administering to the sacrament "did kneel down with the church." (Moroni 4:2.) Some have assumed the meaning that everyone in the congregation knelt down. Although this interpretation is possible, at least one other possibility exists. The statement may mean that the elder or priest did kneel down "in the presence of the members of the church." (See also D&C 20:76.)

Elder Delbert L. Stapley has indicated the importance of keeping the covenants we make with the Lord when we partake of the sacramental emblems:

> Now my brothers and sisters—there are only three prayers that the Lord has revealed to the Church, and two of them have to do with the ordinance of the sacrament, the blessing of the bread and the blessing of the water. These prayers are found in the fourth and fifth chapters of Moroni in the Book of Mormon and also in the 20th Section of the Doctrine and Covenants. While I will not attempt to repeat the sacramental prayers for you, I should like to point out, five important considerations to remember in the revealed sacramental prayers. First, we partake of the sacrament in remembrance of the broken body and spilled blood of Christ. Then we witness unto the Father, and I think we should take note of that, first, that we will take upon us the name of his Son. . . .
>
> If we take upon us the name of Christ, even as we pledge to do—when we partake of the emblems of his body and blood, we agree to keep all the commandments until the end of our days.
>
> Second, we witness or pledge that we will always remember him. As President McKay said, "Always remember him in the home, in business, in society," and I would assume wherever else we might be.
>
> Third, we pledge to keep the commandments which he has given unto us, and last, we have a promise that if we do these

things, and it is assumed that we do so worthily, that we shall always have his spirit to be with us. . . .

In partaking of the sacramental emblems, we should always call to mind Christ's suffering and sacrifice, the death upon the cross, with faithful obedience to his appointed mission. The sacrament is so sacred that it is recommended during the sacramental services, that no music be played, nor should there be any distractions whatsoever during the service. It is a time for meditation, a time for resolve, not a time for visiting, nor the chewing of gum, as so many people do, nor permitting our minds to dwell upon other things foreign to the sacred ordinance of the sacrament itself.

We know that no one but a God could suffer or go through what Christ experienced to redeem men from the effects of the fall. His sacrifice was an infinite sacrifice and that sacrifice was required of a God to satisfy broken law. In the 19th Section of the Doctrine and Covenants the Savior said: [Quotes D&C 19:16-19.]

The Lord makes it very plain that if we keep the commandments that we shall not suffer as he suffered, because he assumed the burden of people's sins, if they would repent, and also atoned for the fall of our first parents in Eden. When the Lord loves us enough to die for us, we should be willing to show our love for him by serving him and keeping all his commandments.

Another important purpose of the sacrament is to renew and keep in force the covenants and obligations which we have entered into with our God. . . . ("The Sacrament," *BYU Speeches of the Year,* 1956.)

MORONI 5:1-2   *The sacramental prayer on the wine (or water)*

In his next brief appendix, Moroni includes the prayer on the sacramental wine or water. Again, the prayer is identical with the one in the Doctrine and Covenants 20:78-79, except for the use of the word *wine* instead of *water.* The authority to use water rather than wine in the sacrament was given to the Prophet Joseph Smith by the Savior in August 1830. In this revelation the Savior states:

. . . it mattereth not what ye shall eat or what ye shall drink when ye partake of the sacrament, if it so be that ye do it with an eye single to my glory—remembering unto the Father my body which was laid down for you, and my blood which was shed for the remission of your sins.

Wherefore, a commandment I give unto you, that you shall not purchase wine neither strong drink of your enemies;

Wherefore, you shall partake of none except it is made new among you; yea, in this my Father's kingdom which shall be built up on the earth.

Behold, this is wisdom in me; wherefore, marvel not, for the hour cometh that I will drink of the fruit of the vine with you on the earth. . . . (D&C 27:2-5.)

This statement by the Savior indicates that the "wine" used in the sacrament is really a fruit juice, as he mentions that in the future he will drink of the "fruit of the vine" with his disciples.

MORONI 6:1-9   *Being cleansed "by the power of the Holy Ghost"*

In his farewell address to the Nephites during his last appearance to them, the resurrected Jesus Christ listed the major purposes of the gospel as follows: "Now this is the commandment: Repent, all ye ends of the earth, and come unto me and be baptized in my name, that ye may be sanctified by the reception of the Holy Ghost, that ye may stand spotless before me at the last day. Verily, verily, I say unto you, this is my gospel. . . . " (3 Nephi 27:20-21.) Here in chapter 6, Moroni indicates that the baptism of the water is not complete until the baptism of the Holy Ghost follows. Also, only when the people were "wrought upon and cleansed by the power of the Holy Ghost, they were numbered among the people of the church of Christ." (Moroni 6:4.)

MORONI 7:1-14   *"A man being evil cannot do that which is good"*

The seventh chapter of Moroni is a brief resumé of Mormon's teachings on faith, hope, and charity. Mormon indicates here that the spirit of the law is extremely important. In fact, he says that if a person keeps a commandment but does it with the wrong spirit or for the wrong purpose, it would not be a blessing to him:

God hath said a man being evil cannot do that which is good; for if he offereth a gift, or prayeth unto God, except he shall do it with real intent it profiteth him nothing.

For behold, it is not counted unto him for righteousness.

For behold, if a man being evil giveth a gift, he doeth it grudgingly; wherefore it is counted unto him the same as if he had retained the gift; wherefore he is counted evil before God.

And likewise also is it counted evil unto a man, if he shall pray and not with real intent of heart; yea, and it profiteth him nothing, for God receiveth none such.

Wherefore, a man being evil cannot do that which is good. . . .   335
(Moroni 7:6-10.)

Essentially this same teaching is contained in the Doctrine and Covenants: ". . . he that doeth not anything until he is commanded, and receiveth a commandment with doubtful heart, and keepeth it with slothfulness, the same is damned." (D&C 58:29.) Here again the person keeps the commandment, but he does it "with slothfulness"; therefore it is not accounted unto him for righteousness.

MORONI 7:15-17   *How to know good from evil*

The "Spirit of Christ," which Mormon tells us "is given to every man, that he may know good from evil" (Moroni 7:16), is not the same as the Holy Ghost. The difference between the Spirit of Christ and the Holy Ghost has been explained by Joseph F. Smith as follows:

The question is often asked, is there any difference between the Spirit of the Lord and the Holy Ghost? . . . The Holy Ghost is a personage in the Godhead, and is not that which lighteth every man that comes into the world. It is the Spirit of God which proceeds through Christ to the world, that enlightens every man that comes into the world, and that strives with the children of men, and will continue to strive with them, until it brings them to a knowledge of the truth and the possession of the greater light and testimony of the Holy Ghost. (*Improvement Era* 11:381-82. Also *Latter-day Prophets Speak,* p. 287.)

If a person is obedient to the commandments of God, however, it is possible for the Holy Ghost also to be with him as a "comforter within." This idea has been expressed as follows by President Wilford Woodruff:

The Holy Ghost . . . is different from the common Spirit of God, which we are told lighteth every man that cometh into the world. The Holy Ghost is only given to men through their obedience to the Gospel of Christ; and every man who receives that Spirit has a comforter within—a leader to dictate and guide him. This Spirit reveals, day by day, to every man who has faith, those things which are for his benefit. As Job said, "There is a spirit in man and the inspiration of the Almighty giveth it understanding." It is this inspiration of God to His children in every age of the world that is one of the necessary gifts to sustain man and enable him to walk by faith, and to go forth and obey all the dictations and commandments and revelations which God gives to His children to guide and direct them in life. (*Journal of Discourses* 13:157. Also *Latter-day Prophets Speak,* pp. 287-88.)

MORONI 7:40-43   *The relationship between faith and hope*

Faith is frequently listed as the first principle of revealed religion. However, Mormon raises the question as to whether or not hope does not precede faith: "How is it that ye can attain unto faith, save ye shall have hope?" (Moroni 7:40.) He next lists what we must have hope for—the atonement of Jesus Christ, the power of his resurrection, a hope in life eternal, etc. Then he continues: "Wherefore, if a man have faith he must needs have hope; for without faith there cannot be any hope." (Moroni 7:42.) Evidently Moroni, who records this sermon given by his father, learns these teachings very well, for in his later writings when he discusses faith and hope, Moroni also concludes: ". . . if there must be faith there must also be hope." (Moroni 10:20.)

MORONI 7:44-48   *Mormon's teachings on faith, hope, and charity*

Some students of the Book of Mormon have asked the question how the teachings of Mormon on faith, hope, and charity (found in Moroni 7) could be so similar to the teachings of Paul on this same subject (1 Corinthians 13:4-8). Although the Book of Mormon does not provide the exact answer to this question, at least two possibilities exist: (1) The statement on faith, hope, and charity may not have been original with either Mormon or Paul; it may have been contained in an ancient record available to both of them, or it may have been included in the teachings of the Savior that are not recorded either in the New Testament or in the Book of Mormon. (2) All revelation is received through the power of the Holy Ghost, and the Holy Ghost may have revealed this idea in essentially the same way to both Mormon and Paul.

MORONI 8:5-24   *Infants should not be baptized!*

Baptism is perhaps the most basic ordinance in Christianity, and the question of the baptism of infants is certainly one of the most fundamental questions related to this ordinance. The largest Christian church in the world today, as well as many other churches, teaches that because of the original sin of Adam and Eve no person can enter heaven without baptism. Thus these churches deny that Jesus Christ atoned for original sin, and they say that little infants and others who die without baptism cannot be saved in heaven.

The Book of Mormon definitely teaches that Jesus Christ did atone for the original transgression of Adam and Eve, and little children do not need to be baptized until they arrive at the age of accountability and are responsible for their own acts.

The teachings of Mormon are clear and definite on this subject, and he says he obtained his information "by the power of the Holy Ghost" (Moroni 8:7) in a direct revelation from the Savior. In his letter to Moroni, Mormon mentions the following fundamental principles:

1. Repentance and baptism should be taught unto those who are accountable and capable of committing sin. (Verse 10.)

2. "Little children need no repentance, neither baptism" (verse 11), and ". . . little children are alive in Christ, even from the foundation of the world" (verse 12).

3. "All little children are alive in Christ, and also all they that are without the law." (Verse 22.)

4. "He that supposeth that little children need baptism is in the gall of bitterness and in the bonds of iniquity, for he hath neither faith, hope, nor charity." (Verse 14.)

5. "He that sayeth that little children need baptism denieth the mercies of Christ, and setteth at naught the atonement of him and the power of his redemption." (Verse 20.)

Mormon also indicates why he is so definite and strong in his teachings on this subject: "I speak it boldly; God hath commanded me." (Moroni 8:21.)

(For further information on topics related to this subject, read the material following: 2 Nephi 2:22-25; Mosiah 3:11, 16-18; 3 Nephi 27:13-18.)

MORONI 8:25-26   *Receiving a remission of sins*

Baptism of water in and of itself does not bring about the remission of sins that comes only through "the fulfilling the commandments; . . . And the remission of sins bringeth meekness, and lowliness of heart; and because of meekness and lowliness of heart cometh the visitation of the Holy Ghost." (Moroni 8:25-26.) Concerning the fact that baptism of water must be followed by the baptism of the Holy Ghost

338   in order to be efficacious, Dr. William E. Berrett has written:

All that man can do is to perform the physical act of baptism which, when performed by one having authority, binds the recipient in a covenant with God, a witness that he will keep God's commandments. But this baptism, in and of itself is valueless if the commandments are not kept and the baptism of the Holy Ghost does not follow. (*Teachings of the Book of Mormon* [Deseret News Press, 1952], p. 93.)

MORONI 9:1-23   *The Nephites "delight in everything save that which is good"*

After listing several of the depraved practices of the Nephites and the Lamanites during their last great struggles, Moroni includes one sentence from his father's letter which seems to epitomize the sad fate of the Nephites: "they delight in everything save that which is good." (Moroni 9:19.)

MORONI 9:20   *Definition of "past feeling"*

Elder Neal A. Maxwell has indicated some of the characteristics of the term "past feeling":

President Harold B. Lee has called our attention to the phrase "past feeling" which is used several places in the scriptures. In Ephesians, Paul links it to lasciviousness that apparently so sated its victims that they sought "uncleanness with greediness." Moroni used the same two words to describe a decaying society which was "without civilization," "without order and without mercy," and in which people had "lost their love, one towards another." Insensate, this society saw violence, gross immorality, brutality and all kinds of "kamikaze" behavior. Nephi used the same concept in his earlier lamentation about his brothers' inability to heed the urgings of the Spirit because they were "past feeling." The common thread is obvious: the inevitable dulling of our capacity to feel renders us impervious to conscience, to the needs of others, and to insights both intellectual and spiritual. Such imperceptivity, like alcoholism, apparently reaches a stage where the will can no longer enforce itself upon our impulses. (*For the Power Is in Them* [Deseret Book Co., 1970], p. 22.)

MORONI 10:4-5   *How to obtain a testimony of the Book of Mormon*

God has made it very clear in his scriptures that he is a God of law. Among other statements he has said: "There is a law, irrevocably decreed in heaven before the foundations of this world, upon which all blessings are predicated—And when we obtain any blessing from God, it is by obedience to that law upon which it is predicated." (D&C 130:20-21.)

The blessing of a testimony of the truthfulness of the Book of Mormon is thus based on law. According to Moroni, the following steps fulfill the law by which one can gain a testimony of the Book of Mormon: (1) read the book and "ponder it in your hearts" (Moroni 10:3), and (2) "ask God, the Eternal Father, in the name of Christ, if these things are not true; and if ye shall ask with a sincere heart, with real intent, having faith in Christ, he will manifest the truth of it unto you, by the power of the Holy Ghost. And by the power of the Holy Ghost ye may know the truth of all things." (Moroni 10:4-5.)

MORONI 10:8-18   *The gifts of the Spirit*

In the concluding chapter of his record, Moroni exhorted the future readers to accept the gifts of God. Elder Bruce R. McConkie has indicated the importance of the gifts of the Spirit:

By the grace of God—following devotion, faith, and obedience on man's part—certain special spiritual blessings called *gifts of the Spirit* are bestowed upon men. Their receipt is always predicated upon obedience to law, but because they are freely available to all the obedient, they are called gifts. They are signs and miracles reserved for the faithful and for none else. . . .

Their purpose is to enlighten, encourage, and edify the faithful so that they will inherit peace in this life and be guided toward eternal life in the world to come. Their presence is proof of the divinity of the Lord's work; where they are not found, there the Church and kingdom of God is not. . . .

Faithful persons are expected to seek the gifts of the Spirit with all their hearts. They are to "covet earnestly the best gifts" (1 Cor. 12:31; D. & C. 46:8), to "desire spiritual gifts" (1 Cor. 14:1), "to ask of God, who giveth liberally." (D. & C. 46:7; Matt. 7:7-8.) To some will be given one gift; to others, another; and "unto some it may be given to have all those gifts, that there may be a head, in order that every member may be profited thereby." (D. & C. 46:29.)

From the writings of Paul (1 Cor. 12; 13; 14), and of Moroni (Moro. 10), and from the revelations received by Joseph Smith (D. & C. 46), we gain a clear knowledge of spiritual gifts and how they operate. Among others, we find the following gifts named either in these three places or elsewhere in the scriptures: the gift of knowing by revelation "that Jesus Christ is the Son of God, and that he was crucified for the sins of the world" (D. & C. 46:13), and also the gift of believing the testimony of those who have gained this revelation;

340   the gifts of testimony, of knowing that the Book of Mormon is true, and of receiving revelations; the gifts of judgment, knowledge, and wisdom; of teaching, exhortation, and preaching; of teaching the word of wisdom and the word of knowledge; of declaring the gospel and of ministry; the gift of faith, including power both to heal and to be healed; the gifts of healing, working of miracles, and prophecy; the viewing of visions, beholding of angels and ministering spirits, and the discerning of spirits; speaking with tongues, the interpretation of tongues, the interpretation of languages, and the gift of translation; the differences of administration in the Church and the diversities of operation of the Spirit; the gift of seership, "and a gift which is greater can no man have." (Mosiah 8:16; Alma 9:21; D. & C. 5:4; 43:3-4; Rom. 12:6-8.) And these are by no means all of the gifts. In the fullest sense, they are infinite in number and endless in their manifestations. (*Mormon Doctrine*, 2d ed. [Salt Lake City: Bookcraft, 1966], pp. 314-15.)

MORONI 10:9-17   *What is a possible explanation of the striking similarity between Moroni 10:9-17 and 1 Corinthians 12:8-11?*

Some people have been bothered by the similarity between the two scriptures listed above inasmuch as the reference in the New Testament was written on the eastern continent in the first century A.D. and the reference in the Book of Mormon was written several hundred years later and without any known access to the New Testament account. Several plausible explanations of this similarity could be given; however, the following possibility seems to be most reasonable: The Savior could have given a great sermon on the manifestations or gifts of the Spirit on both the eastern and western continents. Thus both Paul and Moroni would have been acquainted with the teachings of this sermon, just as they were both acquainted with the teachings of the Sermon on the Mount. Neither the New Testament nor the Book of Mormon claims to contain all the teachings of Jesus Christ. In fact, the Book of Mormon specifically states the "more part" of the teachings of the resurrected Christ were not included on the plates of Mormon (3 Nephi 26:6-11), and John indicates that not all of the teachings of the Savior were contained in the New Testament (John 21:25).

Two other possible explanations of this similarity are as follows: (1) These teachings on the gifts of the Spirit could have been recorded by a prophet in Old Testament times, and thus could have been available to Moroni through the brass plates of Laban and to Paul through one of the manuscripts that has not been included in our Old Testament; (2) the truths of the gospel are revealed to man through the power of the Holy Ghost, and the teachings concerning the gifts of the Spirit could have been revealed to both Moroni and Paul in essentially the same order.

APPENDIX A

The Book of Mormon as a Part of God's System of Witnesses

One of the major purposes of our existence upon this earth is to learn to walk by faith. To help us realize this purpose, the Lord removed our memory of the pre-earthly existence; thus we can truly learn to develop our powers of faith in him here in this life. God does not let our faith go unanswered, however. He has promised that certain *evidences* or *witnesses* shall "follow them that believe" (Mark 16:17-18); therefore, we can know our faith in him is not in vain, and we are encouraged in the further development of faith.

The Book of Mormon plays a unique role in God's system of witnesses because it testifies to man of the actuality of God and also of the truthfulness of his work upon the earth. However, the Book of Mormon is not the only witness provided by God. One of the prophets has stated, *"In the mouth of two or three witnesses shall every word be established."* (2 Corinthians 13:1. Italics added.)

Members of the Godhead testify of each other

The three members of the Godhead apparently follow this same law of witnessing or testifying of each other. In fact, in the New Testament the Savior testifies of the Father and his work so frequently, and indicates that he and the Father are *one*, that traditional Christianity has come to believe that God the Father and Jesus Christ the Son are one in substance as well as in other areas. That such is not the case was made absolutely clear by the first vision of Joseph Smith.

The members of the Godhead are *one* in many respects, however (such as goals, purposes, ideals), and they are also *one in testimony.* Note the significance of the following statement of the resurrected Jesus Christ concerning this matter:

I say unto you, that the Father, and the Son, and the Holy Ghost are one; and I am in the Father, and the Father in me, and the Father and I are one . . . *and I bear record of the Father, and the Father beareth record of me . . . and whoso believeth in me believeth in the Father also;* and unto him will the Father bear record of me, for he will visit him with fire and with the Holy Ghost. And thus will the Father bear record of me, and the Holy Ghost will bear record unto him of the Father and me, for the Father, and I, and the Holy Ghost are one. (3 Nephi 11:27, 32, 35-36. Italics added.)

Here the Savior makes two very important points: (1) the three members of the Godhead are *one* in the sense that they testify or witness of each other, and (2) if we accept or believe in any one of the members of the Godhead, we must accept or believe in the others, for they all testify of each other.

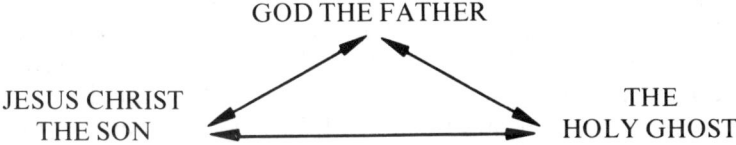

GOD THE FATHER

JESUS CHRIST THE SON   THE HOLY GHOST

The three members of the Godhead testify and witness of each other: "I bear record of the Father, and the Father beareth record of me, and the Holy Ghost beareth record of the Father and me . . . and whoso believeth in me believeth in the Father also." (3 Nephi 11:32, 35.)

The scriptures testify of each other and of the members of the Godhead

The same divine law of witnesses applies also to the holy scriptures. The Holy Bible is one witness to the divinity of Jesus Christ, but where are the second and third witnesses? Latter-day Saints believe the Book of Mormon to be a second witness (the "American" witness) to the divine mission of the Savior, and we believe the third great witness is yet to come forth. The Lord taught of the existence of three scriptural witnesses in these words:

For behold, I shall speak unto the Jews and they shall write it; and I shall also speak unto the Nephites and they shall write it; and I shall also speak unto the other tribes of the house of Israel, which I have led away, and they shall write it; . . . And it shall come to pass that the Jews shall have the words of the Nephites, and the Nephites shall have the words of the Jews; and the Nephites and the Jews shall have the words of the lost tribes of Israel; and the

344   lost tribes of Israel shall have the words of the Nephites and the Jews . . . and my word . . . shall be gathered in one. (2 Nephi 29:12-14.)

Thus there shall be three great scriptural witnesses brought forth by the Lord.

The relationship of these records to each other is also made clear in the Book of Mormon. In his farewell address, Mormon made the following statement to the Lamanites of this dispensation: "Therefore repent, and be baptized in the name of Jesus, and lay hold upon the gospel of Christ, which shall be set before you, not only in this record [the Book of Mormon] but also in the record which shall come unto the Gentiles from the Jews, which record [the Bible] shall come from the Gentiles unto you. For behold, this [the Book of Mormon] is *written for the intent that ye may believe that* [the Bible]; *and if ye believe that* [the Bible] *ye will believe this* [the Book of Mormon] *also.*" (Mormon 7:8-9. Italics added.)

Here Mormon says that one of the major purposes of the coming forth of the Book of Mormon is to testify of the Bible, and he also states that if we honestly accept one of these scriptures, we will accept the other, for the two scriptures testify of each other. This is also the testimony of Brigham Young:

No man can say that this book (laying his hands on the Bible) is true . . . and at the same time say that the Book of Mormon is untrue; . . . There is not that person on the face of the earth who has had the privilege of learning the Gospel of Jesus Christ from these two books, that can say that one is true, and the other is false. No Latter-day Saint, no man or woman, can say the Book of Mormon is true, and at the same time say that the Bible is untrue. If one be true, both are. (*Journal of Discourses,* 1:38.)

In addition to testifying of other scriptures, the Book of Mormon also has the mission to testify of the divinity of Jesus Christ. Nephi, the first major historian in the Book of Mormon, made this comment concerning the relationship between the teachings of Christ and the Book of Mormon: "And now, my beloved brethren, and also Jew, and all ye ends of the earth, hearken unto these words [the Book of Mormon] and believe in Christ; and if ye believe not in these words believe in Christ. And if ye shall believe in Christ ye will believe in these words [the Book of Mormon], for they are the words of Christ. . . ." (2 Nephi 33:10.)

According to the testimonies of these two great 345 prophets—Mormon and Nephi—if we accept the Book of Mormon, we must also accept both the Bible and the divinity of the Savior, for the Book of Mormon testifies of these things. In a like manner, if we accept either the Bible or the divinity of the Savior, then we will also accept the Book of Mormon.

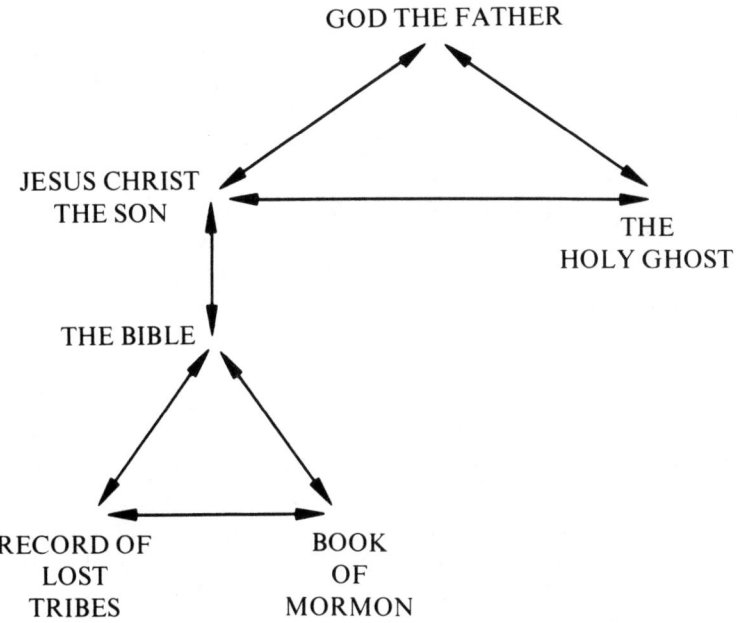

The Book of Mormon is written for the intent that we may believe the Bible; if we believe the Bible, we will also believe the Book of Mormon. (Mormon 7:9.) If we hearken unto the words of the Book of Mormon, we will believe in Christ; if we believe in Christ, we will also believe in the Book of Mormon. (2 Nephi 33:10.)

Special witnesses to the Book of Mormon

The Lord has even provided us with a series of witnesses to the scriptures themselves. In relationship to the Book of Mormon, at least three groups of human witnesses were promised by the Lord and have been provided. (2 Nephi 11:3; 2 Nephi 27:12-14; Ether 5:2-4; and D&C 5:11-15.)

346   First of all, we have the life and testimony of the Prophet Joseph Smith as a witness that the Book of Mormon is true. The Prophet declared that the record was given to him by an angel sent from God and that he translated the record by the gift and power of God. (See Joseph Smith 2:30-54, 59, 67.) Joseph Smith sealed this testimony with his own life.

Second, we have the testimonies of the three special witnesses—Oliver Cowdery, David Whitmer, and Martin Harris. These men testified that the record of the Book of Mormon had "been translated by the gift and power of God, for his voice hath declared it unto us; wherefore we know of a surety that his work is true." They also claimed they had "seen the engravings . . . upon the plates . . . they have been shown to us by the power of God, and not of man. . . . an angel of God came down from heaven, and he brought and laid before our eyes, that we beheld and saw the plates, and the engravings thereon." (See "The Testimony of Three Witnesses" in the front of the Book of Mormon.) None of these three special witnesses ever denied their testimonies of the things they had both seen and heard.

Then we have the testimonies of the eight special witnesses. They said Joseph Smith had shown them the plates and they had handled them with their own hands and had seen the engravings thereon: "And this we bear record with words of soberness . . . that the said Smith has got the plates of which we have spoken." (See "The Testimony of Eight Witnesses" in the front of the Book of Mormon.) Again, none of these men ever denied their testimonies.

These groups of special witnesses not only testify of each other, but they also serve as witnesses to the claims of Joseph Smith, including the truthfulness of the Book of Mormon. If we accept the testimony of any of these groups of human witnesses, we must accept the Book of Mormon and also the Bible and the divinity of Jesus Christ.

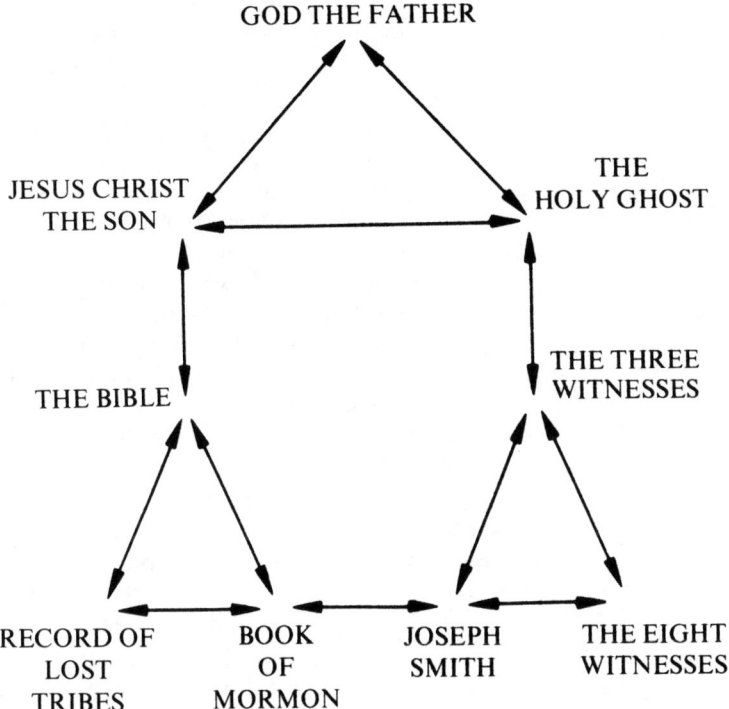

GOD THE FATHER

JESUS CHRIST
THE SON

THE
HOLY GHOST

THE BIBLE

THE THREE
WITNESSES

RECORD OF
LOST
TRIBES

BOOK
OF
MORMON

JOSEPH
SMITH

THE EIGHT
WITNESSES

If we accept the testimony of any of the human witnesses, we must also accept the prophetic calling of Joseph Smith, the Book of Mormon, the Bible, and the divinity of Jesus Christ.

The Holy Ghost testifies of the truth of these things

In addition to the testimony of other people and of the scriptures, however, the Lord has promised us a "more sure witness" of the truth of these things. This more sure witness is the Holy Ghost. Paul tells us that no man knoweth of the things of God except by the Spirit of God (1 Corinthians 2:11), and in 1 John 5:6 we read: ". . . it is the Spirit that beareth witness, because the Spirit is truth."

Thus, the best and most effective way to discover truth in the spiritual and religious realm is to ask God. "Ask, and it shall be given you," the Savior said (Matthew 7:7), and James adds, "let him ask in faith, nothing wavering" (James 1:6).

348   The last writer in the Book of Mormon gives us a specific formula by which we can arrive at a knowledge of the truth of spiritual things, including the knowledge of whether or not the Book of Mormon is true:

Behold, I would exhort you that when ye shall read these things, if it be wisdom in God that ye should read them, that ye would remember how merciful the Lord hath been unto the children of men, from the creation of Adam even down unto the time that ye shall receive these things, and ponder it in your hearts.

And when ye shall receive these things, I would exhort you that ye would ask God, the Eternal Father,[1] in the name of Christ, if these things are not true; and if ye shall ask with a sincere heart, with real intent, having faith in Christ, he will manifest the truth of it unto you, by the power of the Holy Ghost.

And *by the power of the Holy Ghost ye may know the truth of all things.* (Moroni 10:3-5. Italics added.)

Surely the Lord has provided us with ample witnesses in our day that the work of this dispensation is true. He has borne his own testimony to us through his prophets and his divine Son; he has sent angels again to the earth with the glad tidings of the gospel; he has provided scriptural and human witnesses to his great work; and he has promised us the witness of his emissary the Holy Ghost if we are sincere and faithful. As the prophet Moroni stated: ". . . all this shall stand as a testimony against the world at the last day." (Ether 5:4.)

It now behooves us to examine honestly and sincerely these witnesses and their testimonies, and, if we do, the Lord has promised us we shall not find them wanting.

APPENDIX B

Background Information Related to the Book of Mormon

1. Joseph Smith as the "author and proprietor" of the Book of Mormon

Joseph Smith was not the author or writer of the Book of Mormon; he was the translator of this record.

However, in the first edition of the Book of Mormon the following statement appears on the same page as the preface: "By Joseph Smith, Junior, Author and Proprietor." Enemies of the Church have adversely criticized the use of the expression "Author and Proprietor"; they maintain this clearly indicates that Joseph Smith was the real author or writer of the book. However, in using this expression, Joseph Smith was merely employing the terminology of the copyright law then in use. This copyright law was printed in the first edition of the Book of Mormon; note the wording of part of this law: "In conformity to the act of the Congress of the United States, entitled 'An act for the encouragement of learning, by securing the copies of Maps, Charts, and Books, to the authors and proprietors of such copies, during the times therein mentioned.'—R. R. Lansing, Clerk of the Northern District of New York." In subsequent editions of the Book of Mormon, the following appeared on the page with the preface: "Translated by Joseph Smith, Jun."

2. Origin of the section entitled "pronouncing vocabulary"

The "Pronouncing Vocabulary" section of the Book of Mormon (pp. 531-34 of the present edition) came into being as a result of a Book of Mormon convention held at Brigham Young University in May 1903. Some of the arbitrary rules of pronunciation that were formulated at this convention are as follows:

Words of two syllables to be accented on the first syllable.

Words of three syllables to be accented on the second syllable, with these exceptions, which are to be accented on the first syllable; namely: Amlici (c soft); Amulon; Antipas; Antipus; Corihor;

350   Cumeni; Curelom; Deseret; Gazelam; Helaman; Joneam; Korihor; Tubaloth.

Words of four syllables to be accented on the third syllable with the following exceptions, which are to be accented on the second syllable; namely: Abinadi; Abinidom; Amalickiah; Aminadi; Aminadab.

Ch is always to be pronounced as K.

G at the beginning of a name to be always pronounced "hard."

"I" final, always to take the long sound of the vowel. (B. H. Roberts, *New Witnesses for God,* 2:13-14.)

3. A few important dates related to the publication of the Book of Mormon

December 23, 1805:	the birthdate of the Prophet Joseph Smith
Spring of 1820:	the "First Vision"
September 21, 1823:	the first appearance of the angel Moroni
September 22, 1827:	Joseph Smith obtains the Plates of Mormon
February 1828:	Martin Harris visits Professor Charles Anthon
April 5, 1829:	Joseph Smith meets Oliver Cowdery for the first time
May 15, 1829:	the Aaronic Priesthood is restored by John the Baptist to Joseph Smith and Oliver Cowdery
June 11, 1829:	Joseph Smith applies for the copyright to the Book of Mormon
June-July 1829:	the special manifestations to the eleven special witnesses of the Book of Mormon
March 1830:	the Book of Mormon comes off the press.

4. The use of superscriptions in the Book of Mormon

In the current edition of the Book of Mormon, the descriptive or explanatory writings (superscriptions) that appear in italics immediately after the titles of most of the books were on the original plates from which this record was translated. The only exception to this rule is the two-line superscription that appears immediately after the book of Ether; these two lines did not appear on the plates of Mormon.

The following descriptive writings in the current edition also appeared on the plates: (1) the words that appear in italics immediately before Mosiah 9 and 23, Alma 9, 17, 21, 36, 39 and 45, Helaman 7 and 13, and 3 Nephi 11; and (2) the first four lines after Alma 5, the first three lines after Alma 7, and the first two lines after Alma 38, the title of 4

Nephi, and Moroni 9. All other explanatory writings that appear in italics immediately after the chapter headings *did not* appear on the original plates; they were added in later editions, primarily the edition of 1920.

APPENDIX C
The Book of Mormon as a Power of Conversion

Wilford Woodruff

According to the custom of the Mormon elders then, as now, a meeting was appointed at the schoolhouse, and notices were circulated throughout the village. The story of this new experience is told by Wilford Woodruff in a simple and beautiful manner:

Upon my arrival home my sister-in-law informed me of the meeting. I immediately turned out my horses and started for the schoolhouse without waiting for supper. On my way I prayed most sincerely that the Lord would give me his Spirit, and that if these men were the servants of God I might know it, and that my heart might be prepared to receive the divine message they had to deliver.

When I reached the place of meeting, I found the house already packed. My brother Azmon was there before I arrived. He was equally eager to hear what these men had to say. I crowded my way through the assembly and seated myself upon one of the writing desks where I could see and hear everything that took place.

Elder Pulsipher opened with prayer. He knelt down and asked the Lord in the name of Jesus Christ for what he wanted. His manner of prayer and the influence which went with it impressed me greatly. The Spirit of the Lord rested upon me and bore witness that he was a servant of God. After singing, he preached to the people for an hour and a half. The Spirit of God rested mightily upon him, and he bore a strong testimony of the divine authenticity of the Book of Mormon and of the mission of the Prophet Joseph Smith. I believed all that he said. The Spirit bore witness of its truth. Elder Cheney then arose and added his testimony to the truth of the words of Elder Pulsipher.

Liberty was then given by the elders to anyone in the congregation to arise and speak for or against what they had heard as they might choose. Almost instantly I found myself upon my feet. The Spirit of the Lord urged me to bear testimony to the truth of the message delivered by these elders. I exhorted my neighbors and friends not to oppose these men; for they were the true servants of God. They had preached to us that night the pure gospel of Jesus

Christ. When I sat down, my brother Azmon arose and bore a 353
similar testimony. He was followed by several others. (Quoted in
Improvement Era, November 1960, p. 814.)

Willard Richards

At the age of ten years he removed with his father's
family to Richmond, Mass., where he witnessed several
sectarian "revivals" and offered himself to the Congrega-
tional Church at that place at the age of seventeen, having
previously passed the painful ordeal of conviction and
conversion, even to the belief that he had committed the unpardonable sin. But the total disregard of that church to his
request for admission led him to a more thorough investigation of the principles of religion, when he became convinced
that the sects were all wrong and that God had no church on
the earth, but that he would soon have a church whose creed
would be the truth, the whole truth, and nothing but the
truth. From that time he kept himself aloof from sectarian
influence, boldly declaring his belief, to all who wished to
learn his views, until the summer of 1835, when, while in the
practice of medicine, near Boston, the Book of Mormon,
which President Brigham Young had left with his cousin
Lucius Parker, at Southborough, accidentally or provi-
dentially fell in his way. This was the first he had seen or
heard of the Latter-day Saints, except the scurrilous records
of the public prints which amounted to nothing more than
that "a boy named Joe Smith, somewhere out West, had
found a Gold Bible." He opened the book, without regard to
place, and totally ignorant of its design or contents, and
before reading half a page, declared that, "God or the devil
has had a hand in that book, for man never wrote it." He
read it twice through in about ten days; and so firm was his
conviction of the truth, that he immediately commenced settling his accounts, selling his medicine, and freeing himself
from every incumbrance, that he might go to Kirtland, Ohio,
seven hundred miles west, the nearest point he could hear
of a Saint, and give the work a thorough investigation; firmly
believing, that if the doctrine was true, God had some
greater work for him to do than peddle pills. But no sooner
did he commence a settlement, than he was smitten with the
palsy, from which he suffered exceedingly, and was
prevented from executing his design, until October, 1836,

354 when he arrived at Kirtland, in company with his brother (Doctor Levi Richards, who attended him as physician), where he was most cordially and hospitably received and entertained by his cousin, Brigham Young, with whom he tarried, and gave the work an unceasing and untiring investigation, until Dec. 31, 1836, when he was baptized by Brigham Young, at Kirtland. (Andrew Jenson: *LDS Biographical Encyclopedia* 1:53-54.)

Parley P. Pratt

Arriving at Rochester, I informed my wife that, notwithstanding our passage being paid through the whole distance, yet I must leave the boat and her to pursue her passage to our friends; while I would stop awhile in this region. Why, I did not know; but so it was plainly manifest by the Spirit to me. I said to her, "We part for a season; go and visit our friends in our native place; I will come soon, but how soon I know not; for I have a work to do in this region of country, and what it is, or how long it will take to perform it, I know not; but I will come when it is performed."

My wife would have objected to this; but she had seen the hand of God so plainly manifest in His dealings with me many times, that she dare not oppose the things manifest to me by His Spirit.

She, therefore, consented; and I accompanied her as far as Newark, a small town upwards of 100 miles from Buffalo, and then took leave of her, and of the boat.

It was early in the morning, just at the dawn of day, I walked ten miles into the country, and stopped to breakfast with a Mr. Wells. I proposed to preach in the evening. Mr. Wells readily accompanied me through the neighborhood to visit the people, and circulate the appointment.

We visited an old Baptist deacon by the name of Hamlin. After hearing of our appointment for the evening, he began to tell of a *book,* a STRANGE BOOK, a VERY STRANGE BOOK! in his possession, which had been just published. This book, he said, purported to have been originally written on plates either of gold or brass, by a branch of the tribes of Israel; and to have been discovered and translated by a young man near Palmyra, in the State of New York, by the aid of visions, or the ministry of angels. I inquired of him how or where the book was to be obtained. He promised me the perusal of it, at his house the next day, if I would call. I felt a strange interest in the book. I preached that evening to a small audience, who appeared to be interested in the truths which I endeavored to unfold to them in a clear and lucid manner from the Scriptures. Next morning I called at his house, where, for the first time, my eyes beheld the "BOOK OF MORMON"—that book of books—that record which reveals the antiquities of the *"New World"* back to the remotest ages, and which unfolds the destiny of its people and the world for all time to come;—that Book which contains the fulness of the gospel of a crucified and risen Redeemer;—that Book which reveals a lost remnant of Joseph, and which was the principal means, in the hands of God, of directing the entire course of my future life.

I opened it with eagerness, and read its title page. I then read the testimony of several witnesses in relation to the manner of its being found and translated. After this I commenced its contents by course. I read all day; eating was a burden, I had no desire for food; sleep was a burden when the night came, for I preferred reading to sleep.

As I read, the spirit of the Lord was upon me, and I knew and comprehended that the book was true, as plainly and manifestly as a man comprehends and knows that he exists. My joy was now full, as it were, and I rejoiced sufficiently to more than pay me for all the sorrows, sacrifices and toils of my life. I soon determined to see the young man who had been the instrument of its discovery and translation. . . .

This discovery greatly enlarged my heart, and filled my soul with joy and gladness. I esteemed the Book, or the information contained in it, more than all the riches in the world. (*Autobiography of Parley P. Pratt* [Deseret Book Co., 1961], pp. 36-37, 39.)

Hugh B. Brown

Among the volumes of scripture in which we believe, the one most frequently referred to by friends and critics is the Book of Mormon. It has had the largest circulation and has elicited more comment during the past century, favorable and otherwise, than any other modern book.

This book is an inspired text, having been written by

356 various prophets who lived in America at the times of which they write. It is a sacred record of the ancient inhabitants of America, covering in the main that portion of their history from about 600 B.C. to 400 A.D.

Its message was inscribed on metallic plates by various authors. These writings were abridged by the Prophet Mormon, one of the last survivors of a dwindling race. It is therefore known as the Book of Mormon. He entrusted the plates to his son, Moroni, who was the last of the Nephite historians. Moroni deposited the plates in a stone box on a hillside and some fourteen hundred years later he, at that time a resurrected being, revealed their hiding place to Joseph Smith, the prophet, who translated what is said to be reformed Egyptian characters into English by the gift and power of God.

It is doubtless this element of the miraculous which disturbs many who hear of this record and causes some to shrug it off without further interest. It seems strange to us that believers in the Judeo-Christian Bible should be skeptical of the miraculous.

Miracles form an important part of the Old and the New Testaments. The story of the earth life of Jesus of Nazareth continues to grip the hearts and intrigue the minds of men, largely because of the miracle of his birth, the almost daily miracles he performed during his ministry, and the transcendent miracle of his resurrection and ascension. Moreover, he left his apostles and disciples with a promise of a miraculous reappearance in the last days. Paraphrasing the Apostle Paul we ask, "Why should it be thought a thing incredible that God should reveal his will to his servants, the prophets, as he promised to do."

One remarkable fact about this book is its continued popularity and appeal. One hundred thirty years after the first edition was published, it is still a best seller, over thirty-five thousand copies being printed in English each year, and other thousands distributed in the twenty-seven different languages into which it has been translated. Nearly three million copies of this book have been distributed in almost all countries of the world in the last century.

Yes, we do believe the Book of Mormon to be the word of God, and we believe in the miraculous that was involved in its preservation and production. There have been many who have sought to discredit it, many things have been written against it, but in more recent times some of our friends who have made a careful study of the book have made statements which are significant. I shall refer to one or two taken from a little book called, *The Book of Mormon Message and Evidences* by Dr. Franklin S. Harris, Jr. Charles H. Hull, professor of American history in Cornell University, wrote:

"I am perfectly willing to say to anyone that I suppose the Book of Mormon to be one of the most famous and widely discussed books ever published in America."

Says a Rochester newspaper, "The book itself remains on which was founded the greatest religion of the continent and the century. It was not the book itself, but the wonderful influence it had on America that counted."

And a former Secretary of Agriculture, who had read the book carefully, said, "Of all the American books of the nineteenth century, it seems probable that the Book of Mormon was the most powerful. It reached perhaps only one percent of the United States, but it affected this one percent so powerfully and lastingly that all the people of the United States have been affected, especially by its contribution in opening one of our great frontiers."

Now, our declaration regarding the Book of Mormon is a solemn one. If it is false, it is almost blasphemous. If it is true, then all who believe it are under a solemn obligation to its author to proclaim its truth.

One of the prophets of that book emphasized this fact in the following words, and I read from Second Nephi:

"Wherefore, how great the importance to make these things known unto the inhabitants of the earth, that they may know that there is no flesh that can dwell in the presence of God, save it be through the merits, and mercy, and grace of the Holy Messiah, who layeth down his life according to the flesh, and taketh it again by the power of the Spirit, that he may bring to pass the resurrection of the dead, being the first that should rise." (2 Nephi 2:8.)

And further in his same book, after reciting the miraculous events in the history of the Israelites, he said,

". . . I say unto you, that as these things are true, and as the Lord God liveth, there is none other name given under

358 heaven save it be this Jesus Christ, of which I have spoken, whereby man can be saved." (*Ibid.,* 25:20.)

It is the message of the Book of Mormon that has caused people from almost all nations of the earth to accept it as the word of God. Its inspiring theme and divine message, from the title page to the last chapter, constitutes the testimony or witness of a whole nation of people that Jesus is the Christ, the Son of God, the Creator of the world, the Redeemer of mankind. It bears witness to the efficacy of the atonement, of its universal application and its value to all individuals who will accept his word and keep his commandments.

We urge our friends to examine the book itself, to check its claims, listen to its message and to feel of its spirit. (*Conference Report,* October 1958, pp. 61-63.)

Ezra Taft Benson

Ancient American prophets six hundred years before Christ foresaw the coming of Columbus and those who followed. These prophets saw the establishment of the colonies, the war for independence, and predicted the outcome. These prophecies are contained in a volume of scripture called the Book of Mormon. This sacred record, a companion volume to the Holy Bible, which it confirms, is an added witness to the divine mission of Jesus Christ as the Son of God and Redeemer of the world.

How I wish every American and every living soul would read the Book of Mormon. I testify to you that it is true. It tells about the prophetic history and mission of America. It gives the comforting assurance that God has kept this great nation, as it were, in the hollow of his hand in preparation for its great mission. (*Conference Report,* April 1962, p. 103.)

Marion G. Romney

One of the best ways to learn the gospel is to search the scriptures. Our purpose in urging all bearers of the Melchizedek Priesthood to read the Book of Mormon during 1961 was that they might learn more about the gospel. One cannot honestly study the Book of Mormon without learning gospel truths, because it contains ". . . the fulness of the gospel of Jesus Christ to the Gentiles and to the Jews also. . . ." (D&C 20:9) So impressed was the Prophet Joseph with

it that he "told the brethren that the Book of Mormon was 359
the most correct book of any book on earth, and the keystone
of our religion, and a man would get nearer to God by abiding by its precepts, than by any other books." (*DHC* 4:461.)
(*Conference Report,* April 1962, pp. 18-19.)

LeGrand Richards

We had a man here as a tourist on Temple Square a few
years ago, a minister from Texas, and after returning home
he wrote a letter back saying that he had purchased a copy of
the Book of Mormon. He said, "I have a library of important
books that cost me over twelve thousand dollars, but I have
one book that is more valuable than them all because it is
the word of God and it is the Book of Mormon."

Just recently a letter came in to the headquarters of the
Church from a minister in the East. He said he bought a
copy of the Book of Mormon years ago from a Mormon
elder who called at his home. He said, "I put it in my library.
I never read it until recently, and now I have been reading it,
and I have been quoting from it in my sermons." In his letter
he mentioned the words of Alma and the words of Nephi out
of the Book of Mormon which he had used in the preparation of his sermons.

Why cannot the world believe? Why cannot they accept
it? Some of you remember a few years ago how Brother
Nicholas G. Smith told us of being invited by the dean of religion at the University of Southern California in California
to lend him a copy of the Book of Mormon. He gave him a
copy used by the missionaries that had passages underlined
in red ink, or a lead pencil, and that minister invited Brother
Smith and the missionaries to attend his next meeting in his
own parish, and he stood before his people and read verse
after verse that had been underlined by the missionaries, and
then he said something like this:

"Why cannot we fellowship a people who believe in such
wonderful things as I have been reading to you here today?"
And then he went on to say, "We have here a volume of
scripture which has been in our midst a hundred years, and
we have not known anything about it."

I see that my time has gone. I love the Book of Mormon.
I know that no honest soul searching after God can study

360   that book without knowing that it is divine, that it was not written by Joseph Smith; and when it is evident that it is what it purports to be, a volume of scripture that the Bible promised should come forth in our day, then all of the message of the Prophet Joseph Smith is true, then they will open their hearts and their minds to the messages of Moroni, John the Baptist, Peter, James, and John, Moses, Elijah, Elias, the prophets who have visited this earth in the restitution of all things spoken by the mouths of all the holy prophets since the world began, which Peter declared and promised would occur in this world before the coming of Christ.

The Book of Mormon was preserved to be a witness that Jesus is the Christ, the Eternal God, manifesting himself unto all nations. (*Conference Report,* April 1959, pp. 19-20.)

APPENDIX D

The Lamanite and the Gospel
by President Spencer W. Kimball

The history of the American Indian over the past 400 years is one of oppression and exploitation. In the eastern United States the Indians were "used" by the colonists as pawns, as guides, and they were induced to fight on one side or the other of numerous conflicts between colonial powers.

They were pushed and driven and evicted and exiled. They fought the "Battle of America," a continuing battle with some conquests and temporary wins but with infinitely more losses, each one resulting in a further move westward reminiscent of the continuing flight northward by their Nephite victims more than a thousand years earlier. In the eighteenth and nineteenth centuries, the retreat was across the length of the land.

They fought back. Of course, they fought back. This was their homeland—these, their forests; these, their mountains; these, their plains; these, their buffalo and deer and wild turkey; these, their burial grounds. They did not have cannons or guns at first, and they learned to defend themselves and to fight their battles with bows and arrows and spears and fire, their own weapons.

The history of the Indians has been a checkered one, and disturbing and unpleasant, but it has been said "the darkest hour is just before the dawn." And, the dawn has come and the full day approaches.

The greatest and choicest land of all the world had been given by the Lord to the descendants of Lehi as their inheritance forever. Never would they have lost it had they lived the commandments of the Lord, carried forward their culture, and grown and developed as they could and as they did in certain times in their ancient history. But they forgot their benefactor, lost their written language and culture, and degenerated until they were no match for the wily and subtle Europeans.

362   Not long ago, I clipped an advertisement from a magazine. On it is a picture of a sad-faced Indian woman with her blanket wrapped around herself and her little child whom she hugs close to her. The title is "Bad Deal at the Trading Post":

More than 50% of America's farm products today consists of plants used by the Indians before Columbus planted his flag. They include beans, chocolate, corn, cotton, peanuts, potatoes, pumpkins, tobacco and tomatoes. To combat illness, the Indian has given us arnica, cascara, cocaine, ipecac, oil of wintergreen, petroleum jelly, quinine and witch hazel. Botanists have yet to discover, in 400 years, any medicinal herb that was not used by the Indian.

That's what *they* gave *us.* Here's what *we* have *given* them: High infant mortality rate, short life expectancy. Dependency on handouts. Loss of pride. Much illness. Unemployment as high as 80% in some tribes. The 600,000 remaining American Indians are struggling to hang on to the lowest health, education and economic rungs in American life. Somebody better do *something* before those rungs collapse. Remember, you're up there somewhere on that ladder yourself.

This was not the kind of a deal where two peoples jockey back and forth and finally arrive at an amicable arrangement wherein each benefits about equally. This was a deal where power ruled; where the white party of the first part took nearly everything of value—the lands, the water, the mountains, the rivers, the buffalo and the fish, and the homeland and security. The red party of the second part received nearly nothing—limited reservations of stark and barren "badlands," which had been theirs from the first. The white conquerors even took much of that. It was a bad deal.

That bad deal began soon after the pivotal year of 1492 and has never yet ended. It was a unfair one, an unequal one, a treacherous one. Why didn't the Indians rise and demand fair treatment? The answer is, they did. But unorganized, with limited war materiel and uncountable defeats behind them, they could not cope with the situation.

Perhaps of all prophecies ever made, none have been fulfilled more literally and more intensely and more devastatingly than this one from Mormon: "But behold, it shall come to pass that they shall be driven and scattered by the Gentiles. . . ." (Mormon 5:20.)

And what a tragic, literal fulfillment those scriptures had.

Go to the rounded hill standing above the Big Horn and Little Big Horn rivers in Montana. Ride up the hill on a paved road to a government building constructed to memorialize Custer's last fight. Look about you and see the monuments—small marble monuments.

The encyclopedia says:

Custer rode for the heart of the Indian line. A rise across the stream masked the enemy and as Custer swept down, the *savages* rode against him and swarmed around to his rear. Outnumbered twenty to one, the heroic band [that was the white man] still fought their way up to the ridge and a small number with their general reached it. Then a fresh band of one thousand Cheyennes rose up under Rain-in-the-face and not a soul was left. . . . The bodies of the slain division were left as they lay. . . . Forty-two Indians were killed; the battle field has been marked with a small marble monument where each *white* man fell. (*Encyclopedia Americana* 8:336-337; italics added.)

The account reads "not a soul was left alive" from the battle, again fulfilling the scriptures, "They shall be considered as naught." The thousands of Redmen who rode away—this time triumphantly—were not considered souls by the historians.

Another instance: The story of the Cherokees would melt the stoniest heart—driven at the point of a bayonet from their homes and lands, evicted from their country and sent to the swampy, mosquito-ridden area of Indian Territory. The prejudiced historian again said that the Indians were the culprits. Their suffering and death means little; their homes and gardens and farms were expropriated. The "white heroes" evicted and expropriated for their own use (at the point of bayonets) the lands of the "red demons."

We follow the Navajos from their exquisitely beautiful red sandstone lands of northeastern Arizona in their long, pitiful, painful march to central New Mexico, to Bosque Redondo on the Pecos River. We suffer and starve and freeze with them in the lonely four years, and then walk with them back to their homeland after signing their treaties.

In recent times our attention was arrested by a double-page picture in *Life* magazine. It is the dead of winter. Plodding across the thousands of square miles of deep snow and the wind-scoured stubbly plain, two Indian women on their horses make a new deep trail through the snow. It is good

364 that their horses can break trail; it is good that their warm skirts are long to their ankles; it is good that their blankets cover them well and their scarves cover their heads and faces, for the wind is bitter and the cold intense, and the way is long. Thank goodness they have a sense of direction, for if the horses failed, never would they be found alive. They have left in their hogans their children, so they might find food for their families. Their wagon is under a tree, a solitary tree; frozen sheep are here and there half covered in the snow. That frozen one that the boy is dragging is one of over half a million sheep, goats, and cattle that were stranded with no food save that from a lucky drop. They will have food for a few days but soon the carcasses will be spoiled beyond eating.

Why do I return to a rehearsal of the indignities against the Indian? The answer is that we have debt to pay. We are deeply indebted and we shall never have liquidated that debt until we shall have done all in our power to rebuild the Indian and give him back the opportunities that are possible for us to give him.

The glider without an engine lies helpless on the ground until a motorized plane tows it high into the air with a tow line. When the glider is aloft, it is on its own and flies about at the will of its pilot, hundreds of miles in either direction—up and down, even to high altitudes. The pilot finds the updrafts and increases his altitude. He sails from updraft to updraft like a great bird in the air. He remains aloft until he chooses to descend.

Remember that the glider would remain on the ground until it rotted unless some power lifted it. The sailplane is the Indian. The tow line is the Indian program and the gospel of Christ. The members of the Church are the power plane and must do the lifting and the towing. The updrafts are the gospel principles.

And this, of course, reminds us to Paul's statement to Rome:

For whosoever shall call upon the name of the Lord shall be saved.

How then shall they call on him in whom they have not believed? and how shall they believe in him of whom they have not heard? and how shall they hear without a preacher? (Romans 10:13-14.)

We must be the preachers.

As we see the Indians pushed from pillar to post; from the eastern seaboard to the west; from their free, open country to their narrow, limited reservations; from their carefree, open world to their limited lands supposed worthless, we remember Jacob's lament:

. . . the time passed away with us, and also our lives passed away like as it were unto us a dream, we being a lonesome and a solemn people, wanderers, cast out from Jerusalem, born in tribulation, in a wilderness, and hated of our brethren, which caused wars and contentions; wherefore, we did mourn out our days. (Jacob 7:26.)

In our own dispensation, the Indian was vanishing. In the Cherokees' "Trail of Tears," 4,600 died within a very short time on that merciless march from Georgia to Indian Territory. There were no marked graves. Herded like cattle, they traveled ten miles a day.

We were told that 450 years ago, nearly a million American Indians inhabited what is now the United States. By the close of the nineteenth century, sometimes referred to as a "Century of Shame," only 235,000 remained.

I have seen changes myself. On October 23. 1927, the Arizona Temple at Mesa, Arizona, was dedicated by President Heber J. Grant. At that time, I was stake clerk of the St. Joseph Stake and was secretary of the temple fund and collected the tens of thousands of dollars that the people of our stake contributed for the erection of this temple.

In the dedication services, President Grant made reference to the part which the Lamanites would play in this particular temple.

We beseech thee, O Lord, that thou wilt stay the hand of the destroyer among the descendants of Lehi who reside in this land and give unto them increasing virility and more abundant health, that they may not perish as a people but that from this time forth they may increase in numbers and in strength and in influence, that all the great and glorious promises made concerning the descendants of Lehi may be fulfilled in them; that they may grow in vigor of body and of mind, and above all love for thee and thy son, and increase in diligence and in faithfulness in keeping the commandments which have come to them with the gospel of Jesus Christ, and that many of them may have the privilege of entering this holy house and receiving ordinances for themselves and their departed ancestors. (*Temples of the Most High*, p. 173.)

366   It is remembered that the Indian was called, for long years, "the Vanishing American," and disease and hardships and hunger and war had, through the years, taken their heavy toll.

Wilford Woodruff, the President of the Church, in an oft-quoted statement said:

I am looking for the fulfillment of all things that the Lord has spoken, and they will come to pass as the Lord God lives. Zion is bound to rise and flourish. The Lamanites will blossom as the rose on the mountains. I am willing to say here that, although I believe this, when I see the power of the nation destroying them from the face of the earth, the fulfillment of that prophecy is perhaps harder for me to believe than any revelation of God that I ever read. It looks as though there would not be enough [Indians] left to receive the Gospel; but notwithstanding this dark picture, every word that God has ever said of them will have its fulfillment, and they, by and by, will receive the Gospel. It will be a day of God's power among them, and a nation will be born in a day. Their chiefs will be filled with the power of God and receive the Gospel, and they will go forth and build the new Jerusalem, and we shall help them. They are branches of the house of Israel. . . . (*Journal of Discourses* 15:282.)

The Lamanite population of the Americas, at the greatest number, must have run into many millions, for in certain periods of Book of Mormon history, wars continued almost unabated and the soil was covered with the bodies of the slain. Mormon says:

. . . and there had been thousands slain on both sides, both the Nephites and the Lamanites. (Mormon 4:9.)

And it is impossible for the tongue to describe, or for man to write a perfect description of the horrible scene of the blood and carnage. . . . (Mormon 4:11.)

There were the peoples of the Mulekites, all of whom were slain. There were the people of the Jaredites who inhabited the land for centuries and who must have grown to great numbers. Coriantumr, you remember, saw—

that there had been slain by the sword already nearly two millions of his people [Was it ever heard of before or since, two million in a battle?] . . . yea, there had been slain two millions of mighty men, and also their wives and their children. (Ether 15:2.)

As Mormon tells of the last great battle, he tells of his own ten thousand who were hewn down and the ten thousand of Moroni. Then twenty-one other men with their ten thousand each "and their flesh, and bones, and blood lay upon the face of the earth . . . to molder upon the land, and to crumble and to return to their mother earth." (Mormon 6:15.)

The remnants of Israel broke up into numberous tribes and families and the civil war battles continued. It is estimated by some that when Columbus came, there were only about 233,000 of the scores of millions who had been on this continent. They were almost gone and were still vanishing by war and pestilence.

In 1927, when President Grant offered this prayer, they were losing their children, as Mormon said. "They were considered as naught" before the oncoming settlers, and when the smoke of battles dissipated, the dead white men were lauded, numbered, buried, but the Indians were, in fact, uncounted. They had been dying by war and now, after their subjugation in 1868, they were dying from germs and viruses, starvation and freezing. Their health level was at perhaps an all-time low. The infant mortality was terrifyingly high. How could little babes survive? The incidence of tuberculosis and other diseases was unbelievable. The Indians' water supply was contaminated generally, and potentially dangerous; and without waste disposal facilities, viral infections and pneumonia and malnutrition were common and devastating.

Since 1900, the American Indians have climbed back to over 600,000 in number. By 1975, they will have reached their original force; in fact today, Indians comprise the fastest growing ethnic group in America. There is now a significant number of them in every state of the Union. (Gordon H. Fraser, *Moody,* p. 23.)

There are probably nearly as many actual members of the Church today who are Lamanites and Mestizos (people of mixed blood partly Lamanite) as there were total Indians in the United States when the tide turned and the vanishing American began to increase, in line with the prayers and prophecies of the leaders of the Church.

Today they are coming into the Church in large numbers. There are several stakes largely Lamanite, with ward, quorum, and auxiliary leadership from the Lamanites. There are many missions devoted to teaching Lehi's children.

There are some many thousands of youngsters in the Indian seminary program, thousands of Indians in United States universities and a larger number in the Pacific schools and BYU. There are many thousands in schools in Mexico and Chile and in the Pacific and in the Indian placement program.

Many young people have filled missions and thousands are now preparing for them. Numerous Lamanites are receiving their endowments and sealings.

Some of my most happy moments have been when I have been performing marriage ceremonies in the holy temple with two wonderful Indians across the altar.

The Twelve Apostles in their "Proclamation to the World" in 1845 stated:

Thy sons and daughters of Zion will soon be required to devote a portion of their time in instructing the children of the forest, for they must be educated and instructed in all the arts of civil life, as well as in the gospel.

They must be clothed, fed, and instructed in the principles and practice of virtue, modesty, temperance, cleanliness, industry, mechanical arts, manners, customs, dress, music and all other things which are calculated in their nature to REFINE, PURIFY, EXALT, and GLORIFY them as sons and daughters of the royal house of Israel and of Joseph, who are making ready for the coming of the bridegroom.

And so as the sons and daughters of Zion we will soon be required to give a portion of our time, the Lord says through his prophets, to the training and teaching of these Lamanites, who have been deprived so long and who now are beginning to stretch and yawn and awaken from their sleep and come into their own.

As Elder Boyd K. Packer returned from Peru, he told me of his experience in a branch sacrament meeting in Cuzco in the lofty Andes. The chapel was still, the opening exercises finished, and the sacrament in preparation.

A little Lamanite ragamuffin entered from the street. Calloused and chappy were the little feet that brought him in the open door, up the aisle, and to the sacrament table. Here was dark and dirty testimony of deprivation, want, unsatisfied hungers—spiritual as well as physical. Almost unobserved, he slyly came to the sacrament table and, with a seeming spiritual hunger, leaned against the table and lovingly rubbed his unwashed face against the cool, smooth-white linen.

A woman in the front seat, seemingly outraged by the intrusion, caught his eye, and with motion and frown, sent the little ragamuffin scampering down the aisle out into his world, the street.

A bit later the little urchin, seemingly compelled by some inner urge, overcame his timidity and came stealthily, cautiously down the aisle again, fearful, ready to escape if necessary, but impelled as though directed by inaudible voices with "a familiar spirit" and as though memories long and faded were reviving, as though some intangible force were crowding him on to seek something for which he yearned but could not identify.

From his seat on the stand, Elder Packer caught his eye, beckoned to him, and stretched out big welcoming arms. After a moment's hesitation, the little Lamanite ragamuffin was nestled comfortably on his lap, in his arms, the tousled head against the great warm heart—a heart sympathetic to waifs, and especially to little Lamanite ones.

Later, Elder Packer with a subdued voice recalled this incident to me. As he sat forward on his chair, his eyes glistening, emotion in his voice, he said: "As this little one relaxed in my arms, it seemed it was not a single little Lamanite I held. It was a nation, indeed a multitude of nations of deprived, hungering souls, wanting something deep, good and warm they could not explain—a humble people yearning to revive memories all but faded out, of ancestors standing wide-eyed, open-mouthed, expectant and excited. A people reaching for truths they seemed to remember only vaguely; for prophecies which surely would some day be fulfilled; looking up and seeing an holy glorified Being descend from celestial areas and hearing a voice say: 'Behold, I am Jesus Christ, the Son of God . . . and in me, hath the Father glorified his name . . . I am the light and the life of the world.' "

The day of the Lamanite is surely here and we are God's instrument in helping to bring to pass the prophecies of renewed vitality, acceptance of the gospel, and resumption of a favored place as part of God's chosen people. The promises of the Lord will all come to pass; we could not

370   thwart them if we would. But we do have it in our power to hasten or delay the process by our energetic or neglectful fulfillment of our responsibilities. (*Faith Precedes the Miracle,* Deseret Book, 1973, pp. 339-49.)

APPENDIX E

A Pure Heart and Clean Hands
by President Marion G. Romney

My text, "A Pure Heart and Clean Hands," is taken from an impassioned interrogation addressed by Alma, in the year 83 B.C., to backsliding members of the church in the city of Zarahemla. To put it in context I quote the following:

And now . . . I ask . . . you, my brethren . . . have ye spiritually been born of God? . . . Have ye experienced this mighty change in your hearts?

Do ye exercise faith in the redemption of him who created you? Do you look forward with an eye of faith, and view this mortal body raised in immortality, . . . to stand before God to be judged according to the deeds which have been done in the mortal body?

I say unto you, can you imagine to yourselves that ye hear the voice of the Lord, saying unto you, in that day: Come unto me ye blessed, for behold, your works have been the works of righteousness upon the face of the earth?

Or . . . can ye imagine yourselves brought before the tribunal of God with your souls filled with guilt and remorse, having . . . a remembrance that ye have set at defiance the commandments of God? I say unto you, can ye look up to God at that day with a pure heart and clean hands? (Alma 5:14-16, 18, 19.)

Alma is here implying that the "exercise of faith in the redemption" of Christ, sufficient to bring about the mighty change in one's heart, to which he refers, is prerequisite to obtaining "a pure heart and clean hands." He is also implying that if on the great judgment day one can look up to God with a "pure heart and clean hands," he will hear the voice of the Lord saying unto him, "come unto me ye blessed," and that if he cannot do so, his soul will be filled with guilt and remorse.

He uses the phrase "a pure heart and clean hands" to indicate a state of purity—the condition one attains unto, when, through faith in the Lord Jesus Christ, repentance, baptism by immersion, and baptism by fire and the Holy Ghost, he receives forgiveness of sins which works in him a

372 spiritual rebirth, a birth through which he comes back into harmony with, and is sensitive and alive to, the things of the Spirit. *Healed* is the term frequently used in the scriptures to denote the state of such an one.

On that great day, according to Alma, those who have "a pure heart and clean hands" will receive "an inheritance at the right hand" of God, while those who do not will wail and mourn, for they at long last will recognize that they cannot be saved but must await "an everlasting destruction."

We may well ponder Alma's question: "Can ye look up to God at that day with a pure heart and clean hands?" for there can scarcely be another question upon the answer to which so much depends. To me it suggests the same consideration as does the following statement found in the 21st section of the Doctrine and Covenants: "Let virtue garnish thy thoughts unceasingly; then shall thy confidence wax strong in the presence of God" (v. 45).

Realizing that it will not be long now until I shall be summoned to appear before the judgment bar, these scriptures are becoming more and more meaningful to me. Adding to my concern is the fact that if I appear there without "a pure heart and clean hands," I will have no justifiable excuse, because by the power of the Holy Spirit I have been given a knowledge of that "law, irrevocably decreed in heaven" upon which the possession of such a pure heart and clean hands is predicated (D&C 130:20). This law is, of course, of the celestial and not of this world, but its provisions are as fixed and certain as are the laws of the physical universe. If we cannot obey them, we cannot obtain the blessings which obedience to them brings, for the Lord himself has said that "he who is not able to abide the law of a celestial kingdom cannot abide a celestial glory" (D&C 88:22).

The provisions of this celestial law, as already indicated, are "faith in the Lord Jesus Christ, repentance, baptism by immersion and baptism by fire and the Holy Ghost." Because to abide by these principles and ordinances is prerequisite to obtaining, and a guarantee that one will obtain "a pure heart and clean hands," let us take a little closer look at them.

Faith in the Lord Jesus Christ requires belief in him.

That is, acceptance as truth of all that has been revealed concerning him and his mission. For example: That he is the firstborn spirit son of God; that he was chosen and ordained in the great heavenly council to be our Redeemer; that he came to earth in the meridian of time as the Only Begotten of God in the flesh, lived a sinless life, taught the gospel, suffered in Gethsemane, died on the cross, was buried, rose again the third day, and ascended into heaven; that through his victory over death he brought about universal resurrection; and that through his atonement he implemented the merciful plan of salvation whereby men may be forgiven of their sins, which forgiveness creates in them pure hearts and clean hands.

This belief must, however, be more than mental assent. James emphasized this when he said, "Thou believest that there is one God; thou doest well: the devils also believe, and tremble" (James 2:19). It must also be more than the knowledge referred to by Mark in his account of a man with an unclean spirit who, when he saw Jesus, cried out: "What have we to do with thee, thou Jesus of Nazareth? . . . I know thee who thou art, the Holy One of God" (Mark 1:23, 24).

A saving belief or faith in the Lord Jesus Christ is accompanied by some of its fruits. "The ancients quenched the violence of fire, escaped the edge of the sword, women received their dead, etc. By faith the worlds were made. A man who has none of the gifts has no faith" (*History of the Church,* 5:218). Paul says that by faith the elders obtained a good report.

By faith Abel offered unto God a more excellent sacrifice than Cain, by which he obtained a witness that he was righteous. . . .

By faith Enoch was translated that he should not see death: . . .

He that cometh to God must believe that he is, and that he is a rewarder of them that diligently seek him (Hebrews 11:2, 4-6).

The efficacy of a belief that God is and that "he is a rewarder of them that diligently seek him" in producing a "pure heart and clean hands" is conclusively evidenced by the fact that it moves one to repent of his sins and obey the principles and ordinances of the celestial law.

The significance, power, and indispensability of such a faith in the Lord Jesus Christ have been repeatedly declared from the beginning. It was declared to them of the first dispensation by Adam, to whom the Lord said:

> If thou wilt turn unto me, . . . and believe, and repent . . . and be baptized . . . in the name of mine Only Begotten Son, . . . Jesus Christ, the only name which shall be given under heaven, whereby salvation shall come unto the children of men, ye shall receive the gift of the Holy Ghost (Moses 6:52).

Such was the message of all the Old Testament prophets.

It was likewise the message of all the Nephite prophets. "As the Lord God liveth [said Nephi], there is none other name given under heaven save it be this Jesus Christ, of which I have spoken, whereby man can be saved" (2 Nephi 25:20).

In the meridian of time, Jesus said to the Jews, as he taught them in the temple treasury: "If ye believe not that I am he, ye shall die in your sins" (John 8:24).

When Peter and John were being questioned by the Jews concerning the power by which they had healed the impotent man at the gate of the temple, Peter answered:

> Be it known unto you all . . . that by the name of Jesus Christ of Nazareth . . . doth this man stand here before you whole. . . .
> Neither is there salvation in any other: for there is none other name under heaven given among men, whereby we must be saved (Acts 4:10, 12).

In this last dispensation the Lord has repeatedly declared this truth. Through the Prophet, he said to Oliver Cowdery and David Whitmer: "Behold, Jesus Christ is the name which is given of the Father, and there is none other name given whereby man can be saved" (D&C 18:23).

I have quoted these several scriptures which emphasize the preeminent role of faith in the Lord Jesus Christ and in the plan of salvation because of my desire to teach, with all the power at my command, and bear witness to the truth that Jesus is the Son of God, our Savior and our Redeemer, and that a vital, moving faith in him is an indispensable prerequisite to forgiveness of sins, which forgiveness, as above indicated, is the catalyst which heals the sinner and creates in him a pure heart and clean hands.

To me, one of the most direct and persuasive lessons on this point is given in the book of Enos. He begins by saying, "I will tell you of the wrestle which I had before God, before I received a remission of my sins."

Then he recounts how, as he sought food in the forest, the words which [he] had often heard [his] father speak concerning eternal life and the joy of the saints, sunk deep into [his] heart.

And [he continues] my soul hungered; and I kneeled down before my Maker, and I cried unto him in mighty prayer and supplication for mine own soul; and all the day long did I cry unto him; yea, and when the night came I did still raise my voice high that it reached the heavens.

And there came a voice unto me, saying: Enos, thy sins are forgiven thee, and thou shalt be blessed.

And I, Enos, knew that God could not lie; wherefore, my guilt was swept away.

And I said: Lord, how is it done?

And he said unto me: Because of thy faith in Christ, . . . wherefore, go to, thy faith hath made thee whole (Enos 2-8).

So much for faith in the Lord Jesus Christ, the first provision of the law which brings a pure heart and clean hands. We come now to repentance, the second provision.

One who has faith, and the desire which comes with it, to "look up to God at that day with a pure heart and clean hands" will repent, for the commandment as stated by the risen Lord himself to the Nephites is: "Repent, . . . and come unto me and be baptized in my name, that ye may be sanctified by the reception of the Holy Ghost, that ye may stand spotless before me at the last day" (3 Nephi 27:20).

He early renewed this commandment in this dispensation in the revelation recorded in the 19th section of the Doctrine and Covenants.

To repent indicates a "godly sorrow for sin," which produces a reformation of life. It "embodies (1) a conviction of guilt, (2) a desire to be relieved from the hurtful effects of sin, and (3) an earnest determination to forsake sin and in the Lord's appointed way seek forgiveness" (Talmage, *Articles of Faith,* p. 109).

After faith and repentance, the third principle and the first ordinance in the prescribed celestial law for obtaining a pure heart and clean hands is baptism by immersion in water for the remission of sins. Baptism is symbolical. It symbolizes a cleansing, a washing away of sins. It also symbolizes a resurrection.

Know ye not [said Paul] that so many of us as were baptized into Jesus Christ were baptized into his death?

376

Therefore we are buried with him by baptism into death: that like as Christ was raised up from the dead by the glory of the Father, even so we also should walk in newness of life (Romans 6:3, 4).

Baptism is the "water" birth spoken of by Jesus when to Nicodemus he said, "Except a man be born of water and of the Spirit, he cannot enter into the kingdom of God" (John 3:5).

One evidences his faith in the Lord Jesus Christ and his repentance, by being so baptized, by covenanting in the waters of baptism to keep the commandments. Alma, instructing the people of Gideon, put it this way:

Yea, I say unto you come and fear not, and lay aside every sin, which easily doth beset you, which doth bind you down to destruction, yea, come and go forth, and show unto your God that ye are willing to repent of your sins and enter into a covenant with him to keep his commandments, and witness it unto him this day by going into the waters of baptism (Alma 7:15).

Jesus, being sinless, did not need to be baptized for the remission of sins, but nevertheless he insisted that he be baptized, saying unto John, "Suffer it to be so now: for thus it becometh us to fulfill all righteousness" (Matthew 3:15).

Nephi, commenting on the baptism of Jesus, explains what is meant by fulfilling all righteousness and introduces the fourth provision of the celestial law which purifies one's heart and cleanses his hands. He says:

And now, I would ask of you, my beloved brethren, wherein the Lamb of God did fulfill all righteousness in being baptized by water?

Know ye not that he was holy? But notwithstanding he being holy, he showeth unto the children of man that, according to the flesh he humbleth himself before the Father, and witnesseth unto the Father that he would be obedient unto him in keeping his commandments.

Wherefore, after he was baptized with water the Holy Ghost descended upon him in the form of a dove.

And . . . the voice of the Son came unto me, saying: He that is baptized in my name, to him will the Father give the Holy Ghost, like unto me; wherefore, follow me, and do the things which ye have seen me do.

Wherefore, my beloved brethren, I know that if ye shall follow the Son, with full purpose of heart, . . . repenting of your sins, witnessing unto the Father that ye are willing to take upon you the name of Christ, by baptism—Yea, by following your Lord and your Savior down into the water, according to his word, behold, then shall ye receive the Holy Ghost; yea, then cometh the baptism of fire and of the Holy Ghost (2 Nephi 31:6, 7, 12, 13).

This "baptism of fire and of the Holy Ghost" here spoken of by Nephi effects the great change in the hearts of men referred to by Alma. It converts them from carnality to spirituality. It cleanses, heals, and purifies the soul. It is the sealing and sign of forgiveness. It is the spiritual rebirth spoken of by Jesus to Nicodemus. Faith in the Lord Jesus Christ, repentance, and water baptism are all preliminary and prerequisite to it, but it is the consummation. To receive it is to have one's garments washed in the atoning blood of Jesus Christ.

Alma was trying to arouse his hearers at Zarahemla to a realization that their being able to look up "to God at that day with a pure heart and clean hands" would depend upon their experiencing the mighty change wrought in men's hearts by the baptism of fire and the Holy Ghost.

Reminding them that his father had accepted the words of Abinadi and that

according to his faith there was a mighty change wrought in his heart. . . .

And [that he had] preached the word unto [their] fathers, and a mighty change was also wrought in their hearts,

And now behold, I ask of you, my brethren of the church, have ye spiritually been born of God? . . . Have ye experienced this mighty change in your hearts? (Alma 5:12-14).

It was against this background that he put the question: "Can ye look up to God at that day with a pure heart and clean hands?" (Alma 5:19).

This "mighty change" wrought by the baptism of fire and the Holy Ghost should and does, if the proselyte is prepared to receive it, occur when he is baptized by immersion for the remission of sins and receives the laying on of hands for the gift of the Holy Ghost—the two required ordinances for being "born of water and of the spirit."

Alma gave his son Helaman a most graphic account of his being born again. As he

went about with the sons of Mosiah seeking to destroy the church of God [he was called to repentance by an angel who said unto him] . . .

If thou wilt of thyself be destroyed, seek no more to destroy the church of God.

[Whereupon, said Alma] I fell to the earth; ...

And ... I was racked with eternal torment, for ...

I did remember all my sins and iniquities, for which I was tormented with the pains of hell; ...

Oh, thought I, that I could be banished and become extinct both soul and body, that I might not be brought to stand in the presence of my God, to be judged of my deeds.

And it came to pass that as I was racked with torment, while I was harrowed up by the memory of my many sins, behold, I remembered also to have heard my father prophesy unto the people concerning the coming of one Jesus Christ, a Son of God, to atone for the sins of the world.

Now, as my mind caught hold upon this thought, I cried within my heart: O Jesus, thou Son of God, have mercy on me, who am in the gall of bitterness, and am encircled about by the everlasting chains of death.

And now, behold, when I thought this, I could remember my pains no more; yea, I was harrowed up by the memory of my sins no more.

And oh, what joy, and what marvelous light I did behold; yea, my soul was filled with joy as exceeding as was my pain! ...

Yea, methought I saw ... God sitting upon his throne, surrounded with numberless concourses of angels, in the attitude of singing and praising their God; yea, and my soul did long to be there.

But behold, my limbs did receive their strength again, and I stood upon my feet, and did manifest unto the people *that I had been born of God.*

Yea, and from that time even until now, I have labored without ceasing, that I might bring souls unto repentance; that I might bring them to taste of the exceeding joy of which I did taste; that they might also be *born of God, and be filled with the Holy Ghost* (Alma 36:6, 9, 10, 12, 13, 15, 17-20, 22-24; italics added).

In the following three verses of the 4th chapter of Mosiah we have an account of a whole multitude experiencing a new birth.

And now, it came to pass that when king Benjamin had made an end of speaking ... that he cast his eyes round about on the multitude, and behold they had fallen to the earth, for the fear of the Lord had come upon them....

And they all cried aloud with one voice, saying: O have mercy, and apply the atoning blood of Christ that we may receive forgiveness of our sins, and our hearts may be purified; for we believe in Jesus Christ, the Son of God, . . .

And it came to pass that after they had spoken these words the Spirit of the Lord came upon them, and they were filled with joy, having received a remission of their sins, and having peace of conscience, because of the exceeding faith which they had in Jesus Christ (Mosiah 4:1-3).

Everyone who complies with the prescribed conditions is born again. As Alma sought to impress this great truth on his recreant brethren at Zarahemla, he sought also to teach them that being born again does not guarantee one a pure heart and clean hands at the final judgment.

If ye have experienced a change of heart [he said to them], and if ye have felt to sing the song of redeeming love, I would ask, can ye feel so now?

Have ye walked, keeping yourselves blameless before God? Could ye say, if ye were called to die at this time, . . . that ye have been sufficiently humble? That your garments have been cleansed and made white through the blood of Christ? (Alma 5:26, 27).

The implication of these questions is in strict harmony with the teachings of all the prophets and of the Lord himself. They all proclaim that he who can at that great day look up to God with the "pure heart and clean hands," which will qualify him for eternal life, is he who so lives as to retain to the end of his life the forgiveness received through "baptism of fire and of the Holy Ghost." The Savior said it in these words:

Whoso repenteth and is baptized in my name shall be filled [that is, filled with the Holy Ghost]; and if he endureth to the end, behold, him will I hold guiltless before my Father at that day when I shall stand to judge the world.

And no unclean thing can enter into his kingdom; therefore nothing entereth into his rest save it be those who have washed their garments in my blood, because of their faith, and the repentance of all their sins, and their faithfulness unto the end (3 Nephi 27:16, 19).

If time permitted, a proper sequence to the foregoing remarks would be a consideration in depth of the things to be done to retain a remission of sins. To know what they are and do them is as important as obtaining remission of sins in the first place. Since, however, we do not here and now have time for such a consideration, I shall close by quoting

380 Nephi's summary on this important matter:

And now, my beloved brethren after ye have gotten into this straight and narrow path, I would ask if all is done? Behold, I say unto you, Nay; . . .

Ye must press forward with a steadfastness in Christ, having a perfect brightness of hope, and a love of God and all men. Wherefore, if ye shall press forward, feasting upon the word of Christ, and endure to the end, behold, thus saith the Father: Ye shall have eternal life (2 Nephi 31:19, 20).

He who is born of the spirit, and continues to live in a state of repentance from the time he is thus "born again" to the end of his mortal life, will have retained the remission of his sins. After death he will be free from the powers of evil and he will be able to look up to God with "a pure heart and clean hands" and he will hear the great Judge say, "Come unto me ye blessed, for behold, your works have been works of righteousness upon the earth" (Alma 5:16).

That it may be so with each of us, I humbly pray. (*Look to God and Live* [Deseret Book Co., 1971,] pp. 261-73.)

COMPILATION OF THE BOOK OF MORMON

PLATES BROUGHT FROM JERUSALEM	SOURCE MATERIALS USED BY MORMON AND MORONI	PLATES RECEIVED BY JOSEPH SMITH FROM MORONI	BOOK OF MORMON IN ITS PRESENT TRANSLATED FORM
	LARGE PLATES OF NEPHI Book of Lehi	**PLATES OF MORMON** Mormon's abridgment of the Book of Lehi (See *History of the Church*, 1:56. Translation comprising 116 pages lost by Martin Harris.)	
	Book of Mosiah Book of Alma Book of Helaman Book of (Third) Nephi Book of (Fourth) Nephi	**SMALL PLATES OF NEPHI** Book of I Nephi Book of Enos Book of II Nephi Book of Jarom Book of Jacob Book of Omni	Pages 1-133
BRASS PLATES OF LABAN Portions were quoted by writers of the Small Plates of Nephi and to some extent by writers of the Large Plates of Nephi.		**PLATES OF MORMON** **(continued)** Continuation of Mormon's abridgment of the Large Plates of Nephi (Book of Mosiah, Alma, Helaman, III Nephi, IV Nephi, Mormon, chapters 1-7).	Pages 134-472
LARGE PLATES OF NEPHI Made about 590 B.C. soon after arrival at the Promised Land. (See I Nephi 19:1-2.) Used mainly for secular history until Small Plates of Nephi were filled in the days of Amaleki (Omni 30); thereafter they were used for both secular and religious history.	**PLATES OF ETHER** Record of Jaredites engraved on 24 gold plates by Ether.	**PLATES OF MORMON CONTINUED BY MORONI** Book of Mormon (Chapters 8-9). Book of Ether (Moroni's abridgment of the commentary on the Jaredite record). Book of Moroni. TITLE PAGE (Summary Statement).	Pages 473-522
SMALL PLATES OF NEPHI Made about 570 B.C. (See II Nephi 5:28-32.) Contains the religious history of the Nephite people from Nephi to Amaleki. The Words of Mormon were added when the Small Plates of Nephi were included with the plates of Mormon. (See Words of Mormon, verses 1 and 5.)	**PLATES OF MORMON** Called Plates of Mormon because Mormon made them with his own hands. (See III Nephi 5:10-20.) (It should be noted that Mormon's own little book written on the Plates of Mormon is his abridgment of the more extensive account of his life and times that he wrote earlier on the Large Plates of Nephi. See Mormon 1:4; 2:17-18; 5:9.)	**SEALED PORTION**	The diagram dimensions are not representative of true sizes of plates.

The exact place of the Small Plates of Nephi in the plates received by Joseph is not known.

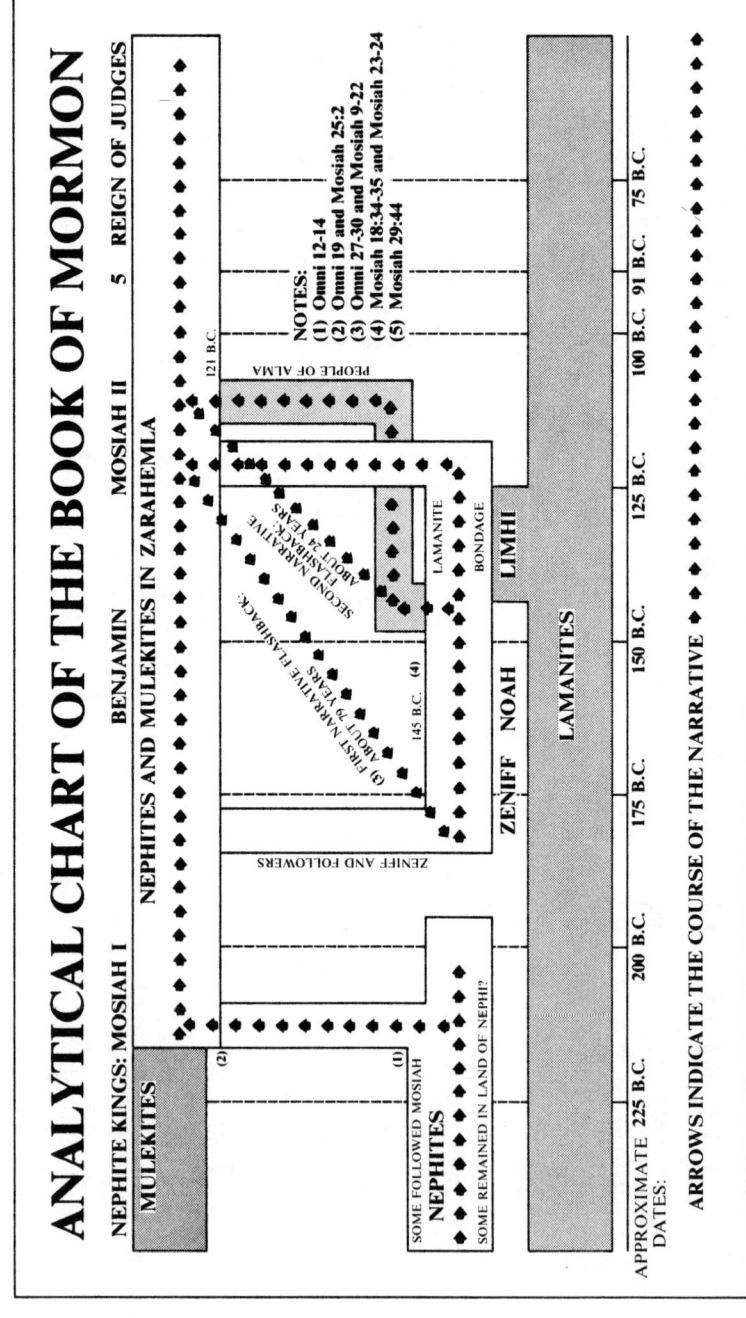

ANALYTICAL CHART OF THE BOOK OF MORMON

NEPHITE KINGS: MOSIAH I   BENJAMIN   MOSIAH II   5   REIGN OF JUDGES

NEPHITES AND MULEKITES IN ZARAHEMLA

NOTES:
(1) Omni 12-14
(2) Omni 19 and Mosiah 25:2
(3) Omni 27-30 and Mosiah 9-22
(4) Mosiah 18:34-35 and Mosiah 23-24
(5) Mosiah 29:44

MULEKITES

PEOPLE OF ALMA

121 B.C.

SECOND NARRATIVE FLASHBACK: ABOUT 24 YEARS

FIRST NARRATIVE FLASHBACK: ABOUT 70 YEARS

145 B.C. (4)

LIMHI

LAMANITE BONDAGE

ZENIFF   NOAH

ZENIFF AND FOLLOWERS

SOME FOLLOWED MOSIAH

NEPHITES

SOME REMAINED IN LAND OF NEPHI?

LAMANITES

APPROXIMATE 225 B.C.   200 B.C.   175 B.C.   150 B.C.   125 B.C.   100 B.C.   91 B.C.   75 B.C.
DATES:

ARROWS INDICATE THE COURSE OF THE NARRATIVE

POSSIBLE BOOK OF MORMON SITES

Possible comparative relationships for some of the sites mentioned in the Book of Mormon based on internal evidences. No effort should be made to identify points on this map with any now existing geographical locations (Cf. 3 Nephi 8:5-18.) Originally prepared by Daniel H. Ludlow with later adaptations by J. Grant Stevenson, F. Kent Nielsen, and Richard Cowan.

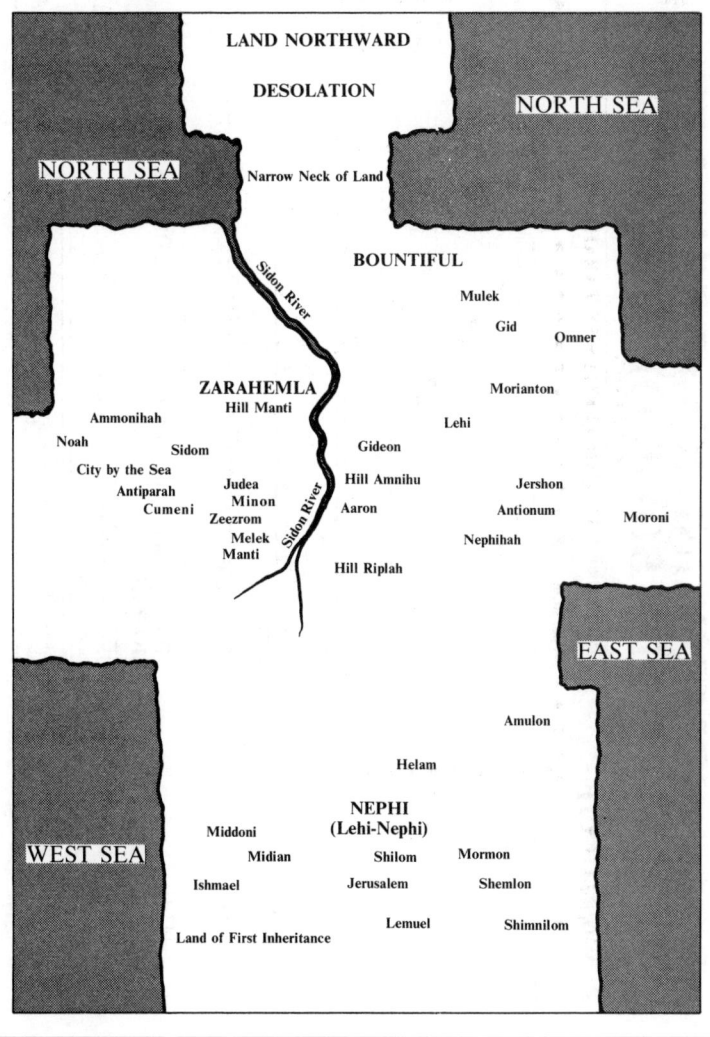

LAND NORTHWARD

DESOLATION

NORTH SEA

NORTH SEA

Narrow Neck of Land

Sidon River

BOUNTIFUL

Mulek

Gid

Omner

ZARAHEMLA

Hill Manti

Morianton

Ammonihah

Lehi

Noah

Sidom

Gideon

City by the Sea

Antiparah   Judea   Hill Amnihu   Jershon

Cumeni   Minon   Aaron   Antionum   Moroni

Zeezrom

Melek   Nephihah

Manti

Hill Riplah

EAST SEA

Amulon

Helam

NEPHI

(Lehi-Nephi)

Middoni

WEST SEA   Midian   Shilom   Mormon

Ishmael   Jerusalem   Shemlon

Lemuel   Shimnilom

Land of First Inheritance

SOME SIGNIFICANT JOURNEYS IN THE BOOK OF MORMON

LAND OF NEPHI

(SOUTH) Helaman 6:10

Established by Nephi
Temple built
(2 Nephi 5:6-16)

Kings in Nephi from
about 200 B.C. to 121 B.C. *

1. ZENIFF
(Mosiah 7:9, 21, 22; 9:1)

2. NOAH
(Mosiah 11:1)

3. LIMHI
(Mosiah 19:26)

* Dates are approximations
Adapted from material originally prepared by Marion/D. Hanks

Most of the important journeys which occur in the Book of Mormon story between 200 B.C. and 74 B.C. are between, or in relation to, Nephi and Zarahemla

Mosiah I leads group from the Land of Nephi. They unite with the Mulekites in Zarahemla. Mosiah becomes king. Before 200 B.C. (Omni 12-15, 19)

First expedition seeking to return to Nephi fails because of internal strife. Before 200 B.C. (Omni 27, 28)

Zeniff leads expedition to Nephi. About 200 B.C. (Omni 29; Mosiah, chapters 9-22)

Ammon leads group of 16 to discover fate of Zeniff and his group. They plan for the escape of Limhi's people from bondage. 121 B.C. (Mosiah, chapters 7 and 22)

Limhi tells Ammon of 43 men sent to get help from Zarahemla. They fail to find Zarahemla but find last of Jaredites, now extinct. They bring back 24 gold plates of Ether. 122 B.C. (Mosiah 8:7-9; 21:25-27; 28:11-17)

Limhi's people escape to Zarahemla. 121 B.C. (Mosiah 22:11-13)

Followers of Alma (Priest of Noah, converted by Abinadi) get to Zarahemla. 121 B.C. (Mosiah 24:25)

MISSIONARY JOURNEY HEADED BY THE SONS OF MOSIAH

Converted sons of Mosiah go on missions to Lamanites. 91 B.C. (Mosiah 27; 28:1-9; also Alma 17-26)

Sons of Mosiah lead converts to Zarahemla; meet Alma the Younger. 74 B.C. (Alma 27:11-16, 20)

LAND OF ZARAHEMLA

(NORTH) Helaman 6:10

Established by
descendants of Mulek,
Son of King Zedekiah

Kings in Zarahemla
from about 200 B.C. to
121 B.C.

1. MOSIAH I
(Omni 19)

2. BENJAMIN
(Omni 23)

3. MOSIAH II
(Mosiah 6:3)

MAJOR LEADERS DURING THE LAST 500 YEARS OF NEPHITE HISTORY 91 B.C. to A.D. 421

YEAR-REIGN OF JUDGES	CHRISTIAN YEAR	CHIEF JUDGE OR GOVERNOR	HISTORIAN AND CHURCH LEADER	MILITARY LEADER
1	91 B.C.	ALMA II (Mosiah 29:44)	ALMA II (Mosiah 29:42)	ALMA II (Alma 2:16)
9	83 B.C.	NEPHIHAH (Alma 4:17, 20)		
18	74 B.C.			MORONI (Alma 43:17)
19	73 B.C.		HELAMAN I (Alma 37:1 and 45:20-23)	
24	68-67 B.C.	PAHORAN (Alma 50:39, 40)		
32	60 B.C.			MORONIHAH (Alma 62:43)
36	56 B.C.		SHIBLON (Alma 63:1)	
39	53 B.C.		HELAMAN II (Alma 63:11)	
40	52 B.C.	PAHORAN II (Helaman 1:1, 5) and PACUMENI (Helaman 1:13)		
42	50 B.C.	HELAMAN II (Helaman 2:1, 2)		
53	39 B.C.	NEPHI I (Helaman 3:37)	NEPHI I (Helaman 3:37)	
62	30 B.C.	CEZORAM (Helaman 4:18 and 5:1)		LAST REFERENCE TO MORONIHAH (Helaman 4:18)
66	26 B.C.	CEZORAM'S SON (Helaman 6:15)		
?	?	SEEZORAM (Helaman 6:39; 9:23)		
92	A.D. 1	LACHONEUS I (3 Nephi 1:1)	NEPHI II (3 Nephi 1:1, 2)	
	A.D. 16			GIDGIDDONI (3 Nephi 3:18)
	A.D. 30	LACHONEUS II (3 Nephi 6:19)		
	?		NEPHI III (Superscription to 4th Nephi)	
	A.D. 110		AMOS I (4 Nephi 19, 20)	
	A.D. 194		AMOS II (4 Nephi 21)	
	A.D. 305		AMMARON (4 Nephi 47)	
	A.D. 321 to C. 335		MORMON (Mormon 1:1-3)	
	A.D. c. 326			MORMON (Mormon 2:2)
	A.D. c. 385		MORONI (Mormon 6:6)	

INDEX

A

Aaronic Priesthood, restoration of, 29-31; Nephites did not hold, 196
Abinadi, prophet among the Nephites, 71, 180; before King Noah, 182-83, 186; testimony of, 187; converted Alma, 187
Abish, 207
Abominable church, 105-7, 110-11
Abraham, 60; record of, found with mummies, 130-31
Adam, 60, 126-28
Adultery, sin of, 157-59, 220-21, 222
Agnostic, definition of, 211-12
Alma, prophet among the Nephites, 71; converted by Abinadi, 187; baptism of, 188; as founder of a church, 189-90
Alma, the younger, as chief judge of Nephites, 72; conversion of, 217-18
"Altar of stones," 93
Amalekites, 208
Amalickiah, 73-74
America, destiny of, 280-81; a choice land, 312; people in, must keep commandments, 313
American Indian, knew Bible stories, 99; progenitors of, came "dancing," 115-16; possible sources of traditions of, 210, 232; oppression of, 361-70; Church program for, 364-70
Amlici, 72, 194
Amlicites, 194-95
Ammaron, 80
Ammon, 70-71
Ammonites, 73
Amulonites, 208
Ancestors of Joseph Smith, 1-4
Angel Moroni. *See* Moroni
Angels, 191
Anthon, Charles, 22-23, 147-48
Anti-Christs, 161-62, 211
Anti-Nephi-Lehies, origin of, 73; meaning of term, 209-10
Apostasy, after signs of birth of Christ, 257-58; steps of, 296-97
Atheist, definition of, 211-12
Atonement of Christ, free agency through, 128; is infinite, 135-36; relationship of, to laws of justice and mercy, 176-77; necessity of, 286-87

B

Baptism, of Joseph Smith and Oliver Cowdery, 29-31; a widely practiced ordinance, 51; Nephites believed in, 139; of Jesus Christ, 153-55; does not ensure spiritual rebirth, 195, 196-98; teachings of Christ on, 262-63; of twelve Nephite disciples, 275; of infants, 336-37; for remission of sins, 337-38; is symbolical, 375-77

Barges built by Jaredites, 82, 313-15   387

Beatitudes, 265

Benjamin, King, 69-70

Benson, Ezra Taft, 358

Bible, Book of Mormon as a witness for, 46-47, 112, 304, 344-45; many
    parts of gospel taken out of, 51, 110-11; is not complete, 109-10, 121;
    as a witness for Christ, 343

Body, resurrection of, 201-2

Book of Mormon, 116; manuscript pages of, were lost, 23-24; process of
    translation of, 27-29, 141-42, 163; three witnesses of, 32-33, 148-49,
    346; eight witnesses of, 38-41, 148-49, 346; publication of, 41-42, 350;
    major editions of, 42-43; as a witness of Christ, 45-46, 302, 343-45; as
    a witness for the Bible, 46-47, 112, 304, 343-45; fulfills biblical
    prophecy, 47-48; to convince Lamanites they are of the house of
    Israel, 48-51; to restore truths of gospel, 51; as a test of faith, 52-53; to
    help those living in the last days, 53-55; of, by, and for house of
    Israel, 117-19; taking of, to Lamanites fulfills prophecy, 122;
    geography of lands of, 209, 236-37, 321-22; climate of lands of, 235;
    as a witness of God, 342; Joseph Smith as witness for, 346;
    "Pronouncing Vocabulary," 349-50; superscriptions in, 350-51

"Born again," importance of being, 196-98; explanation of, 377-79

Brass plates of Laban, 56-57, 95; Lehi sends sons to obtain, 65;
    contained biblical accounts, 98-99; in Egyptian, 173

Brass serpent held by Moses, 216, 243-44

Breastplate, 20

Brother of Jared, name of, 310; Lord helped, build barges, 315-17;
    appearance of pre-earthly Christ to, 317-19; had Urim and
    Thummim, 319-20

Brown, Hugh B., 355-58

C

"Casting of lots," 95

Chariots, 206-7

Chicago Democrat, letter of Joseph Smith to, 13

Children, parents responsible for, 159

Christ. *See* Jesus Christ

Christian churches, contention in, at time of Joseph Smith, 7-8, 149

Church, great and abominable, 105-7

Church of Jesus Christ of Latter-day Saints, as "standard" to be raised
    up, 135; Indian program of, 364-65

Columbus, Christopher, 107-8

Compass, Liahona as a, 116-17

Copyright of first edition of Book of Mormon, 41, 349

Coriantumr, last Jaredite king, 83-84; lived with people of Zarahemla,
    169-70; warned by Ether, 326-27; survived final battle, 328-29

Covenant, definition of, 140; made at baptism, 154; eternal nature of,
    made with Lord, 164-65

Cowdery, Oliver, describes appearance of Moroni to Joseph Smith, 17;
    accompanies Joseph to return plates, 21; becomes Joseph's scribe,

388

25-26; testimony of, 26-27, 34-36; records restoration of priesthood, 30-31; one of three witnesses, 32-33; death of, 36
Creator, Jesus Christ as, 248, 259
"Cross yourself," meaning of, 223
Crucifixion of Christ, sign of, 120; necessity of, 140; date of, 258-59
Cumorah, great Lamanite and Nephite battle on, 81, 302-3
Curtis, Rebecca, 2
Custer, 363

D

Dancing, people came, in their ships, 115-16
Death, 200-1
Democratic government, 193
"Deseret," meaning of, 310-11
Devil, Lucifer as, 145; teaching of no, 151-52
Disciples, twelve Nephite, 291-92
Divorce, teachings of Christ on, 266-67
Dove, as a sign of the Holy Ghost, 104
Dream of Lehi, 98; interpretation of, 100-1

E

Egyptian, brass plates of Laban in, 173
Eight witnesses of the Book of Mormon, 38-41, 148-49, 346
Elders among Nephites, 195-96
Elijah, 284-85
Enos, nephew of Nephi, 67-68
Ephraim, Ishmael was a descendant of, 199
Ether, plates of, 58; Jaredite prophet, 82

F

Faith, Book of Mormon as a test of, 52-53; definition of, 214-15, 324; moving of mountain through, 325; and hope, 336; learn to walk by, 342; necessity of, in Christ, 372-75
Fall of Adam, 126-28
"Feller," meaning of, 145
First Vision of Joseph Smith, 7-13
Five books of Moses, 56, 98-99
Foreknowledge of God, 101-3
Forgiveness of others, 268-69
Fornication, sin of, 157-59
Free-men, 74
Free agency, could be no, without law, 125-26; through atonement of Christ, 128; importance of, 249-51
French, Mary, 1

G

Gadianton, secret band of, 76, 239

Gates, Lydia, 3
Gazelem, 218-19
Gentile, definition of, 111-12; nation to be raised up, 121
Gift of discernment, 202
Gifts of the Spirit, 339-41
God, foreknowledge of, 101-3; "knoweth all things," 138-39, 202
Godhead, 276-77; members of, testify of each other, 342-43
Gold plates. *See* Plates
Gospel, Book of Mormon to restore truths of, 51; to prepare people to be worthy to live with Christ, 55; living laws of, 219; essential doctrines of, 287-89; fulness of, 289-91
Gould, Priscilla, 2
Grandin, Egbert B., first printer of Book of Mormon, 41-42

H

Hagoth the shipbuilder, 76, 238
Harris, Martin, gave Joseph Smith fifty dollars, 22; visits Charles Anthon, 22-23, 147-48; was Joseph's first scribe, 23; loses 116 pages of manuscript, 23-24; as one of three witnesses, 32-33; testimony of, 37-38
Hebrews, Lehi and his colony as, 97-98
Helaman, 73; leads 2,000 warriors, 75, 237-38; Lamanites in days of, 239-40
Hell, 174-75
Holy Ghost, in sign of dove, 104; inspired Columbus, 107-8; "right" to receive, 195, 196-98; disciples received power to give, 274-75; not same as Spirit of Christ, 335; as a witness of truth, 347-48; effects great change in heart, 377
Horses on the American continent, 117, 206-7
"Hosanna," meaning of, 261-62
House of Israel, Lamanites are of, 48-51; origin of, 61; compared to an olive tree, 113; led by Moses, 115; Book of Mormon of, by, for, 117-19; scattering of, 118-19; gathering of, 119, 144-45, 279-80
Humility, 214, 324-25

I

Indian. *See* American Indian
Infants, baptism of, 336-37
Isaac, 60
Isabel the harlot, 220
Isaiah, writings of, 134-35, 141-44
Ishmael, accompanies Lehi from Jerusalem, 65; possible reason for selection to accompany Lehi, 99-100; was a descendant of Ephraim, 199
"Isles of the sea," 121
Israel, 60; origin of house of, 61; descendants of, in bondage to Egypt, 61; house of, compared to an olive tree, 113; exodus of, under Moses, 115; "second" gathering of, 144-45; resurrected Christ appeared to lost tribes of, 271; teachings of Savior on gathering of, 279-80

390 **J**

Jacob, son of Isaac, 60

Jacob, son of Lehi, 67; visited by pre-earthly Savior, 125

Jared, plates of Ether are record of people of, 58; name of brother of, 310; Lord helped brother of, build barges, 315-17

Jaredites, left Middle East at time of tower of Babel, 69; record of, 81; built barges, 82, 313-15; arrived in promised land, 83; had great battle on Cumorah, 84; genealogies of, 309; language of, 309-10; high civilization of, 323-25; war among, 327-28

Jarom, 68

Jeremiah, prophet in Jerusalem, 63, 89-90

Jerusalem, at time of Lehi's departure from, 63, 90-91; after Lehi's departure, 63-64; Lehi departs from, 65, 103; destruction of, 124; Savior born in land of, 196

Jesus Christ, Book of Mormon as a witness for, 45-46; gives reasons for preservation of records, 50; gospel to prepare people to live with, 55; sign of birth of given, 77; sign of crucifixion of, given, 78, 120; appears as a resurrected being, 78-79, 260-61; calls Nephites his "other sheep," 79, 270; names his church, 79, 285-86; visited Jacob, son of Lehi, 125; atonement of, is infinite, 135-36; is "keeper of the gate" of heaven, 140; crucifixion of, 140, 258-59; witness of coming of, 140; baptism of, 153-55; why Jews did not accept, 160; as Father and Son, 183-86; birth of, 196; as Creator, 248, 259; spoke to Nephi day before birth, 253; how to become children of, 259-60; appeared to lost tribes of Israel after resurrection, 271; prayer by, 271-72, 275-76; miracle of, providing bread and wine, 277; pre-earthly, appeared to brother of Jared, 317-19; necessity of faith in, 372-75

Jews, of the Book of Mormon, 95; Old Testament as record of, 108-9; why, did not accept Christ, 160

John the Baptist restores Aaronic Priesthood, 29-31

John the Revelator, 112; revelation of, to come forth, 321

Joseph, son of Jacob, records of, 129; prophecies of, 130-31; coat of many colors of, 234-35

Joseph, son of Lehi, 128-29

Judgment, final, 202-4

Judges, God's system of, 300-1

K

King Benjamin, 69-70

King Lamoni, 72

King Limhi, 70-71

Kingdom of Israel, 61

Kingdom of Judah, 62-64, 89

King-men, 74, 194

Kishkumen, 76

Korihor the anti-Christ, 211-12

L

Laban, brass plates of, 56-57, 98-99, 173; Lehi sends sons to obtain records from, 65; killing of, 96

Laman, 66; River of, 93-94

Lamanites, are of the house of Israel, 48-51, 117; the people who remained with Laman and Lemuel known as, 67; sent missionaries to Nephites, 77; taking of Book of Mormon to, fulfills prophecy, 122; curse upon, 132; blessings of, in last days, 153; meaning of term, 156; Book of Mormon for, 167; kings of, 181; false teachings of, 182, 237; taught Nephite language, 190; Amlicites joined, 194-95; buried their weapons, 210; wars of, with Nephites, 230-31, 236; of 74 B.C., 229; in days of Helaman, 239-40; final division of Nephites and, 296; modern-day, 366-70; urchin, story of, 368-69

Lamoni, King, 72

Lands of the Book of Mormon, geography of, 209, 236-37, 321-22; climate of, 235

Language of the plates, 88-89

Large plates of Nephi, 57, 66, 101, 119-20

Last days, Book of Mormon to help those living in, 53-55; conditions in, 122-23, 142-43, 306-7; blessings of Lamanites in, 153; house of Israel in, 282-83

Law, could be no freedom of choice without, 125-26; given as people are able to live, 152; result of obeying or disobeying, 229-30; importance of spirit of, 334-35

Law of justice, 176-77

Law of mercy, 176-77

Law of Moses fulfilled after resurrection, 145-46, 253-54

Law of primogeniture, 116

Leadership, 156-57

Lehi, took brass plates of Laban to promised land, 56; departs from Jerusalem, 65, 103, 257; death of, 66; a prophet in Jerusalem, 89-90, 91; in the wilderness, 92; and colony as Hebrews, 97-98; genealogy of, 99; dream of, 100; interpretation of dream of, 100-1; has vision of destruction of Jerusalem, 124; was a descendant of Manasseh, 198-99

Lehi-Nephi, Nephites in land of, 70-71; temple in, 180

Lemuel, 66; Valley of, 91, 93-94

Liahona, people of Lehi directed by, 65-66; meaning of, 113-14, 218-19; as a compass, 116-17, 219

Limhi, King, 70-71

Linen, fine-twined, 242

Lord's Prayer, 267-68

Lucifer, 145

M

Mack, Lucy, 3-4, 18-21

Mack, Solomon, 3-4

Malachi, prophecies of, 283

Man, basic nature of, 177-80

392

Manasseh, 198-99
Melchizedek, 204-5
Melchizedek Priesthood, 30-31
Mitchell, Dr., 23, 148
Monarchy, 189
Money, love of, 157
Mormon, purpose of writings of, 47, 49-50; plates of, 57, 58, 173, 300, 307, 320-21; abridged large plates of Nephi, 57, 299-300; told to keep record, 80; selected military leader of the Nephites, 80-81; laments human frailty, 246; boyhood of, 298-99
Moroni, appears to Joseph Smith, 13-17; delivers plates to Joseph Smith, 17-18; gives reasons for preservation of records, 50-51; wrote concerning the last days, 53-55; abridged plates of Ether, 58, 81-82; chief captain of Nephites, 73; made "Title of Liberty," 74, 233-34; recaptured Zarahemla, 75; book of, 84-85; military strategy of, 231-32; writings of, 330-31
Mosiah, discovered people of Zarahemla, 68-69; sons of, became missionaries, 71, 72, 208
Mosiah, son of Benjamin, 69-72
Moses, five books of, contained on brass plates of Laban, 56, 98-99; led Israel out of Egypt, 115; face of, shone, 182-83; carried brass serpent on pole, 216, 243-44; was translated, 233
Mulekites, 69, 169
Mummies, record of Abraham and Joseph found with, 130-31
Murder, of spiritual life, 218; sin of, 220, 222

N

"Nahom," 114-15
Nebuchadnezzar, 63
Nehor, 72, 194
Nephi, gives reason for writing his record, 45-46, 47, 50, 51; small plates of, 57, 67, 101, 119-20, 159-60; large plates of, 57, 66, 101, 119-20; commanded to keep records, 66; told to leave rebellious brothers, 67; anoints a king, 67; vision of, 103-4; saw John the Revelator, 112; had sisters, 131-32; kings named, 156; Savior spoke to, day before birth, 253
Nephite disciples, twelve, 104-5
Nephites, brass plates of Laban scripture for, 56; large plates of Nephi official record of, 57; small plates of Nephi are religious record of, 57; people who followed Nephi known as, 67; escaped land of Lehi-Nephi, 70-71; became very wicked, 77; following Christ's ascension, 79-80; held priesthood, 132-34; practiced ordinance of baptism, 139; meaning of term, 156; high state of civilization among, 167; crops of, 181; records possessed by, 188; language of, taught to Lamanites, 190; did not hold Aaronic Priesthood, 196; monetary system of, 199-200; wars of, with Lamanites, 230-31; led by Moroni, 231-32; calendar system of, 254; are descendants of Zenos and Zenock, 260; resurrected Christ appeared to, 260-61; are "other sheep," 270; to have great power in last days, 277-78; twelve disciples

of, 291-92; lived to old age, 295-96; final division of Lamanites and,   393
296; destruction of, 304-6
New Jerusalem, 281-82, 325-26
Noah, 60
Northern kingdom, 61

O

Oaths, importance of, 95-97; secret, 242-43, 322-23
Old Testament, as a record of the Jews, 108-9; is not complete, 109-10
Olive tree, house of Israel compared to, 113; allegory of tame and wild,
    160-61
Omni, 68
Original sin, doctrine of, 175-76

P

Packer, Boyd K., 368-69
Pahoran, 74-75
Palmyra, New York, 5-6
Paradise, 225
Parents, responsibility of, 159
Plates, Joseph Smith acquires, 17-18; return of, 21, 41; description of,
    28; major sets of, 56-58; language of, 88-89
Plates of Ether, 58
Plates of Jacob, 159-60
Plates of Mormon, 57; given to Joseph Smith, 58; language of, 89;
    contents of, 173; script of, 307; sealed portion of, 320-21
Polygamy, 159, 327
Pratt, Parley P., 354-55
Prayer, 112-13; may not be answered immediately, 165-66; power of,
    192; example of effective, 212; of apostate Zoramites, 212-13; by the
    Savior, 271-72, 275-76; teachings on, 273-74; of ordination, 331; of
    sacrament on bread, 331-33; of sacrament on wine, 333-34
Pride, leads to war, 240-41; leads to apostasy, 257-58
Priestcraft, definition of, 146-47; Nehor taught, 194
Priesthood, Nephites held, 132-34; sealing power of, given to Nephi, 245
Priests among Nephites, 195-96
Primogeniture, law of, 116
Promised land, brass plates of Laban taken to, 56; Lehi's family arrives
    in, 66; kept from other nations, 124; people of, to serve Christ, 311-13
"Pronouncing Vocabulary," 349-50
Prophecies of Samuel, 246-48
Prophecy, Book of Mormon fulfills biblical, 47-48
Purity, 371-72

Q

Quetzalcoatl, 261

394   **R**

"Rabbanah," 207
"Raca," meaning of, 265
"Rameumptom," 213
Religious confusion at time of Joseph Smith, 7-8, 149
Repentance, necessity of, to be saved, 200, 240-41, 375; how long, takes, 208; not to procrastinate, 216-17; deathbed, 217
Resurrection, of everyone, 186-87, 200-1; of the body, 201-2, 226-29
Resurrection of Christ, law of Moses fulfilled after, 145-46, 253-54; those who died before, 225-26; resurrection of others at time of, 249
Revelation, way of receiving, 164
Revolutionary War, 2, 3
Richards, LeGrand, 359-60
Richards, Willard, 353-54
Riches, love of, 157
Rigdon, Sidney, as spokesman for Joseph Smith, 129-30
Righteous, suffering of, 205-6
River of Laman, 93-94
"River of water," 92-93
Romney, Marion G., 358-59

S

Sacrament, a widely practiced ordinance, 51; covenants renewed during, 154; ordinance of, 272-73; do not partake of, unworthily, 274; miracle of Savior providing bread and wine for, 277
Salvation, 180
Sam, brother of Nephi, 131
Samuel, a Lamanite prophet, 77; prophecies of, 246-48
Sariah, meaning of name, 92
Satan, as Lucifer, 145; teaching of no, 151-52
Savior. *See* Jesus Christ
"Scalping," 232
Scriptures, value of, 283; testify of each other, 343-45
Sealing power given to Nephi, 245
"Second death," 162-63
Secret combinations, 322-23. *See also* Oaths
Seer, definition of, 181
Sermon on the Mount, 263-64, 270
Service, 174
Shakespeare, Joseph Smith accused of quoting from, 124-25
"Shazer," meaning of, 114
Sherem, the anti-Christ, 161-62
Shipbuilder, Hagoth the, 76, 238
Sin, 150, 157-59; the unpardonable, 162-63, 221-23; doctrine of original, 175-76; remission of, 337-38
Sisters of Nephi, 131-32
Small plates of Nephi, religious record of Nephites, 57, 67; when Nephi

made, 101, 134; books that came from, 119-20; are "plates of Jacob," **395**
159-60; end of, 170

Smith, Asael, 2

Smith, Emma, works as scribe for Joseph, 24-25

Smith, Joseph, Jr., ancestors of, 1-4; boyhood of, 4-7; leg operation of, 5; mother's account of boyhood of, 7; first vision of, 7-13; testimony of, 12-13; visit of angel Moroni to, 13-17; receives plates, 17-18; returns plates, 21; translates plates, 22-29; gives Martin Harris pages of manuscript, 23-24; Emma as scribe for, 24-25; completes translation of plates, 31-32; receives revelation concerning purpose of Book of Mormon, 45, 49; given plates of Mormon, 58; accused of quoting from Shakespeare, 124-25; Sidney Rigdon as spokesman for, 129-30; found record of Abraham and Joseph with mummies, 130-31; method of, for translating plates, 141-42; as witness for Book of Mormon, 346; as "author" of Book of Mormon, 349

Smith, Joseph, Sr., 2

Smith, Robert, 1

Smith, Capt. Samuel, 2

Smith, Samuel, Sr., 2

Smith, William, 9

Sons of Mosiah became missionaries, 71, 72, 208

Sons of perdition, 162-63

Southern kingdom, origin of, 61-62; Egypt in control of, 62; Babylonians in control of, 62-63

Spirit, gifts of the, 339-41

Spirit of Christ, not same as Holy Ghost, 335

Spiritual death, 136-38, 248-49

Spirit world, where, is, 223-25; divisions in, 225

"Standard" to be raised up, 135

Stevenson, Edward, 12-13

Stick of Joseph, 98, 129

Stick of Judah, 98, 129

Superscriptions in Book of Mormon, 350-51

Susquehanna county, Pennsylvania, 22

Sword of Laban, 65

T

Talmage, James E., 120, 252

Teancum, Nephite leader, 74-75

Temple, in Zarahemla, 174; in land of Lehi-Nephi, 180; writing on wall of, 198

Temporal death, 200-1

Three Nephites, 79

Three witnesses of the Book of Mormon, 32-33, 148-49, 346

"Title of liberty," 74, 233-34

Tithing, 284

Tower of Babel, 60

Town, Jacob, letter of Asael Smith to, 2

Translated beings, nature of, 292-94

396   Translation, process of, of Book of Mormon, 27-29, 141-42, 163

U

Unforgivable sin, 221-23
Unpardonable sin, the, 162-63, 221-23
Urim and Thummim, Joseph Smith receives, 17-18; taken from Joseph, 24; description of, 28; King Mosiah had, 70, 192; brother of Jared had, 319-20

V

Valley of Lemuel, location of, 91; naming of, 93-94; firm and steadfast, 94
Voice "out of the dust," 146

W

War, justification of defensive, 232, 235, 254-56; pride leads to, 240; Mormon's teachings on, 300; Nephites became obsessed with, 301-2; among the Jaredites, 327-28
Weaknesses, mankind is given, 324-25
Wealth, love of, 157
Wentworth, John, letter of Joseph Smith to, 13
Whitmer, David, Joseph Smith completes translation at home of, 31-32; as one of three witnesses, 32-33; death of, 36; testimony of, 36-37, 38
Whoredom, teachings on, 157-59
Wilderness, meaning of, 91-92; Lehi's colony in, 92
Wisdom, 219
Witnesses, of coming of Christ, 140; three scriptural, 153
Woodruff, Wilford, 352-53
Works, man to be judged by his, 52-53

Z

Zarahemla, discovered by Mosiah, 68-69; people of, called "Mulekites," 169; "down" from the land of Nephi, 169; temple in, 174; distance from, to land of Nephi, 189
Zedekiah, as king, 63-64, 89; sons of, killed, 341-42
Zeniff, people of, searched for land of Lehi-Nephi, 70-71; record of, 181
Zenock, 215-16, 260
Zenos, allegory of, of tame and wild olive tree, 160-61; testimony of, 215-16; Nephites were descendants of, 260
Zion, 150-51
Zoram, 65